The Cambridge Companion to Seventeenth-Century Opera

The *Cambridge Companion to Seventeenth-Century Opera* is a much-needed introduction to one of the most defining areas of Western music history - the birth of opera and its developments during the first century of its existence. From opera's Italian foundations to its growth through Europe and the Americas, the volume charts the changing landscape – on stage and beyond – which shaped the way opera was produced and received. With a range from opera's sixteenth-century antecedents to the threshold of the eighteenth century, this path-breaking book is broad enough to function as a comprehensive introduction, yet sufficiently detailed to offer valuable insights into most of early opera's many facets; it guides the reader towards authoritative written and musical sources appropriate for further study. It will be of interest to a wide audience, including undergraduate and graduate students in universities and equivalent institutions, and amateur and professional musicians.

JACQUELINE WAEBER is Associate Professor of Music at Duke University, North Carolina. As a musicologist, her research focuses on French musical culture, from the Baroque Era to early twentieth century. She is the editor of *Musique et Geste en France de Lully à la Révolution* (2009) and author of *En musique dans le texte: Le mélodrame, de Rousseau à Schoenberg* (2006).

CAMBRIDGE COMPANIONS TO MUSIC

Topics

The Cambridge Companion to Ballet
Edited by Marion Kant

The Cambridge Companion to Blues and Gospel Music
Edited by Allan Moore

The Cambridge Companion to Choral Music
Edited by André de Quadros

The Cambridge Companion to the Concerto
Edited by Simon P. Keefe

The Cambridge Companion to Conducting
Edited by José Antonio Bowen

The Cambridge Companion to Eighteenth-Century Opera
Edited by Anthony R. DelDonna and Pierpaolo Polzonetti

The Cambridge Companion to Electronic Music
Edited by Nick Collins and Julio D'Escriván

The Cambridge Companion to the 'Eroica' Symphony
Edited by Nancy November

The Cambridge Companion to Film Music
Edited by Mervyn Cooke and Fiona Ford

The Cambridge Companion to French Music
Edited by Simon Trezise

The Cambridge Companion to Grand Opera
Edited by David Charlton

The Cambridge Companion to Hip-Hop
Edited by Justin A. Williams

The Cambridge Companion to Jazz
Edited by Mervyn Cooke and David Horn

The Cambridge Companion to Jewish Music
Edited by Joshua S. Walden

The Cambridge Companion to the Lied
Edited by James Parsons

The Cambridge Companion to Medieval Music
Edited by Mark Everist

The Cambridge Companion to Music in Digital Culture
Edited by Nicholas Cook, Monique Ingalls and David Trippett

Composers

Instruments

The Cambridge Companion
to Seventeenth-Century Opera

Edited by JACQUELINE WAEBER

Duke University

CAMBRIDGE
UNIVERSITY PRESS

Shaftesbury Road, Cambridge CB2 8EA, United Kingdom

One Liberty Plaza, 20th Floor, New York, NY 10006, USA

477 Williamstown Road, Port Melbourne, VIC 3207, Australia

314–321, 3rd Floor, Plot 3, Splendor Forum, Jasola District Centre, New Delhi – 110025, India

103 Penang Road, #05–06/07, Visioncrest Commercial, Singapore 238467

Cambridge University Press is part of Cambridge University Press & Assessment, a department of the University of Cambridge.

We share the University's mission to contribute to society through the pursuit of education, learning and research at the highest international levels of excellence.

www.cambridge.org
Information on this title: www.cambridge.org/9780521823593
DOI: 10.1017/9781139033077

First published 2023

A catalogue record for this publication is available from the British Library.

ISBN 978-0-521-82359-3 Hardback
ISBN 978-0-521-53046-0 Paperback

Contents

Music Examples

Figures

Tables

Contributors

TIM CARTER (David G. Frey Distinguished Professor of Music, University of North Carolina at Chapel Hill) works on opera and musical theatre from Monteverdi through Mozart to Rodgers & Hammerstein. He has held fellowships at the Harvard Center for Italian Renaissance Studies, the Newberry Library, and the National Humanities Center. In 2013 the American Musicological Society awarded him the Claude V. Palisca Prize and the H. Colin Slim Prize for his publications, respectively, on Monteverdi and on Kurt Weill. In 2017, he was named an honorary member of the Society for Seventeenth-Century Music and of the Royal Musical Association.

AMANDA EUBANKS WINKLER is Associate Professor of Music History and Cultures at Syracuse University. Her publications include the book *O Let Us Howle Some Heavy Note: Music for Witches, the Melancholic, and the Mad on the Seventeenth-Century English Stage* (2006); two editions of Restoration-era theatre music; and, with Linda Austern and Candace Bailey, an essay collection, *Beyond Boundaries: Rethinking Music Circulation in Early Modern England* (2017). Her book *Music, Dance, and Drama in Early Modern England* was published with Cambridge University Press in 2020. Since 2017, she has been the Co-Investigator with Richard Schoch on Performing Restoration Shakespeare, funded by the Arts & Humanities Research Council, UK.

BETH L. GLIXON'S archival research in Venice centres on seventeenth- and eighteenth-century opera theatres and musicians. She has published studies on the composers Francesco Cavalli, Francesco Lucio, Barbara Strozzi, and Antonio Vivaldi, as well as on a number of prominent prima donnas active in mid-seventeenth-century Venice. She and her husband, Jonathan E. Glixon, are the authors of *Inventing the Business of Opera: The Impresario and His World in Seventeenth-Century Venice* (2005), and they are joint editors (with Nicola Badolato and Michael Burden) of Francesco Cavalli's *Erismena* for the new Cavalli edition published by Bärenreiter (2018).

REBECCA HARRIS-WARRICK is Professor of Music at Cornell University in Ithaca, NY. She has published widely on French Baroque music and dance, with excursions into nineteenth-century opera, and has prepared critical editions of ballets by Jean-Baptiste Lully and of Donizetti's opera, *La Favorite*. Much of her scholarly work has been informed by her interests in performance; she has studied early dance and performed as a Baroque flutist. She serves on the editorial boards for *Les Oeuvres complètes de Jean-Baptiste Lully* and the *Journal of the Society for Seventeenth-Century Music*. Her most recent book is *Dance and Drama in French Baroque Opera* (Cambridge, 2016).

CHRISTINE JEANNERET is HM Queen Margrethe II's Distinguished Fellow of the Carlsberg Foundation and works at both the Museum of National History at Frederiksborg Castle and the Centre de recherche du château de Versailles. A musicologist specialising in early modern French and Italian music, she investigates issues in performance, the body on stage, cultural exchanges, and court and gender studies. She was a fellow of the Italian Academy for Advanced Studies in America (Columbia University, 2015–2016), and a principal investigator of *Shared Histories of Italian Opera in the Nordic Countries* (2016–2017).

German musicologist MICHAEL MAUL is Research Director at the Bach-Archiv in Leipzig and since 2018 the director of the Bachfest Leipzig. A specialist in the works of Johann Sebastian Bach and the history of Baroque opera in Germany, he is the author of *Barockoper in Leipzig (1639–1720)* (2009) and *'Dero berühmbter Chor' – Die Leipziger Thomasschule und ihre Kantoren 1212–1804* (2012), translated into English as *Bach's Famous Choir: The Saint Thomas School in Leipzig, 1212–1804* (2019). He published in 2004 the most ancient manuscript known of a German opera, Johann Sebastiani's *Pastorello musicale*, which he discovered in 2001.

MARGARET MURATA, Professor Emerita of Music at the University of California, Irvine, has served as President of the Society for Seventeenth-Century Music and Vice-President of the American Musicological Society; she is an honorary member of both. In 2017 she received the decennial Premio Galileo for her work in the history of Italian music, largely in Baroque opera and vocal chamber music. A catalogue of the Barberini manuscripts of music in the Vatican Library, co-edited with Lowell Lindgren, appeared in 2018.

LAURA NAUDEIX is Professor at the University Rennes 2, Département des Arts du Spectacle. She specialises in seventeenth- and eighteenth-century musical theatre, with emphasis on the dramaturgy of French opera, poetics of the ballet, history of aesthetics, and performance practice. She is the author of *Dramaturgie de la tragédie en musique (1673–1764)* (2004) and the editor of *La Première Querelle de la musique italienne (1702–1706)* (2018) and *Molière à la cour, Les Amants magnifiques en 1670* (2020). She is a contributor to the forthcoming *Histoire de l'opéra en France* (dir. Hervé Lacombe) for the chapters on seventeenth-century spectacles.

COLLEEN REARDON is Professor of Music at University of California, Irvine, and past president of the Society for Seventeenth-Century Music. Her research has centred on musical culture in Siena during the early modern period and has resulted in three books published by Oxford University Press – *A Sociable Moment: Opera and Festive Culture in Siena* (2016), *Holy Concord within Sacred Walls: Nuns and Music in Siena, 1575–1700* (2002), *Agostino Agazzari and Music at Siena Cathedral, 1597–1641* (1993) – as well as numerous articles. Her recent forays into Sienese archives have focused on eighteenth- and nineteenth-century singers.

BARBARA RUSSANO HANNING is Professor Emerita of Music at The City College of New York (CCNY) and the Graduate Center of the City University of New York (CUNY), and has taught in the DMA program of The Juilliard School. She is the author of a book on early opera and of various articles on sixteenth- and seventeenth-century Italian music, the iconography of music, and eighteenth-century French subjects as well as of a textbook, *Concise History of Western Music*, currently in its fifth edition (W. W. Norton). A past president of the Society for Seventeenth-Century Music, she currently serves on the board of the early music ensemble ARTEK.

ROGER SAVAGE, an Honorary Fellow in English Literature at the University of Edinburgh, is the author of *Masques, Mayings and Music Dramas* (Boydell, 2014) and *The Pre-History of 'The Midsummer Marriage'* (Routledge, 2019). He has published essays on the history and practice of opera production, especially in connection with Mantuan-Florentine court entertainments, Purcell's music-theatre, and the works of Pietro Metastasio. He has staged operas by, among others, Monteverdi, Purcell, Handel, and Rameau for the Edinburgh University Opera Club and has broadcast for the BBC on the eighteenth-century opera houses at Drottningholm and Český Krumlov.

SARA ELISA STANGALINO holds a PhD in Musicology from Bologna University. She has published several monographs and articles on literary and musical culture of the 17th and 18th centuries, and is a contributor to the publisher Bärenreiter's and Yale University's Cavalli Gesamtausgabe. Among her main publications are *"Ciro in Armenia" di Maria Teresa Agnesi: tra dilettantismo e professionismo nel Settecento milanese* (Roma, Aracne, 2015); *Nicolò Minato, I drammi eroici veneziani* (Paris, Garnier, 2019); *"Didone abbandonata" versus "Die verlassene Dido": ricezione dell'opera metastasiana in Hamburg e nel ducato di Braunschweig (ca 1725–1739)* (Kassel, Merseburger, 2021). A past researcher at the École française de Rome, she currently is an Alexander-von-Humboldt Experienced Researcher at Jena University.

LOUISE K. STEIN is Professor of Musicology at the University of Michigan and is the author of *Songs of Mortals, Dialogues of the Gods: Music and Theatre in Seventeenth-Century Spain* (1993). She subsequently produced an expanded second edition of Howard Mayer Brown's *Music in the Renaissance* (1999) and has continued to publish and collaborate widely, with interests ranging from European, Spanish, and colonial Latin American music of the early modern era, to particular emphasis on theatre music, the history of singing, opera, and keyboard music.

JACQUELINE WAEBER is Associate Professor of Music at Duke University. She works on dramatic music from opera to film, with emphasis on melodrama, French opera from Lully to Gluck, Jean-Jacques Rousseau, and the philosophy of music during the French Enlightenment. She has published as author *En musique dans le texte: le mélodrame, de Rousseau à Schoenberg* (2005) and as editor *Musique et Geste en France de Lully à La Révolution* (2009), as well as the critical editions of Jean-Jacques Rousseau's staged works, *Pygmalion* (1997) and *Le Devin du village* (2021).

Preface

In the middle of the twentieth century, Joseph Kerman had no major qualms about giving the headline 'The Dark Ages' to one of the chapters of his book, *Opera and Drama*. By this, he meant the period between Monteverdi and Gluck. Granted, the expression may have been chosen *cum grano salis*, and Kerman then seemed to moderate his claim, stressing that this period was also 'the great age of opera'. Song, music, stage design, the 'enormous' amount of libretti – all of these testified to 'unbelievable development and unbelievable activity'. During the Baroque era, the ink of their scores barely dried, operas were staged in an overwhelming cadence, be it on Italian theatres or elsewhere in Europe. This led to the rise of a 'star-system' dominated by the cults of the castrato and the prima donna. The era also saw the advent of operatic spectacularity through the use of extravagant machineries. But in the end, once an opera had lived through a few performances, it was then 'thrown away'.[1] Here was, for Kerman, the crux of the problem. This dazzling operatic hyperproductivity was also its main stigma. However foundational these dark ages may have been, they had not yet entered opera into the hall of the canonic repertoire – that is, until Mozart appeared on stage.

Of course, we need to contextualize Kerman's tirade, originally published in 1956, then maintained in his revised edition of 1988. And we could reply that the 1950s were still the 'dark ages' for most operatic productions, especially for works that fell into the Baroque period before Mozart's *Idomeneo*. Only from the 1970s have we started to study the early fringes of the operatic repertoire through historically based recordings, and (more or less) historically based productions. Much has been done since the collaboration between Nikolaus Harnoncourt and Jean-Pierre Ponnelle in 1975 at the Zurich Opera House for the staging of Monteverdi's trilogy (*Orfeo*, *Il ritorno d'Ulisse in Patria*, and *L'incoronazione di Poppea*, as well as the staged madrigal *Il Combattimento di Tancredi e Clorinda*), or Jean-Marie Villégier's 1987 landmark production of Lully's *Atys*, with William Christie and the Arts Florissants, at the Opéra-Comique in Paris. These productions are now considered historical landmarks in the twentieth-century revival of Baroque opera. Also, the renewed scholarly impulse in opera studies, theatre studies, and cultural history during these recent decades has pursued these efforts. Today, no one would deny that this operatic repertoire has become much more visible and accessible be it on stage or through recorded media. As a result, there is now an enthusiastic audience, within or outside the scholarly sphere, for whom this *Companion* is intended.

Our volume is on 'seventeenth-century opera' rather than 'early opera' or 'Baroque opera', and this is not simply to address more explicitly its chronological boundaries. When it comes to art forms, 'early' often implies the notions of archaism, imperfection, or unachievement, and of experimentalism. These can fuel a problematic teleological connotation, when considering that the history of opera unfolds as a cyclical history of crises, during which the respective priorities of music and words needed to be readdressed and readjusted. By the 1680s, Italian opera was rife for its first important critical moment, the Metastasian reform in the early eighteenth century, in the wake of the ideals promulgated by the Arcadian academy. But in parallel, the new genre of the *tragédie en musique*, France's belated answer to Italian opera, offered a treatment of music and text that in many ways stood much closer to the ideals of the Camerata Bardi in the 1600s than to its contemporary Italian counterpart. Thus, the history of opera should be better understood not so much as a linear development aiming towards a supposed operatic perfection but rather as a series of constant 'returns to' the ideal of an original model.

Our volume offers fourteen essays by distinguished scholars in the fields of seventeenth-century opera and theatre studies. Its intention is to provide the readers – be they interested members of the public, students, or scholars – with a series of thorough yet accessible texts scrutinising opera during the entire seventeenth century, a period that provided the foundational pillars for the development of this genre. The volume is also justified by the specialisation of scholarship and the major renewal of opera studies in these recent decades. Independently from the period chosen, the study of opera has also become increasingly reliant on interdisciplinarity. Much of the recent literature on seventeenth-century opera has involved groundbreaking research highlighting opera's relationships with literature, Classical antecedents, theatrical practices, rhetoric, patronage, political functions, gender issues, and other sociological contexts, and our volume draws on such a multiplicity of approaches.

The four chapters in Part I, 'The Italian Foundations', reflect on the origins of opera in the context of Florentine humanism, and how literary ideals and those of Classical literature led to a recreation of a modern equivalent of ancient Greek theatre. Readers are also introduced to the musical characteristics and dramatic functions of the *recitar cantando, stile rappresentativo*, aria, and chorus, and their relation to poetry. The rise of opera-as-drama is discussed up to its Roman period and along its political dimension as a vehicle for displays of power as well as entertainment for its courtly and aristocratic audiences.

The five chapters of Part II, 'Society, Institutions, and Production', focus on various aspects related to operatic production, the development of stage scenery, and the incorporation of ballet. It also assesses opera as a socio-economic institution, which started with the multiplication of opera houses for a paying public (from 1637 in Venice). Part II scrutinizes the increasing professionalisation of the operatic sphere and its impact on composers, librettists, and stage designers, and the strengthening of Venice as a main model for opera throughout Italy, but it also considers how other Italian centres differed from the Venetian model. Emphasis is given to the singers: the rise of the castrato, the primo uomo and prima donna, and the important yet problematic place occupied by female musicians – from composers to singers – and the social constraints they faced.

Part III, 'National Traditions (outside Italy)', addresses the cultivation of opera, by birth an Italian affair, and its expansion outside the limits of the Italian territories, reaching the rest of Europe and the Americas. Its geographical dissemination and assimilation was not always a smooth process: France, England, and Spain had already strong traditions of theatrical spectacles in which music was prominently featured. All these various strands formed different trajectories in which the primeval Italian model had to be reimagined along specific geographical and cultural traditions that had started to consolidate by the end of the seventeenth century. By then, the rise of the Neapolitan school, while preparing the ground for *opera seria*, also contributed to the dissemination of opera in Spain and the Spanish dominions in Italy and the Americas. In parallel, the German countries saw the rise of operatic centres in cities such as Leipzig and Hamburg; in England, the end of the seventeenth century culminated with the first Golden Age of English opera until Purcell's death in 1695. In France, the period between Lully's death in 1687 and the advent of opéra-comique in the 1710s marked the culmination of the Lullian model before Rameau's first operas in the 1730s.

By generating idiosyncratic musical styles and techniques, these traditions also departed from the Italian norm, preparing the ground for national traditions that would lead in the next century to the Gluckian reform. In that respect, the present volume also invites a broader understanding of the origins and development of seventeenth-century opera and its numerous legacies in the next century.

As anyone would expect, the chronological ambitus of our volume starts with opera's Italian origins, c. 1590s–1600s. It extends up to the 1710s, meaning that we do not include what would still be considered 'Baroque opera', that is, Handel's operas, Metastasio and the rise of *opera seria*, and opera in France following the death of Louis XIV. These topics are covered by the *Cambridge Companion to Eighteenth-Century Opera*, thus avoiding any excessive overlapping.

The music examples as well as the orthography of the libretti have all been modernised. Our chronology encompasses the major works mentioned in the volume and provides specific historical events for their contextualisation. The final bibliography is not redundant with the endnotes, and is mainly intended to guide the reader towards essential publications. However, most of the primary sources (scores, libretti, archival texts including manuscripts) are only mentioned in the chapters' endnotes.

I am most grateful to all the contributors of this volume, who embraced with so much dedication the task of writing for this *Companion* and who accepted the challenge of its long overdue genesis. I am indebted to Kate Brett and Nigel Graves, who both provided invaluable help; to Maximiliano Amici, who realized all the music examples and adapted them to modern notation; to Kirsten Rutschman, who translated Michael Maul's text; and to Laura Williams and Celia Abele, both of whom lightened my task of translating and revising the texts by the three French-speaking contributors of this volume.

Special thanks go to Christine Jeanneret, Laura Naudeix, and Colleen Reardon, who, at various stages of this volume's preparation, helped me and encouraged me to persevere with it, and to Tim Carter for always providing wise and erudite advice.

Notes

1 Joseph Kerman, *Opera as Drama* (New York: Knopf, 1956; rev. edn. Berkeley: University of California Press, 1988), ch. 3, 39.

Chronology

1581	Galilei, *Dialogo della musica antica e della moderna*; *Ballet comique de la Reine* (Paris)
1589	Bargagli, *La Pellegrina* (Florence)
1597/8	Peri, *La Dafne* (Florence)
1600	Peri, *L'Euridice* (Florence); Caccini, *Il rapimento di Cefalo* (Florence); Cavalieri, *La Rappresentazione di Anima, et di Corpo* (Rome)
1600/1	Caccini, *L'Euridice* (print)
1601/2	Caccini, *L'Euridice* (Florence), *Le Nuove musiche* (print)
1607	Monteverdi, *Orfeo* (Mantua); F. Caccini, *La Stiava* (Pisa)
1608	Gagliano, *La Dafne* (Mantua); Monteverdi, *L'Arianna*, *Il Ballo delle ingrate* (Mantua)
1610	Guédron, *Le Ballet de Monseigneur le duc de Vandosme ou Ballet d'Alcine* (Paris)
1613	Lanier, *Somerset Masque* (London)
1614	Monteverdi (?), *Orfeo* (Salzburg); Caccini, *Nuove musiche e nuova maniera di scriverle*
1617	Guédron, *Ballet de la délivrance de Renaud* (Paris); Lanier, *Lovers Made Men, The Vision of Delight* (London); A 'Sing-Comedie' on the life of St. Ignatius of Loyola (Würzburg)
1619	Gagliano, Peri, *Lo sposalizio di Medoro et Angelica* (Florence); F. Caccini, *La Fiera* (Florence); Guédron, *Grand Ballet du Roi sur l'aventure de Tancrède en la Forêt enchantée* (Paris)
1620	Vitali, *Aretusa* (Rome); *Delizie di Posillipo boscarecce e marittime* (Naples)
1621	Schütz, *Glückwünschung des Apollinis und der neun Musen* (Dresden)
1622	F. Caccini and Gagliano, *Il martirio di Sant'Agata* (Florence)
1624	Monteverdi, *Il Combattimento di Tancredi e Clorinda* (Venice)
1624/5	Gagliano, *La regina Sant'Orsola* (Florence)
1625	F. Caccini, *La liberazione di Ruggiero dall'isola d'Alcina* (Florence)
1626	Gagliano, *La Giuditta* (Venice); D. Mazzocchi, *La catena d'Adone* (Rome); Boësset, *Grand Bal de la Douairière de Billebahaut* (Paris)

1627	Piccinini and Monanni, *La selva sin amor* (Madrid); Schütz, *Dafne* (Torgau)
1628	Gagliano, *La Flora* (Florence)
1630	Monteverdi, *Proserpina rapita* (Venice)
c. 1630	Publication of *Il Corago*
1631 or 1632	Landi, *Sant'Alessio* (Rome)
1633	M. Rossi, *Erminia sul Giordano* (Rome)
1636	Sances, *Ermiona* (Padua)
1637	Opening of the Teatro San Cassiano (Venice) with Manelli, *Andromeda*; Marazzoli and V. Mazzocchi, *L'Egisto, ovvero, Chi soffre speri* (Rome)
1638	Manelli, *La maga fulminata* (Venice)
1638/9	Cavalli, *Le nozze di Teti e di Peleo* (Venice); Schütz, *Orpheus und Eurydice* (Dresden)
1639	Opening of the Teatro SS. Giovanni e Paolo (Venice); Ferrari, *Armida* (Venice); Manelli, *La Delia* (Venice); Marazzoli and V. Mazzocchi, *L'Egisto, ovvero, Chi soffre speri* (Rome, revised production)
1640	First opera production at the Teatro S. Moisè (Venice); Doni, *Trattato della musica scenica*; Monteverdi, *Il ritorno d'Ulisse* (Venice); Cavalli, *Gli amori d'Apollo e di Dafne* (Venice)
1641	Inauguration of the Teatro Novissimo with Sacrati, *La finta pazza* (Venice); Monteverdi, *Le nozze d'Enea e Lavinia* (Venice)
1642	Cavalli, *La virtù de' strali d'Amore* (Venice); Sacrati, *Bellerofonte* (Venice); L. Rossi, *Il palazzo incantato* (Rome)
1643	Monteverdi, *L'incoronazione di Poppea* (Venice); Sacrati, *Venere gelosa* (Venice)
1644	Cavalli, *L'Ormindo* (Venice); Staden, *Geistliche Waldgedicht oder Freudenspiel, genant Seelewig* (Nuremberg)
1645	Sacrati, *La finta pazza* (Paris, Petit-Bourbon); Rovetta, *Ercole in Lidia* (Venice)
1646	Marazzoli and V. Mazzocchi, *L'Egisto, ovvero, Chi soffre speri* (Paris)
1647	Grasseschi, *Datira* (Siena); L. Rossi, *Orfeo* (Paris)
1648	Opening of the Teatro SS. Apostoli (Venice)
1649	Cavalli, *Giasone* (Venice)
1650	D'Assoucy, *Andromède* (Paris)
1651	Opening of the Teatro S. Apollinare (Venice); Cavalli, *Calisto* (Venice); Cesti, *Alessandro vincitor di se stesso* (Venice)
1652	Cavalli, *La Veremonda, l'amazzone di Aragona* (Naples)
1653	Cavalli, *La Veremonda, l'amazzone di Aragona* (Venice); Cambefort, Lambert et al., *Ballet Royal de la Nuit* (Paris); Hidalgo (attributed), *Fortunas de Andrómeda y Perseo* (Madrid); Locke, *Cupid and Death*; Provenzale/Cavalli, *Il Ciro* (Venice)

1654	Opening of the theatre San Bartolomeo (Naples); Caproli, *Le nozze di Peleo e di Theti* (*Les Noces de Pélée et de Thétis*, Paris); Cambefort, *Les Charmes de Félicie, tirés de la Diane de Montemayor* (Paris); Flecknoe, *Ariadne Deserted by Theseus and Found and Courted by Bacchus* (London); Staden, *Geistliche Waldgedicht oder Freudenspiel, genant Seelewig* (Wolfenbüttel)
1655	Cavalli, *Erismena* and *Xerse* (Venice); Cesti, *L'Argia* (Innsbruck)
1656	Opening of the Teatro S. Samuele (Venice); Lawes, Locke et al., *The Siege of Rhodes* (London); Cesti, *Orontea* (Innsbruck); Hidalgo, *Pico y Canente* (Madrid)
1657	Ziani, *Le Fortune di Rodope e Damira* (Venice); Cavalli, *Artemisia* (Venice); Cesti, *La Dori* (Innsbruck)
1658	Cavalli, *Hipermestra* (Florence)
1659	Volpe, *La Costanza di Rosmonda* (Venice)
1660	Aureli, *L'Antigona delusa da Alceste* (Venice); Hidalgo, *La púrpura de la rosa* (Madrid); Cavalli, *Xerse*, with additional entrées by Lully (Paris)
1661	Opening of the Teatro S. Salvatore (Venice); Hidalgo, *Celos aun del aire matan* (Madrid); J. Melani, *Ercole in Tebe* (Florence)
1662	Cavalli, *Ercole amante* (Paris); Bontempi, *Il Paride* (Dresden)
1663	Opening of the Drury Lane Theatre (London); Sebastiani, *Pastorello musicale* or the *Verliebte Schäffer-Spiel* (Königsberg)
1664	Cavalli, *Scipione affricano* (Venice); Locke, *Macbeth* (London); Banister, *The Indian Queen* (London)
1665	Cavalli, *Mutio Scevola* (Venice)
1666	Cesti, *Il Tito* (Venice)
1667	Inauguration of the Komödienhaus am Taschenberg (Dresden) with Ziani's *Il Teseo*
1668	J. Melani, *Il Girello* (Rome); Cesti, *Il Pomo d'oro* (Vienna)
1669	Foundation of the Académie d'Opéra (Paris; renamed in 1671 Académie Royale de Musique); Cesti, *Argia* (Siena); Lully, *Ballet de Flore*
1670	Molière and Lully, *Les Amants magnifiques* (Saint-Germain-en-Laye); Molière and Lully, *Le Bourgeois gentilhomme* (Chambord, then Paris)
1671	Opening of the Dorset Garden Theatre (London); Ziani, *Heraclio* (Venice); Cambert, *Pomone* (Paris)
1672	Sartorio, *Orfeo* (Venice); Pasquini, *La sincerità con la sincerità, overo Il Tirinto* (Ariccia); Cesti, *Dori* and *Il Tito* (Siena); J. Melani, *Il Girello* (Siena); Bontempi and Peranda, *Musicalisches Schauspiel von der Dafne* (Dresden)
1673	Lully, *Cadmus et Hermione, Les Fêtes de l'Amour et de Bacchus* (Paris); Bontempi, *Jupiter und Io* (Dresden)

1674	Draghi, *Il ratto delle Sabine* and *Il fuoco eterno custodito dalle Vestali* (Vienna); Lully, *Alceste* (Paris); Cavalli, *Erismena* (?) (London); Locke, *The Tempest* (London); Perrault, *Critique de l'opéra, ou Examen de la tragédie intitulée Alceste*
1675	Legrenzi, *Eteocle e Polinice* (Venice); Lully, *Thésée* (Saint-Germain-en-Laye); Locke, *Psyche* (London)
1676	Sartorio, *Giulio Cesare in Egitto* (Venice); Lully, *Atys* (Saint-Germain-en-Laye)
1677	Opening of the Teatro S. Angelo (Venice); Legrenzi, *Totila* (Venice); Agostini, *L'Adalinda* (Siena); Lully, *Isis* (Saint-Germain-en-Laye)
1678	Opening of the Teatro S. Giovanni Grisostomo (Venice); establishment of the Theatre am Gänsemarkt (Hamburg); Theile, *Adam und Eva* (*Der erschaffene, gefallene und aufgerichtete Mensch*), *Orontes* (Hamburg); Lully, *Psyché* (Paris)
1679	Lully, *Bellérophon* (Paris); Scarlatti, *Gli equivoci nel sembiante* (Rome)
1680	Creation of the Comédie-Française (Paris); Scarlatti, *L'honestà negli amori* (Rome); Lully, *Proserpine* (Saint-Germain-en-Laye); Strungk, *Alceste* and *Die liebreiche, durch Tugend und Schönheit erhöhte Esther* (Hamburg)
1681	Lully, *Le Triomphe de l'Amour* (Saint-Germain-en-Laye); Lorenzani, *Nicandro et Fileno* (Fontainebleau); Steffani, *Marco Aurelio* (Munich)
1682	Lully, *Persée* (Paris)
1683	Legrenzi, *Il Giustino* (Venice); Scarlatti, *L'Aldimiro, o vero Favor per favore* and *La Psiche, o vero Amore innamorato* (Naples); Lully, *Phaëton* (Versailles)
c. 1683	Blow, *Venus and Adonis* (London)
1684	Lully, *Amadis* (Paris)
1685	Lully, *Roland* (Versailles) and *Le Temple de la Paix* (Fontainebleau); Grabu, *Albion and Albanius* (London); Steffani, *Solone, Audacia e rispetto* (Munich)
1686	Lully, *Armide* (Paris); Lully, *Acis et Galatée* (Anet); Lully, *Cadmus* (London); Franck, *Cara Mustapha* (Hamburg); Franck, *Die drey Töchter Cecrops* (Ansbach/Hamburg); Steffani, *Servio Tullio* (Munich)
1687	Lully, *Achille et Polyxène* (Paris); Steffani, *Alarico il Baltha* (Munich)
1688	Charpentier, *David et Jonathas* (Paris); Lorenzani, *Orontée* (Chantilly); Steffani, *Niobe, regina di Tebe* (Munich)
1689	Purcell, *Dido and Aeneas* (London); Collasse, *Thétis et Pélée* (Paris); Krieger, *Die ausgesöhnte Eifersucht oder Cephalus und*

	Procris (Weissenfels); Pallavicino and Strungk, *Antiope* (Dresden); Steffani, *Henrico Leone* (Hanover)
1690	Foundation of the Accademia dell'Arcadia (Rome); Purcell, *Dioclesian* (London)
1691	Purcell, *King Arthur* (London); Conradi, *Die schöne und getreue Ariadne* (Hamburg); Steffani, *Orlando generoso* (Hanover)
1692	Conradi, *Die Verstöhrung Jerusalem* (Hamburg); Kusser, *Ariadne* (Braunschweig); Purcell, *The Fairy-Queen* (London)
1693	Noris, *Nerone fatto Cesare* (Venice); Charpentier, *Médée* (Paris); Desmarets, *Didon* (Paris); Strungk, *Alceste* (Leipzig)
1694	Scarlatti, *Pirro e Demetrio* (Naples); Jacquet de La Guerre, *Céphale et Procris* (Paris); Kusser, *Erindo* (Hamburg)
1695	Scarlatti, *Pirro e Demetrio* (Siena); Collasse, *Les Saisons* (Paris); Desmarets, *Les Amours de Momus* (Paris)
1697	Scarlatti, *La caduta de' Decemviri* (Naples); Campra, *L'Europe galante* (Paris); Destouches, *Issé* (Fontainebleau); Keiser, *Adonis* (Hamburg)
1698	Eccles, *Rinaldo and Armida* (London); Navas, *Destinos vencen finezas* (Madrid)
1699	Campra, *Le Carnaval de Venise* (Paris); Strungk, *Agrippina* (Leipzig)
1700 ?	Kusser, *Adonis* (Stuttgart)
1701	Hidalgo, Torrejón y Velasco, *La púrpura de la rosa* (Lima); Keiser, *Störtebecker* (Hamburg); *Ballet de Narva* (Stockholm)
1702	Raguenet, *Parallèle des Italiens et des Français en ce qui regarde la musique et les opéras*
1703	Albinoni, *Griselda* (Florence); Destouches, *Le Carnaval et la Folie* (Fontainebleau); Keiser, *Claudius* (Hamburg)
1704	Le Cerf de la Viéville, *Comparaison de la musique italienne et de la musique française*
1706	Marais, *Alcyone* (Paris)
1709	Steffani, *Tassilone* (Düsseldorf)
1710	Campra, *Les Fêtes vénitiennes* (Paris); Mattheson, *Boris Goudenow* (Hamburg)
1728	Hidalgo, *Celos aun del aire matan* (Mexico)

Abbreviations

Books
MGG1	*Die Musik in Geschichte und Gegenwart. Allgemeine Enzyklopädie der Musik*
MGG2	*Die Musik in Geschichte und Gegenwart. Allgemeine Enzyklopädie der Musik*, 2nd rev. edn

Journals
COJ	*Cambridge Opera Journal*
EM	*Early Music*
EMH	*Early Music History*
JAMS	*Journal of the American Musicological Society*
JM	*Journal of Musicology*
JRMA	*Journal of the Royal Musical Association*
JSCM	*Journal of Seventeenth-Century Music*
ML	*Music & Letters*
MQ	*Musical Quarterly*
MT	*Musical Times*
PRMA	*Proceedings of the Royal Musical Association*
RIM	*Rivista Italiana di Musicologia*
RM	*Revista de Musicología*
SM	*Studi Musicali*

Library Sigla
E-Mn	Madrid, Biblioteca Nacional
GB-Cu	Cambridge, University Library
GB-Lbl	London, British Library
GB-Lna	London, The National Archives
I-Bc	Bologna, Museo Internazionale e Biblioteca della Musica di Bologna
I-Bu	Bologna, Biblioteca Universitaria
I-Mb	Milan, Biblioteca Nazionale Braidense

I-Nn	Naples, Biblioteca Nazionale Vittorio Emanuele III
I-PESo	Pesaro, Biblioteca Oliveriana
I-Vas	Venezia, Archivio di Stato
I-Vnm	Venezia, Biblioteca Nazionale Marciana
MEX-Mn	México Biblioteca Nacional, Departamento de los manoscritos
US-CAh	Cambridge, MA, Harvard University, Houghton Library
V-CVbav	Città del Vaticano, Biblioteca Apostolica Vaticana

PART I

The Italian Foundations

1 | Opera Is Born

The Wedding of Music and Drama in Late Renaissance Florence

BARBARA RUSSANO HANNING

> I think it would not be useless ... to recall to mind how and when such spectacles had their origin, which without any doubt, since they were received with much applause ... , will at some time or other reach much greater perfection ... all the more if the great masters of poetry and music set their hands to it.[1]

Acknowledging the experimental beginnings of opera and expressing high hopes for its future, Marco da Gagliano (1582–1643) thus reviews the origins of 'such spectacles' in the 1608 preface of his own first effort in the new genre, *La Dafne*, itself a reworking and expansion of the earliest completely sung music drama a decade earlier. He goes on to explain how, after a great deal of discussion concerning the way the ancients had represented their tragedies and about what role music had played in them, the court poet Ottavio Rinuccini (1562–1621) began to write the story (*favola*) of Dafne, and the learned amateur Jacopo Corsi (1561–1602) composed some airs on part of it. Determined to see what effect a (completely sung) work would have on the stage, they approached the skilled composer and singer Jacopo Peri, who finished the work and probably premièred the role of Apollo 'on the occasion of an evening entertainment' during the carnival of 1597/8 and on subsequent occasions. In the invited audience at the first performance were Don Giovanni de' Medici and 'some of the principal gentlemen' of Florence.[2]

Gagliano, Florentine composer and *maestro di cappella* to the Medici court from 1609 until his death in 1643, provides a useful and accurate outline – despite the rivalries and counterclaims surrounding the events (about which more will be said) – of the immediate circumstances of opera's modest beginnings, one that will serve well enough to organise our discussion.

Florentine Origins

His narration infers, first of all, that it was a completely Florentine affair. This is not surprising since Florence had a long tradition of musical theatre in the sixteenth century, manifested principally in the productions known as *intermedi* that were staged between the acts of spoken plays. These were but one of many different types of festivities mounted by courts all over Europe. But unlike other centres, Medicean Florence also had a particularly rich history of 'civic humanism'[3] – that is, of involvement by its more educated citizens in the rediscovery of and allegiance to Classical culture via a network of formal and informal academies that were engaged in critical inquiry and philological pursuits, which involved studying the Greek and Latin texts of the ancients. Moreover, as Gary Tomlinson and others have suggested, Florence was the centre of a particular Renaissance worldview that accorded music a 'magical' role in the cosmos and in man's interaction with it.[4] Before filling in some of the details of Gagliano's outline, we shall examine each of these three elements – *intermedi*, humanism, and musical magic – in order to understand how their confluence at the end of the sixteenth century resulted in Florence becoming the birthplace of opera.

Intermedi

Extravagantly staged pageantry involving sumptuous costumes, special effects, music, dance, and song characterised the sixteenth-century Florentine *intermedi*, which were produced as entr'actes to a theatrical entertainment such as a comedy or pastoral play at court. Sets of *intermedi* were originally a modest and functional feature of North Italian court entertainments: they served to signal the divisions of the spoken drama, since there was no curtain to be dropped; and they suggested the passage of time by employing allegorical characters and themes unrelated to the main plot. At the court of the Medici rulers, however, *intermedi* evolved into an elaborately lavish type of spectacle, planned and rehearsed months in advance, whose cost and impact dwarfed that of the main drama and whose raison d'être was to leave no doubt in the minds of the audience – comprised entirely of invited guests gathered to help celebrate a special family event – about their host's wealth and generosity.

Such an occasion was the marriage in 1589 of Grand Duke Ferdinando de' Medici of Tuscany to the French Princess Christine of Lorraine, a union that had been in negotiation for nearly a year. The *intermedi* devised for this event climaxed a month-long sequence of public and courtly pageantry that mobilised the combined intellectual, artistic, and administrative forces of Tuscany at the height of its wealth, power, and cultural prestige. 'Their splendor cannot be described', wrote one court chronicler, 'and anyone who did not see it could not believe it.'[5] A huge team of artists, artisans, poets, musicians, architects, and technicians was assembled under the intellectual guidance of the prominent Florentine aristocrat and military leader Giovanni de' Bardi (1534–1612), who formulated the underlying conception of the *intermedi*, served as stage director, and coordinated all the thematic and antiquarian aspects of the project.[6] As the moving spirit behind the program, Bardi worked closely with the court poets, principally Rinuccini, who wrote most of the text.[7] Emilio de' Cavalieri (c. 1550–1602), the recently appointed superintendent of music at the ducal court who had been in Ferdinando's retinue while he was still a cardinal resident in Rome, became the show's musical director. The court architect-engineer Bernardo Buontalenti (c. 1531–1608), who only a few years earlier had constructed for the Medici the first permanent indoor theatre with a modern proscenium arch, remodelled it for the occasion, and designed the sets and costumes.[8] The music was largely composed by court organist Cristofano Malvezzi and madrigalist Luca Marenzio, with individual contributions by the young composer-singer Jacopo Peri (1561–1633), by Bardi's protégé Giulio Caccini (1551–1618), and by Bardi himself, among others. Note that both Rinuccini and Peri also figure in Gagliano's narration of opera's origins a decade later.

Bardi conceived the set of six *intermedi* as 'a sort of mythological history of music',[9] fitting for a wedding celebration in that it depicts the descent of Harmony as a gift from the gods and predicts a new Golden Age initiated by the royal couple. Moreover, the individual tableaux are loosely unified by the literary theme of the power of music, a topic of longstanding interest to the Florentines (see 'Musical Magic'). The opening *intermedio* contemplates the harmony of the spheres. The next, which represents the ancient rivalry between the Muses and the Pierides (nine daughters of King Pierus who challenged the Muses to a song contest), dwells on the virtues and virtuosity of song. The third, by enacting the combat between Apollo and the Pythic serpent, prefigures the opening scene from the Rinuccini-Peri *Dafne* about which Gagliano wrote. It thus introduces the first operatic hero, Apollo – god of music and of the sun, and some said father of the legendary musician Orpheus, who became in turn the protagonist of several early opera libretti. The fifth *intermedio* gave a prominent role to Peri, who composed and performed his first piece for solo voice to portray another musician-poet par excellence, Arion; according to myth, Arion was saved from drowning by a dolphin attracted by the dazzling power of his song. In the concluding allegory, harmony and rhythm are bestowed on mortals who, represented by the nymphs and shepherds of Arcadia, are instructed by the gods in the art of dancing during an elaborately choreographed *ballo*.

The 1589 *intermedi* had many of the same players and almost all the ingredients of opera – costumes, scenery, stage effects (for example, the life-size fire-spitting dragon slain by Apollo[10]), enthralling solo singing, colourful instrumental music, large concerted numbers, dance – everything except unified action and the innovative style of dramatic singing yet to be created. It remained for a few pioneering individuals to shape these elements into a new and quite 'noble style of performance'[11] that would, by emulating ancient theatre, revive the power of modern music to move the emotions.

Humanism

The catalyst for their experiments, as Rinuccini explains in his preface to the libretto for the first opera for which the music survives in print (Peri's *Euridice*, 1600[12]), was the belief by some scholars that the ancient Greeks and Romans sang their tragedies on the stage in their entirety.[13] Although Renaissance scholars disagreed among themselves about the role of music in ancient tragedy, the amount of attention focused on the practices of the ancients was typical of humanism. Rinuccini, it seems, subscribed to a kind of Greek revivalism that Tomlinson has called 'ordinary-language humanism' – a view that underlay 'the whole late-Renaissance exaltation of music's affective powers';[14] indeed, it had been manifest in one way or another across the breadth of Renaissance musical culture in the degree of importance given to expressing the meaning of the text. While philological humanism promulgated the transmission, translation, and interpretation of ancient texts, and rhetorical humanism was built on the principles of persuasive oratory, this ordinary-language humanism placed greater emphasis on the ability of language itself – the very sound and shape of the words rather than the eloquence with which they were arranged – to communicate meaning and emotion.

Where did these ideas come from? Rinuccini belonged to the Alterati Academy – its very name (Academy of the Altered Ones) acknowledged the ability of ideas to effect change in human beings – one of a network of associations of artists and thinkers that flourished in Florence during the sixteenth century. Its membership included the widely read and accomplished Count Giovanni de' Bardi, who was a member of long standing by the time Rinuccini was initiated in 1586, three years before they collaborated on the wedding festivities discussed above. Another member was the remarkable scholar Girolamo Mei (1519–1594), who, although Florentine by birth, worked in Rome and made known his ideas about Tuscan prose and poetry along with the results of his research into Greek music through correspondence with Bardi and other academicians. An erudite philologist, Mei developed theories about language that were in fact as central to the genesis of the new dramatic style of singing as his convictions about Greek music were to the origins of opera; for not only was it Mei's belief that poems and plays were always sung in ancient times, whether by soloists or by the chorus, but also that they were sung *monophonically* so that the words as sounding structures could act on the listeners' souls. Finally, the Alterati also counted among its members another Florentine nobleman, Jacopo Corsi, the enthusiastic amateur we first encountered in Gagliano's preface, who partially composed, on Rinuccini's text, and fully sponsored the production of the first completely sung 'favola tutta in musica', *La Dafne,* in 1597/8. These are some of the reasons that justify Claude Palisca's having dubbed the Alterati of Florence 'pioneers in the theory of dramatic music'.[15]

Now, Count Bardi also had his own circle of friends with similar humanist and musical interests, a more informal academy which met in his palace and came to be known as the Florentine Camerata.[16] As the courtier chiefly responsible for organising entertainments for the grand duke, Bardi naturally became interested in theatrical or dramatic music and eagerly cultivated his long-distance relationship with Mei.[17] These two, then, were key players in both the Alterati Academy and the Camerata, and it's easy to see that both groups shared a concern with musical humanism. Bardi's inner circle also included the singer-lutenist-composer Caccini (whom he involved in the 1589 *intermedi*) as well as Vincenzo Galilei (c. 1530–1591), another talented singer-lutenist-composer in his employ. Galilei, father of the revolutionary thinker and astronomer Galileo, had studied with the most famous counterpoint teacher of the age, Gioseffo Zarlino, and had already published a text on how to arrange polyphonic music for solo voice and lute (*Il Fronimo,* 1568), a medium that became increasingly popular during the last quarter of the century.[18] Under the influence of Bardi and Mei, Galilei wrote a treatise that became the Camerata's revolutionary manifesto, for it articulated the principles of ordinary-language humanism in the most radical way imaginable for a sixteenth-century musician: eschew vocal counterpoint altogether and adopt a type of non-polyphonic composition combining (texted) melody and simple accompaniment (which we now call monody).

Galilei published his inflammatory tract in the conventional Renaissance form of a dialogue – a conversation between two friends (one of whom is named after Count Bardi) debating the merits of ancient and modern music (*Dialogo della musica antica e della moderna*, 1581).[19] By 'modern music' he meant the *ars perfecta*, the system of counterpoint he and all the leading composers of his day had learned, directly or indirectly, from Zarlino, whose *Istitutione harmoniche* (1558) was the foremost textbook for writing both sacred and secular music. Galilei challenged the ultimate perfection of counterpoint and advocated instead restoring through a single melody line the expressive powers of which ancient music was capable, judging by the corpus of literature about the Greek modal system that had been revived by Renaissance humanists and was recently newly interpreted by Mei.[20] Why monophony? Because it alone was capable of imitating nature – that is, the 'natural language' of speech, through which a person's character and states of soul are reflected. Mei had contended that ancient music always presented a single affection embodied in *un aria sola* (a single melody). He reasoned that monophony could convey the message of the text through the natural expressiveness of the voice – via the register, rhythms, and contours of its utterance – far better than the contrived delivery of a polyphonic texture.[21] Like Mei, Galilei was persuaded that counterpoint was ineffective because it presented contradictory information to the ear. When several voices simultaneously sang different melodies and words – pitting high pitches against low, slow rhythms against fast, rising intervals against descending ones – the resulting web of sounds was incapable of projecting the semantic meaning or emotional message of the text. Only by returning to an art truly founded on the imitation of human nature rather than on contrapuntal artifice would it be possible for modern composers to approach the acclaimed power of ancient music.

Plato had taught that song (*melos*) was comprised of words, rhythm, and pitch, in that order. From that followed the humanist ideal of music and poetry as two sides of a single language, as well as the idea that song arose from an innate harmony within the words that was muted in normal speech. For this reason, Galilei advocated the art of oratory as a model for modern musicians, urging them to imitate the manner in which successful actors delivered their lines on stage:

Kindly observe in what manner the actors speak, in what range, high or low, how loudly or softly, how rapidly or slowly they enunciate their words ... how one speaks when infuriated or excited; how a married woman speaks, how a girl, how a lover ... how one speaks when lamenting, when crying out, when afraid, and when exulting with joy.[22]

For Galilei, it is clear that 'how one speaks' the words reveals their underlying emotion. For the composers of monody and theatrical song, by extension, it then became a question of 'how one sings' the words to disclose their innate significance.[23]

Twenty years Galilei's junior, Caccini built his long career as a singer, singing teacher, and composer on these precepts, claiming to have learnt more from Bardi's Camerata than from 'more than 30 years of counterpoint'. After composing solo madrigals and airs with figured bass accompaniment and performing them for Bardi's circle, where they were received 'with warm approval' in the 1580s, Caccini issued his pathbreaking collection of madrigals and airs in 1602 with the title *Le nuove musiche* (*The New Music* – more correctly translated as 'musical works in a new style').[24] Caccini's was the first set of *composed and published* monodies, as opposed to the improvised airs that had been 'recited' on formulas suitable for rendering sonnets, epic stanzas, and other fixed poetic forms during the fifteenth and sixteenth centuries; in effect, the new pieces were frozen improvisations. The distinction of being composed also separates them from contemporary solo songs that were actually arrangements of polyphonic compositions. In addition to their new texture, Caccini's works embody Galilei's precepts in two more ways: they abjure the common manner and excessive use of ornamentation, and in melodic contour and rhythmic profile they approach the nuances of speech. In the first instance, Caccini was adamant about using ornamentation only to enhance the affections inherent in the text and melody. And, to approximate the flexibility of speech, he advocated that the performer apply his concept of *sprezzatura* – a sort of nonchalance or casualness of delivery – a concept he adapted from Baldassare Castiglione's *Il libro del cortigiano* (*Book of the Courtier*, 1528), a meditation on the qualities necessary for the ideal Renaissance courtier to cultivate.[25] Caccini's innovations had a far-reaching impact on composers of monody in the early seventeenth century. However, once the theatre became the proving ground of the capabilities of modern music in the late 1590s, Caccini staked his claim to primacy in that arena by composing and rushing into print his own first music drama, *L'Euridice* (1601), in the wake of Peri's and Rinuccini's success.[26]

After Bardi moved to Rome in 1592, having been to some extent unseated at court by Duke Ferdinando's new favourite, Cavalieri, the field was left open for the wealthy merchant Corsi to become the principal patron of music in Florence (after the Medici) and the standard-bearer of the experimental 'movement' in musical theatre.[27] With Rinuccini, fellow academician in the Alterati, and Peri, he produced their first offering, *La Dafne*, in 1597/8.[28] In contrast to the 1589 *intermedi*, performed before several thousand international guests, *Dafne* was a very modest affair. It first played in Corsi's home for a comparatively few invited guests, among whom were 'some of the principal gentlemen' of Florence.[29] It had the distinction, however, of being the first to include the dramatic style of singing now known as recitative. It was soon followed by *L'Euridice* (by Rinuccini and Peri, with some music by Caccini), performed in October 1600, as a small and fairly inconsequential part of the entertainments for the wedding festivities of Maria de' Medici and Henry IV of France.[30] Because Caccini would not allow the singers under his tutelage to perform Peri's music, he inserted his own music for some of the roles. Meanwhile, Cavalieri was claiming the distinction of having composed and produced in 1595 the first completely sung 'pastorals' on texts by a different poet, Laura Guidiccioni (one with whom he had collaborated in the 1589 *intermedi*) – a claim which Peri generously acknowledged in his preface to *L'Euridice*. But Cavalieri's works are not extant, and, judging by the tuneful style of his later musical play, *La Rappresentazione di Anima, et di Corpo*, printed in 1600 and first performed in Rome, Cavalieri shared neither the academic perspective nor the humanistic, ordinary-language aesthetic of his Florentine peers.[31] Still, such private rivalries among musicians were fuelled by the printers who promptly published their works and by the public competition among princes to garner attention with their patronage. These were some of the factors that fostered the endurance of the first completely sung musical tales and their spread to other urban centres – Mantua, Rome, Venice, and elsewhere, both inside and outside the Italian peninsula. Within a decade, the masterful madrigal composer Claudio Monteverdi (bap. 1567–1643) was to make his debut in the field with two dramatic works of his own: *La favola d'Orfeo* (1607), the first opera to achieve a place in the modern repertory, and *L'Arianna* (1608), now lost except for the Lament, which was destined to become the most famous piece of music of the seventeenth century. But Monteverdi's works owe a great deal to Peri's score, particularly in the way they build on and amplify the rhetorical strategies of Peri's innovative style of dramatic singing. However, in order to appreciate fully Peri's accomplishment in inventing recitative, we first need to explore Neoplatonic notions in Renaissance Florence about Orphic singing and its effects.

Musical Magic

More than a century before the first experiments in opera, Angelo Poliziano had dramatised the myth of Orpheus for the Florentine cultural elite. His *Orfeo* (1480), the earliest secular play in Italian, received numerous editions during the sixteenth century and became, in effect, a Medici literary classic, popularising through the Orpheus legend the marvels of ancient music and musicians.[32] The musician par excellence of antiquity, Orpheus had been able to tame the beasts of nature and charm Hades into allowing him to lead Eurydice out of the Underworld – all by means of the power of his spellbinding incantation. Poliziano himself was a member of the Neoplatonic circle surrounding Lorenzo de' Medici (known as the 'Magnificent' because of his brilliance and erudition). The main intellectual figure in his informal academy was another erudite Florentine, Marsilio Ficino (1433–1499), a humanist well versed in Platonic thought. As early as 1489, Ficino postulated a 'music-spirit' theory, which explained the peculiar power of music by the fact that, unlike other sensual stimuli, it is carried by air, which is also the medium of the *spiritus*.[33] This is why Ficino and his fellow Neoplatonists counted among the most prized classical disciplines to have been revived in the Florence of their day the art of singing to the Orphic lyre.

So, in the court culture of Florence during the late fifteenth century and throughout the sixteenth, singing – and especially solo singing – took on very special significance. This derived from Ficino's conviction that the human voice, through music, provided the link between the earthly world and the cosmos. Because Platonic thought held that the individual was connected to the entire universe through harmony, it followed that the best way to express this connection was by giving voice to song. Moreover, the artful singer had the ability to envoice psychological and moral reality and the power to make that reality present to others.[34] This is what underlay the Aristotelian concept of imitation or mimesis. By employing certain patterns of correspondence between micro- and macrocosm, between the motions of the human soul and the hidden harmony of the cosmos, the singer could manipulate the listener's responses. The composer-singer, then, in the guise of the legendary Orpheus, became the expressive agent of that artistic power. And Florentine Neoplatonism, in the artistic manifestation of Poliziano's *Orfeo* – a spoken drama with interpolated song[35] – helped to stimulate a century-long fascination with the expressive powers of music.

It is now possible to comprehend how Mei, Bardi, Caccini, Peri, and Rinuccini, being products of a culture steeped in Neoplatonic musical mysteries, were all heirs to these Renaissance ideas about the magical effects of song. Mei shared some of Ficino's 'music-spirit' theories, particularly that which held hearing to be superior to the other senses in its ability to act on the soul's passions.[36] As we have seen above, Bardi's program for the 1589 *intermedi* revolved around the power of song, while his protégé, Caccini, revitalised the Renaissance ideal of incantatory solo singing for the Camerata. In creating the first opera libretto, Rinuccini, under the weight of Florentine and Medicean tradition, looked back to Poliziano's fable of *Orfeo*. Not only was Orfeo a fitting protagonist for a completely sung music drama aiming to demonstrate the power of song, but also, as Tomlinson points out, its outcome and that of the other earliest tales of opera 'vindicated the occult harmony of the cosmos ... : in the answer of Daphne's just prayers by her magical transformation [into a laurel tree], in the alleviation of Ariadne's woes by the miraculous descent of Bacchus, in the transformative power of song in ... [the] Orpheus librettos'. Like Ovid's tales of metamorphoses from which they were drawn, these were fabrications or fables (*favole*) which, by focusing on timeless myths involving love and loss, sought to dramatise, externalise, or represent human sentiment.[37] And what better way was there of realising the transformative power of song and Orfeo's incantatory magic than through musical speech? This was at the heart of the notion of the representational style (*stile rappresentativo*). Peri's invention of the dramatic style of singing known as recitative, then, was rooted in the belief that musical speech was capable of transmitting an inner, emotional reality and could therefore represent human affections on stage.

Peri's Theory of Recitative

Recitative, the most extreme form of solo song or monody, was without question opera's most radical innovation. It was also the ultimate product of humanism because it sought not merely to place the music in the service of the words, but to eliminate completely the distinction between words and music, between speaking and singing, between art and nature. It did this by synthesising the two elements into an inseparable whole, creating a language which was sui generis – more than speech but less than song, as Peri described it: a language able to communicate simultaneously both to the mind and the body, the intellect and the emotions.

In the preface to the published score of *L'Euridice*, Peri recounted his search for a new kind of singing with which to render dramatic dialogue ('the kind of imitation necessary for these poems [libretti]').[38] Significantly, he recognised this creative effort as an act of imitation – not just emulation of the ancients, which it is also, but imitation of natural speech. The resultant 'theory' of recitative was partly adapted from his understanding of the manner of performance of ancient Greek drama and partly based on his quite remarkable analysis of the oral inflections of modern speech, perhaps stimulated in part by Mei's writings.[39] In his preface, Peri reflected on the distinction made by the ancient Greeks between the 'continuous' or sliding pitches of speech and the 'diastematic' or intervallic motion of song in which discrete pitches are sustained. He noted that the first are usually 'fluent' and 'rapid' while the others are normally 'slow' and 'sustained' but 'could at times be hastened and made to take an intermediate course', or 'could be adapted to my purpose'. He went on to explain how he deployed the bass line under the voice, which constitutes the most original aspect of his theory. This involved recognising that 'in our speech some sounds are pronounced [or intoned with a pitch] in such a way [we would say, "stressed" by a tonic accent] that a harmony can be built upon them, and that in the course of speaking we pass through many other [syllables] that are not so intoned, until we reach another that will support a progression to a new consonance [by virtue of having an identifiable pitch]'. So he placed a consonant harmony in the bass to support the 'intoned' notes of the melody and held it firm, allowing the 'continuous', rapidly declaimed syllables to be uttered over that same harmony while passing 'through both dissonances and consonances' until another 'intoned' note in the melody 'opened the way to a new harmony'.

But Peri also built into his method a device for ensuring that the emotional content of the text was respected and that there would be some degree of variety in the recitative's delivery. 'Keeping in mind those inflections and accents that serve us in our grief, in our joy, and in similar states, I made the bass move in time to these, now more, now less [frequently], according to the affections.'

The opening of the speech from *L'Euridice* in which the messenger brings the news of Euridice's death to Orfeo shows how Peri followed his own prescription for composing recitative (see Example 1.1).[40] The vertical boxes identify the syllables that are sustained or accented in normal Italian pronunciation (usually the third and sixth, or sixth and tenth syllable of a line, depending on its length) and which, because they linger on a discrete pitch, are capable of suggesting a chordal harmony. Depending upon the

Example 1.1 Jacopo Peri, *Le musiche di Jacopo Peri sopra L'Euridice* (Florence: Giorgio Marescotti, 1600 [1601, modern style]), Dafne's recitative, mm. 19–26

Ma la *bel*-la Eu-ri-*di*-ce   But the lovely Eurydice
1 2 3 4   5 6 7

Mo-vea dan-zan-do il *pie* sul ver-de *pra*-to   was prancing around the green meadow
1   2 3 4 5   6 7 8 9 10 11

Quand'ahi *ria* sorte a-*cer*-ba   when—O bitter angry fate !—
1   2 3 4 5 6 7

An-gue *cru*-do, e spie-*ta*-to   a snake, cruel and merciless,
1 2 3 4 5 6 7

Che ge-la-to gia-*cea* tra fio-ri e *l'er*-ba   that lay motionless among flowers and grass
1 2 3 4 5 6 7 8 9 10 11

Pun-se-le il *pie* ...   bit her foot ...
1 2 3 4

degree of calm or excitement he wishes to generate, Peri often uses only one chord per line of text, especially for the shorter lines, and almost always places it under the penultimate syllable. The horizontal boxes contain the syllables that are quickly uttered in speech; these may form dissonances (indicated by asterisks) or consonances with the bass, depending on the affections. The way in which the dissonances are introduced and then left was not an issue for Peri because the new speechlike texture freed the voice from the constraints of counterpoint.

Thus, Peri conceived of recitative as a spontaneous-sounding musical language fusing speech and song that was capable of imitating, expressing, and arousing the emotions. It should be noted that neither Peri nor Caccini actually invented basso continuo texture, which had become widespread as a technique for accompanying non-polyphonic music during the last decades of the sixteenth century. However, Peri's account of the role of the bass in his description of recitative shows that his use of the new texture as a compositional tool was completely revolutionary.[41] In this manner of composing, the bass has no rhythmic profile of its own, and the harmonies adhere to no formal plan; they are there merely to support the voice, which is thus liberated from its contrapuntal framework. Another device which Peri understood to be key to the imitation of speech is the use of ametrical rhythms and phrases, carefully separated by rests and following the flow of Rinuccini's irregularly alternating poetic lines of seven and eleven syllables. But the crucial question must be: how does Peri's music reflect the emotional content of the words? He employs a number of devices, some of which are illustrated in Example 1.1: skilful dissonance treatment (shown by the asterisks), with greater density of dissonance signalling more painful emotions; sudden and irrational shifts of harmony, as in the motion from a G major chord to an E major one in the last measure, to intensify moments of grief; poignant and harmonically unsupported melodic intervals such as diminished fourths and fifths; and adjusting the pace of the delivery of words, with slower rhythms conveying laments and doleful sentiments. In the end, Peri knew that he had not revived Greek music; but he believed he had created a speech-song that not only resembled what had been used in ancient theatre but was also compatible with modern musical practice.

Of course, the first operas were entirely sung, but not only in recitative; more traditional styles of singing were also employed, including airs (where the action called for 'singing' rather than 'speaking') and part-songs or many-voiced madrigals for the choruses, sometimes danced, which marked the separation between scenes and delivered sententious pronouncements about the action and fate of the characters. In this respect, all of the early court operas are alike except, as noted, Cavalieri's *Rappresentatione*, which, significantly, employed a libretto not by Rinuccini. But Caccini's *Euridice* was also different enough from Peri's to give the lie to Caccini's claim of having been the first to use the new style of dramatic singing – if by that we mean real recitative and not just the affective, rhetorical kind of solo singing that was indeed his specialty.[42] However, even when he was intent on emulating Peri's recitative, Caccini's theatrical style resembles his chamber monodies. The dialogue passages in Caccini's *Euridice* are more songlike than speechlike: the bass line is more evenly paced, its function closer to that of a contrapuntal line than of a harmonic support; and the melody shows less subtlety and rhythmic variety than Peri's and uses far less dissonance. Both composers were striving toward the ideal envisaged by Galilei in writing a kind of music that naturalistically reflected 'how an actor delivers his lines' so as to convey the character's emotions. Perhaps the difference between them can be summed up by remembering that Caccini was a singer first and a composer second, whereas Peri was primarily a composer who also sang.[43] Moreover, it is clear to anyone who compares the scores of Monteverdi's *Orfeo* and Peri's *Euridice* that, if Monteverdi can be credited with having brought opera into the future that Gagliano was predicting for it in 1608, he did so by recognising and building on Peri's accomplishments.

Notes

1 Marco da Gagliano, preface to *La Dafne di Marco da Gagliano* (Florence: Cristofano Marescotti, 1608; rpt. Bologna: Forni Editore, 1987). The translation used here is based on that of Carol MacClintock, *Readings in the History of Music in Performance* (Bloomington and London: Indiana University Press, 1979), 188. Further on the 1608 *La Dafne* by Marco da Gagliano, see Tim Carter, 'A Florentine Wedding of 1608', *Acta Musicologica* 55/1 (1983), 89–107, rpt. in Tim Carter, *Music, Patronage and Printing in Late Renaissance Florence* (Aldershot and Burlington: Ashgate, 2000).

2 Gagliano, preface to *La Dafne*; see MacClintock, *Readings in the History of Music*, 188–9. The full text with an English translation (by Tim Carter) may be seen in Tim Carter and Zygmunt Szweykowski (eds.), *Composing Opera: From 'Dafne' to 'Ulisse errante'* (Cracow: Musica Iagellonica, 1994), 46–67.

3 The concept of civic humanism was elaborated in Hans Baron's *The Crisis of the Early Italian Renaissance*, 2 vols. (Princeton, 1955; rev. 1966) and Eugenio Garin's *Italian Humanism: Philosophy and Civic Life in the Renaissance*, trans. Peter Munz (New York: Harper and Row, 1965); see Gary Tomlinson, 'Renaissance Humanism and Music', in James Haar (ed.), *European Music, 1520–1640* (Woodbridge and Rochester: Boydell Press, 2006), 1–19, esp. 9–10. Also see the more recent study of Florentine civic humanism as it concerns the birth of opera: Gaspare De Caro, *Euridice: Momenti dell'Umanesimo civile fiorentino* (Bologna: Ut Orpheus Edizioni, 2006).

4 Gary Tomlinson, 'Pastoral and Musical Magic in the Birth of Opera', in Thomas Bauman and Marita McClymonds (eds.), *Opera and the Enlightenment* (Cambridge: Cambridge University Press, 1995), 7–20. See also Daniel P. Walker, *Spiritual and Demonic Magic from Ficino to Campanella* (London: The Warburg Institute, University of London, 1958) and Ruth Katz, *Divining the Powers of Music: Aesthetic Theory and the Origins of Opera* (New York: Pendragon Press, 1986), esp. 87ff.

5 James M. Saslow, *The Medici Wedding of 1589: Florentine Festival as 'Theatrum Mundi'* (New Haven and London: Yale University Press, 1996), 2. For a summary account of the intermedi, see Alois M. Nagler, *Theatre Festivals of the Medici* (New Haven: Yale University Press, 1964), 58–69. The relevant documentation is also illustrated in a recent exhibition catalogue: Maria Adelaide Bartoli Bacherini, *'Per un regale evento': Spettacoli nuziali e opera in musica alla corte dei Medici* (Florence: Centro Di, 2000). For an edition, see *Les Fêtes du mariage de Ferdinand de Médicis et de Christine de Lorraine: Florence, 1589*, in Daniel P. Walker, (ed.), I: *Musique des intermèdes de 'La Pellegrina'* (Paris: Éditions du Centre National de la Recherche Scientifique, 1963).

6 Further on Giovanni de' Bardi, see Tim Carter, *'Per cagione di bene, et giustamente vivere*: Some Thoughts on the Musical Patronage of Giovanni de' Bardi', in Piero Gargiulo, Alessandro Magini, and Stéphane Toussaint (eds.), *Neoplatonismo, musica, letteratura nel Rinascimento: I Bardi di Vernio e l'Accademia della Crusca; atti del Convegno Internazionale di Studi, Firenze-Vernio, 25–26 settembre 1998* (Paris: Société Marsile Ficin, 2000), 137–46; Claude V. Palisca, 'The Musical Humanism of Giovanni Bardi', in Hagop Meyvalian (ed.), *Poesia e musica nell'estetica del XVI e XVII secolo* (Florence: Artiminio, 1979), 45–72; and Warren Kirkendale, *The Court Musicians in Florence during the Principate of the Medici* (Florence: Olschki, 1993).

7 On Ottavio Rinuccini, see *inter alia*, Barbara Russano Hanning, *Of Poetry and Music's Power: Humanism and the Creation of Opera* (Ann Arbor, MI: UMI Research Press, 1980), esp. chap. 1 (1–19): 'Rinuccini and the Power of Music'; and Russano Hanning, 'Glorious Apollo: Poetic and Political Themes in the First Opera', *Renaissance Quarterly* 32/4 (1979), 485–513.

8 Detlef Heikamp, 'Il Teatro Mediceo degli Uffizi', *Bollettino del Centro Internazionale di architettura Andrea Palladio* 16 (1974), 323–32; Nino Pirrotta and Elena Povoledo, *Music and Theatre from Poliziano to Monteverdi* (Cambridge: Cambridge University Press, 1982), 365–83.

9 The phrase is Richard Taruskin's: see his *Music from the Earliest Notations to the Sixteenth Century*, in *The Oxford History of Western Music*, vol. 1 (New York: Oxford University Press, 2009), 804.

10 The pythic creature is described as greenish-black and covered with sparkling mirrors. It 'was constructed in separate units of papier-mâché modeled over

clay forms and assembled on a wooden framework', and it was operated by a stagehand from inside (Saslow, *The Medici Wedding of 1589*, 231–2).

11 Rinuccini's phrase ('*si nobil maniera di recitare*'), from the dedication (to Maria de' Medici) of his libretto *L'Euridice* (Florence, 1600); Italian text and translation in Carter, *Composing Opera*, 16–17.

12 *Le musiche di Jacopo Peri sopra L'Euridice* (Florence: Giorgio Marescotti, 1600 [1601, modern style]; rpt. Rome: Reale Accademia d'Italia, 1934, and Bologna: Forni, 1969); performing edition, ed. Howard Mayer Brown (Madison: A-R Editions, 1981).

13 See note 11.

14 Tomlinson, 'Renaissance Humanism', 18.

15 Claude V. Palisca, 'The Alterati of Florence, Pioneers in the Theory of Dramatic Music', in William W. Austin (ed.), *New Looks at Italian Opera: Essays in Honor of Donald J. Grout* (Ithaca: Cornell University Press, 1968), 9–38; rpt. in Palisca, *Studies in the History of Italian Music and Music Theory* (Oxford: Clarendon Press; New York: Oxford University Press, 1994), 408–31.

16 Claude V. Palisca, *The Florentine Camerata: Documentary Studies and Translations* (New Haven: Yale University Press, 1989); esp. 1–11.

17 Mei's correspondence to the Camerata is published in Girolamo Mei, *Girolamo Mei (1519–1594): Letters on Ancient and Modern Music to Vincenzo Galilei and Giovanni Bardi: A Study with Annotated Text*, ed. and trans. Claude V. Palisca, 2nd edn. ([Rome]: American Institute of Musicology, 1977 [1960]).

18 Claude V. Palisca, 'Vincenzo Galilei's Arrangements for Voice and Lute', in Gustav Reese and Robert J. Snow (eds.), *Essays in Musicology in Honor of Dragan Plamenac on His 70th Birthday* (Pittsburgh: University of Pittsburgh Press, 1969), 207–32; rpt. in Palisca, *Studies*, 364–88.

19 Vincenzo Galilei, *Dialogo della musica antica et della moderna* (Florence, 1581; rpt. New York: Broude Brothers [1967]); for the English translation, see Galilei, *Dialogue on Ancient and Modern Music*, ed. and trans. Claude V. Palisca (New Haven: Yale University Press, 2003).

20 Mei had definitively established that the ancient Greek modes were different from the church modes by being essentially the same arrangement of tones transposed higher or lower on the Greek gamut; thus, depending on their register, some modes were more relaxed, others more intense – much like our modern scales. See his 'Letter to Vincenzo Galilei, 8 May 1572', in Palisca, *The Florentine Camerata*, 66–7.

21 Further on Mei's theories, see Russano Hanning, *Of Poetry and Music's Power*, 31–41.

22 Translated excerpts from Galilei's *Dialogo* may be found in Oliver Strunk (ed.), *Source Readings in Music History*, rev. ed. by Leo Treitler (New York: Norton, 1998), 462–7, and in Piero Weiss and Richard Taruskin, *Music in the Western World: A History in Documents* (New York: Schirmer, 1984), 166–8. The passage quoted above is taken from the latter, 167–8.

23 Compare the following passage from Bardi's *Discourse on Ancient Music and Good Singing (Sopra la musica antica e'l cantar bene)* addressed to Caccini: 'Those great philosophers and connoisseurs of nature understood well that in the low voice is slowness and somnolence, in the medium quiet, majesty, and magnificence, and in the high shrillness and lament. Now who does not know that the drunken and the somnolent usually speak in a low tone and slowly, and that men of great affairs converse in a medium voice, quiet and magnificent; . . . that in the rhythms are the portraits of anger, mildness, strength, temperance, and of every other moral virtue, as well as of all those qualities which are their contraries.' Quoted and translated in Russano Hanning, *Of Poetry and Music's Power*, 37–8. The entire discourse is printed and translated in Palisca, *The Florentine Camerata*, 90–131. Further on Caccini's relations with Bardi, see Claude V. Palisca, 'The *Camerata fiorentina*: A Reappraisal', *SM* 1 (1972), 203–36.

24 Giulio Caccini, *Le nuove musiche* (Florence, 1601 [1602, modern style]; rpt. Rome: Reale Accademia d'Italia, 1934); the critical and performing edition is edited with a translation of Caccini's important Preface by H. Wiley Hitchcock (Madison: A-R Editions, 1970).

25 Caccini's Preface was printed in Italian in Angelo Solerti (ed.), *Le origini del melodrama* (Turin: Fratelli Bocca, 1903; rpt. Bologna: Forni, 1969); for Hitchcock's English translation, see his edition of *Le nuove musiche*, 43–56. See also Margaret Murata's translation of Caccini's Preface, in Strunk (ed.), *Source Readings*, 608–17.

26 *L'Euridice composta in musica in stile rappresentativo da Giulio Caccini detto Romano* (Florence: Giorgio Marescotti, 1601; facs. Bologna: Forni, 1968). In the dedication to Bardi, Caccini lays claim to 'having been the first to give to the press like kind of songs, and the style and manner of them, . . . composed by me more than fifteen years ago at various times, since I have never used in my works any other art than the imitation of the sentiments of the words' (referring to his new score as well as to the monodies yet to be published in *Le nuove musiche*). The dedication is printed and translated in Carter, *Composing Opera*, 35–41, and trans. in Strunk, *Source Readings*, 606. Caccini's complete score, however, was not performed in its entirety until 1602. (The 1600 performance had been largely of Peri's music).

27 On Jacopo Corsi see Tim Carter, 'Music and Patronage in Late Sixteenth-Century Florence: The Case of Jacopo Corsi (1561–1602)', in *I Tatti Studies in the Italian Renaissance* 1 (1985), 57–104, rpt. in Carter, *Music, Patronage and Printing in Late Renaissance Florence* (Aldershot and Burlington: Ashgate, 2000).

28 William V. Porter, 'Peri and Corsi's *Dafne*: Some New Discoveries and Observations', *JAMS* 18/2 (1965), 170–96. Also see Frederick W. Sternfeld, 'The First Printed Opera Libretto', *ML* 59/2 (1978), 121–38.

29 See the opening of this chapter, and notes 1 and 2.

30 Claude V. Palisca, 'The First Performance of *Euridice*', in the *Twenty-fifth Anniversary Festschrift* (1937–62) [of Queens College], ed. Albert Mell (New York: Queens College of the City University of New York, 1964), 1–23; rpt. with a new introductory headnote in Palisca, *Studies in the History of Italian Music and Music Theory*, 432–51. Further on *Euridice* see, *inter alia*, T. Carter, 'Jacopo Peri's *Euridice* (1600): A Contextual Study', *The Music Review* 43 (1982) 83–103, rpt. in Carter, *Music, Patronage, and Printing*; Kelley Harness, 'Le tre *Euridici*: Characterization and Allegory in the *Euridici* of Peri and Caccini', *JSCM* 9/1 (2003), https://sscm-jscm.org/v9/no1/harness.html; and Bojan Bujić, '"*Figura poetica molto vaga*": Structure and Meaning in Rinuccini's *Euridice*', *EMH* 10 (1991), 29–62; and de Caro, *Euridice: Momenti dell' Umanesimo*.

31 *Rappresentazione di anima, et di corpo novamente posta in musica dal sig. Emilio del Cavalieri per recitar cantando* (Rome: Nicolò Mutii, 1600). This judgement of Cavalieri's work was suggested by the Florentine man of letters Giovanni Battista Doni (1595–1647), perhaps the first historian of early opera. Further on Cavalieri see Claude V. Palisca, 'Musical Asides in the Diplomatic Correspondence of Emilio de' Cavalieri', *MQ* 49/3 (1963), 339–55, rpt. in Palisca, *Studies in the History of Italian Music and Music Theory*, 389–407. For a defence of Cavalieri's contribution to the creation of opera, see Warren Kirkendale, *Emilio de' Cavalieri, 'Gentiluomo Romano': His Life and Letters, His Role as Superintendent of All the Arts at the Medici Court, and His Musical Compositions* (Florence: Olschki, 2001), 185–212.

32 Pirrotta, 'Orpheus, Singer of *strambotti*', in *Music and Theatre*, 3–36.

33 See note 4 and Daniel P. Walker, 'Ficino's *Spiritus* and Music', *Annales musicologiques* 1 (1953), 131–50. For a more extensive treatment of these ideas, see Gary Tomlinson, *Music in Renaissance Magic: Toward a Historiography of Others* (Chicago: The University of Chicago Press, 1993), esp. 101–44.

34 Ficino wrote: 'Remember that song is the most powerful imitator of all things. For it imitates the intentions and affections of the soul'; quoted and trans. by Walker, 'Ficino's *Spiritus* and Music', from the third book of Ficino's *De triplici vita* in 'Ficino's Spritus and Music', 139.

35 On the precise role of music in Poliziano's *Orfeo*, see Pirrotta, 'Orpheus', 19–36.

36 Russano Hanning, *Of Poetry and Music's Power*, 27.

37 Tomlinson, 'Pastoral and Musical Magic', 17. Tomlinson also argues that 'early opera was not a specific version of pastoral drama'; rather, both genres 'arose from a culture whose world still offered magical realms' and grew out of 'the esotericism that burgeoned in Renaissance thought in the wake of the fifteenth-century revival of Neoplatonism'.

38 Italian facs. and English trans. (from Strunk, *Source Readings*) in Peri, *Euridice*, ed. Howard M. Brown, plates II and III and facing pages; Italian and English in Carter, *Composing Opera*, 24–33; English trans. (only) in Strunk, *Source Readings*, 659–62. The best annotated translation, which also includes the Italian in parallel columns, is by Claude V. Palisca; see his 'Peri and the

Theory of Recitative', *SM* 15 (1982), 51–61; rpt. in Palisca, *Studies*, 452–66. A similar commentary by Palisca appeared in his magisterial *Humanism in Italian Renaissance Musical Thought* (New Haven and London: Yale University Press, 1985), 427–33. The following paragraph is greatly indebted to Palisca's interpretation.

39 Some of Peri's ideas resemble Mei's theories on language, as expressed in his manuscript *Trattato sopra la prosa*. Compare this passage from Mei with phrases quoted from Peri's preface in the ensuing paragraph: 'just as, naturally, in the range and interval of the voice called by musicians *diastematic*, in other words, intervallic, the more acute places are a sign of an agitated soul, and the medium ones a tranquil soul, so … in the voice also called by them … *continuous*, the natural highness simply compared to the lowness in words retains proportionately the same qualities' (italics mine). Quoted and trans. by Russano Hanning, *Of Poetry and Music's Power*, 36. John Walter Hill has also proposed an approach to the study of early recitative based on intonational and metric phonology. See his 'Beyond Isomorphism toward a Better Theory of Recitative', *JSCM* 9/1 (2003), https://sscm-jscm.org/v9/no1/hill.html. Further on Peri, see Tim Carter, *Orpheus in the Marketplace: Jacopo Peri and the Economy of Late Renaissance Florence* (Cambridge, MA: Harvard University Press, 2013).

40 The example and my analysis are adapted from Palisca, 'Peri and the Theory of Recitative', *Studies*, 459ff.

41 The following observations are largely indebted to Howard Mayer Brown, 'How Opera Began: An Introduction to Jacopo Peri's *Euridice* (1600)', in Eric Cochrane (ed.), *The Late Italian Renaissance, 1525–1630* (London: Macmillan 1970), 401–43, esp. 421ff.

42 See note 26. Brown's judgement of Caccini's theatrical style is quite negative: 'Caccini's work may well have been the only "spite opera" in the history of music. The score shows signs of haste. It is a badly executed work, inferior in every way to Peri's, and unworthy of the composer of *Le nuove musiche*' (Brown, 'How Opera Began', 421–2). The score of Caccini's *Euridice* has had very few modern editions: it was published as vol. 10 in *Publikation älterer praktischer und theoretischer Musikwerke*, ed. Robert Eitner (Berlin: Trautwein, 1881), and in a performance edition in Lucca by OTOS, c. 2000.

43 More extensive comparisons between Peri's and Caccini's versions may be found in Nino Pirrotta, 'Early Opera and Aria', in *Music and Theatre*, 237–80, esp. 252–7; Russano Hanning, *Of Poetry and Music's Power*, 83–117; Georgie Durosoir, 'L'*Euridice* de Rinuccini: Comparaison des réalisations de Peri et Caccini', in Irène Mamczarz (ed.), *Les premiers opéras en Europe et les formes dramatiques apparentées* (Paris: Klincksieck, 1992), 49–58, esp. 54–5; and Laura Pistolesi, *Del recitar cantando: Per uno studio comparativo dell'Euridice di Jacopo Peri e dell'Euridice di Giulio Caccini* (Milan: Assoc. Amici della Scala, 1990), esp. 61–86.

2   '...e poi le parole'

Towards a History of the Libretto

TIM CARTER

Any attempt to write a history of the libretto is fraught with paradox. Almost without exception, a text is the starting point for any opera. Indeed, before Mozart, and often after, the libretto was normally complete before the composer put pen to paper, for all that it might then be revised according to the musical and other demands made upon it. As we shall see, its poetry usually had quite precise musical implications. Moreover, in early opera the poet was normally the prime mover in the operatic enterprise, not just by devising the subject and fleshing it out with appropriate words, but also given his often standard role as director of the production. The libretto was itself the public face of opera in terms of the artefacts that survive to record a given performance: libretti were usually printed for general consumption inside or outside the theatre, whereas musical scores were, on the whole, regarded as more ephemeral performance materials, to be adopted, adapted, and disposed of at will. Poets also acted as the chief ideologues of opera, promoting and defending the genre against its detractors and inserting it into broader literary and cultural debates. In a very real sense, the history of the libretto is the history of opera *tout court*.[1]

Yet as countless librettists have complained, the words rarely come high on any opera audience's agenda. The music, singers, *mise-en-scène*, costumes, and choreography vie for the attention of the eye and the ear, while the text, if it is held in any regard at all, is dismissed as a trying necessity or a trifling irrelevance. The beauties of a poet's verse are as nothing compared with the beauties of a composer's music, and, in some minds, both pale in comparison to the beauties of a singer's high C. In this light, the history of the libretto is just one relatively minor branch of opera studies.

The point is confirmed by a platitude: the best poetry can rarely be set to music because it is too self-sufficient, with nothing to be added. While this may or may not be true, the more damaging corollary – that any poetry for music must be second-rate – ignores the fact that libretti should be judged not by the canons of 'great' verse (although some are) but, rather, by fitness to purpose. Most theatre poets accepted, gladly or not, that when writing for music, compromises had to be made in terms of plot design and arrangement, and of poetic language, accent, and even vowel sounds (it is hard to sing a melisma on *u*). The mere fact that it always takes longer to sing something than to say it conditions the nature of *poesia per musica*, which, in turn, must always expect completion by something beyond itself. Nahum Tate's verse for his dying Dido (in Purcell's *Dido and Aeneas*) is scarcely great, or even good, poetry:[2]

Thy hand, Belinda, darkness shades me,
    On thy bosom let me rest.
(*Cupids appear in the clouds o'er her tomb.*)
More I would but Death invades me.
Death is now a welcome guest.
When I am laid in earth, my wrongs create
    No trouble in thy breast;
    Remember me, but ah! forget my fate.

However, it serves its purpose well. Why that should be the case is something worth exploring.

'a Poetical Tale or Fiction'

In 1685, the English poet John Dryden published his *Albion and Albanius*, set to music by Luis Grabu as a full-length opera (the first in English to survive). His preface begins with the nature of operatic subject matter:

An *Opera* is a poetical Tale or Fiction, represented by Vocal and Instrumental Musick, adorn'd with Scenes, Machines and Dancing. The suppos'd Persons of this musical Drama, are generally supernatural, as Gods and Goddesses, and Heroes, which at least are descended from them, and are in due time, to be adopted into their Number. The Subject therefore being extended beyond the Limits of Humane Nature, admits of that sort of marvellous and surprizing conduct, which is rejected in other Plays.[3]

This 'marvellous and surprizing conduct' extends beyond the implausible plots and *dei ex machina* so typical of the genre. Still more 'surprizing' is opera's fundamental premise, that drama can be played out in song. The consequent lack of verisimilitude might best be accepted as just a fact of operatic life, but it remained troubling in an age that still paid at least lip service to precepts drawn from Classical poetics, notably the writings of Aristotle and Horace. This explains the subject matter of the earliest operas in the north Italian courts, drawn chiefly from Graeco-Roman myth, where supernatural gods and goddesses could reasonably be expected to differentiate themselves from mere mortals by way of music. It also explains their standard setting in the pastoral utopia of Arcadia, where poetry and therefore music are natural conditions of an idealised life. For Dryden the presence of gods, goddesses, and heroes

hinders not, but that meaner Persons, may sometimes gracefully be introduc'd, especially if they have relation to those first times, which Poets call the *Golden Age*: wherein by reason of their Innocence, those happy Mortals, were suppos'd to have had a more familiar intercourse with Superiour Beings: and therefore Shepherds might reasonably be admitted, as of all Callings, the most innocent, the most happy, and who by reason of the spare time they had, in their almost idle Employment, had most leisure to make Verses, and to be in Love; without somewhat of which Passion, no *Opera* can possibly subsist.

The gradual expansion of operatic subject matter throughout the seventeenth century attenuated the pastoral argument and called for further special pleading in printed prefaces, as well as in the other standard forum for operatic apologias, the prologue. Even before opera went 'public' in Venice in 1637, its subjects were extending beyond the standard mythological–pastoral fare of earlier court entertainment to embrace epic (Homer's *Iliad* and *Odyssey*, Virgil's *Aeneid*, Lodovico Ariosto's *Orlando furioso*, Torquato Tasso's *Gerusalemme liberata*, Giambattista Marino's *Adone*), and even Greek and Roman history. Sacred operas likewise made the transition from the representation of allegorical virtues and vices (Emilio de' Cavalieri's *Rappresentatione di Anima, et di Corpo* of 1600) to quasi-historical accounts of saints' lives (in the operas staged in Rome under the patronage of the powerful Barberini family from the early 1630s onwards).

The appeal of epic is easily explained. Tasso's Rinaldo and Armida first appeared in a set of *intermedi* by Ottavio Vernizzi (Bologna, 1623), followed by Benedetto Ferrari's *Armida* (Venice, 1639), Lully's *tragédie en musique, Armide* (Paris, 1686), and John Eccles's *Rinaldo and Armida* (London, 1698). Characters from Ariosto's *Orlando furioso* appear in Marco da Gagliano and Jacopo Peri's *Lo sposalizio di Medoro et Angelica* (Florence, 1619), Francesca Caccini's *La liberazione di Ruggiero dall'isola d'Alcina* (Florence, 1625), Luigi Rossi's *Il palazzo incantato* (Rome, 1642), Lully's *Roland* (Versailles, 1685), and Agostino Steffani's *Orlando generoso* (Hanover, 1691), to name only a few. The trend increased in the eighteenth century, from Handel's *Rinaldo* (1711) and *Alcina* (1735) through Gluck's *Armide* (1777) and beyond. The line between myth and epic was thin, and both Alcina and Armida owe a clear debt to the classic *femme fatale* of Homer's *Odyssey* and its mythological forbears Circe, save that in the later case – and no doubt to the gratification of seventeenth- and eighteenth-century censors – these pagan sorceresses could ultimately be redeemed by the love of a Christian hero. The chief difficulty in both cases, however, was how to turn epic narration into dramatic representation, which usually involved the introduction of extraneous characters (divine or mortal) to explain the plot.

Any subject drawn from history might seem to cause greater problems, although these may be more apparent than real. Here, the question of verisimilitude comes most to the fore. As the librettist Francesco Sbarra admitted in the preface to his *Alessandro vincitor di se stesso* (1651, set by Antonio Cesti), dealing with Alexander the Great:

I know that some people will consider the *ariette* sung by Alessandro and Aristotile unfit for the dignity of such great characters ... nevertheless it is not only permitted but even accepted with praise ... If the recitative style were not mingled with such *scherzi*, it would give more annoyance than pleasure. Pardon me this license, which I have taken only in order to make it less tiresome for you.[4]

Some 'historical' characters inhabit a hinterland between fact and fiction: the heroes of the Trojan Wars (Achilles, Aeneas, Ulysses) may actually have existed, but they also have strong mythical properties, and they occupy a world shaped by divine intervention. Both Ariosto and Tasso drew inspiration from history (respectively, the time of Charlemagne and the First Crusade), and yet they subjected their heroes to trials and tribulations inspired by Classical mythology and by medieval romance. The kings and queens of ancient Mesopotamia and the Middle East that also started to populate operas were probably not significant historical presences. Even Roman dictators and emperors (Julius Caesar, Claudius Nero) were not necessarily to be viewed in the same light as characters in, say, a Shakespeare 'history play'. Indeed, in all these cases, it is often the exotic otherness of their stories that makes them appropriate for operas, which, in turn, were not to be construed, at least directly, as some kind of lesson in the facts of history, even if they raised important questions about how history might usefully be read.

Much has been made of what has often been called the 'first' historical opera, Monteverdi's *L'incoronazione di Poppea* (Venice, 1643; libretto by Giovanni Francesco Busenello), which is based on the erotic antics of Emperor Nero and his mistress, Poppaea Sabina, and the consequent downfalls of Empress Octavia (sent to exile) and the philosopher Seneca (condemned to suicide). In a preface to his own edition of the libretto, Busenello acknowledged the outline of the events treated in the opera as described by Tacitus. 'But here', he states, 'we represent these actions differently.'[5] Busenello further tempers any claim for historical veracity by typically relying on the intervention of the god of Love ('without somewhat of which Passion, no *Opera* can possibly subsist', says Dryden). Such treatment might or might not be a case of legitimate poetic license, but it does question the extent to which modern critics should judge this famously immoral plot on the grounds of their own historical knowledge (e.g., that both Poppaea and Nero eventually came to sticky ends).

The problem is not restricted to opera. Contemporary spoken drama runs through a similar gamut of genres, styles, and subjects, and seems equally fluid in terms of potential interpretations. So, too, do *commedia dell'arte* scenarios – which range far more widely than just the stereotypical characters and plots often viewed as standard in the genre – and likewise a relatively unexplored source of material for Baroque opera, contemporary novellas and related 'popular' literature. All these establish a number of plot-types that, in turn, prompt variations on a set of standard themes. For example, two young lovers, one or both in an unhappily arranged engagement or marriage, will staunchly resist social and other pressures applied by a pedantic tutor or a busybody nurse, surmounting all obstacles to find true happiness. The fact that this is the foundation of *L'incoronazione di Poppea* as much as it is of, say, Rossini's *Il barbiere di Siviglia* need not cause too much discomfort. But it suggests that originality of invention is not what matters most. In part, this is blatant commercialism: audience familiarity leads to 'brand loyalty' and hence increasing consumption. Furthermore, it permits efficient short-cuts in the re-telling of well-known stories. Finally, it creates a strongly intertextual world where operas are to be compared less with 'real life' than with other similar works.

While earlier librettists such as Ottavio Rinuccini, Busenello, and Giovanni Faustini had tended to write one-off libretti for a small circle of composers – a practice that, of course, remained in use – some later libretti seem to have become reified as 'works' of and for themselves that could therefore gain wider distribution. Giacinto Andrea Cicognini's text for *Orontea* had settings by Francesco Lucio (Venice, 1649), Francesco Cirillo (Naples, 1654), Cesti (Innsbruck, 1656), and Filippo Vismarri (Vienna, 1660). Their complex genealogy has yet to be fully disentangled, and, in general, the mechanisms of libretto transmission have not yet been properly studied: presumably they involved complex networks of personal contacts (among impresarios, poets, composers, and singers) and also, and increasingly, of printed editions whether of single works or of collected *opera omnia*. One result, however, was that some literate audiences might well have started to identify particular works as belonging to their librettists independent of the different musical clothing offered by a succession of composers and singers. The same is true of, say, the libretti of Pietro Metastasio in the eighteenth century, which had a strong literary presence quite apart from their repeated operatic settings.

The latest catalogue of printed opera (etc.) libretti contains some 5,800 entries covering the years 1600–1699, and 24,000 for 1700–1799.[6] It is hard nowadays to conceive the sheer scale of the operatic enterprise in the seventeenth and eighteenth centuries – especially given the highly limited repertory of most modern opera houses – as the burgeoning opera 'industry' created complex infrastructures of supply and demand. But if the various tendencies towards standardisation identified above are certainly to be viewed in this light, they also reflect a codification of genres for further academic and related reasons. Here the need was to resist, rather than promote, certain trends that were coming to be viewed as deleterious to the notion of opera as some kind of drama; it also played into broader debates, such as the *Querelle des Anciens et des Modernes* that animated French (and thence European) cultural discourse from the second half of the seventeenth century into the eighteenth.

For example, the 'Arcadian Academy' was founded in Rome in 1690 for the reform and 'purification' of Italian poetry, in particular the opera libretto. It emerged like many such Roman gatherings from the circles of specific patrons, in this case Cardinal Pietro Ottoboni, although its influence spread widely through Italy and abroad. Librettists associated with the Arcadians included Ottoboni himself, Apostolo Zeno, Gian Vincenzo Gravina, Silvio Stampiglia, and Metastasio. Their spokesmen, including Giovanni Maria Crescimbeni (*La bellezza della volgar poesia*, Rome, 1700) and Ludovico Muratori, ranged widely in their attacks on the abuses of contemporary poetry, advocating a return to Classical simplicity, in part via French models drawn from Corneille and Racine. Giacinto Andrea Cicognini's libretto for Cavalli's *Giasone* (Venice, 1649) came under particularly harsh critique by Crescimbeni:

with it he brought the end of acting, and consequently, of true and good comedy as well as tragedy. Since to stimulate to a greater degree with novelty the jaded taste of the spectators, equally nauseated by the vileness of comic things and the seriousness of tragic ones ... [he] united them, mixing kings and heroes and other illustrious personages with buffoons and servants and the lowest men with unheard of monstrousness. This concoction of characters was the reason for the complete ruin of the rules of poetry, which went so far into disuse that not even locution was considered, which, forced to serve music, lost its purity, and became filled with idiocies. The careful deployment of figures that ennobles oratory was neglected, and language was restricted to terms of common speech, which is more appropriate for music; and finally the series of those short metres, commonly called *ariette*, which with a generous hand are sprinkled over the scenes, and the overwhelming impropriety of having characters speak in song, completely removed from the compositions the power of the affections, and the means of moving them in the listeners.[7]

Thus the Arcadians sought to restore order by regularising opera's structures, themes, and affective content. But their appeal for a more 'moral' form of art went back to Horace's dictum that art should not just entertain but also educate. Lip service to the ideal was conventionally paid in operatic prologues that sought to justify, or at least explain away, the action that followed. According to its prologue, *L'incoronazione di Poppea* is a demonstration of the power of Love over Fortune and Virtue, which, if not 'moral' enough in itself, might at least prompt a satirical reading of the work by negative example. Other morals were even clearer in those operas where ancient heroes exhibited the qualities of bravery, virtue, honour, wisdom, and clemency that, in turn, could stand as allegories for modern princely patrons; this provides a basis for reading most of Lully's *tragédies en musique* as some form of propaganda for Louis XIV. Yet allegory is always a slippery tool. Stories from the appalling life of Nero might well serve pro-Venetian republican propaganda, so one reading of *L'incoronazione di Poppea* goes.[8] But in Antonio Giannettini's *L'ingresso alla gioventù di Claudio Nerone* (Modena, 1692; libretto by Giovanni Battista Neri), the same 'historical' character serves to celebrate the wedding of Francesco II d'Este, Duke of Modena. Either contemporary audiences were able to make subtle and sensitive value judgements about the subjects placed before them, or they did not care much about these subjects at all.

Of course, different members of different audiences would no doubt read different works in different ways. Indeed, such polyvalence was surely an essential condition for opera taking Europe by storm. But if one can perhaps find common ground in what opera 'taught' its consumers, it was probably not so much at the level of grand historical, political, or ethical sermons as it was in more immediate modes of human emotional behaviour. Those who cried or laughed at the characters and actions represented on the stage received a sentimental education in the nature of human feeling through which to construct their lives. Some might view this as social engineering; others might claim it as what is most uniquely liberating about the operatic experience.

'softness and variety of Numbers'

Dryden also discusses the requirements of poetry for music:

If the Persons represented were to speak upon the Stage, it wou'd follow of necessity, That the Expressions should be lofty, figurative and majestical: but the nature of an *Opera* denies the frequent use of those poetical Ornaments: for Vocal Musick, though it often admits a loftiness of sound: yet always exacts an harmonious sweetness; or to distinguish yet more justly, The recitative part of the *Opera* requires a more masculine Beauty of expression and sound: the other which (for want of a proper *English* Word) I must call, *The Songish Part*, must abound in the softness and variety of Numbers: its principal Intention, being to please the Hearing, rather than to gratify the understanding.

Despite the preposterous notion 'That Rhyme, on any consideration shou'd take place of Reason', Dryden says, one can only follow the models established by the masters, in this case, the Italians.

Dryden's 'softness and variety of Numbers' refers to the nature of Italian poetry, defined by the number of syllables in a given line and the position of the final accent.[9] Poetic lines can be from three to eleven syllables in length (thus *ternario, quaternario, quinario, senario, settenario, ottonario, novenario, decasillabo,* and *endecasillabo*): the *endecasillabo* is the 'classic' norm, with its chief component, the *settenario,* in second place. The *verso piano* has the final accent on the penultimate syllable. An accent on the final syllable produces a *verso tronco,* and one on the antepenultimate syllable a *verso sdrucciolo. Versi tronchi* and *sdruccioli* are counted as modified *versi piani:* so, a *settenario tronco* or *sdrucciolo* will have, respectively, six and eight actual syllables. Syllable counts are also affected by various treatments of synaloepha and diphthongs.

The *verso piano* is the standard form, while *versi sdruccioli* and *tronchi* are used in special circumstances. For example, in libretti *versi sdruccioli* often invoke pastoral resonances (on the precedent of Jacopo Sannazaro's *Arcadia* of 1504); they also have a long history of association (usually, in *quinari*) with infernal, demonic, or magic scenes, as in the response of the woodland gods to the summons of the wicked witch Artusia in Benedetto Ferrari and Francesco Manelli's second Venetian opera, *La maga fulminata* of 1638 (Act III scene 3: 'Insana femina') or Medea's 'L'armi apprestatemi' in Cavalli's *Giasone* (Act III scene 9; 1649). The *verso tronco* can be comic – and it is sometimes associated with nonsense syllables – but, on a structural level, it becomes most significant to articulate closure: the result has strong musical implications, given the greater suitability for musically perfect cadences of *versi tronchi* (with a masculine ending, weak–strong) over *versi piani* (with a feminine ending, strong–weak).

Italian opera libretti draw only rarely upon the standard poetic forms of Renaissance Italian (Tuscan) hendecasyllabic verse: for example, Dante's *terza rima* (rhyming *aba bcb cdc...*), Petrarch's fourteen-line sonnet (with two quatrains – *abab abab* – and two tercets, e.g., *cdc dcd*) and the *ottava rima* stanzas of Ariosto and Tasso (*abababcc*). When they do, it is often for special (archaic, moralising, etc.) effect, as with Orpheus's 'Possente spirto, e formidabil nume' in *terza rima* in Act III of Monteverdi's *Orfeo*. Instead, the basis of early libretti – as of the late Renaissance pastoral plays that provided their most immediate precedent – was a mixture of free-rhyming *endecasillabi* and *settenari*, producing *versi sciolti* ('loose' or 'free' verse): more regular rhymes and/or metrical consistency could define structural units within this flow, and lines could be divided between characters to enhance the effect of dialogue. However, one major, and crucial, exception is the strophic canzone/canzonetta, generally in other than seven- or eleven-syllable lines, that appears even in the first operas. Rinuccini, for example, introduced strophic groupings mixing *ottonari* and *quaternari* in *Dafne* (1598) and *Euridice* (1600) specifically for the end-of-'scene' choruses. His model was the anacreontic verse introduced (in part, on French precedent) by the poet Gabriello Chiabrera (1552–1638), who said that he was catering specifically for composers of the 'new music' and their 'arias'. In *Orfeo*, the librettist Alessandro Striggio brought such structures into the acts themselves to produce formal songs – often distinguished as such, whether dramatically (e.g., diegetically) or structurally – that stand apart from the prevailing *versi sciolti* for the recitative. The opening of Act II, for example, has a series of four-line stanzas for Orfeo and his companions (one in *ottonari*, six in *settenari*) separated by instrumental ritornelli, culminating in four quatrains in *ottonari* for Orfeo, producing an aria both in the technical sense (a strophic setting of strophic verse) and in the musical one:

Vi ricorda, o boschi ombrosi,	8	Do you remember, o shady woods,
de' miei lunghi aspri tormenti,	8	my long, harsh torments,
quando i sassi ai miei lamenti	8	when the rocks to my laments
rispondean fatti pietosi?	8	responded having been made pitying?
Dite, all'hor non vi sembrai	8	Tell me, did I not then seem to you
più d'ogn'altro sconsolato?	8	more inconsolable than any other?
Hor fortuna hà stil cangiato,	8	Now Fortune has changed her style,
et hà volto in festa i guai.	8	and has turned troubles into celebration.
etc.		

Eleven- and seven-syllable *versi sciolti* remained standard for recitative (and variants thereof) through the nineteenth century and beyond: their fluidity and flexibility were well suited to its dramatic function and musical style. However, the style of arias (choruses, ensembles, etc.) favoured shorter lines in clear-cut patterns with regular metre and rhyme. From early opera onwards, such dramatic and structural shifts were essentially cued by the librettist, whom the composer could ignore only with potential prejudice to the musical outcome. Thus reading a libretto allows one to predict with a fair degree of certainty what the music is meant to do with it, and therefore also encourages us to be surprised when something different occurs.

Such matters remained fluid throughout most of the seventeenth century as the canons of opera were forged by developing social, political, and even literary contexts. Lodovico Zuccolo (*Discorso delle ragioni del numero del verso italiano*, Venice, 1623) showed clear contempt for the new canzonetta, claiming it to be a mere sop to musicians. More sympathetic theorists of the second quarter of the century, such as the anonymous author of *Il corago* (c. 1630), still felt ambivalent about shifts away from *versi sciolti*: they approved the variety thereby achieved but warned against anti-Classical improprieties. But as opera entered the public domain, the rising fortunes of the aria could scarce be resisted. Thus at the beginning of Act I scene 2 of Cavalli's *Giasone* (1649), Cicognini gives the lovesick hero two stanzas of *senari* (with a refrain and cadential *versi tronchi*) before Ercole interrupts his amorous babble. The strong amphibrachs (weak–strong–weak, two per line) almost force a setting in triple time.

Giasone:

Delizie, contenti,	6	Delights, raptures
che l'alma beate,	6	that ravish the soul,
fermate, fermate:	6	stay, stay:
su questo mio core,	6	on this my heart
deh più non stillate	6	pour no more
le gioie d'amore.	6	the joys of love.
Delizie mie care,	6	My dear delights,
fermatevi qui!	6^t	stop now!
Non so più bramare,	6	I can desire no more,
mi basta così.	6^t	this is enough for me.
In grembo agl'amori	6	In the lap of Cupids
fra dolci catene	6	among sweet chains
morir mi conviene.	6	am I fit to die.
Dolcezza omicida	6	Murdering sweetness

a morte mi guida	6	leads me to death
in braccio al mio bene.	6	in the arms of my beloved.
Dolcezze mie care,	6	My dear sweetnesses,
fermatevi qui!	6^t	stop now!
Non so più bramare,	6	I can desire no more,
mi basta così.	6^t	this is enough for me.

Ercole:

E così ti prepari	7	And is this how you prepare
alla pugna, Giasone?	7	for battle, Jason?
Né temi a far passaggio	7	Do you not fear to pass
dall'amoroso al marziale agone.	11	from amorous to martial struggle?

The structures adopted for 'aria' poetry through the seventeenth century are strikingly varied, at least until the rationalisations prompted by the Arcadians and followed by Metastasio. Here the pattern becomes relatively standard: two isometric stanzas, usually of four or three lines each (*settenari* – sometimes with concluding *quinari* – or *ottonari* tend to be preferred), with regular (and generally parallel) rhyme-schemes, and each often ending with a *verso tronco* rhyming with its counterpart. This then meshed with the musical structure that was emerging to dominate opera in the early eighteenth century, the da capo aria, with one stanza each for the A and B sections and a subsequent return to A, therefore ending with the first part of the text.

A representative example of what one might call an intermediate stage in this long process of development is provided by a scene from Antonio Sartorio's *Giulio Cesare in Egitto*, to a libretto by Francesco Bussani, first performed in Venice in the 1676–1677 season (although the main score that survives comes from a performance in Naples in 1680).[10] Cesare (Julius Caesar) has arrived triumphant in Egypt and is pursued by Cleopatra, who has disguised herself as the maid, Lidia; her servant, Nireno, is also in on the game. In Act I scene 4, Cesare is alone on stage musing on his amorous state – observed by Nireno in hiding – but then is suddenly surprised to hear a voice singing in the distance:

Cesare:

Son prigioniero	5	I am a prisoner
del nudo arciero	5	of the blind archer
in laccio d'or.	5^t	in a golden trap.
Ma non so come	5	But I do not know how
m'hanno due chiome	5	two locks of hairs
legato il cor.	5^t	have bound my heart.

Vaga Lidia, ove sei? Se un sol tuo sguardo	11	Beautiful Lidia, where are you? If just a single glance
trasse quest'alma ad abitarti in fronte,	11	led this soul to fix upon your brow,

fu in sì bel ciel d'amore aquila un occhio, — 11 — then under such a beautiful sky of love, an eagle's was the eye,

e Ganimede un core. . . — 7 — and Ganymede's the heart. . .

Nireno (hidden):
(Ora è il tempo opportuno.) — 7 — (Now the time is right.)

Cleopatra (offstage, singing):
V'adoro, pupille, — 6 — I adore you, o eyes,

saette d'amore. . . — 6 — arrows of love. . .

Cesare:
Qual voce ascolto mai? — $\rightarrow$ — What voice do I hear?

Nireno (to himself):
Questa è Cleopatra. — 11 — This is Cleopatra.

Intendo, del suo amor son arti e frodi. — 11 — I understand: these are the arts and deceits of her love.

Femina inamorata — 7 — A woman enamoured

per discoprirsi amante ha mille modi. — 11 — has a thousand ways of revealing herself as a lover.

Cleopatra:
. . . le vostre faville — 6 — . . . your sparks

son faci del core. — 6 — are torches of the heart.

Nireno:
Signor. . . — $\rightarrow$ — My lord.

Cesare:
Nireno, udisti — 7 — Nireno, did you hear

questa angelica voce? — 7 — this angelic voice?

Cesare begins with two stanzas in *quinari* – which Sartorio sets in ABA' form, repeating the first stanza after the second – and then moves into *versi sciolti* (recitative). Cleopatra's offstage song ('V'adoro pupille') is a single four-line stanza (*senari*) that is interrupted (after line 2) by a brief question in recitative from Cesare ('What voice do I hear?'); Nireno then takes over this poetic line (indicated by the arrow), identifying the owner of the voice for the benefit of the audience ('This is Cleopatra') and then commenting on feminine wiles. The song resumes, and, at its end, Nireno reveals himself (recitative), allowing Cesare to wax rhapsodical over the 'angelic voice' he has just heard.

There are several typical games in play here. Cleopatra's aria is diegetic (performed as a 'real' song meant to be heard as such by the other characters onstage), whereas Cesare's is not (he is just in love); we also have the typically meta-operatic strategy of commenting on the act of singing and on the 'angelic' qualities of the singer. It is a scene that invites a mixture of arousal and wry humour; it also merits comparison with Handel's handling of this same moment in his own *Giulio Cesare in Egitto* (London, 1724).[11]

'they labour at Impossibilities'

Dryden greatly admired the Italian language, 'the softest, the sweetest, the most harmonious, not only of any modern Tongue, but even beyond any of the Learned', one that 'seems indeed to have been invented for the sake of Poetry and Musick', rich in vowels and with a pronunciation that is 'manly' and 'sonorous'. Other nations, however, can only envy the Italians:

the *French*, who now cast a longing Eye to their Country, are not less ambitious to possess their Elegance in Poetry and Musick: in both which they labour at Impossibilities. 'Tis true indeed, they have reform'd their Tongue, and brought both their Prose and Poetry to a Standard: the Sweetness as well as the Purity is much improv'd, by throwing off the unnecessary Consonants, which made their Spelling tedious, and their pronunciation harsh: But after all, as nothing can be improv'd beyond its own Species, or farther than its original Nature will allow: as an ill Voice, though never so thoroughly instructed in the Rules of Musick, can never be brought to sing harmoniously, nor many an honest Critick, ever arrive to be a good Poet, so neither can the natural harshness of the *French*, or their perpetual ill Accent, be ever refin'd into perfect Harmony like the *Italian*.

Dryden's reference to French's 'natural harshness' presumably refers to its consonants, and the 'perpetual ill Accent' to the final *es* left mute in speech but articulated in song. Of course, a seventeenth-century French *académicien* would not have agreed.

The French equivalent of the Italian *endecasillabo* is the alexandrine, with twelve or thirteen syllables, depending on whether the rhyme is masculine (accent on the final syllable) or feminine (accent on the penultimate syllable, followed by a mute *e*). Alexandrines may be subdivided into six-syllable hemistichs by medial caesuras (thus offering the possibility of two parallel musical phrases for a single line of verse). Line-endings tend to alternate between masculine and feminine, often in *rimes croisées* (*abab*), although one can also find *rimes plates* (*aabb*) and *rimes embrassées* (*abba*). But the alexandrine is not always amenable to fluid musical setting given the internal caesura and the strong end-accents; it also seems too long, save where sententiousness or grandeur is required. Accordingly, the French librettist Philippe Quinault tended to opt for freer *vers libre*, mixing lines of different length. The argument between the flirtatious Céphise and her suitor Straton in Act I scene 4 of Lully's *Alceste* (1674) is typical enough (syllable counts ignore feminine endings):[12]

Céphise:

Dans ce beau jour, quelle humeur sombre	8	On this fine day, why so dark a humour
Fais-tu voir à contre-temps?	7	do you display so contrarily?

Straton:

C'est que je ne suis pas du nombre	8	It is because I am not among the number
Des amants qui sont contents.	7	of lovers who are happy.

Céphise:

Un ton grondeur et sévère	7	A grumbling and severe tone
N'est pas un grand agrément;	7	is no great ornament;
Le chagrin n'avance guère	7	anger scarcely advances
Les affaires d'un amant.	7	the cause of a lover.

Straton:

Lychas vient de me faire entendre	8	Lychas has just told me
Que je n'ai plus ton cœur, qu'il doit seul y prétendre,	12	that I no longer have your heart, that he alone can claim it,
Et que tu ne vois plus mon amour qu'à regret.	12	and that now you look upon my love only with regret.

Céphise:

Lychas est peu discret. . .	6	Lychas is indiscreet. . .

Straton:

Ah, je m'en doutais bien qu'il voulait me surprendre.	12	Ah, I did not doubt that he wanted to deceive me.

Céphise:

Lychas est peu discret	6	Lychas is indiscreet
D'avoir dit mon secret.	6	to have told my secret.

Straton is given alexandrines when it comes to voicing his complaint and when he jumps to the (wrong) conclusion that Lychas has lied to him. The opening couplets are nicely balanced, and Céphise's final comment wittily plays off two hemistichs to deflate her importunate lover. Her four seven-syllable lines ('Un ton grondeur et sévère … d'un amant') also mark a generalised moral that Lully sets apart from the prevailing recitative in the manner of a duple-time aria. However, and in general, French verse has fewer clear structural implications for music than Italian, often making it harder to predict from the text what the composer would do with it. This might have been seen as an advantage, given the French preference for more 'natural' and fluid forms of declamation drawing upon (as Lully himself is reported to have done) the rhetorical strategies of spoken drama.

Dryden was equally doubtful about his native tongue:

The English has yet more natural disadvantage than the *French*; our original Teutonique consisting most in Monosyllables, and those incumber'd with Consonants, cannot possibly be freed from those Inconveniences. The rest of our Words, which are deriv'd from the *Latin* chiefly, and the *French*, with some small sprinklings of *Greek*, *Italian* and *Spanish*, are some relief in Poetry; and help us to soften our uncouth Numbers, which together with our *English* Genius, incomparably beyond the triffling of the *French*, in all the nobler Parts of Verse, will justly give us the Preheminence. But, on the other hand, the Effeminacy of our pronunciation, (a defect common to us, and to the *Danes*) and our scarcity of female Rhymes, have left the advantage of musical composition for Songs, though not for recitative, to our neighbors.

The suggestion that 'female Rhymes' (i.e., based on words with strong–weak endings) are important for song is interesting, while Dryden's sense of the 'Effeminacy of our pronunciation' perhaps relates to the lack in English of strong stresses, equally necessary for good melodic writing.

The standard form of 'noble' English verse, the (usually iambic) pentameter, had similar problems to the alexandrine in terms of its length and its tendency to fall into repetitive patterns.[13] As a result, English librettists of the mid-seventeenth century such as Richard Fleckno (*Ariadne Deserted by Theseus and Found and Courted by Bacchus*, 1654) and William Davenant (*The Siege of Rhodes*, 1656) tended to adopt an equivalent of *vers libre* with two-, three-, four- or five-foot lines: Davenant claimed that such variety was 'necessary to recitative music', although the tendency towards rhyming couplets produces a certain sameness. The techniques remained similar in later works. Thus Tate's libretto for Purcell's *Dido and Aeneas* is predominantly in rhyming iambic (weak–strong) and trochaic (strong–weak) tetrameters that become rather plodding (this is typical of German verse, too). Take, for example, Dido's first speech in Act I as presented in Purcell's score (the 1689 libretto has some differences):

Dido:
Ah! Belinda I am prest,
With torment not to be confest.
Peace and I are strangers grown,
I languish till my grief is known,
Yet would not have it guess'd.

Belinda:
Grief increases by concealing.

Dido:
Mine admits of no revealing.

Belinda:
Then let me speak: the Trojan guest
Into your tender thoughts has prest.

Purcell's best option is often to treat this almost as prose, with word repetitions and also a tendency to favour enjambments (thus weakening the rhyme) even at the expense of sense: 'Ah, ah, ah, Belinda, I am prest with torment, / Ah, ah, ah, Belinda, I am prest with torment not to be confest.' In more dance-like sections, however, Purcell seems to enjoy piquant mismatches between textual and musical metre and stress (as in the duet 'Fear no danger to ensue / The hero loves as well as you.')

Given the regularity of much of Tate's libretto, his ending (given towards the beginning of this chapter) is rather strange. Like any good librettist, he provides an appropriate number of key words to prompt the composer ('darkness', 'Death', 'remember me', 'ah!'). But the metre is odd. 'Thy hand, Belinda' is in tetrameters, although the feminine line-endings ('. . . shades me', '. . . invades me') maintain a flow. However, after a reasonably regular quatrain, the metre shifts to a pentameter ('When I am laid in earth, my wrongs create'), a trimeter, and a final pentameter. Tate seems to want to set apart this portion of Dido's final speech, as indeed does Purcell: 'When I am laid in earth' is, of course, Dido's lament, over a ground bass typically based on a descending chromatic tetrachord. However, Purcell does also offer one further intervention that must be his. Tate's syntax is somewhat elliptical, and Purcell seems (consciously or not) to have wanted to clarify the subjunctive, leading to the a-metrical 'When I am laid in earth, *may* my wrongs create'.

* * *

'Prima la musica, e poi le parole' ('First the music, and then the words') was a catchphrase enshrined in the title of a satirical *divertimento teatrale* by Antonio Salieri (1786; libretto by Giambattista Casti). For all that it is a procedural illogicality, it reflects a common aesthetic presumption about the nature of opera. My aim here, however, has been to demonstrate the benefits of taking libretti seriously in terms of their poetic structures, and also, one might add (though I have not covered it here), for what they tell us about staging. Nor are these benefits limited just to early opera. Poetry was the standard format of opera libretti at least until the late nineteenth century and the rise both of *Literaturoper* and of a preference for more 'naturalistic' dramatic and musical prose. Thus the principles established here operated through the Classical and Romantic periods and had no less impact on, say, a Mozart or a Verdi. Ottavio Rinuccini's legacy was powerful indeed.

Notes

1 Compare Paolo Fabbri, *Il secolo cantante: Per una storia del libretto d'opera nel Seicento*, 2nd edn. (Rome: Bulzoni, 2003), which is the best overview for Italian opera in the seventeenth century. Richard Macnutt, 'Libretto (i)', and Brian Trowell, 'Libretto (ii)', in *Grove Music Online*, , www.grovemusic.com, offer broader surveys of the libretto, respectively as a printed artefact and as a genre.

2 The layout, but not the punctuation and spelling, follows what seems to be the spirit, if not quite the practice, of the libretto printed in 1689, reproduced in *The Works of Henry Purcell*, vol. 3, *Dido and Aeneas*, ed. Margaret Laurie (Borough Green: Novello, 1979), xiii–xx. The printer reduced the font size for the last thirteen lines of the text (from 'Great minds against themselves conspire') so as to squeeze it on the page. The indents are also irregular.

3 John Dryden, *Albion and Albanius: An Opera. Perform'd at the Queen's Theatre, in Dorset Garden* (London: Jacob Tonson, 1685), preface.

4 Given in Ellen Rosand, *Opera in Seventeenth-Century Venice: The Creation of a Genre* (Berkeley, Los Angeles, and London: University of California Press, 1991), 421 (my translation).

5 Tim Carter, *Monteverdi's Musical Theatre* (New Haven and London: Yale University Press, 2002), 270.

6 http://corago.unibo.it/ is the most useful resource, also with links to digital copies of libretti where available.

7 Rosand, *Opera in Seventeenth-Century Venice*, 434 (my translation).

8 See Ellen Rosand, 'Seneca and the Interpretation of *L'incoronazione di Poppea*', *JAMS* 38/1 (1985), 34–71; Wendy Heller, 'Tacitus Incognito: Opera as History in *L'incoronazione di Poppea*', *JAMS* 52/1 (1999), 39–96. I offer a counter-argument in my 'Re-Reading *Poppea*: Some Thoughts on Music and Meaning in Monteverdi's Last Opera', *JRMA* 122/2 (1997), 173–204.

9 The discussion here draws upon my contribution to 'Versification' in *Grove Music Online*, www.grovemusic.com. See also my '"In Love's harmonious consort"? Penelope and the Interpretation of *Il ritorno d'Ulisse in patria*', *COJ* 5/1 (1993), 1–16.

10 Antonio Sartorio, *Giulio Cesare in Egitto*, ed. Craig Monson, Collegium Musicum (Yale University), 2nd ser., vol. 12 (Madison: A-R Editions, 1991).

11 Tim Carter, *Understanding Italian Opera* (New York: Oxford University Press, 2015), 95–9.

12 The text is taken from *Philippe Quinault: Livrets d'opéra*, ed. Buford Norman, 2 vols. (Toulouse: Société de Littérature Classique, 1999), vol. 1, 67. For an overview, see Buford Norman, *Touched by the Graces: The Libretti of Philippe Quinault in the Context of French Classicism* (Birmingham, AL: Summa Publications, 2001).

13 For an overview, see Andrew R. Walkling, *English Dramatick Opera, 1661–1706* (London and New York: Routledge, 2019).

3 | Aria, Recitative, and Chorus in Italian Opera

SARA ELISA STANGALINO

Toward a 'nuova maniera di canto': A New Way of Singing

By the end of the sixteenth century, attempts to recover Greek tragedy led to the new genre of the *dramma per musica*. For the Florentine Camerata de Bardi, it meant the reinstatement of the antique *melopoeia* of the Greeks, that is, declamation emphasizing the word and its correct prosody. The Camerata promoted the excellence of monody, echoing the antique doctrine of the *ethos* proposed by the Pythagoricians, according to which modes could elicit different emotional responses in the listener: viewed as natural to man, monody was thus appropriate for the expression of affect. Later, also, Claudio Monteverdi would emphasise monody alongside polyphony, as he would argue in the preface to the *Scherzi musicali* of 1607. There, Monteverdi would define 'Seconda prattica' as a style that asked the music to amplify the affections already expressed by the poem and, in practice, to serve this latter.

Within the Camerata, Jacopo Peri and Giulio Caccini experimented with the new monody, setting to music some of Ottavio Rinuccini's dramas: *Dafne* in 1595 (Peri, Florence; it was set to music in 1608 by Marco da Gagliano as *La Dafne* in Mantua) and, in 1600, *L'Euridice* by Peri and Caccini (Florence). It was no mere coincidence that the beginnings of opera privileged the myth of Orpheus, which is at the core of *L'Euridice* and Monteverdi's *L'Orfeo* (Alessandro Striggio, Mantua, 1607). Other mythological themes not only confirmed the antique literary heritage that was enjoyed by aristocratic elites but also permitted performances to dodge one of opera's thornier issues: theatrical verisimilitude. Constantly sung throughout, opera obviously lacks verisimilitude. Thus, exceptions could be made for mythical or superhuman figures who could assume another mode of expression – supposing that these mythological characters could express themselves through song – and for roles viewed as non-normative in relation to the aristocratic milieu: servants and nurses, and other characters of low social origins who provided comic relief to the main plot.

Peri and Caccini knew that the use of monody required aesthetic justifications. In his preface to *L'Euridice*, Peri explained the use of monody as this 'new way of singing' reflecting the Antique manner, to 'imitate one who speaks through song' (*imitar col canto chi parla*).[1] Monody reaches for a compromise between true singing and oratorical declamation: hence the expression often used to characterise this style – *recitar cantando*, which could be translated as 'recitation in song', or 'to recite while singing', according to Nino Pirrotta.[2] The expression *recitar cantando* appeared for the very first time in the title page of Emilio de' Cavalieri's *Rappresentatione di Anima, et di Corpo nuovamente posta in musica dal Sig. Emilio del Cavalliere per recitar cantando* (Rome, 1600) and in the instructions 'To Readers' of the same.[3] However, for Cavalieri, its meaning was 'to stage through song' (*mettere in scena col canto*): *recitar cantando* identified a kind of spectacle instead of a style or a technique.

As a technique, *recitar cantando* requires vocal flexibility. Its essential feature is the ability to highlight some words through correct pronunciation and diverse techniques of ornamentation. The accompaniment of the voice by the basso continuo should obstruct neither the melody nor the correct perception of the words. Structured by poetic meter, the verbal text allows music to organise itself into a form. The most common verse in Italian poetry is the 'endecasillabo', an eleven-syllable verse (hendecasyllable) with its principal accent falling on the tenth syllable: it was already widely used in sixteenth-century pastoral – Tasso's *Aminta* or Guarini's *Il Pastor fido*, to name only these. Another frequent verse is the heptasyllable (*settenario* in Italian), a seven-syllable verse with its principal accent on the sixth syllable. Heptasyllables and hendecasyllables are often combined (*versi sciolti*; blank verses), mostly because both meters have mobile accents: thus they are able to reproduce the different rhythms of spoken language.

Since the Renaissance, *versi sciolti* were some of the most widespread solutions adopted in poetry, the mobility of their internal accents resembling the delivery of speech and the heightening of expressions. This resemblance is paramount for the foundation of *stile rappresentativo* – the expression appeared in the title page and the dedication of Caccini's *L'Euridice*, published in 1600. In 1699, Andrea Perrucci could still argue that verses 'of seven and eleven syllables [resemble] prose more than others'.[4] In *recitar cantando*, *versi sciolti* result in a syllabic style of song in which the melodic embellishments of song are perceived as transgressive elements signalling dramatic tension, just as the few textual repetitions indicate a change in affect and an intensification of said affect. Due to the flexibility of the verse, the rhythm is rather irregular, while the melodic line remains simple and often proceeds stepwise. Stressed syllables coincide with the downbeat of the measure and are often highlighted by values of greater duration. The melodic arc is modelled on the verse, while the cadences function as punctuation, articulating the unity of the text in its more complex poetic periods. What emerges is a mode of expression organised into segments that respect the syntactic trend in a simple linear style, preserving the essential aspect of monody as conveyor of affect through its imitation of speech, here emphasised through musical intonation, and, above all, respecting the prosody. To the elaborated poetic style corresponds a musical treatment characterised by bare simplicity, essentially made on rather elementary sets of melodic and rhythmic patterns. Within this simple melodic outline, the appearance of an unusual rhythmic figure, a specific ornament, or an unusual melodic contour is sufficient to highlight the dramatic intrusion of the affect.

In Caccini's setting of Rinuccini's libretto for *Euridice*, Dafne's narration of Euridice's death is treated as a monologue in three parts (see Table 3.1). The first part, A, renders the bucolic setting; the second part, B, introduces the long narration of the snake bite and its fatal consequences; and the third part, C, narrates Euridice's death.

The musical outline of this monologue is modelled along these three thematic areas, but, most of all, the outline of the melodic phrase follows the meaning of the syntactic sentence. From the beginning of the first section, the voice lingers on metric syllables and stretches their duration (see Example 3.1).

Shaping the Recitative

In the first half of the seventeenth century, the recitative quickly adapted itself to different needs, as shown for instance with the diffusion of entirely sung dramas in Rome. The use of allegorical figures in the Roman theatre – as in that of Florence – was frequent although here motivated by counter-reformationist propaganda, with historical–hagiographic plots addressing a morally edifying content. In *Rappresentatione di Anima, et di Corpo* (Agostino Manni and Cavalieri; Rome, Oratorio dei Filippini, 1600), the allegorical figures of Body and Soul are subjected to trials of strength and attempt to resist the snares of worldly life. This allegorical action 'per recitar cantando' was intended to be staged, yet with a severe style of recitative in accordance with the nature of the plot. On the other hand, the dramma musicale *Sant'Alessio* (Giulio Rospigliosi and Stefano Landi, Rome, 1631) relies on a recitative style flexible enough to establish different

Table 3.1 Ottavio Rinuccini, *L'Euridice*, Dafne's narration 'Per quel vago boschetto' (1600). Translation slightly reworked from *The Norton Anthology of Western Music*, Volume 1: Ancient to Baroque, 7th ed., ed. J. Peter Burkholder and Claude V. Palisca (New York, London: W. W. Norton & Company, 2014), 73

[A]	[A]
Per quel vago boschetto	In the beautiful thicket
ove rigando i fiori	where watering the flowers
lento trascorre il fonte degl'allori	slowly courses the spring of laurel,
prendea dolce diletto	she took sweet delight
con le compagne sue la bella sposa,	with her companions, the beautiful bride,
chi violetta o rosa	as some picked violets or roses,
per far ghirlande al crine	to make garlands for their hair
togliea dal prato e dall'acute spine,	in the meadow and among the sharp thorns,
e qual posando il fianco	while others, lying on their sides
su la fiorita sponda	on the flowery banks
dolce cantava al mormorar dell'onda.	sweetly sang to the murmur of the waves.
[B]	[B]
Ma la bella Euridice	But the lovely Euridice
movea danzando il piè sul verde prato	dancingly moved her feet on the green grass,
quando, ria sorte acerba,	when, o bitter and angry fate,
angue crudo e spietato	a snake, cruel and merciless,
che celato giacea tra fiori e l'erba	that lay hidden among flowers and grass,
punsele il piè con sì maligno dente	bit her foot with such an evil tooth
ch'impallidì repente	that she suddenly became pale
come raggio di sol che nube adombri,	like a ray of sunshine that a cloud darkens,
e dal profondo core,	and from the depths of her heart,
con un sospir mortale	a mortal sigh,
sì spaventoso 'ohimè!' sospinse fore	so frightful, alas, flew forth,
che, quasi avesse l'ale,	that, almost as if they had wings,
giunse ogni ninfa al doloroso suono,	every nymph rushed to the painful sound,
ed ella in abbandono	and she, fainting,
tutta lasciòssi allor nell'altrui braccia.	let herself fall in another's arms.
Spargea il bel volto e le dorate chiome	Then spread over her beautiful face and golden tresses
un sudor via più freddo assai che ghiaccio.	a sweat colder by far than ice.
[C]	[C]
Indi s'udio il tuo nome	Then your name was heard
tra le labbra sonar fredde e tremanti	from her lips, cold and trembling,
e, volti gl'occhi al cielo,	and, her eyes turned to heaven,
scolorito il bel viso e i bei sembianti,	her beautiful face and features discolored,
restò tanta bellezza immobil gelo.	this great beauty remained motionless ice.

Example 3.1 Giulio Caccini, *L'Euridice composta in musica in Stile Rappresentativo da Giulio Caccini detto Romano*, Dafne's narration 'Per quel vago boschetto' (Florence: Giorgio Marescotti, 1600 [1601, modern style]), mm. 1–14

levels of comedy. In Act II scene 8, the Devil appears to the pageboy Marzio, a simpleton. Mistaking the Devil for a hermit, Marzio begins to mock him. The scene is in two parts, the first with a monologue delivered by the Devil, the second with a dialogue between him and Marzio. The treatment of the recitative differentiates the refined, ironic astuteness of the Devil from the good-natured simplicity of Marzio; during their dialogue, declamation is increasingly treated in a histrionic manner. As for the monologue, the absence of well-defined melodic pattern first evokes a sense of statism. The Devil, however, shows off an unprecedented virtuosity with his *canto di sbalzo*, a style of singing privileging wide intervals and jumps from one extreme to another of the *tessitura*. As shown in Example 3.2, Marzio's intervention causes the mood of the scene to depart from the fearsome gravity of the infernal world, resulting in two different comic

Demonio e Marzio.

Ritorna il Demonio, risoluto di fare ogni sforzo per superare Alessio nel breve spazio
che gli rimane di vita. È sopragionto da Marzio quale, credendolo un eremita
e volendo burlarlo come era solito fare con Alessio, entra seco in discorso, ed adiratosi
con lui, procura di ritenerlo, ma viene in diversi modi schernito dal Demonio.

Example 3.2 Stefano Landi, *Il Sant'Alessio*, Act II, sc. 8, dialogue for Demonio e Marzio
'Già con desir costante' (Rome: Paolo Masotti, 1634), mm. 1–27

tones: on the one hand Marzio's vulgarity, on the other the refined irony of the Devil's witty retorts loaded with subtle double-meanings that escape Marzio.

This search for variety in the recitative is symptomatic of a need to renew musical declamation. Commenting on his own opera *La catena d'Adone* (Ottavio Tronsarelli, Rome, 1626), Domenico Mazzocchi alluded to the negative effects on the audiences of the recitative, which led him to compose *mezz'arie* as a way to 'break the tedium of the recitative'.[5] This led composers and poets to search for alternative modes of musical declamation, for more varied forms with better defined melodic and rhythmic outlines. Giovanni Battista Doni also evoked in his *Trattato della musica scenica* (written 1633–1635), a style 'more vague and adorned than others, and full of varied intervals, which truly requires the scene to avoid tedium and to bring even more delight to the hearers, in order to better express all those different feelings that are subjected to this kind of verse and musical imitation'.[6] As we will see, the recitative would be increasingly submitted to periodic interruptions taking the form of brief episodes with a more singable style in which vocal virtuosity and lyricism would prevail: the aria.

'Like sprouts from the roots': The Aria, Born from the Recitative

In 1744, Francesco Saverio Quadrio wrote that the aria should follow the recitative and have a 'relationship with [it], and rise from the same, as sprouting from the root'.[7] While this describes a well-established practice in eighteenth-century opera, the consolidation of the relation between recitative and aria was strengthened during the previous century.

The text of a libretto alternates between two main formal models assuming different functions: recitative and aria. A quick glance at any printed page of a libretto reveals the different types of verses chosen either for the recitative or the aria. During the seventeenth century, recitative and aria gave rise to hybrid structures. Brief and compact strophes were usually preferred for an aria. The poetic meters of these strophes were of various sorts but remained regulated by rhymes following a fixed pattern that facilitated the identification of the strophe in the flow of the discourse. The aria 'Quanto vale e quanto può' from Antonio Cesti's *Il Tito* (Nicolò Beregan, Venice, 1666) is made up of twelve octosyllables

Table 3.2 Nicolò Beregan, *Il Tito*, Act I, sc. 13, Tito's aria 'Quanto vale e quanto può' (1666)

ATTO I	ACT I
SCENA XIII	SCENE XIII
Galeria con statue.	*Hallway with statues.*
TITO	TITUS
Quanto vale e quanto può [aria]	How mighty and how powerful
bella bocca di cinabro,	is a beautiful vermilion mouth,
s'a goder d'un vago labro	if, to enjoy a sweet kiss
Giove in cigno si cangiò.	even Jove turned into a swan.
Bella bocca di cinabro	Beautiful vermilion mouth,
quanto vale e quanto può.	how mighty and how powerful.
Che non opra e che non fa	What can it not do, what can it not achieve,
il candor di vaga fronte,	the candour of a lovely face,
s'il gran nume d'Acheronte	if the great god of Acheron
fé prigion di sua beltà.	was made a prisoner of its beauty.
Il candor di vaga fronte	The candour of a sweet face,
che non opra e che non fa.	what can it not do, what can it not achieve.
Tito, ma che vaneggi? [recitative]	Titus, but what are you raving about?
Questi i trofei del tuo valor saranno?	Will these be the trophies of your valour?
Dunque chi di Sion domò l'orgoglio,	Thus, he, who tamed the pride of Zion,
chi la Siria atterrò, l'Asia distrusse,	who brought down Syria and destroyed Asia,
fia prigionier d'un guardo, e de la fama	should he be made prisoner by a glance, and of his fame
diràssi in Campidoglio	should it be said on the Capitol
ch'armata di lusinghe, in breve gonna	that, armed with charms, in short skirt,
del mondo il vincitor vinto ha una donna?	a woman overcame the conqueror of the world?
Taci, lingua, che parli?	Be silent, tongue, what are you saying?
Del bell'idolo mio così ragioni?	Is this how you reason about my beautiful idol?
[...]	[...]

(*ottonari*: x_8 a_8 a_8 x_8 a_8 x_8 | y_8 b_8 b_8 y_8 b_8 y_8) followed by a series of heptasyllables and hendecasyllables (see Table 3.2).

A syntactically autonomous form, the aria emphasises the dramatic context of specific situations: displays of lyrical effusion, enunciations of paradigmatic sentences, and other instances of rhetorical effects.

During the seventeenth century, strophes could contain from four to ten verses with poetic meters varying between heptasyllables and hendecasyllables. There were also *quinari* (pentasyllables, i.e., five-syllable verses) and *quaternari* (tetrasyllables, four-syllable verses), often arranged in polymetric strophes. In general, *numeri chiusi* (closed numbers) such as arias and choruses were modelled on the forms of the old *ballata*, the madrigal, and the Anacreontic ode – the latter, popularised in Italy by the poet Gabriello Chiabrera, often used other types of verses than the hendecasyllable usually found in mixed strophes that combined verses of different meters.

Recitative and aria distinguish themselves not only by form and style but also by the varied pace of the plot's progression. The recitative allows for a dynamic integration of the dialogue into the flow of action; the aria, instead, halts the action, allowing externalisation of affect or a contemplative moment of introspection. The relationship between recitative and aria is regulated by a mechanism that allows the tension accumulated during the recitative to be released during the emotional response of the character in the aria. Such displays of affect (anger, joy, despair, etc.) make the aria the culminating point of the scene.

The affect privileged in the aria is made all the more noticeable by the choice of a melodic line easy to remember and frequently repeated in specific verses. However, the vocal line in the aria does not necessarily model itself on the prosody of the poem, nor does it attempt to emphasise the meaning of each verse. Instead, it privileges the general meaning of the strophe or strophes and their main affect. Thus, each aria possesses an unmistakable physiognomy with a distinctive rhetoric and melodic profile.

With the aria, the recitative creates a 'system of contrasts' paramount to the construction and unfolding of the drama. The peripeties of the plot are developed through the contrasting succession of arias along different, if not opposing, moods. The drama unfolds along this succession, so that the spectrum of affects can be ascribable to a paradigmatic system of emotions. A change of meter signals the transition from recitative to aria: the latter is characterised by rhythmic uniformity, the instrumentation is enlivened, and ritornelli are played between each strophe while the basso continuo follows the vocal line with increased animation.

These musical features bring us back to a fundamental issue of verisimilitude on stage, not only complicated by the *recitar cantando* but also by the textual and melodic repetitions which were also considered to be unnatural. Thus, songs that fulfilled a function of *musica di scena* (stage music) – and that would also have been sung in spoken theatre – and other situations that elicited song from the character, be it with a prayer or a moment of invocation, were appreciated: exemplary cases are the aria

'Possente spirto' in Monteverdi's *L'Orfeo* (Act III), in which the hero sings to placate Caronte; Arnalta's 'Oblivion soave' in Monteverdi's *Incoronazione* (Act II scene 12); or Romilda's aria 'O voi che penate' from Francesco Cavalli's *Xerse* (Act I scenes 3–4).

A 'rounded frame': The Function of the *Intercalare*

The first formal models of the aria were borrowed from the traditional forms of Italian poetry – for example, the *terzina* (a three-verse strophe of hendecasyllables using the chain rhyme *aba | bcb | cdc |*, etc.) and the *ottava rima* (a strophe of eight verses usually on the rhyme scheme *abababcc*). The *terzina* was also known as *terza rima*, *terzina dantesca*, or *terzina incatenata* (chained *terzina*), as in the aria 'Possente spirto' in Monteverdi's *L'Orfeo* (see Table 3.3).

The rigorous *terzina* contrasts with more plastic and flexible forms – for example, those addressing a theatrical topos destined to become the object of great emulation: the *lamento*. Originally a literary topos, the *lamento* was known through famous instances: Armida's lament (Tasso, *Gerusalemme liberata*, Canto XVI), or Olimpia and Fiordiligi's laments in *Orlando furioso* (Ariosto, Canto X [*lamento di Olimpia*]; Canto XLIII [*lamento di Fiordiligi*]). The only surviving piece from Rinuccini and Monteverdi's opera *L'Arianna* (Mantova, 1608) is its celebrated *lamento* sung by its eponymous heroine. A long monologue divided in several sections,

Table 3.3 Alessandro Striggio, *La favola d'Orfeo*, Act III, Orfeo's aria 'Possente spirto e formidabil nume' (1607).
Libretto published *in Libretti d'opera italiani dal Seicento al Novecento*, Giovanna Gronda and Paolo Fabbri (Milan: Mondadori, 1997), 37

ORFEO

Possente spirto e formidabil nume,	(a)	Almighty spirit, formidable God,
senza cui far passaggio a l'altra riva	(b)	without whom to pass onto the other bank
alma da corpo sciolta in van presume,	(a)	a soul, freed from its body, presumes in vain,
non viv'io no, che poi di vita è priva	(b)	I do not live, no, since she was deprived of her life,
mia cara sposa, il cor non è più meco,	(c)	my dear wife, my heart is no longer with me,
e senza cor com'esser può ch'io viva?	(b)	and without a heart, how could I be alive?
A lei volt'ho'l camin per l'aër cieco,	(c)	For her I have set foot through the dark air,
a l'inferno non già, ch'ovunque stasis	(d)	yet not into Hades, since where may be
tanta bellezza il paradiso ha seco.	(c)	such beauty, only paradise can be.
[...]		[...]

Arianna's *lamento* adopts mostly a syllabic style for its sinuous and unpredictable vocal line, obeying the poetic prosody. The *recitar cantando* of this *lamento* requires vocal flexibility – the ability to draw attention to the words through emphatic pronunciation and to signal its most poignant moments with diverse vocal techniques. The monologue's organisation does not feature a pre-established formal model: instead, the piece proceeds by juxtaposed sections greatly contrasting with each other. Each section focuses on the presentation of one main affect exacerbated by rhetorical effects that shape the vocal line: anaphora, repetition, peroration, to name only these. Example 3.3 gives the beginning of this *lamento*, with the recurrence of some verses fulfilling the role of a refrain. Monteverdi's later opera, *Il ritorno d'Ulisse in patria* (Giacomo Badoaro, Venice, 1640), also displays a lament for Penelope ('Di misera regina,' Act I scene 1), in which repeated verses also function as refrains. Of course, Monteverdi was not the only one to emulate the theatrical topos of the lament: other examples are found in *La regina sant'Orsola* (Andrea Salvadori, music by Marco da Gagliano; Florence, 1624), *La Flora* (Andrea Salvadori, music by Marco da Gagliano and Jacopo Peri; Florence, 1628), and *L'Andromeda* (Benedetto Ferrari, Francesco Manelli; Venice, 1637).

The refrain became an essential element of the aria. A privileged model is the aria adopting the form of the *ballata*, which relies structurally on the refrain. The *ballata*'s distinctive feature is the repetition of the first verse, or the first couplet at the end of the strophe, and the rhyme between the last verses of the strophe and the first ones of the repeated verse: such repetition is called *intercalare* or ritornello.[8] Arias with *intercalare* were frequent in Venetian operas: an example is Oronta's lament in *Artemisia* (Act III scene 4; Nicolò Minato and Cavalli; Venice, 1657). The aria consists of two strophes separated by an instrumental episode. Its *intercalare* corresponds to the verse given at the beginning and end of the first strophe ('Dammi morte o libertà'); it is then repeated in the final verse of the aria (see Example 3.4).

Seemingly simple at first sight, the structure of these arias with *intercalare* can adopt more complex combinations: the length of the *intercalare* can be extended when made of more than one verse; also, its recurrences can vary. Some arias can have two different texts for the *intercalare*, that is, one for each strophe. An essential feature for the melody of the *intercalare* is its simplicity, making it easily memorable for the listeners and triggering the pleasure of identification.

The aria also took from the sixteenth-century madrigal the epigrammatic character of its final couplet, a very efficient rhetorical expedient.

Example 3.3 Claudio Monteverdi, *L'Arianna*, Arianna's lament 'Lasciatemi morire', adapted from *L'Orfeo, L'Ariana, Il Lamento Di Olimpia*, ed. Anna Maria Vacchelli (Cremona: Fondazione Claudio Monteverdi, 2014), mm. 1–24

Such epigrammatic verses often appear at the beginning of a strophe as a banner for the displayed affect. In Ceffea's aria from *Scipione Affricano* (Act I scene 14; Minato and Cavalli; Venice, 1664), the conclusive couplet functions as the *intercalare* (mm. 22–31 and 63–73; see Example 3.5). The *intercalare* also allows for rhetorical and structural emphasis when used within the blank verses of a recitative. Highlighting specific verses, the

Scena IV

Oronta, *indi* Alindo *con lo scettro d'Artemisia.*

Example 3.4 Francesco Cavalli, *Artemisia*, Act III, sc. 4, Oronta's lament 'Dammi morte o libertà', ed. Hendrik Schulze and Sara Elisa Stangalino (Kassel: Bärenreiter, 2013), mm. 1–87

Example 3.4 (*cont.*)

intercalare creates sections in the textual flow. This can nevertheless
lead to some ambiguities, as it may obscure the relationship between
recitative and aria. In *Scipione Affricano* (Act I scene 13), the
verse 'Chiedi, o bella, che vuoi?' occurs twice during the recitative

Example 3.5 Francesco Cavalli, *Scipione Affricano*, Act I, sc. 14, aria for Ceffea 'Amate pur, amate', transcription from *Italian Opera 1640–1770*, 5, ed. H. Mayer Brown (New York, London: Garland Publishing, 1978), 41r–43r

Example 3.5 (*cont.*)

(see Example 3.6). This osmotic relationship between recitative and aria is one of the most fascinating traits of seventeenth-century opera: it is first of all about poetry – more specifically, about drama structured by poetry.

Example 3.6 Francesco Cavalli, *Scipione Affricano*, Act I, sc. 13, recitative for Scipione 'Dimmi, Ericlea, poss'io', transcription from *Italian Opera 1640–1770*, 5, ed. H. Mayer Brown (New York, London: Garland Publishing, 1978), 38v–39v

Example 3.7 Francesco Cavalli, *Il Xerse*, Act I, sc. 7, *mezz'aria* for Xerse 'Deh rimirate un re', ed. Hendrik Schulze and Sara Elisa Stangalino (Kassel: Bärenreiter, 2019), mm. 17–25

Another technique consists in the poetic arrangement of aggregates of verses within the fabric of the recitative, out of which the composer can write a *mezz'aria* (half-aria), also called *aria cavata*, that is, an aria 'extracted' from the recitative. In this case, the declamatory style proper to the blank verses of the recitative is momentarily abandoned. What emerges instead is a strophic passage characterised by rhythmic periodicity similar to that of the aria. In *Xerse* (Minato and Cavalli; Act I scene 7; Venice, 1655), the king begs for Romilda's love in a short strophe made of heptasyllables. Cavalli singles out this passage from the recitative by treating it as a brief arioso in the very middle of the scene (see Example 3.7).

Such a treatment of the poetic text found its origins in the Monteverdian dramatic recitative, itself reflecting the legacy of the madrigalesque tradition in which blank verses were often declaimed not so much in a brisk manner as at a more sustained tempo, allowing, when necessary, some lingering on a word or on an expression isolated through musical and rhetorical effects. Indeed, the versatile uses of the *intercalare* explain the variety and flexibility of formal models that define the aria during the seventeenth century. Table 3.4 presents the main formal categories determined by the number of strophes in an aria and by the specific uses of the *intercalare* – including instances of formal structures without any *intercalare* (the verses carrying the *intercalare* are underlined in the table).

Table 3.4 Main categories of arias in relation to the use of the *intercalare*

N. Minato–F. Cavalli, *Scipione Affricano*, II, 6 (1664)

Ericlea

   Dite, dite, dolci aurette,   (a)

odorose, placidette,   (a)

perché mai   (b)

son penosi i miei respiri,   (c)

e si cangiano in sospiri?   (c)

Ericlea

   Tell me, tell me, sweet breezes,

fragrant, pleasant,

why on earth

is my breathing so painful,

and has changed into sighs?

N. Minato–F. Cavalli, *L'Orimonte*, I, 12 (1650)

Fleria

   Com'io t'ami non so.   *settenario*

Trovar di te più freddo   "

un amante chi può?   "

Come io t'ami non so.   "

Fleria

   How I can love you I do not know.

Who could find a lover

that is colder than you?

How I can love you I do not know.

B. Ferrari–F. Manelli, *La maga fulminata*, II, 6 (1638)

Pallade

[1st strophe]

   Quand'è in tempesta il mar

teme morte il nocchier;

quando placido appar

ha d'arrichir, non di perir pensier.

Se flagello divin non scote il rio,

ei non conosce più cielo né dio.

Pallade

   When the sea is stormy,

the sailor fears death;

when it appears calm

his thoughts turn to riches, not to peril.

If the divine scourge does not stir the wicked,

he no longer knows neither heaven nor god.

[2nd strophe]

   Ecco femina rea

dorme negli error suoi;

e dall'impura idea

scarcera vizi ed imprigiona eroi.

Ma non usa uno stil sempre la sorte,

e ogni umano piacer termina in norte.

   Lo the guilty woman

sleeping upon her erroneous ways;

and by her impure thought

she releases vices and imprisons heroes.

But fate does not always work in just one way,

and every human pleasure ends in death.

G. Faustini–F. Cavalli, *La Calisto*, I, 2 (1651)

Calisto

   Verginella io morir vo'.

Stanza e nido

per Cupido

del mio petto mai farò.

Verginella io morir vo'.

   Scocchi Amor, scocchi se può

tutte l'armi

per piagarmi,

ch'a la fine il vincerò.

Verginella io morir vo'.

Calisto

   I wish to die a young virgin.

A bed and nest

for Cupid

never will my heart be.

I want to die a young virgin.

   Let Love fire, let him fire, if he can,

all his weapons

to wound me,

for in the end I still will defeat him.

I wish to die a young virgin.*

Table 3.4 (*cont.*)

G. Faustini–F. Cavalli, *Euripo*, III, 5 (1649)

Euripo

[1st strophe]

  Cessate dal piagarmi, occhi omicidi,
troppo barbari siete,
morto voi mi volete:
serbate i dardi a debellar gl'infidi.
Cessate dal piagarmi, occhi omicidi.

[2nd strophe]

  Lontananza non giova, io peno, io moro,
gran trofeo, gran valore
voler estinto un core
che trae da' vostri sguardi il suo ristoro.
Lontananza non giova, io peno, io moro.

Euripo

  Stop wounding me, murderous eyes,
you are too barbaric,
you want me dead:
save your arrows to crush the infidels.
Stop wounding me, murderous eyes.

  Distance does not help, I suffer, I die,
it is a great trophy, a great valour indeed
to wish death upon a heart
that takes its healing from your glances.
Distance does not help, I suffer, I die.

---

[*] Translation slightly reworked from Francesco Cavalli, *La Calisto*, ed. Alvaro Torrente and Nicola Badolato (Kassel, Basel, London, New York: Bärenreiter, 2012), XXXII

Expanding Forms and Structures

In Cavalli's *Xerse*, the aria of Romilda, 'O voi che penate' (Act I scene 3–4), constitutes a fascinating case of *musica di scena*. The aria occurs between two scenes and is interrupted on three occasions by passages in recitative, first by Arsamene, then by Elviro, and finally by Xerse. The form of the aria adapts itself to the unfolding of the plot, following the reactions of the three men to the song of the young Romilda (see Table 3.5).

Arsamene's and Elviro's recitative interjections are inserted twice during the first verses of Romilda's aria 'O voi che penate'. Only later, Xerse enters unexpectedly during the first strophe sung by Romilda. Another aria from the same opera, 'Ombra mai fu', sung by Xerse (Act I scene 1), displays an unusual form of extraordinary effectiveness. The aria occupies the entire scene. Made of four *quinari*, its opening strophe functions as a repeat. The two central strophes, each one made of six verses (*abbaCC*), evoke a madrigalesque form with their hendecasyllabic and heptasyllabic verses, each strophe ending with a rhyming couplet. The contrast with the repeat is highly significant as regards the form and the meter. The instrumental ritornello provides a frame for the different sections of the text (see Table 3.6).

Table 3.5 Nicolò Minato, *Il Xerse*, Act I, sc. 3–4, Romilda's aria 'O voi che penate' (1654).
Translation slightly reworked from Francesco Cavalli, *Il Xerse*, ed. Hendrik Schulze and Sara Elisa Stangalino (Kassel: Bärenreiter, 2019), LI

[*SCENA TERZA*]		[*THIRD SCENE*]	
ARSAMENE	Non ti partir.	ARSAMENE	Do not leave.
ROMILDA	O voi – 〈*Cantando.*〉	ROMILDA	O you … 〈*Singing.*〉
ARSAMENE	Quest'è Romilda.	ARSAMENE	This is Romilda.
ROMILDA	– o voi che penate.	ROMILDA	… O you who suffer …
ELVIRO	Da voi amata?	ELVIRO	Your beloved?
ARSAMENE	Sì, non parlar più.	ARSAMENE	Yes; be quiet.
ROMILDA	O voi che penate per cruda beltà, un Xerse mirate, –	ROMILDA	O you who suffer … for a cruel beauty, look at him, Xerse …
	SCENA QUARTA		*FOURTH SCENE*
	XERSE, ARSAMENE, ELVIRO, ROMILDA 〈*e*〉 ADELANTA *su la loggia.*		XERSE, ARSAMENE, ELVIRO, ROMILDA and ADELANTA *on a balcony.*
〈XERSE〉	(Qui si canta il mio nome?)	〈XERSE〉	(Someone here is singing my name?)

〈ROMILDA〉 –	– che di ruvido tronco acceso sta,
	e pur non corrisponde
	altro al su' amor che mormorio di fronde.
	  Di rami frondosi
	lo sterile Amor,
	con vezzi dannosi
	punge i baci sul labbro al baciator.
	È di Cupido un gioco
	far che mantenga un verde tronco il foco.
		〈ROMILDA〉	… who is in love with a rugged tree
			although nothing answers
			to his wooing but the whisper of the leaves.
			  From the leafy branches
			the cold Amor,
			with harmful caresses
			bites with his kisses the lips of the kisser.
			It is Cupid's game
			to maintain a fire from green wood.

Table 3.6 Nicolò Minato, *Il Xerse*, Act I, sc. 1, Xerse's aria 'Ombra mai fu' (1654). Translation slightly reworked from Francesco Cavalli, *Il Xerse*, ed. Hendrik Schulze and Sara Elisa Stangalino (Kassel: Bärenreiter, 2019), XLIX–L

XERSE		XERSE
Instrumental ritornello		
Ombra mai fu	**A**	Never was a shade
di vegetabile		of any plant
cara ed amabile,		more dear and lovely,
soave più.		more sweet.
Instrumental ritornello		
Bei smeraldi crescenti,	**B**	Beautiful green foliage,
frondi tenere e belle,		tender and lovely branches,
di turbini o procelle		of whirlwinds and storms
importuni tormenti		the unwelcome tortures
non v'affligano mai la cara pace,		shall never afflict your precious peace,
né giunga a profanarvi Austro rapace.		nor should ever the predatory Auster defile you.
Instrumental ritornello		
Mai con rustica scure	**B¹**	Never shall, with rustic cunning,
bifolco ingiurïoso		the harmful yokel
tronchi ramo frondoso;		cut your delicate twigs;
e se reciso pure		and should they be chopped after all,
fia che ne resti alcuno, in stral cangiato		be it that they are changed, as arrows,
o lo scocchi Dïana o'l dio bendato.		to be shot by Diana or the blindfolded god.
Instrumental ritornello		
Ombra mai fu	**A**	Never was a shade
di vegetabile		of any plant
cara ed amabile,		so dear and lovely,
soave più.		more sweet.
Instrumental ritornello		

Another sophisticated instance of the use of the ritornello is featured in an aria from *Sant'Alessio*, 'Se l'ore volano' (Act I scene 2). Hiding in the cellar of his home, Alessio sings of his desire to be freed from the chains of worldly life. The aria is divided into three strophes made of seven verses (pentasyllables and heptasyllables), with a ritornello played between each strophe. Each of its three strophes is subdivided into two sections: the first

Arietta a una voce

Example 3.8 Stefano Landi, *Il Sant'Alessio*, Act I, sc. 2, aria for Alessio 'Se l'ore volano' (Rome: Paolo Masotti, 1634), mm. 1–6

three verses differ for each strophe, while the last four are identical ('Chi l'ali a me darà | tanto ch'all'alto polo | io prenda il volo, | e mi riposi là?'). The melody is identical for each strophe but undergoes a major change on the fourth verse to signal the return of the repeated verses (see Example 3.8).

During the second half of the century, itinerant theatrical companies and cosmopolitan composers disseminated the model of the Venetian opera in Europe, allowing for the development of its forms and vocal styles. In Cesti's operas, the separation between recitative and aria is fully realised, the aria being the culmination of the scene. In Venice, Rome, and Naples, the aria became the privileged locus for lyric effusion, asserting its melodic profile. The expansion of its dimensions went hand in hand with new developments in its formal models. The short *intercalare* of the early Venetian opera, often made of one or two verses, could be extended to the size of a whole strophe and become the focal point of the aria. For instance, Armidoro's aria 'Deh rendetemi, ombre care' (Act III scene 15) from *Difendere l'offensore o vero la Stellidaura vendicante* (Perrucci, Francesco Provenzale; Naples, 1674) is made of two strophes, A and B, the strophe A (repeated after the strophe B) playing the role of an expanded *intercalare* (see Table 3.7).

Both poetic and musical structures are simple: first, the instruments enunciate the melody that will be repeated during the first strophe, section A. Repetition plays a structural role: the instrumental episode that follows the first strophe is based on the melody of the introduction, closing section A and introducing section B. A new melodic material is presented, not so much contrasting with the one presented in strophe A as elaborating the last section of A. The second occurrence of the instrumental interlude is followed by the reappearance of the entire strophe A, now subjected to variations and alterations to the original melodic line. The whole results in a tripartite form: A-B-A', the foundation of the so-called *aria col da capo*, which would become the dominant form of the aria in the eighteenth century.

Table 3.7 Andrea Perrucci, *Difendere l'offensore, ovvero La Stellidaura vendicante*, Act III, sc. 15, Armidoro's aria 'Deh rendetemi, ombre care' (1685)

ARMIDORO

Instrumental introduction

Deh rendetemi, ombre care,	Episode A	Please return to me, o dear shadows,
il mio ben che mi rapiste;		the loved one that you have taken from me;
o bellezze uniche e rare,		o beautiful features, unique and rare,
ahi da me come spariste?		woe, how did you vanish from me?

Instrumental interlude

Rispondetemi, larve cortesi:	Episode B	Answer me, gentle spirits,
chi l'estinta mia rubbò?		who has robbed me of my deceased?
Deh qual nume, ch'io forse offesi,		Please, which god that I might have offended,
da' miei lumi me l'involò?		took her away from my sight?

Instrumental interlude

[Repeat of the first strophe]	Episode A1

During the seventeenth century, an increasing number of formal possibilities and stylistic features allowed arias to become privileged vehicles for the display of affect and emotions: scenes of lament, of madness, of sleep (*aria del sonno*), invocations, and prayers. An important category is the comic aria. In Venetian operas, these arias were integrated within comic episodes, often located at the end of an act or near a change of scenery or action, thus creating an entertaining intermission between the serious episodes of the *dramma per musica*. Comic arias were intended for characters frequently embroiled in quid pro quos or involved in degrading situations, and whose low origin – servants, buffoons, nurses, and the like – originated with stock figures of the *commedia dell'arte*. The verses of comic arias often rely on linguistic manglings, colloquial phonetics, or stuttering, enabling mockeries against the simple-minded or those affected by physical deformities, old bachelors unable to control their lustful desires, and so on.

In *Giasone* (Giacinto Andrea Cicognini and Cavalli, Venice, 1649; Act I scene 7), the servant Demo sings an aria (see Table 3.8), the comic effect of which is ensured by syllables issued in fits and starts – 'so-so-', for example – but also (in dialogue with Oreste) from an obscene allusion: Demo's stuttering prevents him from completing words starting with 'ca-', implying an obscene rhyme with 'strapazzo'.

The 'Epilogue' of the Passion

Demonstrated by their formal variety and their increasing number in operas, arias became from the middle of the seventeenth century the focal point for the musical expression of emotions. Their placement within a scene was also motivated by their dramatic function. An aria could be performed at the opening, at the end, or in the middle of a scene. In the first case, it was called *aria di sortita*; the second case was referred to as *aria d'entrata* or *aria di congedo*; and the third case was *aria mediana*. Presenting the character, the *aria di sortita* possessed a signaletic function. The affect was represented through specific repetitions (*intercalare*, repetition of the first strophe) and rhetorical effects intended to impress the memory of the listener. The *aria d'entrata* (or *di congedo*) reasserted the scene's dominant affect and constituted its climax. Located at the end of the scene, it allowed the singer to gather applause without interrupting the action. Such risk of interruption was much higher with the *aria mediana*: thus, its frequency diminished by the end of the century while the *aria d'entrata* became predominant; by singing the aria before leaving

Table 3.8 Giacinto Andrea Cicognini, *Giasone*, Act I, sc. 7, Demo's aria 'Son gobbo, son Demo' (1649).

Libretto published in *Libretti d'opera italiani dal Seicento al Novecento*, Giovanna Gronda and Paolo Fabbri (Milan: Mondadori, 1997), 129–30

	[*ritornello*]		
DEMO	Son gobbo, son Demo,		I am a hunchback, I am Demo,
	son bello, son bravo,		I am handsome, I am great,
	il mondo m'è schiavo,		the world is my servant,
	del diavol non temo,	[*ritornello*]	I don't fear the devil,
	son vago, grazioso,		I am attractive, graceful,
	lascivo, amoroso;	[*ritornello*]	lascivious, loving;
	s'io ballo, s'io canto,		when I dance, when I sing,
	s'io suono la lira,		when I play the lyre,
	ogni dama per me arde, e so- so-		every woman will burn for me and he-
	so- so- arde, e so- so- so-		he- he- burn for me and he- he- he-
ORESTE	E sospira.		and heave a sigh.
DEMO	So- so- so- so- so- so-		He- he- he- he- he- he-
DEMO *e* ORESTE	Arde e sospira.		burn and heave a sigh.
	[*ritornello*]		
ORESTE	Linguaggio curioso.		Odd language.
DEMO	Sei troppo, troppo, troppo frettoloso,		You are too, too, too hasty,
	e se farai del mio parlar strapazzo,		and if you mock my speech within these walls,
	la mia forte bravura		my tough bravery
	saprà spezzarti il ca-		will know to kick you in your ba-
ORESTE	Oibò.		oh my!
DEMO	Il ca - po in queste mura.		. . . backside.

the stage, the character did not interrupt the action but rather put it on 'stand-by'. Furthermore, the *aria d'entrata* could ideally represent an affect as a universal, absolute quality. As a result, the more the aria focused on such universal truths, the more it could be recontextualisable in another operatic work: thus, arias could be removed from the original *dramma per musica* and reused in another opera. It could also happen that a singer might favour a specific aria particularly apt to showcase his or her vocal abilities; singers would integrate such arias in their own repertoire, with the possibility of performing these on different occasions: this introduced the concept of the *aria di baule*, which gained popularity during the eighteenth century.[9]

Indeed, the *aria d'entrata* became the prevalent type during the eighteenth century, but it was also the object of criticism. Emblematic is the case of Ludovico Antonio Muratori (*Della perfetta poesia italiana*; Modena, Soliani, 1706), who described the aria as a 'ridiculous thing', since it entailed the repetition of verses even when the action required a character's immediate departure from the scene. Muratori's objection is exemplary of the issues surrounding the nature of *inverosimiglianza* raised by the defenders of Italian poetry, who considered these poetic repetitions an obstacle to the unfolding of the dramatic action.

Nevertheless, the aria performed at the end of the scene became the most appreciated formula: in 1715, Jacopo Martello writes that 'a musician ought never depart without a trill of roundelay. Whether plausible or not is of little concern'.[10] As summarised in 1783 by Stefano Arteaga, such an aria was 'the climax or epilogue of the passion',[11] and should therefore not be placed at the beginning of the scene nor in the middle: the aria had to be placed at the end of the scene, for it would not be acceptable (*verosimile*) to have at the beginning of a scene a character already at the height of their passion. The affect should increase during the scene, through the use of dialogues, for instance; thus its climax should be reached with the aria at the end of the scene.

The Verse as Index of Affect

Specific dramatic situations or roles such as otherworldly spirits, satirical or pastoral figures, or comic characters can be efficiently emphasised through the poetic means of proparoxytone verse (*verso sdrucciolo* in Italian), in which the antepenultimate syllable is stressed. The *verso sdrucciolo* is also used in structural scenes, such as prologues or finales of acts. In the prologue of *L'Orimonte* (Minato and Cavalli, 1650), infernal allegorical characters sing a duet of proparoxytone verses (see Table 3.9), heightening a sense of terror.Medea's scene in Cavalli's *Giasone* (Act I scene 15) is another instance that relies on the *verso sdrucciolo* for the invocation of spirits (see Example 3.9). Comic situations also benefit from the expressive power of proparoxytone verse. In Cavalli's *Artemisia* (Act I scene 16), Alindo sings an aria expressing his great delight in receiving a flower from Artemisia, since he hopes that she will return his love. Four scenes later (Act I scene 20), in the same garden, the servant Niso sings the very same *intercalare* previously sung by Alindo (see Table 3.10). Old Erisbe then sings the strophes, while Niso, snatching some flowers, mocks the woman, alluding to her withered face. Bitter disillusionment at the loss

Table 3.9 Nicolò Minato, *L'Orimonte*, Prologue, Confusione and Volturio Spirito's duet 'Saprò confondere' (1650)

CONFUSIONE	CONFUSION
Saprò confondere	I shall confuse
gl'arbitri e l'anime,	free will and souls,
il mostro essanime	the bloodless monster
non caderà.	shall not fall.
VOLTURIO SPIRITO	SPIRIT OF GREED
Saprò diffondere	I shall spread
tempesta orribile,	horrible storms,
l'angue terribile	the terrible snake
non perirà.	shall not perish.
[…]	[…]

of youth emerges from the sententious couplet that closes both stanzas, while the *intercalare* is sung by Niso in an obviously mocking fashion.

Back to the Greeks: Prologues and Choruses

At least until the middle of the century, the *dramma per musica* was introduced by a prologue populated by allegorical or mythological figures. Its strophic structure attests to its derivation from spoken theatre, where prologues were also sung, at least originally. In the prologue of Peri's *Euridice*, the allegorical figure Tragedy declares in seven quatrains of hendecasyllables in *rima crociata* (ABBA) her wish to ban the retelling of the cruellest events and to arouse instead 'sweeter emotions in the heart' by tempering the singing on 'happier chords' (see Table 3.11). As is typical in allegorical prologues, homogeneity characterises poetry and music: in *Euridice*'s prologue, the first verse of each quatrain enunciates a well-defined melodic line, which proceeds with regularity if not placidity; indeed, the allure of the prologue must be adapted to the solemnity of the occasion. An instrumental ritornello separates strophes sung on the same melodic line; only the use of some improvised variations, such as melismas affecting the dynamics and melodic turns, enliven these other-wise identical strophes. While not notated in the score, these improvised melismas function not only as ornamentation but also as signals: they are strategically located at the end of each quatrain on the stressed syllable,

Table 3.10 Nicolò Minato, *Artemisia*, Act I, sc. 16, Alindoro's aria 'Cari, cari vegetabili', and Act I, sc. 20, Niso and Erisbe, 'Cari, cari vegetabili' (1657). Translation slightly reworked from Francesco Cavalli, *Artemisia*, ed. Hendrik Schulze and Sara Elisa Stangalino (Kassel: Bärenreiter, 2013), XLIX–L, LX–LXIV

Act I, scene 16

ALINDO	ALINDO
Cari, cari vegetabili,	Dear, dear plants,
se ben rigida	though unyielding is she
è colei ch'a me vi diè,	who gave you to me
pur da me séte adorabili.	you still are adorable to me.
Cari, cari vegetabili.	Dear, dear plants.
[...]	[...]
Vezzi amabili	Lovable instruments
di chi fa col suo rigor	of her who, with her hardness,
nel mio cor piaghe insanabili.	causes in my heart incurable wounds.
Cari, cari vegetabili.	Dear, dear plants.

Act I, scene 20

NISO	NISO
Cari, cari vegetabili.	Dear, dear plants.
ERISBE	ERISBE
I danni	The damage
degl'anni	caused by the years
sono, o belle, irreparabili:	is, oh beauties, irreversible:
le beltà non son durabili.	beauty is not durable.
Pur liete	Yet happily
godete	let's enjoy
pria che fuggan gl'anni labili:	before the fleeting years go past:
le beltà non son durabili.	beauty is not durable.
NISO	NISO
Cari, cari vegetabili.	Dear, dear plants.

---

highlighting the ending of the strophe and the beginning of the instrumental ritornello.

Interspersed with instrumental ritornelli, this strophic structure was a frequent arrangement during the first half of the seventeenth century. Later, the prologue would assume more flexible and elaborate forms, often incorporating the dialogue. In the 1660s, the prologue would begin to

Table 3.11 Ottavio Rinuccini, *L'Euridice*, Prologue, La Tragedia, 'Io, che d'alti sospir vaga' (1600)

LA TRAGEDIA	TRAGEDY
Io, che d'alti sospir vaga e di pianti, (A) spars'or di doglia, or di minacce il volto, (B) fei negl'ampi teatri al popol folto (B) scolorir di pietà volti e sembianti, (A)	I, who, eager for loud sighs and tears, my face now filled with sorrow, now with threats, once made the faces of the crowd in great theatres turn pale with pity,
non sangue sparso d'innocenti vene, non ciglia spente di tiranno insano, spettacolo infelice al guardo umano, canto su meste e lagrimose scene.	no longer of blood shed by innocent veins, nor of eyes put out by the insane Tyrant, unhappy spectacle to human sight, do I sing now on a gloomy and tear-filled stage.
Lungi via, lungi pur da' regi tetti, simolacri funesti, ombre d'affanni: ecco i mesti coturni e i foschi panni cangio, e desto nei cor più dolci affetti.	Away, away from this royal house, funereal images, shades of sorrow: behold, I change my gloomy buskins and dark robes to awaken in the heart sweeter emotions.
Or s'avverrà che le cangiate forme non senza alto stupor la terra ammiri, tal ch'ogni alma gentil ch'Apollo inspiri del mio novo cammin calpesti l'orme,	Should it now come to pass that these great forms in the world admired with great amazement, so that each gentle spirit that Apollo inspires will thread in the tracks of my new path,
Vostro, Regina, fia cotanto alloro qual forse anco non colse Atene o Roma, fregio non vil su l'onorata chioma, fronda febea fra due corone d'oro.	Yours, Queen, will be so much laurel, that perhaps not even Athens or Rome gathered more, an ornament worthy of those honoured tresses, a frond of Phoebus between two crowns of gold.
Tal per voi torno, e con sereno aspetto ne' reali imenei m'adorno anch'io, e su corde più liete il canto mio tempro, al nobile cor dolce diletto.	Thus, changed, I return, and with a serene countenance I, too, adorn myself for the royal wedding, and temper my song with happier notes, sweet delight to the noble heart.
Mentre Senna real prepara intanto alto diadema onde il bel crin si fregi, e i manti e seggi degl'antichi regi, del tracio Orfeo date l'orecchia al canto.	While the royal Seine is preparing a lofty crown to adorn your lovely hair, and the mantles and thrones of ancient kings, lend an ear to the song of the Thracian Orpheus.

disappear, while the opening scene's significance would increase. Altercations and squabbles between divinities would be abandoned in favour of opening scenes featuring a civil community with a chorus celebrating the actions of the hero.

Example 3.9 Francesco Cavalli, *Il Giasone*, Act I, sc. 15, aria for Medea 'Dell'antro magico', transcription from ms. [c. 1664–1660], I-Vnm, mss.It.IV.363 (=9887), 58v–59v

Commentative Voices

Choruses organised in strophes with well-defined melodies are usually favoured for entrance scenes and finales of acts or demarcative scenes, that is, scenes which separate individual episodes. When interpolated within the dramatic action, the chorus assumes a generic function of commentary,

Example 3.9 (*cont.*)

following the tradition of antique tragedy but with more restraint than in its original model.

In one of the choruses of *L'Orfeo*, Monteverdi avoided declamation and favoured instead a moment of pure spectacle: it occurs at the end of the third act as an intermede between two episodes (Orfeo's dialogue with Caronte and the dialogue between Proserpina and Plutone). After having made Caronte fall asleep, Orfeo descends into the Underworld where the chorus of spirits comments on the virtues of mankind. Setting the first strophe to a five-voice imitative polyphony characteristic of the late Renaissance madrigal with its dense interweaving of voices, Monteverdi creates a grandiose aural effect. The second section of the chorus brings a new musical texture, its sixth verse split in the typical manner of the Venetian *coro battente* or *spezzato*, before all voices reunite again in the seventh verse with some concession to vocal virtuosity (see Example 3.10).

Venetian opera of the second half of the century provides instances of the chorus in opening scenes being assigned to a collective entity or to conflict episodes such as battles, which justify the presence of people or

Example 3.10 Claudio Monteverdi, *L'Orfeo*, Act III, chorus for the Spirits 'Nulla impresa per uom', adapted from *L'Orfeo, L'Ariana, Il Lamento di Olimpia*, ed. Anna Maria Vacchelli (Cremona: Fondazione Claudio Monteverdi, 2014), mm. 337–347

Example 3.10 (*cont.*)

armed men, respectively, rather than otherworldly figures. In these instances, the function of the chorus contextualises and exalts historical events. Devoid of a prologue, *Muzio Scevola* (Minato and Cavalli; Venice, 1665) starts in medias res with an entrance scene (Act I scene 1) depicting the battle near the Tiber: '*Tiber at the Sublician bridge. MELVIO, HORATIUS COCLES fighting on the bridge. PUBLICOLA, Roman soldiers and sapers cut the bridge from one side. PORSENNA, TARQUINIUS SUPERBUS and the army of Tuscany from the other.*' A chorus delivers a series of *senari* (six-syllable verses with the main accent on the fifth syllable): 'Si rompa, si franga, | reciso dall'onda | a l'oste ch'innonda | il varco rimanga. | Si rompa, si franga … '.

Finally, one may wonder at the horizon offered by the complex spirit of experimentation proper to the seventeenth century and its legacy at the dawn of the Arcadian reform. Setting aside all considerations regarding the 'purification' of Italian poetry and its forms, I believe that the answer lies in attempts to conceive musical forms aimed at the expression of human affections in an increasingly universal and standardised sense. This resulted in a reduction of the variety of poetic and musical forms, and in the consolidation of a paramount structural dichotomy: the clear-cut distinction between recitative and aria, and the rise of the *aria col da capo* as the imitation of affect able to provide for the audience an edifying purpose and a cathartic effect: indeed, in order to be able to recognise the passions in ourselves, it helps to observe them on stage. Which was, after all, the very raison d'être of Greek theatre.

Appendix | Table of the Most Common Italian Poetic Verse Meters, as Well as Some Useful Remarks about How They Are Used

Italian Name	Description	Example
quaternario	4-syllable verse with *accento tonico* (i.e., primary stress, coinciding with the last stress of the verse) on the 3rd syllable (in its 'piano' form; see explanation under 'NB')	Ecco il mondo (Arrigo Boito, *Mefistofele*)
quinario	5-syllable verse with *accento tonico* on the 4th syllable (in its 'piano' form)	Muta d'accento (Francesco Maria Piave, *Rigoletto*)
senario	6-syllable verse with *accento tonico* on the 5th syllable (in its 'piano' form)	Speranze, fuggite (Giacinto Andrea Cicognini, *Il Giasone*)
settenario	7-syllable verse with *accento tonico* on the 6th syllable (in its 'piano' form)	Frondi tenere e belle (Nicolò Minato, *Xerse*)
ottonario	8-syllable verse with *accento tonico* on the 7th syllable (in its 'piano' form)	Bella figlia dell'amore (Piave, *Rigoletto*)
novenario	9-syllable verse with *accento tonico* on the 8th syllable (in its 'piano' form)	Vaghe fonti che mormorando (Vincenzo Grimani, *Agrippina*)
decasillabo	10-syllable verse with *accento tonico* on the 9th syllable (in its 'piano' form)	Va', pensiero, sull'ali dorate (Temistocle Solera, *Nabucco*)
endecasillabo	11-syllable verse with *accento tonico* on the 10th syllable (in its 'piano' form)	Pari siamo! Io la lingua, egl'ha il pugnale (Piave, *Rigoletto*)

Note that there are several rules governing syllable count. One of them is *sinalèfe* (synalepha), where consecutive vowels are merged into one syllable: 'Ecco il mondo' = 4 syllables; 'Frondi tenere e belle' = 7 syllables; 'Voi ch'ascoltate in rime sparse il suono' = 11 syllables (Petrarch, *Canzoniere* 1).

NB: In order to understand Italian verse, one needs to distinguish such concepts as *accento tonico, parole tronche, parole piane, parole sdrucciole,* and *parole bisdrucciole.*

Accento tonico is an increase in the volume of the voice when pronouncing a specific syllable in a word: the syllable, and the vowel, on which the stress falls are called *tonico.*

According to the position of this *accento tonico* within a word, we distinguish:

- *tronco* (oxytone): words in which the *accento tonico* falls on the last syllable (for example, 'virt*ù*'; 'ciel'; c*o*r).
- *piano* (paroxytone): words in which the *accento tonico* falls on the penultimate syllable (for example, 'am*o*re'; 'tes*o*ro').
- *sdrucciolo* (proparoxytone): words in which the *accento tonico* falls on the antepenultimate syllable (for example, 'l*i*rica'; 'sdr*u*cciolo').
- *bisdrucciolo*: words in which the *accento tonico* falls on the pre-antepenultimate syllable (for example, 'gi*u*ramelo'; 'ti*e*nitelo').

Accordingly, a verse may end as *tronco*, *piano*, *sdrucciolo*, or *bisdrucciolo*, depending on whether the *accento tonico* of its last word falls on the last, penultimate, antepenultimate, or pre-antepenultimate syllable (this last case is exceedingly rare in Italian librettos).

'Virtù'	Vir - t**ù** *parola tronca*	Accent on last syllable
'Amore'	A - m**o** - re *parola piana*	Accent on penultimate syllable
'Lirica'	L**i** - ri - ca *parola sdrucciola*	Accent on antepenultimate syllable
'Giuramelo'	Gi**u** - ra - me - lo *parola bisdrucciola*	Accent on pre-antepenultimate syllable

Here are examples for different types of *settenario*:

settenario tronco	sguardo cercando il ciel	(Alessandro Manzoni, *Morte di Ermengarda*)
settenario piano	Va lusingando Am**o**re	(Metastasio, *Didone abbandonata*)
settenario sdrucciolo	Ei fu. Siccome imm**o**bile	(Manzoni, *Il cinque maggio*)

On a practical note, the number of syllables in a verse is always counted as if the verse was *piano* (i.e., up to the last stressed syllable and then one additional syllable). Thus, a *settenario tronco* in reality only has six syllables (with no syllable following the last stressed syllable), whereas a *settenario sdrucciolo* has actually eight syllables (with two more syllables following the last stressed syllable):

Ei		fu.		Sic		co		me_im		mo		bi		le
1		2		3		4		5		6		7		8

The only case when a verse actually has the number of syllables that its name indicates is when it is *piano*: a *settenario piano* has seven syllables; an *endecasillabo piano* has eleven syllables, and so on.

Notes

1 Jacopo Peri, 'To Readers', in *L'Euridice* (Florence: Marescotti, 1600), n.p.

2 Nino Pirrotta, 'Early Opera and Aria,' in Nino Pirrotta and Elena Povoledo, *Music and Theatre from Poliziano to Monteverdi* (Cambridge: Cambridge University Press, 1982), 241–5. See also Lorenzo Bianconi and Giorgio Pagannone, *Piccolo glossario di drammaturgia musicale*, in Giorgio Pagannone (ed.), *Insegnare il melodramma. Saperi essenzali, proposte didattiche* (Lecce-Iseo: Pensa MultiMedia, 2010), 201–63: 247.

3 'To readers', in *Rappresentatione di Anima, et di Corpo nuovamente posta in musica dal Sig. Emilio del Cavalliere per recitar cantando* (Rome, 1600), n.p.

4 Andrea Perrucci, *Dell'arte rappresentativa premeditata ed all'improvviso* (1699), ed. Anton Giulio Bragaglia (Florence: Sansoni, 1961), 101. Quoted in Paolo Fabbri, *Metro e canto nell'opera italiana* (Turin: EDT, 2007), 8.

5 The mention appears in the last page of the score: *La catena d'Adone, posta in musica da Domenico Mazzocchi, con privilegio* (Venice: appresso Alessandro Vincenti, 1626). On Falsirena's *mezz'aria* in *La catena d'Adone*, see Chapter 4.

6 Giovanni Battista Doni in his *Trattato della musica scenica*, in Giovanni Battista Doni, *Lyra barberina: De' trattati di musica* [...], ed. Anton Francesco Gori (Florence: Stamperia imperiale, 1763), vol. 2, 23–4.

7 Francesco Saverio Quadrio, *Della storia e della ragione d'ogni poesia* (Milan: Agneli, 1744), 446. Quoted in Paolo Fabbri, *Il secolo cantante. Per una storia del libretto d'opera in Italia nel Seicento*, 2nd ed. (Rome: Bulzoni, 2003), 244.

8 Loreto Mattei, *Teorica del verso volgare e prattica di retta pronunzia* (Venice: Albrizzi, 1695), 78–9. Quoted in Fabbri, *Il secolo cantante*, 253.

9 See Pierpaolo Polzonetti, 'Opera as process', in *The Cambridge Companion to Eighteenth-Century Opera* (Cambridge: Cambridge University Press, 2009), 3–23; 9.

10 Pier Jacopo Martello, *Della tragedia antica e moderna* (Rome: Gonzaga, 1715). Quoted in Fabbri, *Il secolo cantante*, 245.

11 Stefano Arteaga, *Le rivoluzioni del teatro musicale italiano dalla sua origine fino al presente* (Bologna: Trenti, 1783), vol. 1, 321–2. Quoted in Fabbri, *Il secolo cantante*, 244.

Opera as Spectacle, Opera as Drama

MARGARET MURATA

The 'old regimes' in Europe marked happy occasions such as births, birthdays, and weddings as conspicuously as they could, often in a series of sumptuous events. For the general public, there might be street processions, races, jousts, and religious rites made special by richly decorated liturgical spaces and extraordinary music. The nobility, however, expected private festivities suited to their place in society. They held banquets and balls for each other and often prepared staged entertainments. Across Europe, the nature of such private amusements varied from palace to palace and court to court; but it is as one of the varieties of occasional celebrations at court that opera began, borrowing and transforming different features from them. It shared with them song, dance, instrumental music, and poetic texts delivered by costumed figures. A set of songs and dances could be held together loosely by a theme. Recited poems and solo songs could pepper a pantomimic ballet; musical *intermedi* could lighten a spoken play. Any representation could focus on astonishing stage machines – flying dragons and chariots for gods and goddesses, sudden transformations of scenery, or the spouting of fountains. Poetic recitations or musical tableaux could justify or merely adorn these technical wonders. Although opera took on features of court spectacle, it never displaced the other forms. Not only were its special requirements onerous – a stable of singers with the time and ability to memorise and deliver extended roles – but it also demanded acceptance as poetic drama.

Court Spectacles

At both family and formal occasions, children, relatives, and palace pages often gave recitations and danced. Performers could also come from the larger circle of the court and those who served it. A few instances, from modest to elaborate, must serve to illustrate the widespread continuance of this practice from the sixteenth century and the equal importance of reciting and dancing. For a 1609 carnival party in Rome, the sons of Mario Farnese, Duke of Latera, and the nephews of Cardinal Bevilacqua acted in a pastoral written by their tutor that had musical *intermedi* with 'balletti'.[1] When the Spanish royal family visited the estate of the Duke of Lerma in 1614, the royal children and twelve ladies-in-waiting performed Lope de Vega's play *El premio de la hermosura* outdoors. The prince (and future King of Spain Philip IV) played the role of Cupid, and he and his sister danced between the acts. After the play, the ladies-in-waiting danced a choreographed máscara.[2] At the wedding of Henry of Lorraine and Margherita Gonzaga in Nancy in 1606, the guests heard recitations by costumed 'slaves', Cupid, and Classical goddesses, who sang and danced to the music of violins and lutes. The noble performers unmasked before the last two ballets and joined the court in attendance.[3] The princes of the house of Savoy journeyed to Casale Monferrato in 1611 for the birthday of their sister Marguerite, wife of its governor, Francesco Gonzaga. Musicians and actors from the Gonzaga court in Mantua performed the five-act *Il rapimento di Proserpina,* which had music by Gonzaga's *maestro di cappella,* Giulio Cesare Monteverdi (brother of the more famous composer). Three days later, at a villa outside the castle walls, nymphs and shepherds danced to music on the garden paths, with choreography by Gonzaga himself. Back in the city, they witnessed another five-act representation, one on the Classical myth of Psyche, with choruses, music by instrumental ensembles, and stage machines. Venus entered in a chariot drawn by doves; Etna erupted; and the stage became a sea for the entrance of a chariot drawn by sea horses, atop which Neptune sang.[4]

From London to Warsaw and Nancy to Naples, letters, newsletters, and published commemorative descriptions provide abundant, if incomplete, evidence of such entertainments. We call the most lavish of them 'court spectacles', a term that also encompasses horse ballets and staged naval battles. Even for those occasions that depended on a script or poems, the texts were more often than not 'disposable', composed without pretence to lasting literary value. Though literary enough in style, few were intended to be 'literature'. After a long description of one Neapolitan occasion, a diarist wrote

After the dance with the torches was finished, ... [twenty-four cavaliers] danced with the women, and then with the other cavaliers, they continued to dance until the ninth and tenth hours of the night, which ended the *festa.* I won't write out the verses that were sung; rather I've just alluded to them since they are not worth remembering.[5]

Published descriptions of events, given out as souvenirs, served to publicise their magnificence to other, rival, courts. Neither comprehensive nor critical accounts, the booklets themselves were also part of the occasion, often adding a veneer of learned cachet to images of magnificence and largesse – music and figural choreography symbolising harmony and social order, the flourishing of the arts under peaceful government, the Classical gods bestowing their gifts on the reigning houses, or their godly fractiousness yielding to the might and grace of modern rulers, and so on. The full texts of English masques, by comparison, such as those of Ben Jonson and Thomas Campion, were often printed. Jonson especially elevated the ephemeral form, trying to integrate poetry, visual design, music, and dancing into symbolic and philosophical programmes.[6]

Given the lavish surroundings of the great halls in many palaces, costumes alone could create a sense of the 'theatrical'. Decorated chariots – effectively, processional vehicles brought into the great hall – were appropriate means for the entrances of gods and goddesses. (This was an age in which the lavishness of one's horse-drawn carriage denoted one's social status). To construct a temporary stage capable of stage machines or multiple scene changes (by means of revolving or sliding panels) entailed preparation and enormous costs. Not surprisingly, patrons often commemorated the results in engravings of the scene designs. Those for a 1608 Medici wedding in Florence, for example, show a simple woodsy set for the spoken play *Il guidizio di Paride* by Michelangelo Buonarroti, the younger; but for the six *intermedi* between the acts, Giulio Parigi designed elaborate pavilions; gardens; ruins; Vulcan's forge in Hades; the boat of Amerigo Vespucci approaching palm-studded tropical cliffs; and a grandiose, Classical Temple of Peace.[7] Similar engravings later appeared to commemorate operatic productions. The first opera for which we have engraved scene designs is in fact from Florence, *La regina Sant'Orsola* of 1624–1625 (libretto by Andrea Salvadori, music by Marco da Gagliano). Its sets were also by Parigi, who had designed the *intermedi* of 1608.[8] Although they are more idealised than faithful 'snapshot' views of any production, they show us the effects of stage machines (such as figures in clouds), preferred architectural styles, costumes, some notion of the blocking, and a generalised notion of bodily comportment, as well as the figures made by dancers and the positions of their arms and hands. For example, the engraving for Act III scene 4 of the 1636 *Ermiona* (music by Giovanni Felice Sances, c. 1600–1679) staged in Padua shows Apollo and the Muses on clouds and a 'ballo' of six Theban couples on stage. Each couple holds the hand of the other; the wrists of their free arms are bent inward and rest on their hips. The Classical military costumes completely expose the men's legs; the women's fairly simple shifts are mid-calf in length. Thus, all their footwork would have been quite visible.

Whether social dancing by the guests, theatrical dancing by members of the court, or choreographies executed by professionals, solo, pair, and ensemble dance was loved across Europe; and in the early seventeenth century, the French did not have the dominant influence they were later to have. The continued popularity of French *ballets,* staged Italian *balli,* Spanish *saraos,* and masque-like presentations in all countries can also partly be explained by the fact that dancing allowed participation by the ladies of the court. Few noblewomen received formal educations. While not unknowledgeable, many were hardly literate. (Some actresses and female singers must have been much more lettered than many of the duchesses and princesses whose praises they extolled). Formal dancing offered women one of the few opportunities for public self-display at court. Noblemen welcomed the chance, too; it was not rare for noblemen to dance solo.

'Spectacle', then, did not mean that courtiers watched as mere spectators; they were part of it. Opera, however, limited participation by courtiers, unless dancing followed it, as it often followed spoken plays. Tim Carter has gone so far as to say that the detachment created by the 'conceptual and physical barriers between the stage action and the audience' in opera meant that 'opera failed to meet the demands of courtly entertainment.'[9] This is in part why it could never supplant court spectacle.

Due to their occasional nature, the musical components of these events – from the most modest to the most costly – have by and large disappeared. Music for choruses and dances was the most functional and could be created quickly or even improvised. Simple, chordal music could also be the basis for a solo delivery, made elaborate by embellishments added by the singer. The solo *récits* by Pierre Guédron, for example, would appear to parallel Florentine recitative, but their accompaniments are full-textured, and their vocal lines do not borrow Italian techniques of expression. (The French would not adopt basso continuo accompaniments until mid-century).

Sometimes selections were later published in collections, mixed in with non-theatrical music, or preserved in privately held manuscripts. One unusual print was the description of the *Delizie di Posillipo boscarecce e marittime* (*Sylvan and the Seaside Delights of Posillipo*) staged in Naples in 1620.[10] In this carnival extravaganza for the viceregal court of the Duke of Ossuna, dances for wild men, monkeys, and swans are interspersed with vocal music for nymphs and shepherds, sirens, Venus, Pan and his satyrs, and Cupid. The music was by at least five different composers (Giovanni Maria Trabaci, Francesco Lambardi, Pietro Antonio Giramo, Andrea Anzalone, and Giacomo Spiardo), which was not at all unusual, given the haste with which most court festivities were pulled together. Pan and his satyrs sing in Spanish, with poetic feeling for the hills and flora that surround the Bay of Naples. Cupid's final solo, though in Italian, uses a Spanish musical style to remind the spectators that Venus rose from the sea, as he presents twenty-four real cavaliers to the ladies of the court, whose dancing finishes the 'delights' of the evening.

Since operas were not published with the aim of either sales or future performances, the fact that more operatic music has been preserved than music for more typical entertainments like the *Delizie di Posillipo* says the obvious – namely, that the music in musical dramas was of particular importance and its patrons had reason to make it known. A series of public and private events can be described in a printed *descrizione;* the lavishness of a spectacle can be represented in engravings. But *scores* were generally published either for professional use in church or as music for informal amateur performance (songs, madrigals, lute and guitar pieces) and teaching. Court spectacles were typically one-time and exclusive presentations; why, then, publish any of their music? The Medici wedding spectacles of autumn 1600 present an instructive case. The principal production, *Il rapimento di Cefalo* (Giulio Caccini, libretto by Gabriello Chiabrera) had music by at least three different composers and remained unpublished as a whole.[11] Jacopo Peri's opera *Euridice,* however, was published in full. Although Peri himself and Giulio Caccini had been developing their new manner of solo singing for years and singing in varied declamatory styles in chamber, devotional, and theatrical venues, the publication of Peri's score connected his new manner of expressive singing indissolubly with ancient Greek drama. Even though the work *Euridice* was performed at court in the context of a grand wedding, then, the audience for its score was not the wedding guests. It belongs to a third category of musical prints, which, like the madrigals of Gesualdo, was analogous to the learned books of philosophers or historians, representing, one might say, advances in the science of the art of music.

Opera, then, not only was a kind of court spectacle but it also shared almost all of its components with such presentations and continued to do so. Apart from the fact that all of its texts were sung, opera was distinguished by the new kinds of recitative – and the way they were accompanied. Nevertheless, recitative did not remain exclusive to opera; it, too, was soon absorbed into every type of occasional festivity. Delightful as it is, however, *Le delizie di Posillipo* has a theme but tells no story. It was theatrical, but it was not a 'drama'. It was rather in the realm of drama that opera went through its growing pains and became more than a curiosity. This was in the staging of written plays – a part of the education of gentlemen and a growing number of nobles in the seventeenth century. As we shall see, both Peri's *Euridice* and Claudio Monteverdi's *Orfeo* belonged more naturally in this tradition.

Play-Acting, Spoken and Sung

Reciting plays was a common teaching device in the late sixteenth and early seventeenth centuries. Boys in noble households memorised plays written by their tutors. Boarders in colleges performed more elaborate projects with larger casts, often with stage sets, machines, and incidental music provided by outside professionals. In Spain, Italy, France, Flanders, Poland, Catholic Germany, and Austria, Jesuit colleges staged verse plays annually, and many a young nobleman acquired his passion for the theatre from being in them. Short skits and five-act tragedies were given at regular times during the academic year, and especially during carnival time. Nobles and other clerics attended the performances, rarely women. At first they were in Latin, but in the course of the seventeenth century, French, German, and Italian took over. Most included some incidental music, such as songs and choruses composed by the college master of music.

The unexpected notion of *singing* a school play throughout arose in Rome, where choirboys-in-training were often attached to colleges. Completely sung plays were staged by the boys of the Roman Seminary as early as 1606 and by students at the German and Hungarian College in Rome in 1613 and 1628.[12] Pope Urban VIII (Maffeo Barberini) founded the Vatican Seminary in 1637 to train boys for service in St. Peter's. Among their carnival plays were three operas in Italian composed by Virgilio Mazzocchi, music director of the basilica.[13] The performances included humorous *intermedi* with schoolboy pranks;[14] and one had a braggart Spanish captain in its cast, a musical portrayal of a *commedia dell'arte* character. Needless to say, treble voices dominate the casts in these musical dramas, which anticipate by centuries the twentieth-century works for children by Benjamin Britten.

Student actors grew into noble- and gentlemen who produced plays for themselves in private associations and academies. Having recruited Peri and Jacopo Corsi, poet Ottavio Rinuccini created *La Dafne* between

1595 and 1598 as a 'simple test of what the song of our age might be capable', offering the *pastorale* in three successive carnival seasons in the merchant's home.[15] Furthermore, Carter says of a later 1600 performance of Peri's *Euridice* in which Corsi played the harpsichord, 'Indeed, *Euridice* has the air of a family venture.'[16] By the end of 1602, however, many of the original collaborators in the invention of opera had either left Florence or died. A few reconstituted themselves in 1607 as the Accademia degli Elevati, under the patronage of Cardinal Ferdinando Gonzaga, resident in Florence.[17] Among their first carnival projects was another revised and re-set version of the same *Dafne*, with some music by the cardinal himself, which was given for the Gonzaga court in Mantua during carnival of 1608.[18] Interestingly, Rinuccini's libretto was chosen for the wedding celebrations in April of 1627 at Castle Hartenfels (Torgau) of Princess Eleonora of Saxony and Georg II, Landgrav of Hessen. But in a land not yet familiar with Italian recitative, the German adaptation of *Dafne* was produced as a 'musical comedy', that is, as a traditional German *Sing-Comoedie* with spoken dialogue, songs and dances (the German play was by Martin Opitz, the music by Heinrich Schütz).[19]

During the previous carnival, the Mantuan court had enjoyed a spoken play 'on the usual stage and with the expected magnificence'. As a side entertainment, the Accademia degli Invaghiti staged the Greek legend of Orpheus as a 'favola cantata', probably with an all-male cast, in one of the former apartments of the duke's sister.[20] The unusual performance of *Orfeo* with music by Monteverdi pleased so much that the duke ordered a second performance for the ladies of Mantua. This scrap of information indicates the restricted and initially male audience for the Gonzagas' (and Monteverdi's) first completely sung drama. Heard as a chamber work with five or six soloists, the fineness of the poetry and the subtleties of the singing could well be appreciated. Later, the composer introduced *Orfeo* to one of the duke's correspondents, who wrote back to Mantua:

Both poet [Alessandro Striggio] and musician have depicted the inclinations of the heart so skillfully that it could not have been done better. The poetry is lovely in conception, lovelier still in form, and loveliest of all in diction; ... The music, moreover, observing due propriety, serves the poetry so well that nothing more beautiful is to be heard anywhere.[21]

Monteverdi had success on a grander scale with several theatrical commissions from the Gonzaga court for the prince's wedding in May 1608. The 'mainstage' production was a play, Giovanni Battista Guarini's *Idropica*, in a three-hour version with a prologue also by Monteverdi, five additional new *intermedi* by other different composers, eight scene changes, machines, and *balli*. Again as an additional work, Monteverdi wrote an opera on the story of Ariadne, a Cretan princess abandoned by the Greek Theseus. Unlike *Orfeo*, it was not for performance in a chamber but intended for a temporary stage set up in a courtyard to be heard by a huge number of guests.[22] The platform stage allowed no scene changes, and the duchess apparently thought the original conception too plain. She requested additional scenes for Venus and Cupid with the usual mechanical devices for their entrances, nudging the work toward the diversity and symbolism of 'spectacle'. In addition to a hunting party and mock naval battle, the guests also enjoyed two *balletti* in which the Gonzagas and other members of the court danced. Among them was Monteverdi's *Ballo delle ingrate*, whose lead role was performed by Virginia Ramponi Andreini (1583–1629 or 1630), the same actress who played the role of Ariadne in the opera. Thus, the wedding guests heard music by Monteverdi in multiple genres and venues on the same occasion. All had some recitative; it is hard to imagine that they thought to distinguish between them. Tellingly, the score to *Orfeo*, the academic project, was published, but not the score to *Arianna*, one item accommodated to the duchess's desires, on a menu of wedding entertainments.

It was not so much within the realm of celebratory spectacle that opera came into being as musical drama. Instead of emblematic figures warbling pleasant or flattering verse in scenic tableaux, in plays, characters with human qualities experience changing situations that evoke varying emotional responses and demand that they make choices. Monteverdi's Orpheus reacts with shock to the news of his bride's death; his grief turns to resolve as he decides to win Eurydice back from Hades; he despairs upon losing her a second time. Characters interact with each other in drama, sometimes with persuasion or deceit, or out of pure lust. They think out loud in soliloquies, sometimes collapsing under the intensity of their conflicting feelings. To deliver such emotive moments, early opera drew on the freedom of rhythm, harmony, and vocal line afforded by the new Italian *stile rappresentativo*. Monteverdi's Mantuan *Orfeo* and *Arianna* created musical models for such moments, even as their recitative was modelled on Peri's. As with many other court productions, the complete music for *Arianna* has not been preserved, but 'Lasciatemi morire', its famous surviving recitative lament sung by the abandoned Ariadne, was emulated time and again and absorbed into the vocabulary of opera.[23]

Florence and Rome in the 1620s

The 1620s in Italy were dense with academic and court theatricals of every genre, on pastoral, religious, historical, sentimental, and comic subjects. After the death of the Grand Duke Cosimo II de' Medici in 1621 left his widow Maria Magdalena of Austria co-regent of Tuscany with her mother-in-law Christina of Lorraine, a series of spectacles at the Florentine court continued to project Medici strength, and also their piety, by taking three female heroines as subjects: Saint Agatha in Jacopo Cicognini's *Il martirio di Sant'Agata* (music by Giovanni Battista da Gagliano and Francesca Caccini, 1622); Saint Ursula in *La regina Sant'Orsola*, mentioned earlier; and Judith, slayer of Holofernes in Salvadori's *La Giuditta* (1626).[24] Their well-known stories made strong dramas, with scenes of sexual advances resisted, the slaughter of war, and martyrdoms – all familiar situations from Jesuit plays about Christian heroes and heroines. For Catholics at war with both Protestants and Muslims, such stories – with their pagan and pastoral romances – reflected how much more was at stake than in the decades just past. New plays and libretti were grounded in history and called forth both human tragedy and victory. Although saints' lives had long been staples of both popular and collegiate theatre, the shift from the portrayal of Classical myths in music opened up all of drama to musical treatment on a grand scale. Saint Ursula's 'heroic action', it was noted, was staged 'with the pomp worthy of the grandeur of ancient Rome'. Its author Salvadori noted that his text could also be performed as a play, without music, which points out the dramaturgical closeness of many verse and musical dramas of the 1620s and 1630s.

Cicognini's *Il Martirio di Sant'Agata* illustrates a typical opportunistic conflation of musical script, drama, and spectacle. It had begun life in 1614 as a verse libretto for music. During carnival of 1622, it was performed as a largely spoken prose play given by the Compagnia di Sant' Antonio di Padova. Five months later, for a visit to Florence by the Spanish ambassador Don Manuel de Zuñiga, it was transformed into a court spectacle with choruses, machines, dances, and women singers. Giovanni Battista da Gagliano and Francesca Caccini composed its sung choruses and arias; Parigi designed the scenes. Bearing no resemblance to the classicising tableaux of the earlier 'favole in musica', Cicognini's play has prison and brothel scenes; a woman, disguised as a man, who rescues her beloved; a braggart captain from the *commedia dell'arte*; an allegorical figure (who represents Free Will); the destruction of a statue of Venus; an earthquake; and the announcement of the death of a Roman proconsul by an angel. Several of Cicognini's other inventions – combined with elements of *Crispus* (Bernardino Stefonio, 1597), a standard school play in the Jesuit repertory – were put together compellingly in Giulio Rospigliosi's opera libretto *I santi Didimo e Teodora,* given in Rome by Cardinal Francesco Barberini in 1635 and 1636.[25]

Illustrations of the scenes for *La regina Sant'Orsola* appeared in one of the three editions of its libretto (see Figure 9.1, representing the battle between Romans and Huns). And although scores were published for two other Florentine spectacles, engravings of their sets were likewise issued with their libretti. (These were Francesca Caccini's *La liberazione di Ruggiero dall'isola d'Alcina* – a *balletto* offered to Prince Władysław of Poland during in 1625 – and a grand spectacle in 1628 to celebrate the wedding of Margherita de' Medici and the Duke of Parma, Odoardo Farnese: Marco da Gagliano's opera *La Flora* on a libretto by Salvadori, whose *intermedi* were danced by the court). The Barberini family in Rome emulated these Florentine productions. In 1631/2, they chose as the subject of their first opera the life of a celibate Roman saint (echoing the choices of the Grand Duchess Maria Magdalena, with Ursula and Judith as allusions to herself). Stefano Landi's score to the last Roman staging of *Il Sant'Alessio* (1634) was the first to be published with engravings of its stage sets.[26]

An example of what secular Rome was willing to undertake in the 1620s was an academy production for carnival 1626 of *La catena d'Adone,* under the aegis of Prince Giovanni Giorgio Aldobrandini. As with the Florentine *Sant'Orsola,* a ten-page scenario was issued, followed by six editions of the libretto by Ottavio Tronsarelli, from five different publishers. Domenico Mazzochi published his score in October of the same year, dedicating it to Farnese and an Aldobrandini nephew. The libretto was adapted from Giambattista Marino's epic poem *Adone,* the plot made to fit into the classicist's span of one day and to suit the use of stage machines, which were engineered by Francesco de Cuppis.

In contradistinction to court spectacle, extraneous entr'actes were omitted. The librettist wrote in the dedication, 'This tale is presented … not filled up by tiresome stretches of empty intermedi, which, by distracting the minds of the listeners, obscure the action more than they enhance it.'[27] Perhaps, then, partly compensating for the lack of the usual songs and dances of the *intermedi,* Mazzocchi added more tuneful music within the scenes themselves. He called these *mezz'arie* ('half arias'), that is, non-strophic songs. Their purpose was 'to break the tedium of the recitative' without delaying the narrative with songs of repeated stanzas. Example 4.1

Example 4.1 Domenico Mazzocchi, *La catena d'Adone*, favola in musica (Rome, 1626), Act II, sc. 2, *mezz'aria* for Falsirena (Venice: Alessandro Vincenti, 1626), mm. 237–59

comes from the end of Act II scene 2 of *La Catena d'Adone*. At his bedside in the golden palace, the sorceress Falsirena has succumbed to temptation and decided to enchain the Adonis she loves. Her previous indecision is transformed into a happy song over a rhythmically moving bass, but only for a single quatrain in poetic metres for recitative. She turns to regard the sleeping Adonis, now 'speaking' in tender recitative over a slow bass ('since it is for love'; 'che per amor intanto'). The bass line then resumes its motion for Falsirena's poetic closing lines, as she sings a languid descent of surrender 'to enchain the one who has sweetly enchained my soul' ('*per incatenare chi dolce incatenò l'anima mia*'.) Though *mezz'arie* were not an original invention on Mazzocchi's part, his naming and use of them recognised that passages in simple recitative had a different cumulative effect in a full-length drama than in the few short scenes of a pastoral. Mazzocchi's short passages in aria style acknowledged that, among spectacles, the different genres posed different problems in pacing and movement; the option of creating *mezz'arie* freed the composer from the internal divisions of speech and song created by the dramatic poet.

Accommodating Spectacle, Drama, and Music

An anonymous treatise entitled *Il Corago, o vero, Alcune osservazioni per metter bene in scena le composizioni drammatiche* (*The Choragus, or Some Observations for Staging Dramatic Works Well*) gives us an inside view of producing drama at court in the 1620s.[28] Its author had lived in Florence before 1621 and was writing some time after 1628.[29] We do not know what kind of circulation, if any, this treatise may have had in its time; nevertheless, its discussion ranges from the ideal script to stage movement and lighting, with unusually detailed opinions by someone who had seen court productions in Florence, Mantua, Ferrara, and Parma; had knowledge of stage engineering; and most likely had supervised performances himself.

The author knew that what keeps an audience pleased is variety and vivacity. What made a production spectacular, however, were its machines.[30] The technical illustrations for the stage machines, however, are missing in the source manuscript: five ways of handling a proscenium curtain, six mechanisms for changing scenery, and two ways to represent the sea; using moving *carri* and clouds; figures and machines that emerge from below; birds and other things that move through the air (e.g., a falling Lucifer); and, above all, transformations to make the audience marvel. Important as they were, though, machines alone could not make a drama. The author advises the playwright to compose stageworthy pieces between three and five hours in length.[31] He tells writers that a work best performed in a short version can always be published later in its 'full' length. Too many solo speeches can bring displeasure, especially if they are more narrative than expressive, and even emotional laments should be varied.

Surprisingly, the first kind of musical recitation the treatise takes up consists of a voice speaking over instrumental accompaniment, a practice for which we have no musical evidence. The second kind of 'recitation' consists of strophic arias in suitably different moods. One advantage of arias, says the treatise, is that listeners do not remember tunes after only one hearing but come to remember and enjoy them more in second and subsequent stanzas. Too many strophes, however, will bore listeners, for a happy aria stays happy for all of its strophes, and individual words that differ from the main mood cannot be expressed musically.[32] The third type is not tied to a repeated air, but

line for line, or even word by word, agrees with the meaning of the poetry in every possible aspect, doing so in a diatonic mode full of semitones, or in semitones, if necessary. This kind of melodic modelling *(modulazione)* is considered perfect when it imitates best the intonation of the words *(la mutazione delle voci)* that a consummate actor would consider for this kind of poetry.[33]

For singing in this 'recitative style', the author recommends 'qualche poco d'armonia' – a thin accompaniment, since the aim is 'to express ordinary speech most naturally'.[34] Speaking from experience, the author also describes the disadvantages of this 'true' recitative style, namely, the relatively flat contour of the vocal line; the deadening effect of too many cadences ('especially if not all the audience particularly enjoys music'); the lack of response from the audience, if the singer should lack expressivity in voice and movement; and the absence of vocal embellishments. It is up to the poet to help the composer avoid these dangers.

The choices discussed in each chapter of *Il Corago* illustrate how the theatrical genre that opera became resulted from specific and often circumstantial decisions. The treatise represents the accommodation of drama and language to musical performance and to the Baroque love of the elements of spectacle – movable scenery, stage machines, music, and dancing. It does not acknowledge the tensions between them per se but points to the problems by the nature of the advice it gives. A published description of the three-act *Arione* staged in Turin in 1628 apologises for the necessity to accommodate drama and music to each other: 'In order not to incur tedium due to the length of the music, it was necessary to shorten the material, leaving the two fishermen Millo and Mirino in the story hanging, and not much conclusion in the end for [the character] Aci.'[35] In 1635 Calderón de la Barca's first theatrical undertaking was a collaboration with the Florentine engineer Cosimo Lotti. The Spaniard complained that the Italians cared more about the invention of the machines than the play.[36]

Although we have few similar statements about dramaturgical concerns from librettists and composers, many of the aesthetic issues associated with early opera inform a series of learned writings by Giovanni Battista Doni (1595–1647), a Florentine jurist and antiquarian who served as secretary for Cardinal Barberini in Rome until he returned to Florence in 1640. His several Lessons and *Trattato della musica scenica (Treatise on Theatrical Music)* discuss ancient drama hand in hand with general critiques of modern musical spectacles.[37] In terms of dramaturgy, Doni correctly maintained that the ancients spoke dialogues in one metre and sang monodies, or *cantica*, in a variety of lyric metres for emotional soliloquies. After twenty-odd years of hearing varying sorts of dramas in music, Doni claimed that one person in ten would confess to 'a certain tedium and excess, that does not satisfy the ear. They would say perhaps that the fault is the composers', who still haven't found a kind of melody suited to the stage that would have all the desired richness and quality.'[38] It was not setting a text to music that made it too long, he asserted, but the fact that too much of the poetry was 'languid', whereas ancient drama had lively back-and-forth dialogue, threats, insults, and the like. Basically, Doni argued, dialogue must actively portray strong feelings or the music cannot. He advocated a combination of spoken dialogue, using the best actors for non-singing roles, and the most expressive music for fewer, but choice, singers, who could also act. 'We would not at times then', he wrote, 'see people going onstage who either can't be heard for their weak voices or who are so inept and clumsy in movement that they cause more laughter than delight.'[39] He also counselled against having unrelated *intermedi* between acts, advocating that scene changes, machines, and choruses be incorporated into the main action, and that a short, pleasant 'commedietta' close off the evening (which would parallel the closing satyr play of antiquity).[40] Doni's main objections pertained to the presentation of serious dramas. He considered pastorals, in contrast, to be a delightful modern invention, which, being entirely about love, entirely fictitious, and without disasters and revolutions (!), were better suited to be entirely sung.[41]

Libretto after libretto and score after score, recitative, aria, and dance music accommodated to each other, discovering the plasticity required for dramatic music. Since so few scores were published or circulated, composers had few models to learn from (only ten opera scores were published before 1630). It is remarkable that, in this still-trial phase, opera was sampled in foreign courts, although it took root in none of them. We have already mentioned the non-operatic adaptation of Rinuccini's *Dafne* performed in Hessen in April of 1627.[42] That same spring some Florentines in Madrid were preparing to introduce opera to the Spanish court. In December they staged *La selva sin amor,* 'a little machine play in the Florentine manner' commissioned from Lope. It had been set to music – with difficulty – by an Italian lutenist, Filippo Piccinini, who had come to Madrid in 1613.[43] The king, Philip IV, was pleased, but the work was no threat. Madrid, London, and Paris, unlike Italy, had strong traditions of public theatre, which defined the locus of their 'national' dramas. In Spain the *comedia nueva*, performed outdoors in *corrales*, was popular at all levels of society and – with its mix of humour, music, philosophy, and moral propositions – proved impossible to supplant. Neither Italian opera nor even the idea of opera took root in Spain until the end of the century.

It appears that Monteverdi's *Orfeo* was staged in the Austrian city of Salzburg in 1614. Three years later, an original 'Sing-Comoedie' on the life of St. Ignatius of Loyola was staged by students at the Jesuit seminary in Würzburg, Germany.[44] It was not until 1627 that a probable opera was heard at the imperial court in Austria. The work in question was not an experiment in the local language but an Ovidian pastoral in Italian performed by the professional troupe of actors from Mantua led by Giovanni Battista Andreini.[45] The following year Monteverdi would send music from Venice for a *mascherata*. Also in Italian were the efforts of the prince of Poland. First staged in Florence in late 1624, *La regina Sant'Orsola* was given again early in 1625 with a different cast for the prince's visit there. When he became King Władysław IV in 1632, he established a court theatre, which presented twelve Italian operas between 1635 and 1648 in Warsaw, Vilnius, and Danzig.[46]

Venice had numerous private academies, but in 1622 only a few public theatres where professional actors played. The social lives and preferred entertainments of the wealthy of this republic were discreet and remain little known. We do know that Monteverdi composed music (now lost, except for a trio, 'Come dolce oggi l'auretta') for a post-banquet *Proserpina rapita* for the wedding of Lorenzo Giustiniani and Giustiniana Mocenigo in 1630 (Venice). The published text by Giulio Strozzi calls it a 'drama per musica' and mentions the dance master and the stage designer, Giuseppe Alabardi.[47] Alabardi would later be involved in the earliest operas given in the public Teatro S. Cassiano, but this is seven, eight years in the future, a story that starts another chapter with the arrival in 1637 of a troupe of Roman musicians.

Influenced by regency spectacle and opera in Florence, the Barberini sponsored at least one musical drama every eligible carnival from 1631 to 1643. Their *Sant'Alessio*, produced modestly in 1631, was given more grandly in 1632 in the newly completed Palazzo Barberini alle Quattro Fontane. In 1633, Don Taddeo, the married brother, offered a more secular opera, *Erminia sul Giordano*, based on Tasso's crusaders' epic *Gerusalemme liberata*, with music by Michelangelo Rossi (1601/2–1656) and libretto by Rospigliosi.[48] *Erminia sul Giordano* also moved toward spectacle with the engagement of the Ferrarese stage engineer Francesco Guitti, whose inventions spurred the alterations to the 1634 *Sant'Alessio*, which in turn appear to have been reused in the 1635 *Didimo e Teodora* (libretto by Rospigliosi; composer unknown).[49] The more modest spiritual operas for the Vatican seminarians of 1638–1639, 1641, and 1643 have already been mentioned.

In 1637, the Barberini turned in a very different direction when they offered a rather non-spectacular production, but one based on a tale by Boccaccio, to which Rospigliosi added three dialect-speaking characters from the *commedia dell'arte*, as well as two extra romantic subplots. So many aspects of the libretto of *L'Egisto, ovvero, Chi soffre speri* are different from the earlier Rospigliosi texts for the Barberini, it is tempting to speculate that some may have resulted from taking Doni's opinions as challenges. New are the quick repartee and a variety of levels of speech; the lessened melodiousness and speeding up of the recitative dialogue; music from more than one composer – Mazzocchi and Marco Marazzoli, the first operatic undertaking for both – and the integration of the *intermedi* with the main story. Furthermore, the complex plot lines in *Chi soffre speri* increased both the number of solo roles and the occurrences of intercutting scenes necessary to carry the subplots forward. It was the first of the Barberini operas to have the language, pacing, and clever *intreccio*, or interdependence of plotlines, of Venetian opera of the future, as well as a cast of distinct social groups. Its principal figures were landed gentry; servants provided humour.[50] Both sets of characters sing mostly in plot-driving recitative and have few songs. Sweet longings are expressed by a third group of generic, pastoral would-be lovers, who provide the most lyric music. Innovative as it was, the realism of the non-pastoral characters in *Chi soffre speri* significantly reduced the opportunities for melody.[51]

When *Chi soffre speri* was revived in 1639, the revised production was mounted in an annex building to the Barberini palace that Rospigliosi reported could seat 3500. New *intermedi* were written for the pastoral and comic characters of the main play, with special stage effects by the most famous sculptor, architect, and stage engineer in Rome, Gian Lorenzo Bernini (1598–1680). The second *intermedio*, 'La fiera di Farfa' ('Market day in the town of Farfa'), became the most famous part of the production, with its lighting that mimicked the rising and setting of the sun, booths for vendors hawking their wares (much as in madrigals composed of 'cries of London'), animals for sale, and a climactic 'combattimento' as a mocking skirmish between the comic Zanni and a cavalier (who while dancing had struck a dog).[52]

A comparison with *La Galatea*, an opera published in 1639 by one of the Barberinis' own singers, castrato Loreto Vittori, shows how different

Rospigliosi's libretti were from the pastoral works still common in the European courts.[53] Its central figures – Acis, Galatea, Polyphemus, Venus, and Cupid – are from Classical myth; Vittori added a gratuitous subplot of an older shepherdess in pursuit of a young hunter. Its first recorded performance is for carnival of 1644 in the palace of Prince Cariati in Naples. Thus what is apparently the first opera given in Naples was created by a Barberini musician and organised by a Roman prelate, but was by then not typically Roman.

The 1642 Barberini opera brought in a huge cast of separated lovers from Ariosto's romance epic *Orlando furioso*. Rospigliosi's libretto, *Il palazzo incantato*, presents a dizzying number of minor subplots surrounding the love triangle of Bradamante, Ruggiero, and Angelica. The many subplots are tangential, but they do allow much more lyrical singing. The composer Luigi Rossi (?1597/8–1653) was the recognised chamber lyricist of the age, but general gossip deemed his first opera too long and too lachrymose.[54]

Barberini opera spurred the migration of Italian opera to the French royal court, due to the strenuous efforts of the Roman Cardinal Mazarin, who had acted in Jesuit plays at the Collegio Romano and had heard the Barberinis' *Didimo e Teodora* in 1635.[55] From 1644 Mazarin used his position as Prime Minister of France to bring Italian musicians, scene designers, and engineers to Paris. Just as a professional acting troupe from Mantua had first brought opera to Vienna in 1627, it was a mixed group of Italian professionals who performed at the Salle du Petit Bourbon in December of 1645, presenting a partly spoken and partly sung *La finta pazza*, in a version of a Venetian repertory piece of the troupe called the Febiarmonici.[56] The fact that almost all the comments by the French centred on Giacomo Torelli's stage machines, the like of which had not been seen before in France, lessens the likelihood that the work was presented as 'an opera', as opposed to an elaborate evening created by the comedians and stage engineer.[57] Candidates for the first completely sung operas heard in Paris appear rather to be the Roman *Chi soffre speri* in 1646, noted above, and Luigi Rossi's second opera, *Orfeo*, composed expressly for Paris in 1647 (libretto by Francesco Buti). These two were performed in the Palais Royal, and with them court opera finally came to the court that defined court culture for the era.

Mazarin had no opportunity, however, to produce another Italian opera until 1654, after his political return from the upheavals of the Fronde. From the extensive correspondence and public reports on *Les noces de Pélée et de Thétis*, it is clear that one cannot think of it as primarily a musical work by a single composer (the Roman Carlo Caproli).[58] The 'comedy' was sung in Italian, a language the French court had come to detest, by a cast composed of soloists from the Savoy court and from Rome, with mostly French singers in the ensembles. It was given at least ten times at the Petit Bourbon, for an audience that extended beyond the court. The ten ballet entrées were not *intermedi* to the play but were prompted by each scene. They had their own airs and music written entirely by the French. The ballets were, of course, danced by members of the court, including the King Louis XIV himself.[59] In March of 1621, *Glückwünschung des Apollinis und der neun Musen* (*Tribute by Apollo and the Nine Muses*) had greeted Johann Georg I, the Elector of Saxony, on his birthday, singing music by Schütz.[60] In 1654 the King of France made his entrance at the Petit Bourbon as Apollo himself, descending in a machine, with an entourage of Muses, all noblewomen (among them Princess Henriette of England, as the English court was still in exile in France). That the score was never published is not surprising, since the genre of the entire presentation was a pure political competition, which the Italians lost.

Notes

1 The carnival season extended from Epiphany to Fat Tuesday. The notice comes from weekly or semi-weekly manuscript newssheets known as the *Avvisi di Roma* (4 March 1609, in V-CVbav Urbinati latini 1078, fol. 107).

2 Louise K. Stein, *Songs of Mortals, Dialogues of the Gods: Music and Theatre in Seventeenth-Century Spain* (Oxford: Clarendon Press, 1993), 78–9.

3 François-Georges Parisot, 'Le Mariage d'Henri de Lorraine et de Marguerite de Gonzague-Mantoue 1606. Les fêtes et le témoignage de Jacques Bellange', in Jean Jacquot (ed.), *Les fêtes de la Renaissance. Journées internationales d'études Abbaye de Royaumont, 8–13 juillet 1955* (Paris: Éditions du CNRS, 1956), 153–89: 173.

4 For a full description, see Isabella Data, 'Il "Rapimento di Proserpina" di Giulio Cesare Monteverdi e le feste a Casale nel 1611', in Paola Besutti, Teresa M. Gialdroni, and Rodolfo Baroncini (eds.), *Claudio Monteverdi. Studi e prospettive: atti del convegno, Mantova, 21–24 ottobre 1993* (Florence: Olschki, 1998), 333–46. Music does not survive for either work; their genre(s) remain undetermined.

5 ' ... *per non esserno molti degni di memoria*'; from the *Aggiunta alli giornali di Scipione Guerra*, entry for 17 October 1630, quoted in Domenico Antonio D'Alessandro, 'La musica a Napoli nel secolo XVII attraverso gli *avvisi* e i giornali', in Lorenzo Bianconi and Renato Bossa (eds.), *Musica e cultura a Napoli dal XV al XIX secolo* (Florence: Olschki, 1983), 145–64: 161.

6 On English masques in the seventeenth century, see Peter Walls, *Music in the English Courtly Masque, 1604–1640* (Oxford: Clarendon Press, 1996).

7 For Parigi's set designs, see Arthur R. Blumenthal, *Giulio Parigi's Stage Designs: Florence and the Early Baroque Spectacle* (New York and London: Garland Publishing, 1986), figs. 1–13. The surviving music connected to the 1608 wedding has been recorded by Il Complesso Barocco on the CD *La notte d'amore*, Stradivarius STR 33636 (2003), with music edited and directed by Victor Coelho and Alan Curtis. It includes music from the third (Jacopo Peri) and fifth (Marco da Gagliano) *intermedi* to the Buonarroti play. See also Tim Carter, 'A Florentine Wedding of 1608', *Acta Musicologica* 55/1 (1983), 89–107, rpt. in his *Music, Patronage and Printing in Late Renaissance Florence* (Aldershot and Burlington: Ashgate, 2000).

8 *La regina Sant'Orsola* was first prepared for 1620/21 but cancelled due to the death of the grand duke. For the scene designs, see Blumenthal, *Giulio Parigi's Scene Designs*, figs. 32–8.

9 Tim Carter, 'The North Italian Courts', in Curtis Price (ed.), *The Early Baroque Era. From the Late 16th Century to the 1660s* (Houndmills and Basingstoke: Palgrave Macmillan, 1993), 23–48: 43.

10 *Delizie di Posillipo boscarecce e marittime* in *Breve racconto della festa a ballo fattasi a Napoli* (Naples: C. Vitali, 1620; rpt. T. Longo [1620?]).

11 See Tim Carter, 'Rediscovering *Il rapimento di Cefalo*', *JSCM* 9/1 (2003), http://sscm-jscm.org/v9/no1/carter.html.

12 The score to *Eumelio* in Italian, with music by the Seminary's Sienese music director Agostino Agazzari, was published Rome in 1606; for Agazzari's Preface in Italian and English, see Tim Carter and Zygmunt M. Szweykowski (eds.), *Composing Opera: From 'Dafne' to 'Ulisse errante'*. (Cracow: Musica Iagellonica, 1994), 89–95. A transcription of the 1613 Latin libretto (Alessandro Donati) to *David musicus* (Ottavio Catalani) is in Piotr Urbański, 'Pierwsze łacińskie libretto operowe *David musicus* Alessandra Donatiego', in *David musicus i inne studia z pogranicza tradycji antycznej i historii opery* (Kraków: Wydawnictwo Benedyktynów Tyniec, 2013), 13–39. Catalani's score is lost, as is the music by Lorenzo Ratti for *Ciclope* of 1628.

13 *San Bonifazio* (1638, repeated in 1639), *La Genoinda* (1641), and *Sant'Eustachio* (1643) were all by Giulio Rospigliosi and were set to music by Virgilio Mazzocchi. The performers included both seminarians and Mazzocchi's private pupils. Only a few arias survive for *Genoinda*; full ms. scores exist for the other two. See Bernhard Schrammek, *Zwischen Kirche und Karneval. Biographie, soziales Umfeld und Werk des römischen Kapellmeisters Virgilio Mazzocchi (1597–1646)* (Kassel: Bärenreiter, 2001); Margaret Murata, *Operas for the Papal Court, 1631–1668* (Ann Arbor: UMI Research Press, 1981); Frederick Hammond, *Music and Spectacle in Baroque Rome: Barberini Patronage under Urban VIII* (New Haven: Yale University Press, 1994), 231–5. The libretto to *Bonifazio* is available in Giulio Rospigliosi,

Melodrammi sacri, ed. Danilo Romei (Florence: Studio Editoriale Fiorentino, 1999), 71–138. On *Eustachio,* see also Robert Kendrick, 'What's So Sacred about "Sacred" Opera? Reflections on the Fate of a (Sub)Genre', *JSCM,* 9/1 (2003), http://sscm-jscm.org/v9/no1/kendrick.html.

14 See Margaret Murata, '*Dal ridicolo al diletto signorile.* Rospigliosi and the Intermedio in Rome', in Caroline Panel-Giron and Anne-Madeleine Goulet (eds.), *La Musique à Rome au XVIIe siècle* (Rome: École française de Rome, 2012), 269–89.

15 For the several performances of *Dafne,* including one at court, see Warren Kirkendale, *The Court Musicians in Florence during the Principate of the Medici* (Florence: Olschki, 1993), 194–202.

16 Tim Carter, 'Music and Patronage in Late Sixteenth-Century Florence: The Case of Jacopo Corsi (1561–1602)', *I Tatti Studies in the Italian Renaissance* 1 (1985), 57–104; rpt. in Carter, *Music, Patronage and Printing in Late Renaissance Florence* (Aldershot and Burlington: Ashgate, 2000).

17 See Edmond Strainchamps, 'New Light on the Accademia degli Elevati of Florence', *MQ* 62/4 (1976), 507–35. Rinuccini's non-operatic stage works with music far outnumber his few opera libretti; see Francesca Chiarelli, 'Before and after: Ottavio Rinuccini's *Mascherate* and their Relationship to the Operatic Libretto', *JSCM* 9/1 (2003), http://sscm-jscm.org/v9/no1/chiarelli.html.

18 This was the setting by Marco da Gagliano discussed by Barbara Russano Hanning in Chapter 1. See Marco da Gagliano, *Dafne* (Florence: Cristofano Marescotti, 1608; rpt. Bologna: Forni Editore, 1987).

19 An argument for regarding the German *Dafne* as an opera is in Elisabeth Rothmund, '"Dafne" und kein Ende: Heinrich Schütz, Martin Opitz und die verfehlte erste deutsche Oper', *Schütz-Jahrbuch* 20 (1998), 12–47.

20 On the cast, see Tim Carter, 'Singing *Orfeo*: On the Performers of Monteverdi's First Opera', *Recercare* 11 (1999), 75–118. Silke Leopold envisions the performance as 'only concertante': Leopold, *Geschichte der Oper,* vol. 1: *Die Oper im 17. Jahrhundert* (Laaber: Laaber-Verlag, 2006), 66. The best general survey of the opera remains John Whenham (ed.), *Claudio Monteverdi: Orfeo* (Cambridge: Cambridge University Press, 1986). The exact site within the ducal palace remains uncertain, but a no longer existing ground floor room in the Corte Vecchia is the current candidate; see Paola Besutti, 'The "Sala degli Specchi" Uncovered: Monteverdi, the Gonzagas and the Palazzo Ducale, Mantua', *EM* 27/3 (1999), 451–65.

21 Cherubino Ferrari to Duke Vincenzo Gonzaga, Milan, 22 August 1607, quoted in Iain Fenlon, 'Appendix 1. Correspondence Relating to the Early Mantuan Performances', in Whenham (ed.), *Orfeo,* 167–72: 172.

22 On the location for *Arianna,* see Elena Tamburini, 'A partire dall'"Arianna" monteverdiana pensando ai comici. Luoghi teatrali alla corte di Mantova', in Paola Besutti, Teresa M. Gialdroni, and Rodolfo Baroncini (eds.), *Claudio Monteverdi. Studi e prospettive* (Florence: Olschki, 1998), 415–29.

23 There is an extensive literature on the lament. For contextual and interpretive points of view, see the special issue devoted to laments of *Early Music* 27/3 (1999), with essays by Tim Carter, 'Lamenting Ariadne?' 395–405; Anne MacNeil, 'Weeping at the Water's Edge', 406–17; Leofranc Holford-Strevens, '"Her Eyes Became Two Spouts": Classical Antecedents of Renaissance Laments', 379–93; and Suzanne Cusick, '"There Was Not One Lady Who Failed to Shed a Tear": Arianna's Lament and the Construction of Modern Womanhood', 21–43. See also Anne MacNeil, *Music and Women of the Commedia dell'Arte in the Late Sixteenth Century* (New York: Oxford University Press, 2003), ch. 4, 'The Politics of Description.'

24 On these important works, for which only a little music survives for *Sant'Agata*, see Kelley Harness, *Echoes of Women's Voices: Music, Art, and Female Patronage in Early Modern Florence* (Chicago: The University of Chicago Press, 2006), chs. 3 and 4.

25 Its composer remains unknown and no music has yet been found. See Murata, *Operas for the Papal Court*, 28–31, 253–7; and Hammond, *Music and Spectacle*, 224–6. A modern edition of one manuscript version of the libretto is in Rospigliosi, *Melodrammi sacri*, 7–70.

26 Facsimiles of all three scores have been published: Francesca Caccini, *La liberazione di Ruggiero dall'isola d'Alcina* (Florence: Pietro Cecconcelli, 1625; rpt. Florence: Studio per Edizioni Scelte, 1998, with a facsimile of the undated libretto and its plates), modern edn. by Doris Silbert (Northampton: Smith College, 1945); Marco da Gagliano, *La Flora* (Florence: Zanobi Pignoni, 1628; rpt. Bologna: Forni Editore, 1969), modern edn. by Suzanne Court (Middleton: A-R Editions, 2011); Stefano Landi, *Il S. Alessio, dramma musicale* (Rome: Paolo Masotti, 1634; rpt. Bologna: Forni Editore, 1970), reissued in 2003 with an introduction by Arnaldo Morelli and all plates. On the ballet, see the six essays in Christine Fischer (ed.), *'La liberazione di Ruggiero dall'isola d'Alcina'. Räume und Inszenierungen in Francesca Caccinis Ballettoper (Florenz, 1625)* (Zürich: Chronos Verlag, 2015).

27 Dedication by Ottavio Tronsarelli to Giovanni Giorgio Aldobrandini, 30 March 1626, in Domenico Mazzocchi, *La catena d'Adone* (Rome: Fr. Corbelletti, 1626; rpt. Bologna: Forni Editore, 1969), 5–6. The lack of *intermedi* did not mean that *La catena d'Adone* lacked visual effects. A forest is transformed into a garden, which itself gives way to a view with a fountain. A palace of gold miraculously appears, with a series of rooms; another scene takes place in Hades. The changes of scene by Francesco de Cuppis were so successful that a spoken play, *La selva incantata*, was written so that they could be enjoyed again by the academy to which scene painter, engineer, authors, and patron all belonged.

28 The ancient Greek *choregos* produced the festival plays, in the sense of financing them. The Roman's *choragus* served more as a stage manager. The treatise was discovered and edited by Paolo Fabbri and Angelo Pompilio (eds.), *Il corago, o vero alcune osservazioni per metter bene in scena le composizioni*

drammatiche (Florence: Olschki, 1983). Excerpts in English are in Roger Savage and Matteo Sansone, '*Il corago* and the Staging of Early Opera: Four Chapters from an Anonymous Treatise *circa* 1630', *EM* 17/4 (1989), 494–511, and translated by Margaret Murata in Oliver Strunk (ed.), *Source Readings in Music History*, rev. edn. Leo Treitler (New York: W. W. Norton, 1998), 121–6.

29 The latest plausible attribution is to Ferdinando Saracinelli, the 'producer/director' of many Florentine events of this period, including Francesca Caccini's balletto mentioned above, in Harness, *Echoes*, 112–13 note 6.

30 An essay on the relation of stage machines and drama in this period is Sara Mamone, 'La macchina o l'indifferenza del mito', in Marie-Thérèse Bouquet-Boyer (ed.), *Les Noces de Pélée et de Thétis, Venise, 1639–Paris 1654. Actes du colloque international de Chambéry et de Turin, 3–7 novembre 1999* (Bern, etc.: Peter Lang, 2001), 219–35.

31 To which he adds, 'even if some think that, if the action is filled with things other than acting, the length could be up to seven hours', Fabbri and Pompilio (eds.), *Il corago*, 25.

32 Ibid., 57–60.

33 Ibid., 61.

34 Ibid., 43. The number of instruments playing the accompaniment would vary, however, depending on whether the ensemble was closer to the audience or to the singer, and over the course of the production, would change when accompanying a soloist or an ensemble, ibid., 83.

35 Quoted in Marco Emanuele, '*Arione* e il melodrama alla corte di Savoia', *SM* 26/2 (1997), 313–29: 321–2.

36 Sara Mamone, *Dèi, semidei, uomini. Lo spettacolo a Firenze tra neoplatonismo e realtà borghese (XV–XVII secolo)* (Rome: Bulzoni, 2003), 205–6, citing Norman D. Shergold, 'The First Performance of Calderón's *El mayor encanto amor*', *Bulletin of Hispanic Studies* 35/1 (1958), 24–7.

37 The Lessons were published posthumously, but not always accurately, with his collected theoretical writings as *Lezioni sopra la musica scenica* in Giovanni Battista Doni, *Lyra barberina* αμφιχορδος [*amphichordos*], ed. Anton Francesco Gori, 2 vols. (Florence: Stamperia Imperiale, 1763; rpt. Bologna: Forni, 1974), vol. 2: *De' trattati di musica*. See also Hammond, *Music and Spectacle*, 99–102.

38 Doni, *Lezione V*, 'Sopra la musica scenica', in Doni, *Lyra barberina*, vol. 2, 198.

39 Ibid., 201.

40 Doni, *Lezione III*, 'Sopra il mimo antico', in Doni, *Lyra barberina*, 2, 187.

41 Doni, *Trattato della musica scenica* [early version], in Doni, *Lyra barberina*, vol. 2, appendix, 7.

42 See the several studies by Bettina Varwig, including her 'Echos in und um *Dafne*', in *Schütz-Jahrbuch* 33 (2011), 105–10; and her 'Schütz's *Dafne* and the German Operatic Imagination', in Nikolaus Bacht (ed.), *Music, Theatre and Politics in Germany, 1850–1950* (Aldershot: Ashgate, 2006), 117–38.

43 See Lope de Vega, *La selva sin amor*, ed. Maria Grazia Profeti (Florence: Alinea Editrice, 1999); Stein, *Songs of Mortals*, 191–205; Álvaro Torrente, *La música en el siglo XVII* (Madrid: Fondo de Cultura Económica, 2016), 343–9; Danièle Becker, '"La selva sin amor": Favola pastorale, illustración de las teorías de Doni', *RM* 10/2 (1987), 517–27.

44 See Irmgard Scheitler, 'Würzburg, der Jesuitenorden und die Anfänge der Oper', *Schütz-Jahrbuch* 37 (2015), 39–62: 44–5.

45 *Calisto e Arcade* by Cesare Gonzaga, prince of Guastalla; see Herbert Seifert, *Die Opera am Wiener Kaiserhof im 17. Jahrhundert* (Tutzing: Schneider, 1985), 28–9. There are also scattered notices of musical representations elsewhere in Austria, for example, a *Maddalena peccatrice* in Italian with music in '*stile rappresentativo*' by Stefano Bernardi, in 1628 in Salzburg; see Seifert, 'Italienische Opera des Barocks in Österreich', in Alberto Colzani, Norbert Dubowy, Andrea Luppi, and Maurizio Padoan (eds.), *Il melodramma italiano in Italia e in Germania nell'età barocca. Atti del V. convegno internazionale sulla musica italiana nel secolo XVII, Loveno di Menaggio (Como), 28–30 giugno 1993* (Como: A.M.I.S., 1995), 107–14: 110–11.

46 See Wiarosław Sandelewski, '*Teatr dworski Wladyslawa IV (Il teatro di corte di Ladislao IV)* by Karolina Targosz-Kretowa', *RIM* 4 (1969), 151–6; Margaret Murata, 'Encountering Opera', in Michael Klaper and Nastasia Tietze (eds.), *The Beginnings of Opera in Europe* (Turnhout: Brepols, forthcoming).

47 See the 'Chronological List of Spectacles Held in Venice from 1593 to 1642' in the Appendix to Elena Povoledo, 'Una rappresentazione accademica a Venezia nel 1634', in Maria Teresa Muraro, (ed.), *Studi sul teatro veneto fra Rinascimento ed età barocca* (Florence: Olschki, 1971), 119–69: 154–66.

48 Its score was also later published with engravings of the scene designs: see Michelangelo Rossi, *Erminia sul Giordano* (Rome: P. Masotti, 1637; rpt. Bologna: Forni Editore, [1969]). One ms. libretto (of many) was edited by Monica Farnetti in Rospigliosi, *Melodrammi profani*. It received a second production in Pistoia in 1638 by the Accademia dei Sollevati and a modern performance in Pistoia in 2000.

49 For a detailed and wide-ranging discussion of the scenography and theatre architecture in the Barberini productions, see Davide Daolmi, 'La drammaturgia al servizio della scenotecnica. Le "volubili scene' dell'opera barberiniana,"' *Il Saggiatore Musicale* 13/1 (2006), 5–62; see an expanded version at www.examenapium.it/barberini/barberini.pdf (accessed 19 April, 2019).

50 Two pages in Rospigliosi's *Sant'Alessio* are typically cited as examples of comedy in Roman opera, and, indeed, in the 1634 version, one has an encounter with the Devil who turns into a bear. Pages, however, are young nobles, not servants. Their cheekiness in this libretto derives from schoolboy traditions; boys filled their roles.

51 See the facsimile edition of the manuscript copy V-CVbav Barb. lat. 4386 of *L'Egisto, ovvero, Chi soffre speri*, ed. Howard Mayer Brown and Eric Weimer

(New York: Garland Publishing, 1982); facsimile editions of one of several ms. libretti and the 1639 printed *argomento* are in the collection *Italian Opera Librettos: 1640–1770*, ed. Howard Mayer Brown, vol. 14 (New York: Garland, 1983). A modern edition of the libretto by Massimiliano Chiamenti is in Rospigliosi, *Melodrammi profani*. Its expenses are discussed in Lorenzo Bianconi and Thomas Walker, 'Production, Consumption, and Political Function of Seventeenth-Century Opera', *EMH* 4 (1984), 209–96. On a score for the opera recently found in France and a 1646 French staging, see Barbara Nestola, 'L'Egisto *fantasma di Cavalli: nuova luce sulla rappresentazione parigina di* Egisto ovvero Chi soffre speri *di Mazzocchi e Marazzoli* (1646)', *Recercare* 19/1–2 (2007), 125–46.

52 See Frederick Hammond, 'Bernini and the "Fiera di Farfa,"' in Irving Lavin (ed.), *Gianlorenzo Bernini: New Aspects of His Art and Thought* (University Park: Pennsylvania State University Press, 1985), 115–78, which includes text, translation, and the score of the *intermedio*; and Hammond, *Music and Spectacle*, 235–40.

53 *La Galatea, dramma del cav. Loreto Vittori [...] dal medesimo posta in musica* (Rome: Vincenzo Bianchi, 1639). The modern edition by Thomas Dunn (Middleton: A-R Editions, 2002) includes the libretto and a translation into English.

54 Luigi Rossi, *Il palazzo incantato*. For the facsimile edition of V-CVbav Chigi Q.V.51, one of four ms. scores, see Luigi Rossi, *Il palazzo incantato, overo, La guerriera amanta*, ed. Howard Mayer Brown (New York: Garland, 1977). A facsimile edition of another Roman source, I-Bc ms. Q. 50 is Luigi Rossi, *Il palagio d'Atlante overo la Guerriera amante* (rpt. Bologna: Forni Editore, 1983). A ms. libretto (I-PESo MS 168, one of several) and printed *argomento* are available in the vol. 8 of *Italian Opera Librettos: 1640–1770*.

55 See Murata, 'Encountering Opera.'

56 See Michael Klaper, 'Der Beginn der Operngeschichte in Paris? Anmerkungen zu *La finta pazza* (1645)', in Laurine Quetin and Albert Gier (eds.), *Le livret en question. [Actes d'un colloque tenu à Bamberg du 18 au 20 janvier 2007 sur le thème 'Perspectives de la librettologie']. Musicorum* 5 (2006–2007) (Tours: Presses universitaires François-Rabelais, 2007), 77–104, and Margaret Murata, 'Why the First Opera Given in Paris Wasn't Roman', *COJ* 7/2 (1995), 87–105. The Petit Bourbon, a permanent theatre, was razed in 1660. On the Febiarmonici, see Bianconi and Walker, 'Production and Consumption.' The sole musical source of *La finta pazza* has been reproduced in a facsimile edn. with introductions by Lorenzo Bianconi, Wolfgang Osthoff, and Nicola Usula in Giulio Strozzi and Francesco Sacrati, *La finta pazza*, ed. Nicola Usula (Ricordi: Milan, 2018).

57 Henry Prunières, *L'opéra italien en France avant Lulli* (Paris: H. Champion, 1913), 66–77.

58 See especially, Jérôme de la Gorce, '*Les noces de Pélée et de Thétis* d'après les relations des contemporains', in Bouquet-Boyer (ed.), *Les noces de Pélée et de Thétis*, 33–49.

59 The names and roles of almost all the dancers are known; see Nathalie Lecomte, 'Les danseurs des *Noces de Pelée et de Thetis*', in Bouquet-Boyer (ed.), *Les noces de Pélée et de Thétis*, 237–68.

60 *Glückwünschung des Apollinis und der neun Musen, ...* in *Musik ubersetzt durch Henrich Schützen* (Freiberg: Georg Hoffman, 1621), cited in Helen Watanabe-O'Kelly, *Court Culture in Dresden: From Renaissance to Baroque* (Houndmills, Basingstoke, and New York: Palgrave, 2002), 62.

Society, Institutions, and Production

5 | Opera for a Paying Public (Italy c. 1637–c. 1700)

BETH L. GLIXON

In 1663 Giustiniano Martinoni, in his updating of Francesco Sansovino's *Venezia città nobilissima et singolare*, wrote of one of Venice's most important ornaments, its theatres. As Martinoni explained,

> In Venice there have been erected four principal theatres, one of them on the Fondamente nuove (called SS. Giovanni e Paolo, as it is located near there) built by Giovanni Grimani. . . . He also built another theatre at S. Samuele. The other two theatres are at S. Salvatore, and at S. Cassiano. In the [Theatre] at SS. Giovanni e Paolo during carnival they perform musical operas with marvelous mutations of sets, majestic and most rich costumes, and miraculous flights; one sees on a regular basis resplendent heavens, gods, seas, palaces, forests, and other lovely and delightful images. The music is always exquisite, offering the best voices to be heard in this city, and also bringing singers here from Rome, Germany, and other places, especially women, who with their beauty, the richness of their costumes, and the charm of their voices, and with the interpretation of their roles, bring about stupor and wonder.[1]

'Public opera' famously commenced in Venice in 1637 at the Teatro S. Cassiano, owned by the Tron family, with *Andromeda* (libretto by Benedetto Ferrari, c. 1603–1681; music by Francesco Manelli, 1595–1667). In this account, that theatre's foundational role in the history of opera scarcely matters to the author, for the most important opera theatre in Venice in 1663 was SS. Giovanni e Paolo. The other opera theatre, S. Salvatore (also known as S. Luca), had only presented its third season and, quite possibly, its first one of excellence. (The man in charge that year was Vettor Grimani Calergi, cousin to Giovanni Grimani, and a seasoned connoisseur of music, theatre, and singers).

Martinoni's description speaks of opera as practiced in Venice in 1663, rather than retelling the two-and-a-half decades now past as the opera chronicler and librettist Cristoforo Ivanovich would do two decades later in his *Memorie teatrali di Venezia* (1681; 2nd edn. 1688; Ivanovich's book was dedicated to Grimani's nephews and successors Giovanni Carlo and Vincenzo Grimani).[2] Moreover, to the modern scholar the blank spaces between Martinoni's words reveal something of the fragility of the system, for a number of theatres from the first two decades of public opera were not worthy of mention: S. Moisé (where Monteverdi's *Arianna* was performed in 1639), SS. Apostoli, and S. Aponal (also known as S. Apollinare, Aponal in the Venetian dialect), which had operated for seven years in the 1650s. Martinoni's inclusion of S. Cassiano is, in the end, a nod to its importance in Venice's theatrical history, as that theatre had ceased to present opera with the departure of impresario Marco Faustini to Giovanni Grimani's theatre after the 1659/60 season.

Opera at the Grimani theatre began during S. Cassiano's third year – the 1638/9 season – and Giovanni Grimani's dedication to Venice's operatic enterprise was unfailing. His passion for his theatre must have contributed a sense of stability to Venice's burgeoning but shaky opera industry. Indeed, the family seems to have made a conscious decision that their enterprise would not fail. As far as we know, of all the Venetian theatres operating until the time of Giovanni's death, only SS. Giovanni e Paolo remained more or less immune from notarial and legal disputes. This is not to suggest that the Grimani theatre did not suffer financial or artistic setbacks: no theatre could have been immune from those difficulties. Rather, Giovanni Grimani must have resolved to settle nearly all claims internally. This level of commitment is suggested by his tax declaration in 1661 for the theatre, two years before Martinoni's encomium to him:

In calle della Testa, a theatre built by me in these last years so that I might mount operas, with its contiguous house where the theatre custodian lives, and which also serves for the convenience of the musicians. And so that this theatre might render me some profit, I spend significant amounts of money in large salaries to singers that I bring here from foreign lands. And as is well known to Your Excellencies, at times I suffer considerable losses . . . thus I declare that according to the expenses, when the theatre is in operation I can hope to gain two hundred ducats.[3]

Giovanni Grimani might be looked upon as one of the heroes of what had become that staple of Venetian entertainment – public, commercial opera. Financing and running these theatres was at best unpredictable: S. Cassiano, for instance, saw many problems during its first decade.[4] When Francesco Cavalli (1602–1676) agreed in 1648 to come back to the theatre, then operating under a new management team, he did so with extraordinary perks, a sure sign that he had wavered, given that his librettist, Giovanni Faustini, was by then mounting operas across town at S. Moisé.[5] For much of the century, S. Cassiano would present opera only sporadically, and it never again matched the consistency and excellence it boasted during its first decade of operation.

Although publicity such as that provided in libretti would have served to broadcast the allure of public opera, the timing of the opera season during the carnival itself increased the odds of success, as this event occurred when the city teemed with visitors, and at a magical time when masks lent an aura of mystery and excitement to the city: Venice's tradition of carnival entertainment, and its existing theatres supplied with boxes, made the transition from comedy to the production of opera easier than it might otherwise have been.[6] (A secondary season sometimes took place at the time of the Ascension fairs, when the city was filled with merchants from a wide area of Italy).

SS. Giovanni e Paolo, S. Salvatore, S. Cassiano, S. Moisé, and S. Aponal had at one time hosted *commedia dell'arte* troupes. All of them would eventually be called into service as opera theatres, some of them alternating between comedy and opera. Other occasional opera theatres included the Saloni and the Teatro Cannaregio. Three more theatres, the Novissimo, S. Angelo, and S. Giovanni Grisostomo were built new in order to present opera. What is clear is that each theatre might operate according to a different model and change even from season to season. We have seen how Giovanni Grimani was intimately involved in the running of the theatre (as would be his nephews), though many theatre owners for all intents and purposes removed themselves from the management altogether, relying on impresarios, and sometimes even other noblemen to manage and promote their theatres.

New Theatres

What began at S. Cassiano with the Tron family soon spread to other spaces in Venice. The Grimani family opened SS. Giovanni e Paolo in 1638. In 1640, in advance of the fifth season of public opera in Venice, came the Teatro Novissimo, unique in the history of Venice's theatrical life: it was built on the grounds of the Dominican monastery of SS. Giovanni e Paolo (so that it was quite near to the theatre that bore that name), not on the property of a private family. The theatre was built, apparently, by Girolamo Lappoli, a Tuscan businessman who had resided in Venice from the early 1630s and formed contacts with Venetian noblemen. In recent decades the theatre has been associated with Giovanni Francesco Loredan's academy, the Incogniti, to the point that it has been called by some the 'Incogniti theatre'.[7] While it is true that three Incogniti members wrote libretti to be performed there – Giulio Strozzi (1583–1652), the Messinese author

Scipione Errico (1592–1670), and Maiolino Bisaccioni (1582–1663) – and that Giacomo Badoaro (1602–1654), one of Monteverdi's librettists, later had some connection with the theatre, the financial underpinnings of the enterprise are far from clear. Various creditors, from artisans and artists to other 'benefactors', deluged the impresario Lappoli with their demands to be repaid. One of Lappoli's associates was Joseph Camis, a Jewish doctor who had guaranteed the fees of the singer Anna Renzi (c. 1620–d. after 1661) at a time when she might otherwise have gone to sing at a different theatre. Late in the theatre's life Lappoli attempted to turn it over to Bisaccioni.

For its inauguration in 1641 the Teatro Novissimo presented Francesco Sacrati's (1605–1650) *La finta pazza* on a libretto by Giulio Strozzi. This first production was extensively praised (especially in *Il canocchiale per la finta pazza* published by Surian in 1641). *La finta pazza* not only made a star out of its prima donna, Renzi, but it became the first Venetian opera to travel not only to various cities in Italy, but also to Paris. The publicity that emanated from the pens of the Incogniti must have helped to increase the viability of the theatre (despite the frequent debts that went unpaid by Lappoli), but it also would have served to augment attendance at the other theatres. Yet, no matter the excellence of its artists and its operas, there was no family to stand behind the theatre: after several years of wrangling between the Dominican friars and the impresario, the Novissimo was torn down, by which time two of its stars, the scenographer Giacomo Torelli (1608–1678) and dancer and choreographer Giovan Battista Balbi (fl. 1636–1654, formerly of S. Cassiano), had moved to Paris.

Also extraordinary was the eventual sharing of personnel between the Novissimo and SS. Giovanni e Paolo. Lappoli later rented the Grimani theatre, and artists such as Torelli and Renzi, who had gained their initial fame at the newer theatre, worked at both, most famously with Renzi's performance as Ottavia in *L'incoronazione di Poppea* during the 1642/3 season.

As mentioned above, theatres such as the Teatro S. Moisé (under the ownership of the Zane family for much of the seventeenth century) and S. Cassiano (the Tron theatre), alternated between comedy and opera. S. Aponal, once a comedy theatre (most likely in the late 1620s and early 1630s), rose to great heights under the direction of Giovanni Faustini, and then his brother Marco. But, as Marco later moved on to other venues, S. Aponal eventually ceased to operate altogether in that capacity.[8] It was not until the 1670s that two new theatres were built in Venice – each important in different ways and quite opposite in terms of size, repertoire, and management – and both long lived, unlike the Novissimo. They opened in 1677 and 1678, respectively: S. Angelo (built by Francesco Santurini on land owned by the Marcello and Cappello families), then S. Giovanni Gristomo, built by Giovanni Carlo and Vincenzo Grimani to serve as their second opera theatre, a more luxurious and elite theatrical venue. S. Giovanni Grisostomo was known for its 'high' libretti and the excellence of its singers. S. Angelo often served as an entry point for young singers, and it offered a wider range of types of libretti.

The Financing of Operas

Commercial opera in Venice began with musicians who had travelled there from other regions, that is, it had not come into being as a result of a local desire to promote a new sort of carnival entertainment. Many of the artists had earlier mounted the festa teatrale *Ermiona* in Padua (1636; score by Giovanni Felice Sances, c. 1600–1679, on a libretto by Pio Enea degli Obizzi, 1592–1674).[9] The production of opera depended on a theatre (and in the case of Venice, all the theatres were permanent rather than temporary structures), a librettist, a scenographer, carpenters, painters, a composer, dancers, and musicians. To this could be added a dedicated impresario, though, during the first season at S. Cassiano, the artists had no need of one, as they served as a self-contained unit. When they needed capital, one of the singers agreed to make a loan of 100 ducats. Surely the company needed much more.

The dedication of the next opera at S. Cassiano, *La maga fulminata* (libretto and music once again by Ferrari and Manelli) referred to an overall cost of 3,000 ducats, but the company may have recouped much of their 'investment' from box rentals and ticket receipts.[10] It is likely, however, that Ferrari and Manelli did at some point seek investors from Venetians of various stripes. During the next few years we see evidence of loans from a variety of noblemen. Often the company had difficulty repaying them, and the interested parties would end up in court. In other cases help came not in a formal loan but through a guarantor, who would promise payment when members of a company were short of funds. These guarantors were essential to the success of the opera business, as, for the most part, liquid cash was not available until the season was underway, through box rentals and the sales of tickets and refreshments.[11]

Some of the early companies were sustained through investments of a small group of partners, as we see in Marco Faustini's at S. Aponal and

S. Cassiano. Here any profits and losses would be shared by the members, which in Faustini's case varied between *cittadini*, noblemen, and artisans. Later companies were sustained through a more general financing system called *carati*, or carats (the purchasers of these carats were called *caratadori*), whereby a number of investors supported a business scheme, thus spreading among the group any given individual's profit or loss. This fundamental practice of business in Venice dated back to at least the fifteenth century. At least in theory, it protected both the investors and those in need of payment (in this case the theatre owner, artisans, and all the musicians), and it resembles the practices of academies who sponsored opera theatres in other parts of Italy.[12]

The box system provided the surest source of income, whether for the theatre owner or for the impresario. Indeed, the fees for individual boxes came to be the source of funds payable to creditors of all types. In the latter part of the seventeenth century, the Grimani brothers, having hundreds of boxes in three theatres under their control, frequently transferred the box income, sometimes to singers, but also to tradespeople or many others who held credits. Eventually the boxes would become an even greater source of income for the theatre owners when they were put up for sale, in essence becoming the property of a buyer who could transfer the box or pass it down to his or her descendants.

While the 'orchestra' (ground-floor seats) would be rented by a wide variety of people, both Venetians and foreigners, the boxes were occupied by Venetian nobles (in the prime locations), and, higher up towards the ceiling, less wealthy nobles and a number of *cittadini*. Some boxes were rented on a more or less permanent basis by visiting dukes such as the Hanover Brunswicks.[13] Others were chosen by lot, by the doge himself, for the benefit of ambassadors serving in Venice.[14] The boxes offered a modicum of privacy, especially when the spectators wore masks. They also provided an opportune location from which to launch printed sonnets in honour of favourite singers. They might also prove to be places of violence, whether by means of fists or pistols, or places for amorous assignations. The opera box, then, served as a locus for passions of varying kinds.

At S. Aponal, in the 1650s, impresario Marco Faustini personally held the rights to the box income: even if the company lost money over the season, he, at least (rather than his partners), was guaranteed an income. Naturally, he was free, but not required, to reinvest those funds in order to cover debts. But what, or who, was an impresario? He (or she) 'ran' the company, arranged for the musicians, and paid everyone involved with the enterprise.[15] Yet the responsibilities might well vary from theatre to theatre. In the case of Faustini, the most well-documented impresario in seventeenth-century Venice, his duties varied according to the theatre. At S. Aponal (1651–1657) and S. Cassiano (1657–1660) he pretty much ran the show. Despite the difference in social rank his importance in the company was greater than that of his noble partners. In both cases the theatre owners had little to do with the company other than to see their rental fees well in hand. At SS. Giovanni e Paolo (1660–1663), though, the situation could not have been more different. Here Faustini was not responsible for the rent, and he would have dealt with the most knowledgeable theatre owner in the city. Giovanni Grimani would have had strong views on the singers to be hired and, most likely, the repertoire. During the end of Faustini's career as an impresario, the owners were the teenagers Giovanni Carlo and Vincenzo Grimani, so that Faustini would have been the one with far greater experience.

Venice continued to welcome other men who ran theatres over long periods of time, such as Santurini and Giovanni Orsato. Impresarios in Venice included artisans, librettists, noblemen, and businessmen, but, generally, except for Francesco Cavalli around the cusp of 1640, not composers, at least until the time of Antonio Vivaldi in the early 1700s.

Making Opera

Librettists of Venetian Opera

During the seventeenth century in Venice, the librettist was not paid by the company. Rather, he reaped the benefit from ticket sales and (it was to be hoped) from a gift from the person or persons to whom he dedicated the work. Dedicatees might be Venetian or foreign nobles and dukes, ambassadors, or, on occasion, the patrons or owners of the opera theatres. In the case of a revival, where the librettist was deceased, any profits would have gone back to the impresario or the company at large.

The very earliest libretti came from the pen of the poet, composer, and theorbist Benedetto Ferrari (c. 1603–1681). In the third season came the librettist Orazio Persiani, a Florentine who had ties with Venetians dating back to the 1630s, with *Le nozze di Teti e di Peleo*, 1638/9, set by Cavalli at S. Cassiano. That same year saw Giulio Strozzi's first libretto (*La Delia*, 1639, SS. Giovanni e Paolo, music by Manelli); he was also of Florentine heritage, but born in Venice and an active member of the Incogniti. Soon, members of the Venetian nobility and upper classes entered into the fray, chief among them (during the 1640s) Giovanni Francesco Busenello (1598–1659), Giacomo Badoaro (with two libretti), and Giovanni Faustini (1615–1651).

Busenello, also a member of the Incogniti, came from an old Venetian family of the *cittadino* (citizen) class, many of them high-ranking civil servants. An avid versifier, not just of libretti, but of poems, he practiced not as a secretary, however, but as a lawyer. Of his five libretti, only Monteverdi's *L'incoronazione di Poppea* (Venice, Teatro SS. Giovanni e Paolo, 1643) was set by a composer other than Cavalli. [16]

The most prolific librettist of the 1640s came from an entirely different mould. Giovanni Faustini was the younger son of a Venetian *cittadino*. Though of the same rank as the family of Busenello, the Faustini clan could not claim the same prominence that the Busenellos enjoyed. As far as we know, Giovanni never took up a profession and lived with his brother Marco, a lawyer who encouraged his brother's activities, and himself became an impresario upon the death of Giovanni.

Giovanni Faustini entered the arena as the fourth librettist at S. Cassiano (after Ferrari, Persiani, and Busenello), with *La Virtù de' strali d'Amore* (1641/2), set by Cavalli, and the two continued to work together until the librettist's premature death in 1651. Within a ten-year span, Giovanni wrote numerous libretti and drafted even more. In 1647 he left S. Cassiano to take up the smaller S. Moisé, which had presented opera only sporadically during the 1640s (with Faustini at S. Moisé, Cavalli's *Giasone*, the opera presented at S. Cassiano during the 1648/9 season, was penned by Giacinto Andrea Cicognini, 1606–1649). Eventually the owner of S. Moisé (Almorò Zane) must have tired of the vicissitudes of the opera trade, and the third year of Faustini's contract went unfulfilled when Zane hired a *commedia dell'arte* company. His passion for opera undeterred, Faustini soon took over S. Aponal, a theatre that, as we have seen, had been devoted to comedy in earlier years, but had for some indeterminate time served merely to store oil (on the ground floor). There Faustini instituted an ambitious plan in which he would mount two operas per season, each of them with a score by Cavalli – who at this time also supplied some operas for other theatres.

Count Nicolò Minato (c. 1620/5–1698) and Aurelio Aureli (fl. 1652–1708) were both lawyers who began to write libretti during the 1650s. Another member of the *cittadino* class, Matteo Noris (d. 1714), joined them during the 1660s. All three enjoyed remarkably long lives and continued to write libretti through the end of the seventeenth century, two of them into the eighteenth –although after 1669 Minato wrote his libretti

for Vienna rather than for Venice, as imperial poet. Aureli remained in
Venice and served a wide range of theatres and composers aside from
several years spent at the Farnese court of Parma and a year spent in
Vienna in 1659.

Noris's last libretto was produced a year before his death in 1714. He
wrote many works for the Grimani brothers, both at SS. Giovanni e Paolo
and S. Giovanni Grisostomo, but he served other theatres as well, including
S. Salvatore, S. Angelo, and S. Luca (formerly known as S. Salvatore); he
also provided Prince Leopoldo de' Medici with several libretti for his
theatre at Pratolino, outside Florence. Especially vibrant was Noris's collaboration with Carlo Francesco Pollarolo (c. 1653–1723), which persisted
well into the eighteenth century. Many other librettists entered the fray,
including the reformists Domenico David (d. 1698), Count Girolamo
Frigimelica-Roberti (1653–1732), and Apostolo Zeno (1668–1750).

Venice's Libretti

The earliest libretti set in Venice were based in mythology and ancient
history, while making use of comic and lower-class characters added spice
to the adventures and dilemmas of their 'betters'. Giovanni Faustini took a
different path, using newly invented characters. His libretti followed what
has been called the 'Faustini formula', typically two couples at odds finally
reunited by the end of the opera. Only in his last libretto, *Calisto* (Cavalli,
S. Aponal, 28 November 1651), did he turn to a mythological plot with
stunning results – even if the opera was a financial failure.

One magnificent interloper was Giacinto Andrea Cicognini, who arrived
in Venice in 1646 and was soon drawn into the city's intellectual elite.[17]
The son of the dramatist Jacopo Cicognini, he was the only librettist active
in Venice with profound experience as a playwright. As his father before
him, he drew on various Spanish sources in a number of his works, most of
them unacknowledged. Giovanni Faustini, Minato, and Aureli would continue in this vein.[18]

Beginning in the 1653/4 season, Minato formed a close alliance with
Cavalli, and, in the late 1660s, when Cavalli retired from Venetian opera,
he served Antonio Sartorio (1630–1680). Minato's Venetian libretti are
historically based. Unusually, he set out his dramas in acts of twenty scenes
each, something that became his trademark. Generally, he informs the
reader of his sources and then sets out the complications that enter into
the plot. Minato was known for the lively conversation between characters,
his deft use of comedy, and his fine aria texts – which served Handel well

when he reset Minato's *Xerse* via Silvio Stampiglia's adaptation for Giovanni Bononcini (Rome, Teatro di Tordinona, 1694).

Aureli's subjects ranged farther than Minato's. His *Erismena* of 1655/6 (Cavalli, Venice, S. Aponal) was fictional in the vein of Faustini's libretti – and even borrowed from his *L'Ormindo* (Cavalli, Venice, Teatro S. Cassiano, 1644), but many of his works drew on either mythological or historical subjects, always perverting his sources and adding comic effects. At his most outrageous, Aureli turned opera's time-honoured hero Orfeo into a jealous husband whose actions provoke the death of Euridice (*L'Orfeo*, Sartorio; S. Salvatore, December 1672).[19] Librettists tended to complain about Venice's audiences, who prized novelty. *L'Orfeo* shows Aureli willing to topple audiences' expectations by serving up the unusual and, in this case, the unthinkable.

Composers

In some theatres a house composer might have a multi-year contract; in that case, the impresario's task was lessened. Cavalli served as house composer in several theatres, though his loyalties shifted from time to time. In the 1650s he went from S. Cassiano to S. Aponal, then to SS. Giovanni e Paolo, and eventually back to S. Cassiano, now under the direction of Marco Faustini. When Cavalli left SS. Giovanni e Paolo for S. Cassiano, Giovanni Grimani hired Francesco Lucio (c. 1628–1658) and Giovanni Battista Volpe (Rovettino, c. 1620–1691), though not as house composers.

Pietro Andrea Ziani (1616–1684) began to write operas in the mid-1650s and changed theatres according to the activities of Marco Faustini. He served at S. Aponal, S. Cassiano, and SS. Giovanni e Paolo. Cavalli was the most well paid among the composers, much to Ziani's regret. These two – as well as Giovanni Rovetta (c. 1596–1668), Volpe, Lucio, Sartorio, and Pollarolo – were all either Venetian or had worked there for many years. Others – such as the early composers Manelli, Ferrari, and Marco Marazzoli (c. 1602–1662) – came from other regions, as did Antonio Cesti (1623–1669) and Giovanni Antonio Boretti (c. 1638–1672).

As the decades passed, the music of many more 'foreigners' was welcomed onto Venetian stages. Nor did the composer need to be on-site at the time of the opera production. A number of Ziani's operas were produced in those years he served in Bergamo and Vienna; no evidence yet suggests that Giovanni Domenico Freschi (1634–1710), *maestro di cappella* at the cathedral in Vicenza, was present when his operas were performed at S. Angelo. When on location in Venice, the composer would attend rehearsals, direct the orchestra, and make necessary additions and adjustments to the opera as required by any number of contingencies. Many composers were paid 150 ducats for their efforts, an amount that remained constant for many decades.

In Venice, as in other cities, opera was a lucrative 'second job' for composers: all of them had employment elsewhere, whether in churches or conservatories within Venice, or in any number of institutions outside of Venice, even at the imperial court of Vienna, or various duchies through-out Italy and the German lands. What is certain is that any composer who found himself in Venice would likely aspire to have an opera mounted there: the city eventually saw operas from the pens of Alessandro Scarlatti (1660–1725), German composers such as George Frideric Handel (1685–1759) and Johann David Heinichen (1683–1729), as well as 'ama-teur' composers such as Tomaso Albinoni (1671–1750/1) and Giovanni Maria Ruggieri (fl. c. 1690–1714).

Singers and Competition among the Theatres

Unlike opera in France and some Italian cities, a chorus did not figure into Venetian opera during the seventeenth century. Rather, operas might end with an ensemble featuring the main characters. 'Extras' did figure into the opera, but their role was to add grandeur to the stage in scenes where the 'people' were present, not to augment the musical forces. Nor did audiences hear 'big' orchestras such as that featured in Monteverdi's *Orfeo*. Through the 1660s they heard an ensemble of strings (and an occasional brass instrument) accompanied by continuo instruments. Later in the century, winds and brass would routinely find their place in the orchestra.

Every opera needed a corps of singers, often from ten to twelve, so that over the years many singers passed through Venice. Some of them, whether Venetian or from elsewhere, sang both in Saint Mark's Chapel and on the stage. Although several Venetian women (including Elena Passarelli, Margarita Pia, and, later, Vittoria Tarquini and Faustina Bordoni) sang in the theatres of their native city, most female roles were filled by women from Rome, Bologna, and elsewhere. In Venice, female roles were played by women, whereas in many other locales they would have been played by castrati.

Some singers, both male and female, had careers in Venice that lasted for more than a decade, while others sang there only rarely. As noted by

Martinoni in the description that opened this chapter, singers were brought in not only from Italy, but from Germany and Austria (that is, Italian singers employed by various foreign courts). Indeed, impresarios in Venice sought the best they could afford, no matter where they might be found: by the end of the century, especially owing to the growing number of theatres, hundreds of singers had passed through Venice, had built up reputations, and were then available to sing elsewhere. One never knew when the next singer would arrive who would ignite the passions of both listeners and impresarios, as the Roman Anna Renzi had done earlier at the Teatro Novissimo in the 1640s.

The debut of the Roman Vincenza Giulia Masotti in the 1662/3 season was one of these occasions. It occurred at S. Salvatore, newly led by Vettor Grimani Calergi, when Masotti performed in Cesti's *Dori* (Giovanni Filippo Apolloni, Innsbruck, Hof-Saales, 1657). Giuseppe Ghini, a member of the cast, wrote to his patron:

The opera is so praised that one can hardly remember a similar circumstance. The evening of the premiere they took in 913 tickets, a number which has never been seen in the entire time that opera has been done in Venice. The Roman girl ... receives such applause that they hardly let her finish, for all the shouting. Each night so many sonnets in praise of her fly through the air that they impede the view of the spectators.[20]

This account emphasises the singing, pure and simple, of a new singer who would change the dynamics of impresarial dealings for years to come, for Masotti was the singer impresarios lusted over. One of Marco Faustini's colleagues declared that the efforts to hire her in the mid-1660s had driven him mad.[21] Masotti sang at S. Salvatore during Grimani Calergi's years there, and then at SS. Giovanni e Paolo after the death of Giovanni Grimani. Masotti's ascendance, perforce, upset the status quo at the two opera theatres in Venice: Caterina Porri, prima donna at SS. Giovanni e Paolo since 1653, would find her way to S. Salvatore. Faustini, in his prolonged and fruitless efforts to hire Masotti for SS. Giovanni e Paolo for the 1665/6 season, would have to 'make do' without either Porri or Masotti: in the last weeks before the opening of the season, he was forced to settle on women with lesser reputations.[22]

The Visual Element: Scenery, Costumes, Dancers, and Extras

Spectacle on the Venetian Stage

The opera 'experience' provided much more than instrumental and vocal music. The visual element was paramount, and it was this aspect that, in part, separated opera from the *commedia dell'arte*. Working with the scenographer and the costumer, the impresario brought to fruition the librettist's conception. At least during the years of Marco Faustini's management, scenery was made new each year, the specific scenes drawn from the various possibilities of exterior and interior views: campgrounds, gardens, city views, sea views, prison scenes, music rooms, and so on.[23] This aspect could be rather costly; thus when Venetian operas, such as *La finta pazza* travelled to other cities, the spectacular elements might well be pared down.

Matteo Noris was remarkable in his ability to conjure up apposite scenes, such as those that presented the varied populace of a locale, including rulers, subjects, and dissidents, and the incorporation of various machines aimed to leave audience members in a state of marvel. Naturally other librettists also suggested such scenes according to the desires of the impresario and theatre owners. With the conception of any opera, the librettist, along with the scenery designer and the costumer, would chose those visual elements they felt best suited their drama, but economics would have played a significant role in the case of the scenery and the 'extras' that increased the grandeur seen on stage.

The Grimani theatres were especially known for their desire to include such pomp: for Giovanni Carlo and Vincenzo, the resultant splendour outweighed the costs necessary to realise these creations. An eyewitness account of a scene from Nicola Beregan's *Heraclio* (music by Ziani, 1670/1) brings this spectacle to life:

As to the news, it appears in these days of carnival that the world at large revolves around the small world of the theater. No one talks of anything except the opera at S. Zuanepolo [SS. Giovanni e Paolo] .... . There's the first scene with the triumphal carriage drawn by big, life-sized elephants with a structure on it that reaches up to the level of the architrave. And on the structure at the first level there is the emperor Foca with numbers of actual warriors, soldiers, and pages, and on the neck of the elephant an imprisoned king in chains; this carriage is followed by two other large elephants with big turrets on their backs, also filled with armed cavaliers. The theater is surrounded by warriors; and the scenery is laid out so that until the end of the horizon of the perspective, one sees a vast army. And then one hears a great clamor of military sinfonie, trumpets, drums, pifari, cornetti, and artillery, all in music. The warriors, soldiers, pages, with a noble, yet distant military confusion, all sing, as if they were speaking in a hostile camp. All of this brings the greatest magnificence to the eye, and great satisfaction to the mind. The said elephants are so lifelike that one would say they are real; and it seems that this first set is not even one of the best compared to many of the others in this opera, a sign that the Signori Grimani can pride themselves for having spent lavishly . . . . They say in Venice that such spectacle has never before been seen in the theater . . . the attendance in the theater is such that not only Venice, but all of the cities of the *terra ferma* are emptied of the nobles, who run to see the opera.[24]

In December 1672, the singer Giuseppe Ghini, once again in Venice, wrote about a scene from Boretti's *Domitiano* at SS. Giovanni e Paolo (libretto by Noris), mentioning 'a most beautiful naumachia, a banquet scene with Domitiano as Jove that is incomparable, and the last scene . . . is esteemed as beautiful as is possible, so much so that they say at the Piazza: to S. Luca to hear, to SS. Giovanni e Paolo to see'.[25]

Dancers and Costumes

In the first opera at S. Cassiano, the company paid Balbi for several choreographies, and one of the pieces called for twelve dancers. Dances in Venetian opera tended to appear at the end of the first and second acts, rather than occurring more frequently, as would be the case in French opera. Marco Faustini tended to employ several different choreographers, presumably according to their availability (during this period the names of the individual dancers are unknown). In the earliest years of opera in Venice, Balbi was the outstanding dancer and choreographer. His travels to France and other cities in Italy necessitated the presence of other professionals such as Giovanni Battista Martini, Battista Artusi, Olivier Vigasio, and Agostino Ramaccini.[26] Regarding costumers, impresarios relied on a number of them, some quite renowned in the field – such as Horatio Franchi at the Grimani theatre – but others little known aside from several pay records. These costumers were most involved with outfitting the major characters, as generic costumes could often be obtained through jobbers at a much lower cost.[27]

Venetian Opera and the Venetian Republic

Opera in Venice differed from that mounted in other duchies and kingdoms regarding who or what was being honoured or celebrated. If in France, it was designed to reflect the splendour of the Sun King, Louis XIV, and in various duchies that of the reigning duke; in Venice it could be said to celebrate the magnificence of the Most Serene Republic, whether overtly or not. Most likely, the doges would only have known opera in

Venice from those years preceding their reign, when they were free to socialise in their families' boxes: Venice's power resided not in the doge – practically a prisoner in the Doge's Palace – but in its governing bodies made up of nobles of ancient lineage, who filled most of the boxes.

If it could be said in the late 1630s that in Venice one could see such splendour as was normally seen in the palaces of kings, comparisons were no longer necessary as opera became firmly established. An overview of opera libretti published both in and outside of Venice is revealing. A libretto dedication served multiple functions, one of which was to enrich the purse of either the librettist or the opera company. But with one early exception (written by Benedetto Ferrari, a native of Reggio, in 1639, for *L'Armida*) no libretto was dedicated to a doge. Rather, most were dedicated either to visiting princes and dukes and their families, or to Venetian nobles. In both cases Venice's reputation was enhanced: theatres were graced by the 'patronage' of important personages, and, moreover, dedications to nobles often pointed to the service of their families to the Republic. Just as a libretto such as Busenello's *L'incoronazione di Poppea* might celebrate the superiority of the 'republic' over a corrupt emperor, so too could Venice's opera industry serve to shine light on a republic which, despite a loss of power compared to the supremacy of earlier centuries, still emanated an aura of independence and wealth.[28]

'Public' Opera outside of Venice

Opera began at Italy's courts, and private entertainments of various stripes would continue throughout the century. The Barberini family's dedication to opera started during the reign of Urban VIII in the 1620s and continued after the pope's death[29]. Other families (such as the Colonna and the Chigi) and institutions such as embassies would continue the practice, given that public opera was generally discouraged in Rome. Gradually theatres offered up opera in other cities and towns. Often they were 'sponsored' by a local ruler, who might supply some, but not necessarily all of the funds. In Florence, several theatres operated under the sponsorship of academies, whereby the costs were borne by their members, but various Medici princes were active in their support of them.[30] In times of civic celebration, such as during the marriage of the future Grand Duke Cosimo III to Margherita Luisa d'Orléans in 1661, the celebratory opera was *Ercole in Tebe* by Giovanni Andrea Moniglia (1624–1700) and Jacopo Melani (1623–1676). Also presented that year was the Venetian *Erismena* by Aureli and Cavalli.

Then, in turn, Moniglia's libretto travelled to Venice ten years later for the 1670/1 season, revised by Aureli in order to please Venetian audiences, and newly set by Boretti.[31] Whether travelling from or to Venice, both the libretto and the score were malleable, adapted to the occasion and the strengths of the performers.[32]

The establishment and growth of the opera industry in Venice either directly or indirectly led to an expansion of the entertainment. As more and more singers were recruited to sing there, they would have been available for hire in other locales during other seasons; as these singers' popularity waned, they could be hired to sing during the carnival season outside of Venice. In some cases the spread of certain operas seems to have been promoted by singers. Aureli and Ziani's *Le fortune di Rodope e Damira* (Venice, S. Aponal, 1657) circulated widely throughout Italy until the last known performance in Reggio in 1674. In a number of the early performances (Bologna, Milan, Bergamo, and Turin), though not in the original, the role of Rodope was performed by Anna Felicita Chiusi (c. 1635–1664), who also signed the libretto dedication in Milan in 1660 (as well as the dedication for Aureli and Volpe's *Costanza di Rosmonda* in Milan the next year). Yet Chiusi was one of the prima donnas in the opera performed the previous year in Venice at S. Aponal, *Erismena*, by Aureli and Cavalli. Given that *Erismena* was also performed in Milan around the same time (1661), it is likely that she performed in it as well.

Chiusi is one example of a new breed of female singers who would help to mount opera in cities across Italy – as she was living in Venice at the time of her death (1664), she would have maintained numerous contacts with the musicians of that city. The Roman Anna Francesca Costa (fl. 1640–1654), under the protection of Cardinal Giovanni Carlo de' Medici, brought Moniglia's *Ergirodo* (composer unknown) to Bologna in 1652.[33] Another was Elena Passarelli, a Venetian who had performed at S. Cassiano in the 1650s. Having already appeared in Siena in Cesti's *Argia* in 1669 to great popularity, she signed a dedication for a performance of the same composer's *Dori* in Florence in 1670. She had been prepared to have *Dori* mounted in Siena, where she would have served as 'impresaria', but the performance had to be cancelled, and she took it 'elsewhere'.[34] Much of the history of these travelling productions remains to be written.

Public opera, or rather opera that was in part commercial and in part subsidised, spread to many cities and towns throughout Italy. In the seventeenth century, Bologna had two theatres, the Formagliari and the Malvezzi: both presented operas previously performed in Venice, along with others.[35] Opera in Milan flourished at the Teatro Ducale, with a mix of Venetian revivals and works by local composers and librettists, including Carlo Maria Maggi (1630–1699). The types of operas presented throughout Italy, and the interactions between theatre and city, changed from town to town. The next section looks briefly at two examples, Siena and Naples.

Siena

As recently shown by Colleen Reardon, the nature of operatic production in a particular locale could change over time. In Siena – a city with a rich theatrical tradition – it went from being a product of the patronage of a reigning government (as represented by Prince Mattias de' Medici) to an entertainment in part sponsored by an important local family (the Chigi), and then to a more typical impresarial and commercial model.[36]

Datira, a work by Pietro Salvetti and the Medicean singer Michele Grasseschi, was sponsored by Mattias at enormous cost in a theatre renovated by him; the opera was performed in 1647. This type of enterprise was not to be repeated: the more permanent establishment of opera in Siena came about later and arose through a more organic and more local motivation.

Not until 1669 was another opera presented there. Cesti's *Argia* (Giovanni Filippo Apolloni, Innsbruck, 1655), was mounted in a theatre restored with the help of funds from the Roman Chigi, as well as many other Sienese families. Related to Pope Alexander VII who reigned 1655–1667, this branch of the Chigi (principally Cardinal Flavio Chigi and the younger Cardinal Sigismondo) were noted sponsors of music both in Rome and at their villa at Arriccia, just outside the Holy City. Although they helped to choose the opera, the whole production was very much a communal effort, with financial support coming from many of the city's noble families. *Argia*'s prima donna was Passarelli, whose enthusiastic reception, replete with generous gifts, must have encouraged her to return to Siena the next year.[37]

Perhaps the pinnacle of opera production in Siena occurred in 1672, when three works were presented to celebrate the visit of Princess Maria Virginia Borghese Chigi. They were Cesti's *Dori*, the same composer's *Tito* (Nicola Beregan, SS. Giovanni e Paolo, 1666), and Melani's *Girello* (Filippo Acciaiuoli, Rome, Palazzo Colonna, 1668), all of them connected in some way with Rome and some with the Contestabile Lorenzo Onofrio Colonna, a frequent ally of the Chigi regarding issues of musical patronage. The whole enterprise was pulled together by the librettist and impresario (at the

Roman theatre the Tordinona) Filippo Acciaiuoli (1637–1700), in Siena for the duration of the productions.

The next decade brought a number of operas, most of them pastoral in nature and often mounted in connection with Chigi visits to Siena. One of them, Bernardo Pasquini's *La sincerità con la sincerità, overo Il Tirinto* (1673), had previously been mounted at the Chigi villa in Ariccia at great expense. The production of these Sienese operas was always facilitated through the assistance and support of a number of local academies, and, in the case of *Il Tirinto*, by the ad hoc 'L'Accademia del Tirinto', who signed the dedication of the libretto to Virginia and Olimpia Chigi, two of the nieces of Pope Alexander who had remained in Siena.

By the end of the century, Chigi involvement lessened and that of one of the Sienese academies, the 'Rozzi', increased, beginning with a revival of Scarlatti's *L'honestà negli amori* (Rome, 1680) in 1690. Then in 1695 came the noted playwright and historian Girolamo Gigli, born in Siena in 1660. As impresario, he would guide Sienese opera into the next century.[38]

Seventeenth-century Siena embraced opera, supremely conscious of how it operated within what Reardon has called the city's 'sociable' network, which would fade after Gigli's time, when opera would become a more occasional entertainment with less involvement by the Sienese populace and more reliance on travelling companies.

Naples

Opera in Spanish-ruled Naples often took place at the pleasure of the Viceroy of Naples, a Spanish representative of the King of Spain. As in Milan, also under Spanish rule, the same entertainments were frequently presented in two venues, first at the royal palace and then in the public theatre, the most prominent of them S. Bartolomeo. One important way in which opera production in Naples (and Milan) differed from that in the rest of Italy was the result of a Spanish law dating from 1583, by which a percentage of the box income went to a charitable institution: in the case of Naples, the Ospedale degli Incurabili (which had, in 1621, played a part in the building of the theatre). Moreover, no tickets could be sold to public performances without the permission of that institution.[39] In this way, Neapolitan opera could not have been more different from that of Venice.

Lorenzo Bianconi and Thomas Walker examined the early history of public opera in Naples and explored how opera flourished under the auspices of Count Oñate, who, rather than relying purely on local artists, made use of a travelling company of musicians, the Febiarmonici. A number of operas performed there came by way of Venice, including *La finta pazza*, *L'incoronazione di Poppea*, and Cavalli's *La Veremonda* (often, in the 1650s, through the direct intervention of the dancer and choreographer Balbi).[40] But viceroys came and went (eleven of them during the second half of the seventeenth century), and the fortunes of opera in Naples were in large part dependent on the interest of the viceroy. The repertory mixed the music of local talents such as Francesco Provenzale (c. 1626; d. Naples, 6 September 1704) with Venetian scores such as those by Cavalli. In the 1670s, S. Bartolomeo largely specialised in operas from Venice by Ziani, Cesti, Boretti, and Carlo Pallavicino (c. 1640–1688). This theatre enjoyed some notoriety as a result of its impresaria, the former prostitute Giulia De Caro, who had first appeared there as a singer. Here was another difference from Venice, where singers were not impresarios, nor were women.

As Louise K. Stein has shown, during the last quarter of the seventeenth century the patronage and support for opera at the palace and at S. Bartolomeo emanated in large part from the coffers of the viceroy himself, and some of the funds came from the Spanish government.[41] The financing behind Neapolitan opera, then, was inevitably a mix of private and public support, with the management of the 'public' theatre undertaken by an independent impresario.

Some viceroys arrived in Naples with little knowledge of Italian opera, and their support varied widely. However, Gaspar de Haro y Guzmán, Marquis del Carpio (1629–1687), had been an important patron of drama in Spain and had seen opera in Venice. He came to Naples from his ambassadorship in Rome, where he had come to know the music of the young Scarlatti. Carpio placed his stamp on opera in Naples, and he saw personally to many aspects of the operas mounted during his tenure; he also helped to bring Scarlatti to Naples, where his fame and importance would grow. A link between Carpio's activities as a patron in Spain and then in Naples lies in three of the operas presented there, based on the same Spanish plays by Pedro Calderón de la Barca that he had had produced in Spain and then in Rome. Nine years after Carpio's residence in Naples came Luis Francisco de la Cerda y Aragón, Duke of Medinaceli, who also had previously been the Spanish ambassador in Rome and was able to use contacts from the Holy City, Venice, and Florence in order to recruit top musicians to Naples. As in the case of Carpio, Medinaceli's patronage of Scarlatti was particularly significant for the history of opera there.[42]

A Night at the Opera

In Venice as elsewhere in Italy, months of preparation culminated in the première and subsequent performances of an opera. In the end, the audience dictated the success or failure of a production. Was the music pleasing? Did the singers live up to their reputations? Would hisses and boos force the librettist and composer back to their desks, or would the management decide, after nights of cheering audiences, to add new arias to delight the listeners? Anything was possible. In Venice there were those operas that closed after one night, and others whose success defied the odds. Some listeners would even move from theatre to theatre in one night to catch their favourite singer or aria. Indeed, the diversity of the city's offerings not only made such nocturnal wanderings possible but also added to the richness of the carnival season, to the sense of competition, and to questions of which theatre would mount the best show, whatever that might mean. The experience differed in other cities, where, generally, only one opera could be seen at any one time. Yet the spread of public opera – however that might be defined – in all its myriad manifestations meant that, all across and down the Italian peninsula, this expensive and multi-layered entertainment could be enjoyed. Listeners could experience astonishment and wonder, or they could just enjoy a night out with friends and watch the others who made up the audience. And, despite the passage of more than three hundred years, little has changed.

Notes

1 *Francesco Sansovino, Venezia città nobilissima et singolare descritta in XIIII. libri* (Venice, 1581), rev. edn. Giustiniano Martinoni (Venice: Steffano Curti, 1663), 397.

2 Cristoforo Ivanovich, *Memorie teatrali di Venezia*, ed. Norbert Dubowy (Venice: Nicola Pezzana, 1688; rpt. Lucca: LIM, 1993).

3 I-Vas, Dieci sopra le decime in Rialto, b. 218, Castello, no. 1036.

4 Giovanni Morelli and Thomas Walker, 'Tre controversie intorno al San Cassiano', in Maria Teresa Muraro (ed.), *Venezia e il melodramma nel Seicento* (Florence: Olschki, 1976), 97–120.

5 Ibid., and Beth L. Glixon, 'Behind the Scenes of Cavalli's *Giasone* of 1649', in Ellen Rosand (ed.), *Readying Cavalli's Operas for the Stage: Manuscript, Edition, Production* (Aldershot: Ashgate, 2013), 137–52.

6 For other contributing factors to Venice's success as a venue for public opera, see Edward Muir, 'Why Venice? Venetian Society and the Success of Early Opera', *Journal of Interdisciplinary History* 3/36 (2006), 331–53.

7 Ellen Rosand, *Opera in Seventeenth-Century Venice: The Creation of a Genre* (Berkeley, Los Angeles, and London: University of California Press, 1991), Lorenzo Bianconi and Thomas Walker, 'Dalla *Finta pazza* alla *Veremonda*: storie di Febiarmonici', *RIM* 10 (1975): 379–454.

8 Beth L. Glixon and Jonathan E. Glixon, 'Oil and Opera Don't Mix: The Biography of S. Aponal, a Seventeenth-Century Venetian Opera Theater', in Susan Parisi (ed.) with collaboration of Ernest Harriss II and Calvin M. Bower, *Music in the Theater, Church, and Villa: Essays in Honor of Robert Lamar Weaver and Norma Wright Weaver* (Sterling Heights: Harmonie Park Press, 2000), 131–44.

9 Rosand, *Opera in Seventeenth-Century Venice*, 67–70.

10 Beth L. Glixon and Jonathan E. Glixon, *Inventing the Business of Opera: The Impresario and His World in Seventeenth-Century Venice* (Oxford and New York: Oxford University Press, 2006), 69.

11 Ibid., 16.

12 Ibid., 11. See also Michael Talbot, 'A Venetian Operatic Contract of 1714', in *The Business of Music*, ed. Michael Talbot (Liverpool: Liverpool University Press, 2002), 10–61: 19–22.

13 Colin Timms, 'George I's Venetian Palace and Theatre Boxes in the 1720s', in Nigel Fortune (ed.), *Music and Theatre: Essays in Honour of Winton Dean* (Cambridge: Cambridge University Press, 2005), 95–130.

14 For a famous description of the box system, see Cristoforo Ivanovich in his *Memorie teatrali*, 403–4.

15 See, for example, John Rosselli, *The Opera Industry in Italy from Cimarosa to Verdi: The Role of the Impresario* (Cambridge: Cambridge University Press, 1984).

16 The newest study on Busenello is Jean-François Lattarico, *Busenello, un théâtre de la rhétorique* (Paris: Garnier, 2013).

17 Beth L. Glixon, 'Cicognini, Giacinto Andrea', in *Grove Music Online*.

18 Fausta Antonucci and Lorenzo Bianconi, 'Plotting the Myth of Giasone', in Rosand (ed.), *Cavalli's Operas on the Modern Stage*, 201–27. Sara Elisa Stangalino, 'I drammi musicali di Nicolò Minato per Francesco Cavalli' (Ph. D. dissertation: University of Bologna, 2011); Maria Grazia Profeti (ed.), *Commedia e musica tra Spagna e Italia* (Florence: Alinea, 2009).

19 Ellen Rosand, 'L'Orfeo: The Metamorphosis of a Musical Myth', *Israel Studies in Musicology* 2 (1980), 101–30.

20 Beth L. Glixon, 'Giulia Masotti, Venice, and the Rise of the Prima Donna', *JSCM* 17/1 (2011), http://sscm-jscm.org/jscm-issues/volume-17-no-1/giulia-masotti-venice-and-the-rise-of-the-prima-donna/, par. 3.10.

21 Glixon and Glixon, *Inventing the Business of Opera*, 212.

22 Ibid., 212.

23 Ibid., ch. 9.

24 Glixon, 'Giulia Masotti', par. 7.3.

25 Ibid., par. 8.1.

26 Glixon and Glixon, *Inventing the Business of Opera*, 216–20. On dance in Venetian opera, see Irene Alm, 'Winged Feet and Mute Eloquence: Dance in Seventeenth-Century Venetian Opera', ed. Wendy Heller and Rebecca Harris-Warrick, *COJ* 15/3 (2003), 216–80.

27 Glixon and Glixon, *Inventing the Business of Opera*, 280.

28 See Wendy Heller, 'Tacitus Incognito: Opera as History in *L'incoronazione di Poppea*', *JAMS* 52/1 (1999), 39–96.

29 Margaret Murata, *Operas for the Papal Court, 1631–1668* (Ann Arbor, MI: UMI Research Press, 1981).

30 The most comprehensive source for opera in Florence is Robert Lamar Weaver and Norma Wright Weaver, *A Chronology of Music in the Florentine Theater, 1590–1750: Operas, Prologues, Finales, Intermezzos and Plays with Incidental Music* (Detroit: Information Coordinators, 1978).

31 Lorenzo Bianconi, 'L'Ercole in Rialto', in Maria Teresa Muraro (ed.), *Venezia e il melodramma nel Seicento* (Florence: Olschki, 1976), 259–72.

32 See Jennifer Williams Brown, 'On the Road with the "Suitcase Aria": The Transmission of Borrowed Arias in Late Seventeenth-Century Italian Opera Revivals', in Beth L. Glixon (ed.), *Studies in Seventeenth-Century Opera* (Farnham: Ashgate, 2010), 261–81.

33 Teresa Megale, 'Altre novità su Anna Francesca Costa e sull'allestimento dell'*Ergirodo*', *Medioevo e Rinascimento* 7/n.s. 4 (1993), 137–42.

34 Colleen Reardon, *A Sociable Moment: Opera and Festive Culture in Baroque Siena* (New York: Oxford University Press, 2016), ch. 1.

35 Corrado Ricci, *I teatri di Bologna nei secoli XVII e XVIII: storia aneddotica* (Bologna: Successori Monti, 1888).

36 Reardon, *A Sociable Moment*.

37 Ibid., 78.

38 Ibid., chs. 7–9.

39 Louise Stein, 'A Viceroy behind the Scenes: Opera, Production, Politics, and Financing in 1680s Naples', in Susan McClary (ed.), *Structures of Feeling in Seventeenth-Century Cultural Expression* (Toronto: University of Toronto Press, 2013), 209–49: 221.

40 Bianconi and Walker, 'Dalla *Finta pazza* alla *Veremonda*'. Nicola Michelassi, '*La Finta pazza* a Firenze: Commedie "spagnole" e "veneziane" nel teatro di Baldracca (1641–1665)', *Studi secenteschi* 41 (2000): 313–53; Michelassi, *La doppia 'Finta pazza': Il viaggio di un dramma veneziano nell'Europa del Seicento*, 2 vols. (Florence: Olschki, forthcoming).

41 Stein, 'A Viceroy behind the Scenes', 209–49.

42 José María Domínguez Rodríguez, *Roma, Nápoles, Madrid: Mecenazgo musical del Duque de Medinaceli, 1687–1710* (Kassel: Edition Reichenberger, 2013).

6 | 'Una bella voce, un bel trillo, ed un bel passaggio'

Opera Singers in Seventeenth-Century Italy

COLLEEN REARDON

The birth of opera around 1600 is intimately tied to singers. Jacopo Peri and Giulio Caccini are known not only as composers of the first complete published operas but also as superb vocalists. In October 1600, as part of the Florentine celebrations for the wedding of Maria de' Medici to Henry IV of France, Peri starred as Orfeo in his own setting of Ottavio Rinuccini's *Euridice*.[1] On stage with him were Caccini's daughters, Francesca (1587–after 1641) and Settimia (1591–c. 1660), who, instead of performing Peri's music, sang the settings their father had insisted upon inserting. In future years, Francesca would go on to be celebrated for both her vocal prowess and her compositional acumen: she was the first woman to compose an opera, *La liberazione di Ruggiero dall'Isola di Alcina* (1625).[2] The spread of opera thus cannot be separated from the talented performers who brought the works to light on the stages of courts and public theatres over the course of the century.

That said, Sergio Durante has noted that the career of opera singer was 'a professional role that really came into being only gradually'.[3] Such a change could happen only after opera had vaulted to the public stage in Venice in the late 1630s and after cities all over Italy began to mount such works on a regular basis throughout the year (and not just in carnival season). The careers of Peri and Caccini played out before this sea change. They were both initially employed at the Medici court in Florence for their skill as singers and instrumentalists, but their duties also comprised the composition of many different kinds of works, including instrumental pieces, songs, and court entertainments. After 1600, Peri worked mostly as a composer, collaborating with Marco da Gagliano (1582–1643) on both operas and *sacre rappresentazioni*. Caccini was a sought-after voice teacher – he had a hand in training both of his daughters – and later in life he dedicated himself to gardening. Singing in opera was but one small facet of their storied careers.

It was only in the last decades of the seventeenth century that it was possible for a singer to devote a career to opera; some well-known vocal stars, however, chose not to do so. The castrato Matteo Sassani (or Sassano, c. 1667–1737), for example, began and ended his professional life singing in serenatas and religious services; he mounted the operatic stage for about ten years of his long career, more rarely than other great singers of the time.[4] Pier Francesco Tosi (1654–1732), who sang perhaps once on the operatic stage in the 1680s and who went on to write a highly regarded treatise on the voice, noted that all singers should be able to sing recitative in three styles: one for church, one for chamber, and one for opera.[5] Even in the late seventeenth century, then, singing opera was sometimes just one part of a larger professional life that arose out of a confluence of talent, training, and patronage.

Training

The institutions that offered musical instruction were already well established in Italy by the time opera rose to importance and included churches, conservatories, and seminaries (especially the national colleges in Rome).[6] Boys entered or were recruited to those organisations at very young ages and learned their foundational skills there. Pedagogical programs doubtless taught them the techniques that are the basis of any vocal training, even today: how to produce a healthy tone, how to sing in tune, how to develop vocal flexibility, how to enunciate clearly, and how to avoid grimacing. Since the ability to decorate a vocal line was so important in the seventeenth century, students needed to practice how to apply and sing various ornaments, such as trills.[7] Boys also received instruction on the keyboard and learned basic theory and counterpoint as well.

The need for male sopranos in church choirs was so great that the administrators at some cathedrals began to recommend talented young boys with beautiful voices as candidates for castration and either to pay directly for the procedure or to reimburse parents who had already had it done. The attraction of the operatic stage was so powerful that churches issued contracts specifying a standard length of service before the boy could leave the choir and seek his fortune as an opera singer. In Siena, for example, boys had to serve the cathedral choir for six years before they could leave the employ of the institution; otherwise, they had to repay half of the cost of the operation and half of the salary they had earned.[8] As long as the boys remained on the payroll most of the year, however, the administrators at Siena Cathedral did allow them to take short leaves of absence to sing on the stage; in this, they were much less severe than their peers at San Francesco in Assisi, whose rules forbade castrati to perform in opera until the tenth year of their service.[9]

Talented girls in Italy could not avail themselves of this kind of comprehensive, institutional education unless they were placed in convents with active and lively traditions for musical performance. Nuns were some of the most highly regarded singers on the Italian peninsula during the seventeenth century, and some sang theatrical works in the convent.[10] In 1670, for example, the Grand Duchess of Florence consigned to a Sienese nunnery a young girl 'highly predisposed' to music, perhaps in the hope that she would blossom into an excellent performer.[11] The Duke of Savoy adopted a similar strategy in 1688 when he sent the singer Diana Aureli (fl. 1691–1696) to a Milanese convent to perfect her vocal technique.[12] Since the majority of convents in Italian urban centres during this period were, however, intended for 'surplus' women of aristocratic birth whose status would not permit them to sing on stage, not many professional opera singers came out of this environment.

Most girls had to receive their training privately, and, in this, some were more fortunate than others. The Caccini sisters, for example, were raised in a musical household (both Giulio and his wife Lucia di Filippo Gagnolanti were singers) and probably began their musical apprenticeship at a very young age. Other parents made different decisions. Silvia Galiarti (c. 1629–c. 1677), whose mother was a talented opera singer unattached to a court, entrusted her daughter's musical education to a private tutor, whose seduction of the young woman sparked a legal case.[13] The gifted Caterina Martinelli (1589 or 1590–1608), on the other hand, found a good home away from home. She came to Mantua from Rome as a thirteen-year-old and boarded with Claudio Monteverdi (1567–1643), who took on the responsibility of teaching her and subsequently wrote the title role in *Arianna* for her.[14] Her unfortunate death from smallpox at the age of eighteen forced the composer to look elsewhere, and he turned to a woman best described as an actress with an excellent voice, Virginia Ramponi Andreini (1583–1629 or 1630). The trend of using actress-singers in opera did not, however, persist into the mid- to late-seventeenth century, as the musical skills required became more specialised.

The case of Lucrezia d'Andrè (fl. 1694–1704) is illustrative in this regard. In 1694, the Roman noblewoman Lucrezia Colonna Conti wrote to Cardinal Francesco Maria de' Medici in Florence, seeking to induce him to hire d'Andrè for an opera. Her letter briefly describes the background and character of the young woman (she was the daughter of one of Colonna Conti's servants and was modest and hard working) but is most effusive as to her musical training. The young woman had learned her vocal technique from Giuseppe Fede (1639 or 1640–1700), an accomplished castrato singer in the papal choir, a veteran of operatic performances, and an admired teacher. She had studied harpsichord with Bernardo Pasquini (1637–1710), a keyboard virtuoso and a renowned composer of oratorio and opera. Colonna Conti also notes that another famous opera composer, Giovanni Bononcini (1670–1747), and a singer under the protection of the Medici, Giuseppe Canavese (fl. 1684–1707), had heard her perform, undoubtedly at the Colonna household. By the late seventeenth century, it appears that (with some exceptions) a high level of musical training, as well as a good stage presence, was necessary to be able to sustain a career on the operatic stage.[15]

Beyond her training, a woman who wanted to perform in opera could unleash another weapon in her arsenal, if she possessed it: the 'lovely letter of recommendation' in her face.[16] John Rosselli quotes a 1663 document concerning the requirements for female singers at the Venetian theatre of SS. Giovanni e Paolo: 'beauty' and 'rich clothes' were the first items on the list and only then was 'attractive singing' mentioned.[17] In her plea to Francesco Maria, Colonna Conti made sure that the cardinal knew of d'Andrè's physical charms in addition to her good character and first-rate musical education. When the Bolognese singer Angela Cocchi ('la Linarola', d. 1703) arrived in Parma in late 1697 to perform a role in *L'Atalanta*, the castrato Giovanni Battista Tamburini (1669–after 1719) observed that if her voice were equal to her beauty, she would be marvellous.[18] That said, beauty went only so far. A Sienese correspondent once described Vincenza Giulia Masotti (c. 1651–1701) as an extremely ugly woman ('una gran brutta figliola'), but audiences went into raptures during her performances, and she was one of the most highly regarded singers of her time.[19]

Many singers made their débuts on the operatic stage at a relatively young age: Masotti first appeared in Venice when she was probably eleven or twelve years old, and Vittoria Tarquini ('la Bombace', 1670–1746) made her première at age fourteen.[20] The alto castrato Francesco Bernardi (1686–1758), the singer for whom Handel would write some of his most celebrated works, was thirteen when he first mounted the stage in his native Siena. Girolamo Gigli, the impresario for the production, was probably responsible for adding the part tailored just for him in the libretto, and the local chapel master, Giuseppe Fabbrini, doubtless set those new additions with music suited to his young voice. Bernardi then continued his instruction at Siena Cathedral under Fabbrini for another eight years before going off to seek his fame and fortune.[21] Anna Renzi

(c. 1620–after 1661), on the other hand, was probably near twenty when she first sang in opera; nonetheless, her voice teacher, Filiberto Laurenzi, accompanied her to Venice for her début.[22] Voice lessons thus could continue after singers were launched in opera, especially if they were young; at times, however, such training could extend into adulthood.

Tamburini provides an interesting example of a singer whose schooling we can follow for many years. He was one of the numerous boys for whom the religious authorities at Siena Cathedral paid the expenses of castration and provided a foundational education in music. His tenure at the institution lasted from 1683 to 1695, that is, from the age of fourteen to the age of twenty-six. He came under Cardinal Francesco Maria de' Medici's protection sometime in his early twenties and mounted the stage in minor roles for productions in Florence and Siena from 1690 to 1695. Then the cardinal packed him off, first to Rome and then to Parma, to study under the composer Bernardo Sabadini (d. 1718). Tamburini sang in several operas during this further period of study. When Sabadini left for Madrid in 1700, Francesco Maria sent his protégé to the composer Carlo Antonio Benati in Bologna, despite the fact that Tamburini was nearly thirty-one years old and had already performed in sixteen operas. It is true that the lessons in Parma probably consisted primarily of Sabadini coaching the singer on the music he had written especially for him and perhaps also refining his acting skills. Tamburini did, however, tell his patron that 'sometimes my teacher will have me sing scales to make sure my technique is secure'. Although we have some insight into singers' basic training during the seventeenth century, we still know little about how they continued to perfect their craft once they were established on the operatic circuit.[23]

One additional category of singer deserves mention here: the talented dilettante. In small cities with strong academic traditions, noblemen sometimes took the stage for local performances. In Siena, for instance, we know of at least two productions featuring a mix of professional and amateur performers: *L'Adalinda* (Apolloni, Agostini, 1677) and *L'innocenza riconosciuta* (1698). In the latter opera, three members of the Sienese patrician class mounted the stage alongside Pietro Mozzi (fl. 1686–1729) and his son, the young castrato Giuseppe Mozzi. One of them, Tolomei, perhaps less skilled than the others, lost his voice during the last act of the second performance and accused the elder Mozzi of instructing the instrumentalists to play so loudly as to drown him out.[24] Such were the perils of the lack of professional training.

Patronage

Opera singers depended on powerful patrons for protection. Italian rulers in numerous urban centres hired and maintained salaried singers to use in operas performed under their aegis. The ecclesiastical courts in Rome also patronised singers. But if Peri's *Euridice* was mounted in Florence using singers on the Medici payroll, the performance of Monteverdi's *Orfeo* only seven years later depended on the talents of at least one performer who was not part of the musical establishment at Mantua. The Florentine court loaned one of Caccini's pupils, the castrato Giovanni Gualberto Magli (d. 1625), to the Mantuan court for the opera; he sang at least two and probably three roles in *Orfeo*.[25] When public operas began to be staged in Venice starting in the late 1630s, it was paramount that singers be able to move from one city to another to take advantage of the opportunities to sing. This was especially true for female singers in Rome, who were forbidden from taking the stage in that city.

Several solutions to the problem presented themselves. In the first half of the seventeenth century, self-financing touring companies, sometimes called Febiarmonici, travelled from city to city to put on operatic performances. Ellen Rosand has noted that such troupes (often with Roman singers) were responsible for the first operatic performances in Venice; after carnival season, they then took their shows on the road.[26] By the 1680s or so, when opera was well established as a feature of cultural life all over the Italian peninsula, performers were the star attractions. Impresarios wanted to hire the best, and a number of rulers with singers under their protection often responded to requests to send them to perform elsewhere. Thus was the ducal or gentlemen's circuit born – with the enthusiastic participation of courts in Florence, Mantua, Ferrara, Parma, and Rome (to name but a few), whose rulers loaned out musicians to one another as well as to impresarios in the public theatres of Venice. The system benefitted everyone. Rulers who loaned out one of 'their' coveted singers symbolised their social rank through a display of 'good taste and knowledge', thus earning honour for themselves as well as the more prosaic right to borrow a singer from another member on the circuit for their own productions. The singer had the protection of the ruler as a guarantee against ill treatment, an opportunity to perform in a new setting with new colleagues, and the chance to earn more than he or she ever could as a court employee.[27]

Some patrons kept a tight rein on their protégés. Rosand describes how Pietro Dolfin, a librettist and composer in Venice, exercised his power over the singer Lucretia, a young woman who came to live in his house in the late 1660s. Dolfin controlled all the young woman's contracts, refusing to allow her to sing when he thought the part too small or the cast mediocre.[28] Francesco Maria de' Medici did the same with Tamburini, arranging for his début in Florence in 1690, informing him (through a proxy) that he was to turn down a role in a 'dreadful, feeble work' in Rome in 1697, and instructing Sabadini on the operatic environment in which his protégé was likely to shine: as the singer of a secondary role (*parte di mezzo*) in an opera with a cast of excellent singers.[29]

Tamburini's situation was not unlike that of many singers in the later seventeenth century. Francesco Maria paid Sabadini for his role as Tamburini's teacher and for the expenses of housing and feeding the singer in Parma; he also gave his protégé a modest yearly annuity until about 1705. Tamburini was, however, never resident in Florence as a court employee; instead, he spent his life on the road.[30] The same was true for other singers of the time, such as the contralto Francesca Vanini (or Venini; d. 1744), Maria Maddalena Musi ('la Mignatta', 1669–1751), and Barbara Riccioni (fl. 1684–1707), who received small stipends as court musicians in Mantua but spent most of their time travelling the Italian peninsula to perform in opera.[31] Although some dukes and princes served as agents, many functioned simply as clearinghouses for their singers. It is thus ironic that during the last years of the century, libretti start to emblazon the names of not only the singers in operatic productions but also those of their patrons: 'Elena Garofalini, Bolognese, *virtuosa* of the Most Serene Duke of Mantua', 'Diana Caterina Luppi of Ferrara, *virtuosa* of Count Ercole Estense Mosti', and 'Signora Diamante Scarabelli, *virtuosa* del Sereniss. Di Mantova' (see Figure 6.1), and so on.

The Rise of the Prima Donna

At opera's birth, Rosand notes, singers were 'merely the mouthpiece[s] of the librettist and composer'.[32] That began to change by mid-century, with the woman who has been called the first prima donna of opera, Anna Renzi. Renzi came from Rome to Venice to create the role of Deidamia in the Giulio Strozzi/Francesco Sacrati opera *La finta pazza* (1641). Later, she would première the role of Ottavia in Monteverdi's *L'incoronazione di Poppea* (1643). A book was issued in her honour in 1644, praising her voice, her acting, and her ability to embody a character through gesture and spontaneity of expression. Her fame and popularity meant that during the

Figure 6.1 *Giuditta di Baviera* (Siena, Stamperia del Publico, 1702). The dedication of the libretto (librettist and composer unknown), to Count Francesco Sansebastiani, is dated 3 July 1702.
Detail of the cast and beginning of the libretto, 8–9. Image from Biblioteca Comunale degli Intronati, Siena

1643–1644 season, she was able to command a far higher salary than any other woman who had sung on the Venetian stage up until that point.[33]

The control singers had over the very fabric of opera began to be audible by the 1660s and into the following decades with the proliferation of arias.[34] By this time, singers could request that the composer make changes and additions to their parts, and were able to reject arias they did not like and substitute them with works of their choosing – even if not by the composer of the opera – that they felt showed off their voices to greater advantage. The practice of performers repeating arias on stage when an enthusiastic audience demanded it also became a commonplace.

As singers' fame and influence grew, so did their power to negotiate all manner of things relating to the production. Masotti offers a good case study of a singer who knew her worth and knew how to work the patronage system to her best advantage.[35] She was obviously a talented young woman; in Rome, Margherita Branciforte, Princess of Butera, had taken her under her wing and Masotti had received her musical training in the princess's home from Giacomo Carissimi (1605–1674), one of Rome's most celebrated composers and *maestro di cappella* at S. Apollinare. A Tuscan resident in Rome, Torquato Montauto, became her protector and probably helped arrange her début in Venice at the Teatro San Luca for the 1662–1663 season. Despite the fact that Giulia was no older than twelve, she made a huge splash in the title role of *La Dori*, an opera with a libretto by Giovanni Filippo Apolloni (c. 1635–1688) and music by Antonio Cesti (1623–1669). She reluctantly returned in 1663–1664 to perform in two operas, one of them Francesco Cavalli's *Scipione affricano*. Around this time, she gained new patrons: the Contestabile Lorenzo Onofrio Colonna and his wife, Maria Mancini.

Masotti refused to go back to Venice in the 1664–1665 and 1665–1666 seasons, but the impresario Marco Faustini (1606–1676) insistently requested her presence for 1666–1667. Using the Contestabile Colonna and the Venetian nobleman Girolamo Loredan as intermediaries, Masotti dug in her heels and once again refused to go until promised a salary that was twice as much as she had been offered (and had turned down) in 1665. She also received travelling expenses and was given lodging with the Grimani family. She was similarly shrewd in her negotiations for the 1668–1669 opera season in Venice, using both the Colonna and her new patrons, members of the Chigi family, to guarantee herself a large salary and other concessions. She must have been gratified that the opera chosen that season was a revival of *L'Argia*, a work by her preferred librettist, Apolloni, with music by her favourite composer, Cesti. In 1671, in fact, she tried to persuade Cardinal Sigismondo Chigi to ask Apolloni for a new libretto with a 'part that does me honor above everyone else'. This was one of her few requests that came to nothing. Throughout her career, she managed to convince impresarios to mount operas that she liked and to cast her in the roles she wanted to sing. In other words, although she depended upon patrons to protect and help her, she was in charge of her own professional life.

Other singers sometimes took hold of the reins in an even more authoritative manner. Elena Passarelli ('la Tiepola', fl. 1658–1673) was not only a well-respected singer, but also cast herself at least once in the role of impresario, perhaps in tandem with her husband, Galeazzo. In 1670, she signed the libretto issued for a Florentine revival of Cesti's *La Dori*, dedicating the work to Margherita Luisa d'Orléans, the Grand Princess of

Tuscany, whose marriage to Cosimo III was then in a final period of reconciliation. Passarelli and her company mounted the opera in Florence and then were scheduled to go on to Siena, where the singer had performed the previous year in a revival of *L'Argia*. She astutely supposed that an opera by the same librettist–composer team that had triumphed in Siena a year previously with her in the lead role would be sure to please the Sienese, who were indeed waiting with impatience for the performances. Unfortunately, the show was cancelled due to the death of Grand Duke Ferdinando II in 1670. A correspondent in Siena observed that Passarelli was responsible for the company and since the show could not be staged there, she would pay the salaries and take the cast on to the next performance.[36] In 1704, in Siena, the singers Maria Anna Garberini Benti ('la Romanina', c. 1684–1734) and Vittoria Costa (fl. 1701–1719), aided by the Florentine chapel master Giuseppe Maria Orlandini (1676–1760), decided to serve as impresarios for a little pastoral opera, taking the lead roles, establishing the ticket prices, and hoping to make a profit from the enterprise.[37] Their plans may not have come to fruition, but they show that more than one female singer was unafraid to venture into new realms to direct her own career.[38]

Payment and the Gift Culture

The first singers of opera performed those works as part of their normal court duties. That changed once an operatic circuit was established and it was necessary for singers (or their agents) to negotiate salaries. As is clear from the discussion of Masotti above, singers who had to journey to foreign cities also often asked for travelling expenses and requested free lodging with the impresario or with a nobleman; otherwise, they might not have taken much money home after a long season. No one formula determined how much a singer could make, and salaries varied according to the locale and the size or importance of the role, as well as the reputation of the singer. Women were the most coveted performers during this period and generally earned higher salaries than men, an imbalance that would change in the eighteenth century when the castrato rose to great prominence. One thing appears to be true for opera productions throughout the Italian peninsula in the late seventeenth century: the costliest items on the budget were the salaries paid to the singers.[39]

Although private agreements between an impresario and a singer were by far the most common throughout Italy, a few publicly registered contracts for singers in Venice survive and help clarify some of the details of payment and the expectations placed on singers and impresarios. A contract for Renzi from the 1643–1644 season, for example, establishes a payment schedule, which seems to have been the normal one for that city: the singer was to receive the honorarium divided into three portions and distributed at the beginning, middle, and end of the opera's run. If she were to fall ill, she would collect only a portion of her salary. She also received the use of a box in the theatre at the expense of the impresario and all the costumes she would need (although these remained with the impresario at the end of the run). In return, she agreed to attend all rehearsals and performances.[40] What may be the first printed contract for singers, issued in Siena in 1703, lays out basically the same expectations, although it specifically excludes payments for travel and food.[41] Even with a contract in place, if a show did not succeed as planned, singers might receive only a portion of the contracted fee and have to lodge complaints or initiate legal cases to collect what was owed them.[42]

Payment in cash was, however, only one form of remuneration that performers acquired during the run of an opera. Both men and women (but especially women) expected to receive gifts, including rings; bracelets; necklaces; watches; earrings made of gold and silver and often encrusted with precious jewels; and items of clothing comprising hats, gloves, ribbons, and stockings. The cash portion of the payment to a singer, especially a beautiful female singer, sometimes paled in comparison to the presents she received from admirers. When Passarelli performed the title role in the Sienese revival of *L'Argia* (1669), the women of the town ordered culinary delicacies from Florence for her on a continual basis, and over thirty gentlemen contributed money to buy her a gift worth 700 *lire*. She left town at the end of the opera's run with 2,800 *lire* in cash and gifts, probably more than she had earned in Venice in the early 1660s. From accounts of the revival of Bononcini's setting of Silvio Stampiglia's *Camilla, regina de' Volsci* in Siena in 1700, we know that the star performer, Maria Domenica Pini ('la Tilla', 1670 or 1671–1746), carried away about 1,400 *lire* in cash and almost 600 *lire* in gifts. Her colleague, Maria Maddalena Vittori ('la Marsoppina', fl. 1699–1704), went home with about 400 *lire* in cash and perhaps as much as 600 *lire* in gifts.[43]

Critical Assessment

It is difficult to find true critical assessments of an opera singer's voice in the seventeenth century; most comments tend to the generic, comparing singers to swans or sirens, or waxing lyrical about how divinely or magnificently or wonderfully they perform.[44] The quotation given in the title of this essay – 'una bella voce, un bel trillo, ed un bel passaggio' – comes from a letter penned by Leonardo Marsili about the singer 'Aloisia', and it begins in typical fashion: she had a 'beautiful voice, a beautiful trill, and beautiful ornamentation'. He does go on to note that the singer was able to modulate her voice depending on the size of the room; that is, she knew to sing more softly in a chamber setting than on the operatic stage. Sometimes observers commented on the strength of the voice; Caterina Galerati (fl. 1701–1721), for instance, apparently had a small instrument but compensated for its size through the use of trills and other musical ornaments.[45]

Stage deportment and acting skills were also addressed and evaluated, as in a commentary from a performance of *Pirro e Demetrio* (Adriano Morselli; Alessandro Scarlatti) in Siena in 1695: Maria Rosa Bracci ('l'Acciaiola', fl. 1695–1726) was the technically superior singer, but Maria Domenica Marini ('la Cappona', fl. 1695–1702) made the best impression because she moved naturally and nobly. In the same cast, a tenor from Pistoia was judged to be a good actor with a terrible voice.[46] It is clear, however, that assessments of a singer's acting skills were situational. The Siena 1704 carnival season featured two works with the same cast of singers: revivals of Scarlatti's *La caduta dei decemviri* and of Tomaso Albinoni's *La Griselda*. In the Scarlatti opera, Anna Maria Coltellini ('la Serafina', fl. 1691–1704) was praised as the singer who held the show together and was superior to all, but Maria Maddalena Fratini (fl. 1690–1705) was disparaged for poor acting skills, despite a pleasant voice. In the Albinoni opera, however, Coltellini cut a poor figure because she did not know how to act her part, whereas Fratini was lauded for her acting skill; the commentator asserted that no one would recognise her as a woman when she was onstage in a pants role.[47]

Public Images

In the culture of Renaissance and Baroque Italy, silence was understood as a sign of a woman's chastity. The eloquent woman was in danger of being considered unchaste; indeed, the famous courtesans of the period were renowned for their skills in both rhetoric and music. Female singers on the operatic stage thus faced a dilemma; they had to be eloquent to be successful in their careers, but their very powers of musical persuasion marked their virtue as suspect. A female singer thus was in jeopardy of being considered little better than a prostitute – her profession required her to 'speak' in song and to do so in front of a paying public.[48] To be sure, some were courtesans, although, for the most part, their careers seem not to have lasted long.[49] Female singers thus had to be vigilant about their image. They often travelled with family members (mothers, husbands, and brothers) as protection and took care to manage their offstage behaviour in a way that was above reproach.

Notwithstanding their precautions offstage, female opera singers on stage often aroused sexual desire, a desire that could be intensified by the adoption of pants roles, in which women cross-dressed as young men. Wendy Heller has illuminated the ways in which operatic heroines embodied seventeenth-century ideas about female sexuality and anxieties about the fluid gender boundaries between men and women. Heroines on the Venetian stage ran the gamut from the chaste but undesirable Ottavia; to the nymph Calisto rejoicing in her amorous same-sex encounter; to the virile, cross-dressing warrior queen Semiramide; to the sexually rapacious Messalina. Singers who brought these heroines to life were both 'desired and condemned' for their erotic power and control, and they often risked creating a public image that might have greatly diverged from their private identity.[50] Renzi's portrayal of the scheming and vengeful Ottavia in Monteverdi's *L'incoronazione di Poppea*, for instance, was so incongruous with her own character that several critics provided interpretations of the role that 'transcend[ed] the virtues and vices of her own musico-dramatic representation'.[51]

Castrati also had to deal with a public image that might have been at odds with their own private personae. In their glorious artificiality, castrati were understood as 'purely sensual' creatures 'frozen' in the state of everlasting boyhood. In the one-sex system of the day, that meant that they stood somewhere between a submissive woman and an adult man who had gone through puberty; their eternally soft, attractive features rendered them the objects of desire for both men and women.[52] Their status was often reflected in the affectionate and slightly condescending use of diminutives for their stage names: Luigi Albarelli (fl. 1692–1707) was 'il Luigino', Francesco Bernardi was 'il Senesino', and Matteo Sassani was 'Matteuccio'.

The cult of the castrato took hold in the last half of the seventeenth century, just as the penchant for lyrical display in aria accelerated in operatic scores. Castrati were cast as 'effeminate' men; that is, as men too much preoccupied with loving women and with erotic adventures rather than with proper masculine activities such as war. The 'lush vocalism' inherent in aria style rather than the 'lyric restraint' characteristic of recitative, helped make the voice type the pre-eminent choice for operatic heroes at the end of the seventeenth century and into the following century as well.[53]

Private Lives

The life of an opera singer was not an easy one, despite the fame and adulation that could come with it. It often involved tiring travel, protracted and vexing negotiations with impresarios, quarrels with composers and librettists, and the possibility of not receiving promised payments. All who chose the profession faced these frustrations, but women were in a much more precarious position at a time when, as John Rosselli so succinctly puts it, most men operated under the assumption 'that almost any woman was available for fumbling at the first opportunity'.[54] Beth L. Glixon has documented the dangers that lay in wait for young women at the earliest stages of their careers. Giovanni Carlo del Cavalieri not only seduced his thirteen-year-old pupil, Galiarti, but also hoped to kidnap the girl and poison her mother. In 1685, the father of the then fourteen-year-old Tarquini complained to the Council of Ten in Venice that she had been raped.[55]

Now, it is true that some singers were in thrall to powerful men, often their patrons. Ferdinando de' Medici seems to have carried on sexual relationships with both the castrato Francesco De Castris (c. 1650–1724) and with Tarquini.[56] Most female singers, however, chose to marry at some point in their careers, although their reasons varied. Some wed while still professionally active and chose husbands in their field. Elena Lorenzoni married Galeazzo Passarelli, who served as impresario for productions featuring his wife and who seems to have toured with her when she was performing outside Venice. Some took husbands out of convention and lived apart from them; Dionora Luppi (also known as Leonida Presciani) is a case in point, as is Tarquini. Galiarti married Pietro Manni at age sixteen when her mother's death left her alone and unprotected in Venice; her husband might have been an impresario or possibly a singer.[57] Some women waited to marry until they decided to leave the Italian circuit. Masotti retired from the Venetian stage in 1673 at the young age of twenty-two or twenty-three and took up a court position in Vienna. Two years after her arrival, she met and married her younger husband, the violinist Ignaz Leopold Kugler. Their union produced four children, including a daughter whom Masotti trained as a singer.[58]

Castrato singers were in an especially circumscribed position, especially if they wanted to form a family, because the Catholic Church denied them the sacrament of marriage. One castrato who managed to wed did so outside the Italian realm. Bartolomeo Sorlisi (1631 or 1632–1672) spent his adult career in Munich and Dresden and was so well regarded at court that Elector Johann Georg II suggested he retire in Saxony. While looking for appropriate property to buy in the early 1660s, he fell in love with Dorothea Lichtwer, and she with him. After a long battle with Lutheran ecclesiastical authorities, the two wed in 1667.[59] The same option was not open to castrati working in Italy. At the age of thirty, for example, Tamburini fell in love with Vanini, who apparently had returned his affection at some point. It is possible that the patrons of both singers did their best to quash the blossoming love affair; a description of Tamburini's fruitless attempts to meet and speak with Vanini after an operatic performance in autumn of 1699 is heartbreaking.[60] Castrati were created to be singers; once their operatic careers were over, some returned to live near extended family, some sought out adoptive sons, and some created an extended network of close relationships through teaching. As Rosselli has eloquently noted, 'the chief hazard' for a castrato singer after retirement 'was probably loneliness'.[61]

Epilogue

It remains to remind the reader that seventeenth-century composers did indeed cast roles for natural male voices. The tenor Peri created the role of Orfeo in his own setting of *Euridice*; Gagliano praised the manner in which he could make his listeners 'weep or rejoice' through the grace and style of his singing and his interpretation of the emotions latent in the text.[62] Monteverdi likewise cast the role of Orfeo in his eponymous opera for a tenor, Francesco Rasi (1574–1621). By the end of the century, however, casting tenors in primary roles happened more rarely. It is notable, however, that among the many women and castrati Tosi cites in chapter seven of his treatise on the voice, he names only one man with a natural voice, the tenor Giovanni Buzzoleni (fl. 1682–1722), whom he praises for his ability to ornament while keeping a steady tempo.[63] Buzzoleni was in the service of the Mantuan court and sang in opera during the last two decades of the seventeenth century, often in main roles.[64]

Basses generally played older men in important positions, such as generals and counsellors.[65] Sometimes these were title roles (even if they were not the largest in the opera). The talented and irascible bass Pietro Mozzi, for example, took on the part of the Roman king Tullo Ostilio in *Alba soggiogata da' Romani* (music by Ziani; Pisa, 1701), but could more often be found in secondary roles. Mozzi had a remarkably long career, first mounting the stage in the mid-1680s. Later in life he transitioned to playing comic characters, and his last known appearances in opera took place in 1729.[66]

Natural male voices would come into their own during the eighteenth century, but during the seventeenth century, high voices – both male and female – ruled the stage.

Notes

1 Tim Carter has shown that Peri's *Euridice* actually saw its first performance in May 1600 in a room in the Pitti Palace; see 'The Staging of Peri's *Euridice* (1600)', a paper presented at the Annual Meeting of the American Musicological Society, Louisville, Kentucky, 14 November 2015.

2 Articles on Peri and members of the Caccini family, as well as many of the singers mentioned in this essay, are available at *Grove Music Online* and *Oxford Music Online*.

3 Sergio Durante, 'The Opera Singer', in Lorenzo Bianconi and Giorgio Pestelli (eds.), *Opera Production and Its Resources*, trans. Lydia G. Cochrane, *The History of Italian Opera*, vol. 4 (Chicago and London: The University of Chicago Press, 1998), 345–417: 346.

4 John Rosselli, *Singers of Italian Opera: The History of a Profession* (Cambridge: Cambridge University Press, 1992), 43.

5 *Opinioni de' cantori antichi e moderni* (Bologna: Lelio dalla Volpe, 1723; rpt. New York: Broude Brothers, 1968), 41–2. See also the English translation of Tosi's treatise by J. E. Galliard, *Observations on the Florid Song: Or Sentiments on the Ancient and Modern Singers*, 2nd edn. (London: J. Wilcox, 1743), 66–7.

6 Rosselli, *Singers of Italian Opera*, 41–3; 97.

7 Rosselli summarises Tosi's recommendations in ibid., 104–5.

8 Colleen Reardon, 'Siena Cathedral and its Castrati', in Kristine K. Forney and Jeremy L. Smith (eds.), *Sleuthing the Muse: Essays in Honor of William F. Prizer* (Hillsdale: Pendragon, 2012), 201–7: 202–3.

9 Cristina Pampaloni, 'Giovanni castrati nell'Assisi del Settecento', *Musica/ Realtà* 8 (1987), 133–54: 138. Pampaloni's documents come from the first half of the eighteenth century, when the cult of the castrato was at its height.

10 On this topic, see Reardon, *Holy Concord within Sacred Walls: Nuns and Music in Siena, 1575–1700* (Oxford and New York: Oxford University Press, 2002), 131–53; Reardon, *A Sociable Moment: Opera and Festive Culture in Baroque Siena* (New York: Oxford University Press, 2016), 149; and Jonathan Glixon,

Mirrors of Heaven or Worldly Theaters? Venetian Nunneries and Their Music (Oxford and New York: Oxford University Press, 2017), 250–61.

11 Reardon, 'Getting Past No or Getting to Yes: Nuns, Divas, and Negotiation Tactics in Early Modern Italy', in Karen Nelson (ed.), *Attending to Early Modern Women: Conflict and Concord* (Newark: University of Delaware Press, 2013), 23–43: 26.

12 Rosselli, *Singers of Italian Opera*, 97–8.

13 Beth L. Glixon, 'Scenes from the Life of Silvia Galiarti Manni, a Seventeenth-Century *virtuosa*', *EMH* 15 (1996), 97–146: 101–11.

14 Edmond Strainchamps, 'The Life and Death of Caterina Martinelli: New Light on Monteverdi's "Arianna,"' *EMH* 5 (1985): 155–86.

15 Reardon, 'Getting Past No or Getting to Yes', 33–8. Rosselli, *Singers of Italian Opera*, 93, cites the case of one seventeenth-century bass with a fine voice who was musically illiterate.

16 See Reardon, *A Sociable Moment*, 240.

17 Rosselli, *Singers of Italian Opera*, 58.

18 Reardon, 'Launching the Career of a *secondo uomo* in Late Seventeenth-Century Italy', *JSCM* 16/1 (2010), www.sscm-jscm.org/v16/no1/reardon.html, par. 5.5.

19 Reardon, *Holy Concord*, 126.

20 Beth L. Glixon, 'Giulia Masotti, Venice, and the Rise of the Prima Donna', *JSCM* 17, no. 1 (2011), pars. 3.1–3.11, http://sscm-jscm.org/jscm-issues/volume-17-no-1/giulia-masotti-venice-and-the-rise-of-the-prima-donna/; Glixon, '*Supereminet omnes*: New Light on the Life and Career of Vittoria Tarquini', *Händel-Jahrbuch* 62 (2016), 385–98: 403.

21 Reardon, '*Camilla* in Siena and Senesino's Début', *SM* n.s. 2/2 (2011), 281–325: 305–6, 311–18.

22 Claudio Sartori, 'La prima diva della lirica italiana: Anna Renzi', *Rivista musicale italiana* 2/3 (1968), 430–52: 435–8.

23 Reardon, 'Launching the Career of a *secondo uomo*', pars. 3.1–3.7.

24 Reardon, *A Sociable Moment*, 205.

25 Joachim Steinheuer, '*Orfeo* (1607)', in John Whenham and Richard Wistreich (eds.), *The Cambridge Companion to Monteverdi* (Cambridge: Cambridge University Press, 2007), 119–40: 122.

26 Ellen Rosand, *Opera in Seventeenth-Century Venice: The Creation of a Genre* (Berkeley, Los Angeles, and London: University of California Press, 1991), 2–3; Lorenzo Bianconi and Thomas Walker, 'Dalla *Finta pazza* alla *Veremonda*: Storie di Febiarmonici', *RIM* 10 (1975), 379–454.

27 For the ducal or gentlemen's circuit, see Robert Lamar Weaver and Norma Wright Weaver, *A Chronology of Music in the Florentine Theater, 1590–1750: Operas, Prologues, Finales, Intermezzos, and Plays with Incidental Music* (Detroit: Information Coordinators, 1978), 65–71, and Beth L. Glixon and Jonathan E. Glixon, *Inventing the Business of Opera: The Impresario and His*

World in Seventeenth-Century Venice (Oxford and New York: Oxford University Press, 2006), 180–9. The observation on patronage is taken from Claudio Annibaldi, 'Towards a Theory of Musical Patronage in the Renaissance and Baroque: The Perspective from Anthropology and Semiotics', *Recercare* 10 (1998), 173–82: 174.

28 Rosand, *Opera in Seventeenth-Century Venice*, 236.

29 Reardon, 'Launching the Career of a *secondo uomo*', pars. 8.2–8.6.

30 See the Tamburini Career Chronology published as an appendix to ibid.

31 Paola Besutti, *La corte musicale di Ferdinando Carlo Gonzaga, ultimo Duca di Mantova: Musici, cantanti e teatro d'opera tra il 1665 e il 1707* (Mantua: Gianluigi Arcari Editore, 1989), 12–18.

32 Rosand, *Opera in Seventeenth-Century Venice*, 244.

33 Ibid., 227–37; and Glixon and Glixon, *Inventing the Business of Opera*, 202.

34 Rosand, *Opera in Seventeenth-Century Venice*, 243–4.

35 The discussion here is based on a series of articles in the *JSCM* 17/1 (2011) that exhaustively examined Masotti, her life, and her career: see Reardon, 'Letters from the Road: Giulia Masotti and Cardinal Sigismondo Chigi', http://sscm-jscm.org/jscm-issues/volume-17-no-1/letters-from-the-road-giulia-masotti-and-cardinal-sigismondo-chigi/; Beth L. Glixon, 'Giulia Masotti, Venice'; Valeria De Lucca, 'The Power of the Prima Donna: Giulia Masotti's Repertory of Choice', http://sscm-jscm.org/jscm-issues/volume-17-no-1/the-power-of-the-prima-donna-giulia-masottis-repertory-of-choice/; Janet Page, 'Sirens on the Danube: Giulia Masotti and Women Singers at the Imperial Court', http://sscm-jscm.org/jscm-issues/volume-17-no-1/sirens-on-the-danube-giulia-masotti-and-women-singers-at-the-imperial-court/.

36 Reardon, *A Sociable Moment*, 82–3.

37 Ibid., 250–4.

38 See Glixon and Glixon, *Inventing the Business of Opera*, 7, for the names of other female impresarios.

39 Rosand, *Opera in Seventeenth-Century Venice*, 223, notes that singers were generally paid more than composers. See also Lorenzo Bianconi and Thomas Walker, 'Production, Consumption, and Political Function of Seventeenth-Century Opera', *EMH* 4 (1984), 209–96: 224, 230–1, 284–5.

40 Glixon and Glixon, *Inventing the Business of Opera*, 199–200.

41 Reardon, *A Sociable Moment*, 244–6.

42 Beth L. Glixon, 'Private Lives of Public Women: Prima Donnas in Mid-Seventeenth-Century Venice', *ML* 76/4 (1995), 509–31: 522, and 'Scenes from the Life of Silvia Galiarti Manni', 113–15, 131, 133.

43 Reardon, *A Sociable Moment*, 78, 216. For more on singers and gifts, see Rosselli, *Singers of Italian Opera*, 81–2.

44 Rosand, *Opera in Seventeenth-Century Venice*, 228, 230; Durante, 'The Opera Singer', 357–8.

45 Reardon, *A Sociable Moment*, 37, 240.

46 Ibid., 173.

47 Ibid., 249.
48 For an introduction to the subject, see Wendy Heller, *Emblems of Eloquence: Opera and Women's Voices in Seventeenth-Century Venice* (Berkeley, Los Angeles, and London: University of California Press, 2003), 9–17.
49 Rosselli, *Singers of Italian Opera*, 62–3; Beth L. Glixon, 'Private Lives of Public Women', 522–4.
50 Heller, *Emblems of Eloquence*, 85.
51 Ibid., 174–6.
52 Roger Freitas, 'The Eroticism of Emasculation: Confronting the Baroque Body of the Castrato', *JM* 20/2 (2003): 196–249.
53 The description of the singing styles is from Heller, *Emblems of Eloquence*, 135.
54 Rosselli, *Singers of Italian Opera*, 52.
55 Beth L. Glixon, 'Scenes from the Life of Silvia Galiarti Manni', 100–12, and 'New Light on the Life and Career of Vittoria Tarquini', 403–4.
56 Beth L. Glixon, 'New Light on the Life and Career of Vittoria Tarquini', 409.
57 See Glixon and Glixon, *Inventing the Business of Opera*, 192; Beth L. Glixon, 'Scenes from the Life of Silvia Galiarti Manni', 116–19, 127–30.
58 Page, 'Sirens on the Danube', pars. 5.1–5.4.
59 Mary E. Frandsen, '*Eunuchi conjugium*: The Marriage of a Castrato in Early Modern Germany', *EMH* 24 (2005), 53–124.
60 Reardon, 'Launching the Career of a *secondo uomo*', pars. 6.4–6.5.
61 Rosselli, *Singers of Italian Opera*, 47–50, 53.
62 Richard Wistreich , '"La voce è grata assai, ma. . .": Monteverdi on Singing', *EM* 22/1 (1994), 7–20: 16.
63 Tosi, *Opinioni de' cantori*, 65. It is interesting that Galliard, the translator of Tosi's work into English, knew by reputation most of the female singers and castrati the author mentioned but could report nothing on Buzzoleni. See *Observations on the Florid Song*, 100–4.
64 See Bianconi and Walker, 'Production, Consumption, and Political Function of Seventeenth-Century Opera', 277–8.
65 Glixon and Glixon, *Inventing the Business of Opera*, 176.
66 See Rosselli, *Singers of Italian Opera*, 29, for a caricature of Mozzi in his old age.

7 | Opera, Gender, and Voice

CHRISTINE JEANNERET

The invention of opera not only introduced musical, dramatic, and aesthetic innovations, but it also prompted unexpected changes in gender roles and social relationships, in particular the appearance of the first women to sing on the operatic stage as professionals and the rise of the castrato. The stricter gender roles of early modern society meant that a professional female singer appearing in public was perceived to be committing a significant transgression. The public sphere was primarily a male space where men could act professionally and still maintain their honour and prestige, whereas the reputation of a woman who performed on stage was considerably more precarious: her career was likely to be viewed as indistinguishable from prostitution. The embodiment of an object of desire, the female singer was viewed as both threatening and appealing. Crossing the border between public and private spheres was therefore a bold move for a woman and exposed those who did it to all kinds of attacks. In everyday life, chastity, moderation, silence, and invisibility were the major virtues associated with an honest woman. Female opera singers became visible and professionally active by exhibiting themselves onstage; they also transgressed the border between silence and voice.[1]

Castrati were not subjected to the same social bans on their behaviours, though they were certainly ambivalent figures both in gender and sexual terms. Controversies about the morality of opera, bans on women's voices, and the paradoxical figure of the castrato were also influenced by medical discourses on the body, sexuality, and gender. As such, it is necessary first to assess how the body was understood in medical terms and to examine how it defined gender and sex distinctions in the seventeenth century.

Gender, Sex, Voice, and Morality

Until the end of the eighteenth century, natural philosophy and medicine were still largely based on Hippocratic and Galenic doctrines, themselves conceived in accordance with the theory of the humours.[2] Physical and psychological health depended on a balance of blood, phlegm, and yellow and black bile. The sexual difference between men and women was determined by 'vital heat', or innate heat: women (and children) had less vital heat than men, and were thus colder and weaker. It was believed that vital heat was produced by the heart: maintained by the *pneuma* (air in motion, breath, and, by extension, spirit or soul in early modern medicine), vital heat circulated throughout the body via the blood vessels. It was considered to be an intelligent organ that controlled and directed all the others, shaping the body and the humours. Sexual difference was not understood as qualitative but quantitative, in gradual and hierarchical terms. The male represented anatomical perfection, while the female was a lesser, imperfect version of man. Both were situated on a continuum, called the 'one-sex model' by historian Thomas Laqueur.[3] The castrato was positioned exactly in the middle: not as perfect as the uncastrated man, but less imperfect than the woman. Due to a lesser amount of vital heat and its ensuing retention within the body, female genitalia were considered identical to male ones, but turned inside instead of outside.[4] These anatomical considerations also determined divergent psychological attributes for both sexes: dry and hot were viewed as male qualities; wet and cold defined female ones. A man was naturally inclined to honour, bravery, and strength of spirit, whereas a woman was predisposed to instability, depravity, and an uncontrollable sensuality. In this one-sex model, male and female did not exist as binary or even distinct sexual entities: being a man or a woman was first and foremost a difference in gender and behaviour, not an ontological difference between the sexes. Moreover, the relative positioning and incremental continuity of the sexes across this one-sex continuum created a space for fluidity, though at the same time gendered and social constructions accentuated the difference between them.[5]

The emergence of the castrato was linked, first, to the ban on women's voices in the church and, second, to the rise of opera.[6] Roger Freitas defines the castrato as a 'temporally extended boy' who embodies a suspension between masculinity and femininity.[7] Physically and spiritually viewed as superior to women, boys represented the supreme ideal of love for men. In the early modern world, friendships, sometimes involving tutoring, between adults and young boys were common. Such relationships could remain chaste, be eroticised, or also take sexual expression, even though the Church had condemned sodomy as an act against nature since the late Middle Ages.[8] With their round baby faces devoid of facial hair, their soft skin and high voices, castrati embodied the ideal boy. Castration prevented the production of sex hormones that normally stopped bone growth, which explains why castrati were usually taller than average and had extraordinary lung capacity. Trained since childhood, their only viable career path was to become professional singers. That said, some did perform diplomatic missions, working as spies for their patrons, thus using their singing career as a ladder to achieve a better position in society.[9]

The castrato did not occupy the middle ground of the continuum alone; it was also populated by ambivalent creatures such as hermaphrodites, effeminate men, and virile women. Stories of spontaneous physiological sex changes abounded, underscoring how the passage from one end of the continuum to the other could easily be achieved.[10] It should come as no surprise that cross-dressing games and ambivalent figures such as the castrato and the female professional singer were key to the popularity of opera in the seventeenth century.

From Aristotle until the early eighteenth century, the voice was viewed merely as a wind instrument. It was only in 1741 that the French surgeon and anatomist Antoine Ferrein discovered the vocal cords – a term he also coined, describing his discovery in his treatise *De la formation de la voix de l'homme* (1741). Before the eighteenth century, it was widely believed that women and children had high voices because they were weak and could only move a small quantity of air, while men's low voices were attributable to their greater strength. Castrati, again, occupied a middle ground, demonstrating feminine vocal qualities, yet with more strength. According to Galenic medical theories, physical activities such as singing, exercising, playing, or acting onstage produced heat, which was conveyed through the body by the animal spirit. Made of blood and air, the animal spirit originated in the brain and circulated through the whole body by way of the arteries. Its role was to maintain the body's natural heat; it also conveyed the passions, impressing them in the mind and body.

Medically, singing was recommended in several situations, for instance as a form of physical exercise that stimulated the pulse and balanced the humours. It was also thought to be beneficial for digestion and relaxation before sleeping; and it was thought to facilitate childbirth as well.[11] By singing, imperfect creatures such as women or effeminate castrati could increase their bodily temperature, thus becoming similar to men. In so doing, they transgressed a border, stepping into the territory of masculine identity. Advocates of opera as well as its moral detractors considered this transgression either appealing or disgusting, either sensual or threatening: yet everyone agreed on the eroticism conveyed by women performing onstage. The marvellous and sensual effects of song were always described from a masculine point of view and thus always relied on the same trope: seeing and hearing a female singer moved an audience to rapture.

Medical considerations with misogynist undertones led to the construction of highly differentiated gendered roles in society. Social behaviour was subjected to moral scrutiny, especially for women, and even more so for women who acted as men, such as professional opera singers. Therefore, moral condemnations of theatre and opera were not rare; the most fervid attacks were directed at women performing onstage. In his pamphlet *Il puttanismo romano* (1668) depicting an imaginary conclave of prostitutes electing the pope, the Jesuit Gregorio Leti condemned the nepotism of the papal court and ferociously attacked women playing a public role. Among the latter were aristocrats such as Princess Olimpia Aldobrandini, Queen Christina of Sweden, Mazarin's niece Maria Mancini, and the singer Leonora Baroni:

Ladies and Whores have almost always been one and the same, and one could not find anyone, apart from some poor peasant who did not understand that under the word Lady is the word Whore, and encompassed under the word Whore is the word Lady. And if you hadn't known it before, understand it now, so you do not make yourself appear to be simple: you will find no other difference but that the Lady is a private Whore and the Whore a public Lady.[12]

It is no coincidence that these noblewomen were also involved in opera patronage.[13] Giovanni Domenico Ottonelli, another Jesuit who authored a book on the danger of keeping company with women, 'especially singers', and no less than six volumes condemning theatre, affirms:

Our modern comedians and mountebanks, who wish for the effective enticement of the crowd on stage and on the bench, should abandon the practice of presenting women speaking of lascivious love; because it is a means quite dangerous and pernicious to many. I mean that the comedian or mountebank, presenting a frivolous and lasciviously adorned woman for enticement commits a grave error because, even if he does not expect it nor perhaps think of it, nor want to think of it, nonetheless places with real effect a great diabolical and infernal trap before many souls and they are led to the penitential fire of eternal damnation.[14]

Crossing the line between private and public, between silence and singing, led many female singers to be equated, at best, with courtesans and, at worst, with prostitutes. In fact, some of them actually were courtesans, including, for instance, Barbara Strozzi[15] and the Neapolitan prima donna Giulia De Caro, detta La Ciulla (1646–1697). The latter, described as 'singing actress, harmonious whore and princess of the brothel' in a contemporary text, became famous by interpreting ribald songs with a company of mountebanks, abandoning her husband, and becoming a member of the Febiarmonici, the first opera company in Naples.[16] Between 1673 and 1675, De Caro had also been impresario of the Teatro S. Bartolomeo, Naples's first opera house. Her career, however, exemplifies the trend of professional singers needing to develop self-fashioning strategies to elevate their reputation – even when not engaged in prostitution.

Myth or reality, notorious rumours of affairs abounded between male and female singers, involving aristocrats or prelates.[17] Scandals did not spare the stages, as is shown by the famous controversy around the production of Domenico Mazzocchi's opera *La Catena d'Adone* (Rome, 1626; libretto by Ottavio Tronsarelli), commissioned by Prince Giovanni Giorgio Aldobrandini (1591–1637). A heated rivalry opposed two famous Roman singers regarded as courtesans, Margherita Costa and Cecca del Padule, about the respective importance of their roles as Venus and the enchantress Falsirena. The scandal grew even further in notoriety, passionately dividing the Roman nobility. Finally, it was resolved by the patron's mother, Olimpia Aldobrandini Borghese the elder, who dismissed both female singers and had them replaced by two castrati.[18]

Singers who were not engaged in prostitution were not spared accusations of debauchery, and had to preserve and defend their moral integrity. It is not surprising, then, that even artistic praise had to be expressed according to masculine standards. For instance, the singer, instrumentalist, and composer Adriana Basile (c. 1580–1583, d. after 1642) and even more so her daughter Leonora Baroni (1611–1670), who had moved to Rome in 1633, were praised by their admirers as 'virtuose',[19] a term that draws on the classic Roman ideal of manliness ('vir') and, later, the Renaissance ideal of masculine 'virtù'. Thus, women or castrati praised as 'virtuosi' involved a transgression, a shift from the feminine to the masculine as they exhibited themselves in the public or semi-public sphere, increasing their body temperature through the act of singing.

Staging the Passions in Italy: Female Singers and Castrati

The first professional women onstage were actresses, such as Isabella Andreini (1562–1604). Along with her husband, she directed a *commedia dell'arte* troupe called *La Compagnia dei Gelosi*, which performed the celebrated *intermedi* of *La Pellegrina* at the wedding of Christina of Lorraine and Gran Duke Ferdinando I de' Medici in Florence in 1589. Isabella was the star of the festivities with her stunning performance of the mad scene in *La pazzia di Isabella*, an improvised comedy in which she sang several pieces.[20] She also was the mother-in-law of Virginia Ramponi Andreini (1583–1629/30; known as 'la Florinda'), actress, singer, and poet, and the first wife of Giovanni Battista Andreini, with whom she founded the *Compagnia dei Fedeli*.[21] In Mantua in 1608, during the festivities for the wedding of Francesco Gonzaga and Margherita of Savoy, Ramponi sang the title role in the première of Monteverdi's opera *Arianna* and also played the part of an Ungrateful Lady in the first production of his *Ballo delle ingrate*.[22] Her performance of Arianna's lament was so moving that 'not one lady present failed to shed a tear'.[23]

Tears pouring from the singer onstage and from the female audience clearly allude to humoural humidity in women. As a topos in opera, tears signal the achievement of Aristotelian catharsis through drama.[24] They also represent the submission of women to the will of men and the ritual of lamenting at wedding ceremonies as a mark of women's sacrifice and subjugation to men.[25] Like Ramponi, Anna Renzi (c. 1620–after 1661) – the first prima donna in opera – was famous not only for her virtuoso singing technique but also for her acting skills.[26] She performed exceptionally in Francesco Sacrati's (1605–1650) *La finta pazza* (1641). *Il Cannocchiale per la finta pazza*, an elaborate account of the opera, its machinery, and the singers' performance, described her as follows: 'Signora Anna Renzi from Rome, a young woman as skillful in acting as she is excellent in music, as cheerful in feigning madness as she is wise in knowing how to imitate it, and modest in all her habits.'[27] In the preface to the libretto, Strozzi describes her as 'a most gentle siren, who sweetly steals the heart and charms the eyes and ears of the listeners'.[28] In the description of Sacrati's *Bellerofonte* (Vincenzo Nolfi, 1642), Giulio Del Colle characterises her as the 'true embodiment of music and the only marvel of the stage, who, during the course of the performance first gave vent to, then hid, then disguised, then revealed, and then lamented her amorous passions'.[29]

The fascination exerted by female high voices on audiences was constantly described in erotic terms. Interestingly, the same effect was achieved by castrati but not by lower male voices. The castrato Atto Melani (1626–1714) who had played the role of Achille in *La Finta pazza* along with Renzi, is described in such gendered terms: 'a young castrato from Rome of beautiful appearance, who resembles an Amazon in his mixture of warlike spirit and feminine delicacy'.[30] The following description from *Il Cannocchiale* demonstrates the effect his singing had on his listeners:

The youth, who was a most valorous little singer from Pistoia, began to sing so delicately that the souls of the listeners, as if exiting through the portals of the ears, raised themselves to heaven to assist in the enjoyment of such sweetness.[31]

Pietro Della Valle affirms that castrati 'cloaking themselves in the affects, ... enrapture the listener'.[32] All singers – and especially those with high voices such as female singers and castrati – were often admired for their virtuosity, but the rapture was caused by an association of both aural and visual effects. The affects expressed by the text were not only sung but also staged, appealing to the eyes and the ears of the spectators simultaneously. In his description of the female consorts employed at the courts of Mantua and Ferrara (the *concerto delle donne* developed in late Renaissance, originally at the court of Ferrara), Vincenzo Giustiniani gives us a valuable insight into how these singers had such a powerful effect on their audience:

Furthermore, they moderated or increased their voices, loud or soft, heavy or light, according to the demands of the piece they were singing; now slow, breaking off with sometimes a gentle sigh, now singing long passages legato or detached, now groups, now leaps, now with long trills, now with short, and again with sweet running passages sung softly, to which sometimes one heard an echo answer unexpectedly. They accompanied the music and the conceit with appropriate facial expressions, glances and gestures, with no awkward movements of the mouth or hands or body, which might not express the conceit of the song.[33]

According to the Neoplatonic theory of love, sight was the sense that allowed the image of the beloved to penetrate the soul: entering through the eyes, it literally took possession of the lover's soul.[34] Female singers and castrati represented symbolic embodiments of the lover onstage: they had a similar effect on their audience. Thus, opera was considered the most appealing expression of the affects, while still considered a threat to the spectators' souls.

Empowering the Female Voice: Francesca Caccini and *La liberazione di Ruggiero* (1625)

Even when women were seen to be transgressing their gendered role by stepping onstage, their presence was certainly acknowledged, whether they were praised or despised. The growing popularity of public opera made them all the more visible, and heard. Composing, however, was an entirely different matter as it was almost exclusively a male domain and prerogative. One remarkable exception was Francesca Caccini (1587–1641), who worked at the Medici court in Florence and was the first woman to compose an opera, *La liberazione di Ruggiero dall'isola d'Alcina* (*The Liberation of Ruggiero from Alcina's Island*, 1625).[35] She was raised in a musical household; her father Giulio Caccini (1551–1618) was her teacher; her mother Lucia di Filippo Gagnolanti, her stepmother Margherita della Scala, and her sister Settimia (1591–c. 1660) were all gifted singers. Francesca served the Medici from 1607 until 1627 as a singer, instrumentalist, and music teacher; she was also the most prolific female composer of her era. The musician with the highest salary on the Medici payroll, she composed the music to at least thirteen court entertainments. Her unique role as a female composer is undoubtedly linked to the joint female regency (1621–1630) in Florence and to the destinies of two outstanding women, the Grand Duchess Christina of Lorraine, widow of Ferdinando I de' Medici, and her daughter-in-law, the Archduchess Maria Magdalena of Austria, widow of Cosimo II. The contrast between the two of them could not have been more marked. A delicate, elegant French aristocrat with a dominant and controlling attitude towards power, Christina had been the de facto sovereign of Tuscany since 1607 and during her son's reign. Maria Magdalena, on the other hand, was an unusually robust and manly woman – an accomplished dancer, horsewoman, and huntress. Both, however, were united in legitimising their unprecedented female regency, and one privileged means was patronage of the arts. Continuing a Medici tradition of myth-building and self-fashioning through pictorial, musical, and textual productions, the female regents adapted it to the purpose of gender politics by portraying positive models of female leaders; theatrical spectacles played a central role in this campaign. In 1607, Christina commissioned *La Stiava* (*The Female Slave*, libretto by Michelangelo Buonarroti the Younger), Francesca's first opera and also her very first composition. Unfortunately the score is lost, but it was described as having 'marvelous music'.[36] The grand duchess was involved in the preparations and had the librettist rewrite the script to transform the female slave from an object of male desire to a sovereign kidnapped by pirates, and from a mute object to a singing subject. The political justification of the female voice was essential to Christina as a legitimisation of her regency: as Cusick puts it, the opera was 'a conquest of disorder by sonic order'.[37]

The Archduchess Maria Magdalena commissioned *La liberazione di Ruggiero dell'isola d'Alcina* in 1625 to celebrate the visit of her Polish nephew, Prince Władysław, hoping to arrange a marriage with her daughter Margherita – the plan was destined to fail. The opera was performed at the Villa Poggio Imperiale, the family's summer residence, which had just been redecorated at Maria Magdalena's request with female imagery of Amazon warriors, heroines of ancient history, and female saints. Maria Magdalena attended nearly every rehearsal to maintain control over the production. Drawing on both Ariosto and Tasso, the libretto by Ferdinando Saracinelli (d. 1640) is an allegory of female power, staged as a struggle between two sorceresses to win Ruggiero. The benevolent Melissa eventually succeeds in freeing him from the charms of the evil and sensual Alcina, who has kidnapped him. The character of Ruggiero is utterly passive, prey to the two women's contradictory desires. Allegorically, the opera stages a struggle between chaos and order, between Alcina's uncontrollable and threatening sexuality characterised by her immoderate behaviour, and Melissa's forceful call to duty and eventual restoration of Ruggiero at the head of the Christian armies. Musically, Caccini uses various styles and modes to depict gender. Alcina and her attendants sing in flat keys; Ruggiero and his male attendants sing in sharp keys; the bi-gendered Melissa – first appearing as Atlante, a male warrior, then shifting into the role of a female benevolent sorceress – sings mostly in C natural.[38]

Francesca chose specific musical genres: canzonettas for a trio of sopranos; an evocation of the *concerto delle donne*; elaborate strophic arias for the lovers' duet with ornamentation inspired by her father's collections of monodies, *Le Nuove musiche* (1602) and *Nuove musiche e nuova maniera di scriverle* (1614); musically dispassionate recitatives for the narration; and a five-part madrigal for the chorus of the enchanted plants. To restore masculinity to power, Melissa dissociates herself from her gender: she first appears onstage in male disguise as the non-Christian prince and warrior Atlante and musically appropriates male speech and reasoning.[39]

Published in 1625 and dedicated to Maria Magdalena, *La liberazione* is one of the few operas to have been published at that time, which attests to its political importance. It is also rare for its inclusion of five engravings of stage designs by Alfonso Parigi. One of the political purposes of *La liberazione* had much to do with the legitimisation of Maria Magdalena's regency: intended to contribute to her self-fashioning as a benevolent cross-gendered ruler, the work reinforced her image as the dynastic guardian of Medici sovereignty. Saracinelli's allusion to Maria Magdalena's manly manners must have been unequivocal to the audience. Her call to duty 'Atlante a te se'n vien' ('Atlante is coming to you') is set as a diatonic, slow recitative in a narrow range: it follows the words, emphasising the domination of the rational male sphere of the *logos* over the lascivious female sphere of the *melos*. Her speech condemns sensual love, glorifying war and manly duties. She shames Ruggiero for his effeminacy, and calls him to action once he has regained his virility. By adopting a male disguise and voice, Melissa convinces Ruggiero to abandon his lover. Alcina's long lament 'Ferma ferma crudele' ('Stop, stop cruel one') is on the contrary musically excessive and immoderate – two typical female vices. Switching rapidly from intense pain to joy and laughter, the libretto evokes extreme passions, enhanced by a musical setting based on melodic and harmonic extravagances.

Confronting her unfaithful lover in a chromatic complaint, Alcina constantly switches from one affect to another. Florid passages alternate with bursts of anger, erratic melodic motions with grief-stricken lamentations. Extreme dissonances, chromatic passages, and abrupt modal changes characterise her long lament. Failing to regain Ruggiero's love by the beauty of her sensual song, she unleashes demons and fire against him, failing again to avenge herself. On the contrary, the moderate Melissa ultimately triumphs and restores the male power of Ruggiero.

In the hands of two powerful women who desire him, Ruggiero remains effeminate and passive. Overtly emotional and confused by passion, his song acquires a feminine quality in his love duet with Alcina, 'Quanto per dolce'. His vagaries are set to capricious music, featuring erratic changes in the melodic line and in the harmony (see Example 7.1). Melissa reproaches him for his immodesty, a typical feminine flaw: sensual excess has transformed him into a womanish figure.

The Situation in France: Hatred of Castrato Voices

The court of Louis XIV was by no means a gynocentric form of government, and it certainly did not favour female artists as the Florentine regents did. To escape the predatory misogyny of the court, the *précieuses* – women belonging to the French nobility and advocating a new, sophisticated literary style referred to as 'précieux' (precious) – created alternate spaces known as *ruelles* where the arts were cultivated. Their refined language and activities, including parlour games, exuded exquisite elegance and manners. A form of resistance against the coarseness of the Court, the *ruelles* allowed them to discuss controversial political topics, focusing on women's independence from social and sexual submission, and on improving their access to knowledge.[40] The *air de cour* was their favoured musical genre, much more than opera, which was strongly tied to the politics of absolutism.

Example 7.1 Francesca Caccini, *La liberazione di Ruggiero dal'isola d'Alcina, baletto* (Florence, 1625), Ruggiero, 'Quanto per dolce' (Florence: Pietro Cecconcelli, 1625), mm. 138–62; 223–37

One exceptionally talented woman who performed regularly at Versailles – the first and only female composer to write a *tragédie en musique* – was Élisabeth-Claude Jacquet de La Guerre (1665–1729). A child prodigy born into a family of musicians, she performed on the

Example 7.1 (*cont.*)

harpsichord from the age of five and sang at the court of Louis XIV under the protection of his mistress, Madame de Montespan. In 1684, she married the organist Martin de La Guerre and left the court to give lessons and concerts in Paris. In 1691 she wrote a ballet for the King, *Les Jeux à l'honneur de la victoire* (music lost).[41] *Céphale et Procris*, her only *tragédie en musique*, was performed in 1694 in Paris at the Théâtre du Palais Royal, but it met with little success. Its failure can be attributed to several factors, the first of which was a confused plot with weaknesses in the libretto written by Joseph-François Duché de Vancy, a protégé of the king's morganatic wife, Madame de Maintenon, but not the best poet.[42] Second, in the 1690s, the king, influenced by the religious conservatism of Madame de Maintenon, had started to show less interest in opera. Third, the church intensified its attacks on the theatre and particularly opera in 1693, condemning it as inappropriate and excessively sensuous.[43]

Duché's libretto does not feature strong female characters, but rather a love triangle with traditional gender roles. Céphale and Procris' love is thwarted by the gods, who declare that Procris will marry Borée. Attempting to intervene in a fight between her two male rivals, Procris is inadvertently killed by Céphale. Musically, the overall structure of this opera follows the conventions of the *tragédie en musique* of Lully and Quinault. The modal organisation – its style and structure – adheres to and depicts the characters' passions but does not establish gender distinctions, as was the case in Caccini's opera. About to be married to Borée, Procris invokes death to escape her destiny in a lament, 'Funeste mort, donnez-moy du secours', set to the descending tetrachord in F with many dissonances illustrating her defeat.

Jacquet de La Guerre was the only woman to appear among the composers listed in Évrard Titon du Tillet's chronicle *Le Parnasse françois* (1732). However, Titon du Tillet mentions several other women with less important positions, mostly singers on the Parisian stage, where professional female singers did not have to share the limelight with castrati, as was the case in Italy. The French distaste for castrati was first and foremost moral and sexual; aesthetic considerations only came second. None of their detractors objected to the quality and virtuosity of their singing, but the mutilation they endured and the resulting gender ambiguity caused physical disgust among women and sexual anxieties among men.[44] Castrati's physical appearance and their manners were perceived as extravagant by the French, whose culture privileged language and declamation over sheer vocal beauty. Castrati seemed unconvincing from a dramaturgical point of view, especially in cross-dressed or heroic male roles. The poet and librettist Pierre Perrin (1620–1675) described them as 'the horror of women and the laughing stock of men' and advised banning castrati from opera, where they offended decorum and verisimilitude.[45] Moreover, contrary to Italian practice, the French did not privilege high-pitched voices, and the pure vocality embodied by the female singer was frowned upon: the female voice was perceived as a threat to *logos*, since it conveyed overwhelming passions that deformed the semantic content of the text.[46]

Anne Chabanceau de La Barre (1628–1688), daughter of the organist Pierre de La Barre, sang in the French production of Luigi Rossi's *Orfeo* in 1646 and Francesco Cavalli's *Ercole amante* in 1662 as La Bellezza (The Beauty).[47] She was praised for her excellence in both the French and Italian styles, as well as in court ballets and Italian operas. Queen Christina invited her to the court of Sweden in late 1652 or early 1653, where she remained until the queen's abdication in 1654; she then briefly performed at the court of Denmark.[48] In 1661 she was appointed *ordinaire de la musique du roi* – the first time such a title was granted to a female musician.[49] Her marriage in 1667 signalled the end of her career, as was the tradition for female singers once married.

Marie Le Rochois (c. 1658–1728) sang at the Paris Opéra from 1678 until 1698, where she premièred all the major female roles in several of Lully's operas – *Proserpine* (1680), Mérope in *Persée* (1682), Arcabonne in *Amadis* (1684), Angélique in *Roland* (1685), *Armide* (1686), and Galatée in the *pastorale héroïque Acis et Galatée* (1686). Her portrayal of Armide made her famous and caused quite a stir. The French critic Jean Laurent Le Cerf de la Viéville (1674–1707) affirmed that 'he had never been moved so deeply' and that he still shivered when he remembered Le Rochois's marvellous voice and performance.[50] Titon du Tillet describes her as

the most perfect model for declamation who had appeared on stage. ... Even though she was fairly short, very dark, and looked very ordinary outside of the theatre, with eyes close together which were, however, large, full of fire, and capable of expressing all the passions, she effaced all the most beautiful and more attractive actresses when she was on stage.[51]

On the other hand, François Raguenet, an ardent defender of the Italian style, wrote in his *Parallèle des Italiens et des Français* (1702) that 'if a principal actress such as Le Rochois should step aside, not only Paris but all of France would not be able to find another one that could replace her'.[52] In the English translation of Raguenet's text (1709), the translator added that Le Rochois was 'a wretched Actress, and sang insufferably out of Tune'.[53] In Titon's description, however, Le Rochois fell in line with French expectations, advocating more realistic staging and less florid singing.

Marie-Louise Desmatins (fl. 1682–c. 1708) sang together with Le Rochois in several secondary roles from Lully's *tragédies*, alternating with her in the title role of Destouches's *Issé* (1697), a *pastorale héroïque*. She sang Médée in Lully's *Thésée* in the 1698 revival and the title-role in *Armide* in 1703. Although Desmatins is referenced in very few sources, she is prominently featured in *La musique du diable ou le Mercure Galant dévalisé* (Paris: Robert le Turc, 1711). Just as the Italian Jesuits had before, this cautionary pamphlet criticised opera and the decadence of theatre. *La musique du diable* was written as an attack on women performing onstage and offers a satirical depiction of an afterlife in hell in which Desmatins, together with Lully and the most famous musicians of the king, are transformed into porpoises.[54] Rumoured to have had her fat removed by a butcher, Desmatins then organises a dinner where she serves food prepared with her own fat and dies soon after. At the outset of Pluto's reign, she faces a host of serious charges. Accused of prostitution, transmitting venereal diseases, spoiling marriages, robbing respectable merchants, poisoning prelates and fellow actresses, neglecting confession for twenty years, and having had four abortions, she replies: 'I have done nothing that an opera girl as tolerably pretty as I should not have done.'[55] Pluto eventually welcomes her to hell with the highest honours.

Fanchon Moreau (1668–1743) made her début in the prologue of Lully's *Phaëton* in 1683. She premièred the roles of Oriane in Lully's *Amadis* (1684) and Créuse in Charpentier's *Médée* (1693); she also sang in Campra's *L'Europe galante* (1697), in Destouches's *Issé* (1697), and in several Lully revivals. Her elder sister Louison was also a singer, and both were mistresses of the dauphin, Louis de France.[56] But no singer's life was as tumultuous as that of Julie d'Aubigny, or La Maupin (c. 1673–1707). She started her career by giving fencing exhibitions and singing in roadside taverns in France, and made her operatic début in a revival of Lully's *Cadmus et Hermione* in 1690; she then sang in new productions by Henri Desmarets, Destouches, Campra, and La Barre. Her voice was a 'bas-dessus' (more akin to our modern mezzo-soprano). Claude and François Parfaict's *Dictionnaire des théâtres* described her voice as being of unequaled beauty.[57] Married and openly bisexual, she often cross-dressed and was an accomplished swordswoman. Her idiosyncrasies were such that already during her lifetime many unverified stories circulated about her. Her tumultuous love affair with Fanchon Moreau also inspired the imagination of her biographers – according to a rather dubious anec-dote, La Maupin attempted suicide when Fanchon rejected her.

La Maupin's unusual vocal range, her acting skills, and her androgynous appearance made her a favourite of French audiences. Since a fundamental principle of the operatic genre in France was its adherence to the rules of classical theatre, the singer's principal task was not so much to sing well ('le beau chant') but to act well in order to represent the drama.[58] The sung voice, and especially the female one, expressed extreme passions that were conceived as a threat to eloquence and to the verisimilitude of the *tragédie en musique*. A shift in perspective during the eighteenth century eventually enabled the female singer to become a diva, as musical listening was increasingly understood as a form of sensory and emotional participation, creating a liberating space for female voices that had previously been restrained.[59] Through her daring personality and overtly sexualised image,

La Maupin highlights some of the changes that took place during the seventeenth century with respect to female musicians.

The Exportation of the Italian Model to the Germanic Countries and England

While the French started their own national tradition with the *tragédie en musique* and their decisive rejection of castrati, the rest of Europe imported the Italian genre, along with its style and, most importantly, its performers. The diaspora of Italian singers spread in the early seventeenth century to the German-speaking countries.[60] Vienna and Innsbruck became outposts of Venice for operatic production. The *Compagnia dei Fedeli*, who had premièred Monteverdi's *Arianna* in Mantua in 1608, was at the service of the imperial court of Vienna from 1626–1628. Antonio Cesti (1623–1669) was chapel master and opera director in Innsbruck from 1652–1658 and 1661–1665, premièring among others his celebrated *Argia* in 1655 for the conversion to Roman Catholicism of Queen Christina of Sweden.

Women were always chaperoned and usually travelled around Europe with companies to perform operas. Typically, they were married to other singers. Some exceptionally gifted singers were appointed to northern courts. Invited by Maria de' Medici, Ramponi performed with the *Compagnia dei Fedeli* in France; they also toured in Prague and Vienna. Margherita Basile (d. after 1639), sister of Adriana Basile, started her career in Mantua from 1615–late 1620s and was appointed to the imperial court of Vienna in 1631. She also accompanied one of Emperor Ferdinand II's daughters to Poland in 1637. The prima donna Giulia Masotti abandoned her operatic career in Italy in 1673 to enter the service of Empress Claudia Felicitas as a chamber musician in Vienna. There, she encountered a very different setting than the spectacular one offered by the Italian stages to which she was accustomed. Also, she was an anomaly at the Habsburg court, where female singers had little public presence and did not usually appear on the operatic stage. Giulia performed in at least two operatic productions by Antonio Draghi, *Il ratto delle Sabine* and *Il fuoco eterno custodito dalle Vestali* (both 1674), with additional music by Emperor Leopold and Johann Heinrich Schmelzer. She stayed at the court after the death of the empress, but no records of her musical activity have survived.[61]

In England, the operatic tradition started later, and the celebrity culture surrounding operatic singers only developed at the turn of the eighteenth century in London. Cavalli's *Erismena* (Venice, 1655) may have been performed in an English version in London in 1674;[62] Lully's *Cadmus et Hermione* (Paris, 1673) was given there in 1686, probably in the public theatre of Dorset Garden by a French company.[63] Like the French, the English had an enduring tradition of plays and court masques combining music, dance, and scenic spectacles with spoken dialogue instead of recitative. By the end of the century, resistance to Italian opera was not only motivated by aesthetic and patriotic considerations but also by what the English saw as a lack of dramatic coherence, and by issues surrounding gender in tandem with recurring arguments against castrati and the poor moral reputation of female singers.[64]

The Italian soprano (Francesca) Margherita de L'Epine (c. 1680–1746), who had started her operatic career in Venice in the 1698–1700 seasons, arrived in London in 1702 as the mistress of the German composer Jakob Greber (d. 1731). She became the first leading female singer in London, just at the time when Italian opera was beginning to be produced on the English stage.[65] Immensely popular and courted by many English aristocrats, she had a brilliant career as a singer and dancer, and could sing in both Italian and English.

L'Epine's first known London performance in an opera was Haym's adaptation of Bononcini's *Camilla* at Drury Lane in 1706. She then appeared in almost all operatic productions in London until 1714, often playing male parts because of her looks. Burney described her as 'so swarthy and ill-favored that her husband used to call her Hecate . . . But with such a total absence of personal charms, our galleries would have made her songs very short, had they not been executed in such a manner as to silence theatrical snakes, and command applause.'[66] The anti-theatrical newspaper *The Observator* wrote in 1706: 'Can we help laughing and weeping at the same time, to see a secretary retiring from the great affairs of state to an alcove with Donna Margaritta de la Pin [*sic*], alias Pegg Thorn, to hear her sing "Colly my cow" and "Uptails all"?'[67] As was the case in France and Italy, attacks against female singers were common and were directed at the sexual threat they represented.[68]

* * *

Opera, whether in its Italian homeland or as an exported genre, always raised aesthetic and moral concerns. Along with castrati, female performers embodied this peril, which explains the simultaneous singling out of female singers as the worst examples of debauchery while showering them with praise for their angelic voices. On stage, their acting bodies – projecting sound and conveying passions to an audience – were powerful tools for the sensuality of music, which could threaten reason and dramatic coherence. Librettists, composers, and critics alike tried in various ways to repress the voice, containing or sublimating its dangers, whether because of its unhinged nature and ensuing threat to *logos*, or because of the performers' excessive display of virtuosity.

In the wake of Catherine Clément's influential study, *Opera, or the Undoing of Women* (published originally in French in 1979), opera has long been considered a place of defeat for women. Yet, through its performative aspect, opera also became a space for the empowerment of the female voice. Conventional scenes in early opera often feature a female protagonist gripped by passions, a lament scene, a mad scene, or an incantation scene – from Monteverdi's lament of Arianna to Armide's scene 'Enfin, il est en ma puissance' in Lully's eponymous *tragédie en musique*. Through their colourful careers, opera performers were the embodiment of the characters they represented onstage. With its proliferation of crossed-dressed female warriors or lamenting heroines, effeminate or virile characters, seventeenth-century opera offers a most fertile ground for studying the performance of gender.

Notes

1 Wendy Heller's *Emblems of Eloquence: Opera and Women's Voices in Seventeenth-Century Venice* (Berkeley, Los Angeles, and London: University of California Press, 2003), a study of operatic heroines, presents how women were depicted in the social and political context of Venetian opera.

2 Vivian Nutton, 'Humoralism', in William F. Bynum and Roy Porter (eds.), *Companion Encyclopedia of the History of Medicine*, 2 vols. (New York: Routledge, 1993), vol. 1, 281–91; Nancy Siraisi, *Medieval and Early Renaissance Medicine: An Introduction to Knowledge and Practice* (Chicago: The University of Chicago Press, 1990).

3 Thomas Laqueur, *Making Sex: Body and Gender from the Greeks to Freud* (Cambridge: Harvard University Press, 1990). Michael Stolberg argues for the emergence of sexual dimorphism during the Renaissance: 'A Woman down to Her Bones: The Anatomy of Sexual Difference in the Sixteenth and Early Seventeenth Centuries', *Isis* 94/2 (2003), 274–99. Lorraine Datson and Katharine Park criticise Laqueur's view as an oversimplification: 'The Hermaphrodite and the Orders of Nature: Sexual Ambiguity in Early Modern France', in Louise Fradenburg and Carla Freccero (eds.), *Premodern Sexualities* (New York: Routledge, 1996), 117–36: 118–19. See also Helen King, *The One-Sex*

Body on Trial: The Classical and Early Modern Evidence (Farnham: Ashgate, 2013). However, all agree on a dominant view of medicine still following Galen.

4 Galen formulated the identity of male and female genitalia, and his formulation remained a commonplace until the eighteenth century: see Laqueur, *Making Sex*, 4, 79–82.

5 Dorinda Outram, 'Gender', in Katherine Park and Lorraine Daston (eds.), *Cambridge History of Science: Volume 3, Early Modern Science* (Cambridge: Cambridge University Press, 2006), 797–817; Karen Harvey, 'The Substance of Sexual Difference: Change and Persistence in Representations of the Body in Eighteenth-Century England', *Gender & History* 14/2 (2002), 202–23.

6 Sergio Durante, 'The Opera Singer', in Lorenzo Bianconi and Giorgio Pestelli (eds.), *Opera Production and Its Resources*, trans. Lydia G. Cochrane, *The History of Italian Opera*, vol. 4 (Chicago and London: The University of Chicago Press, 1998), 354–417; Roger Freitas, 'The Eroticism of Emasculation: Confronting the Baroque Body of the Castrato', *JM* 20/2 (2003), 196–249; Giuseppe Gerbino, 'The Quest for the Soprano Voice: Castrati in Renaissance Italy', *SM* 33/2 (2004), 303–56; John Rosselli, 'The Castrati as a Professional Group and a Social Phenomenon', *Acta Musicologica* 60/2 (1988), 143–79; Katherine Bergeron, 'The Castrato as History', *COJ* 8/2 (1996), 167–84.

7 Freitas, 'The Eroticism of Emasculation', 218, 223.

8 See notably John Boswell, *Christianity, Social Tolerance, and Homosexuality: Gay People in Western Europe from the Beginning of the Christian Era to the Fourteenth Century* (Chicago: The University of Chicago Press, thirty-fifth anniversary edn. 2015); Stephen J. Milner, *At the Margins: Minority Groups in Premodern Italy* (Minneapolis: University of Minnesota Press, 2005); Michael Rocke, *Forbidden Friendships: Homosexuality and Male Culture in Renaissance Florence* (New York and Oxford: Oxford University Press, 1996).

9 Roger Freitas, *Portrait of a Castrato: Politics, Patronage, and Music in the Life of Atto Melani* (Cambridge: Cambridge University Press, 2009).

10 Outram, 'Gender', 804ff; King, *The One-Sex Body on Trial*, 97–127.

11 Penelope Gouk, 'Music, Melancholy, and Medical Spirits', in Peregrine Horden (ed.), *Music as Medicine: The History of Music Therapy since Antiquity* (Aldershot: Ashgate, 2000), 173–94.

12 Gregorio Leti, *Il puttanismo romano ovvero conclave generale delle puttane della corte; per l'elettione del nuovo Pontefice* (Cologne: [s.n.], 1668), 202–3. Translations are mine, unless otherwise stated.

13 Valeria De Lucca, 'Strategies of Women Patrons of Music and Theatre in Rome: Maria Mancini Colonna, Queen Christina of Sweden, and Women of Their Circles', *Renaissance Studies* 25/3 (2011), 374–92. Baroni spent her all career in Rome and is not known to have performed operas.

14 Giovanni Domenico Ottonelli, *Della christiania moderatione del theatro libro primo, detto la Qualità delle comedie per dichiarare quale sia la lecita a' buoni Christiani...*

(Florence: Bonardi, 1655), first book, 102; *Della pericolosa conversatione con le donne, o poco modeste, o ritirate, o cantatrici, o accademiche* (Florence: Francheschini & Logi, 1646).

15 On Strozzi, see Ellen Rosand, 'Barbara Strozzi, *virtuosissima cantatrice*: The Composer's Voice', *JAMS* 31/2 (1978), 241–81; David Rosand and Ellen Rosand, 'Barbara di Santa Sofia and Il Prete Genovese: On the Identity of a Portrait by Bernardo Strozzi', *Art Bulletin* 63/2 (1981), 249–58; and Beth L. Glixon, 'New Light on the Life and Career of Barbara Strozzi', *MQ* 81/2 (1997), 311–55.

16 Innocenzo Fuidoro, *Giornali di Napoli dal 1660 al 1680*, ed. Franco Schlizer, Antonio Padula, and Vittoria Omodeo, 4 vols. (Naples: Società napolitana di Storia Patria, 1934–1939), entry dated 08/11/1671, quoted in Benedetto Croce, *I teatri di Napoli: Dal Rinascimento alla fine del secolo decimottavo* (Milan: Adelphi, 1992), 168. Paologiovanni Maione, 'Giulia de Caro "seu ciulla": da commediante a cantarina: osservazioni sulla condizione degli "armonici" nella seconda metà del seicento', *RIM* 32/1 (1997), 61–80.

17 Cardinal Antonio Barberini was rumoured to have had affairs with both Leonora Baroni and the castrato Marcantonio Pasqualini; Duke Carlo II of Mantua with Atto Melani; Countess Elena Forni with Giovanni Francesco Grossi (detto Siface); Grand Prince Ferdinando de Medici with the castrato Francescode Castris (detto Cecchino); and Cardinal Camillo Pamphili with Leonora Baroni. See Freitas, 'The Eroticism of Emasculation', 216, and Amy Brosius, '"Il suon, lo sguardo, il canto": Virtuose of the Roman Conversazioni in the Mid-Seventeenth Century' (Ph.D. dissertation: University of New York, 2009), 335.

18 The anecdote is related in Gian Vittorio Rossi [Iani Nicii Erithraei], *Pinacotheca Imaginum Illustrium*, 3 vols. (Cologne: Kalcovium, 1648), vol. 3, 150–1, with his usual malicious misogyny.

19 *Applausi poetici alle glorie della signora Leonora Baroni* (Bracciano: Francesco Ronconi, 1639); Franca Trinchieri Camiz, '"La bella cantatrice": I ritratti di Leonora Barone e Barbara Strozzi a confronto', in Francesco Passadore and Franco Rossi (eds.), *Musica, Scienza e idee nella Serenissima durante il Seicento* (Venice: Edizioni Fondazione Levi, 1996), 285–94; Brosius, '"Il suon, lo sguardo, il canto"'; Christine Jeanneret, 'Gender Ambivalence and the Expression of Passions in the Performances of Early Roman Cantatas by Castrati and Female Singers', in Tom Cochrane, Bernardino Fantini, and Klaus R. Scherer (eds.), *The Emotional Power of Music. Multidsciplinary Perspectives on Musical Arousal, Expression, and Social Control* (Oxford: Oxford University Press, 2013), 85–101, appendix 359–69.

20 Anne MacNeil, *Music and Women of the Commedia dell'Arte in the Late Sixteenth Century* (Oxford and New York: Oxford University Press, 2003), and MacNeil, 'The Divine Madness of Isabella Andreini', *JRMA* 120/2 (1995), 195–215.

21 Emily Wilbourne, *Seventeenth-Century Opera and the Sound of the Commedia dell'Arte* (Chicago: The University of Chicago Press, 2016), 29.

22 Tim Carter, 'Lamenting Ariadne?' *EM* 27/3 (1999), 395–405 (the whole issue is dedicated to female laments).

23 Federico Follino, *Compendio delle sontuose feste fatte nell'anno 1608 nella città di Mantova* (Mantova: Osanna, 1608), 30.

24 MacNeil, *Music and Women*, 149.

25 Anne MacNeil, 'Weeping at the Water's Edge' *EM* 27/3 (1999), 406–17; Suzanne Cusick, '"There Was Not One Lady Who Failed to Shed a Tear": Arianna's Lament and the Construction of Modern Womanhood' *EM* 22/1 (1994), 21–43.

26 See Beth L. Glixon, 'Private Lives of Public Women: Prima Donnas in Mid-Seventeenth-Century Venice', *ML* 76/4 (1995), 509–31.

27 Maiolino Bisaccioni, *Il cannocchiale per La finta pazza drama dello Strozzi* (Venice: Giovanni Battista Surian, 1641), quoted in Ellen Rosand, *Opera in Seventeenth-Century Venice: The Creation of a Genre* (Berkeley, Los Angeles, and London: University of California Press, 1991), 96.

28 Rosand, *Opera in Seventeenth-Century Venice*, 94.

29 Vincenzo Nolfi, *Bellerofonte: Descrittione degli apparati del Bellerofonte di Giulio del Colle* (Venice: [s.n.], 1642), quoted in Rosand, *Opera in Seventeenth-Century Venice*, 101.

30 Rosand, *Opera in Seventeenth-Century Venice*, 96.

31 Nolfi, *Bellerofonte*, 12, quoted in Rosand, *Opera in Seventeenth-Century Venice*, 415.

32 Pietro Della Valle, *Della musica dell'età nostra* (1640), partially trans. Margaret Murata in Oliver Strunk (ed.), *Source Readings in Music History*, rev. edn. by Leo Treitler (New York: Norton, 1998), 544–51.

33 Vincenzo Giustiniani, *Discorso sopra la musica de' suoi tempi* (1628), transl. Carol MacClintock (Rome: American Institute of Musicology, 1962), 69.

34 Ioan P. Couliano, *Eros and Magic in the Renaissance* (Chicago and London: The University of Chicago Press, 1987), 21–30.

35 Kelley Harness, *Echoes of Women's Voices: Music, Art, and Female Patronage in Early Modern Florence* (Chicago: The University of Chicago Press, 2006); Suzanne Cusick, *Francesca Caccini at the Medici Court: Music and the Circulation of Power* (Chicago and London: The University of Chicago Press, 2009). Although both Harness (152) and Cusick (192) insist that *La liberazione* is not an opera because it is entitled 'balletto a cavallo', it can definitely be placed in the tradition of Florentine theatrical spectacles. Those were only later labelled 'operas'. The first mention of an 'opera' as such dates from 1639 in the libretto of *Le Nozze di Teti e Peleo* (Orazio Persiani and Francesco Cavalli). Before, 'operas' were characterised as 'dramma per musica, favola in musica, favola pastorale, festa teatrale, tragedia, tragicommedia, or balletto in musica': see Rosand, *Opera in Seventeenth-Century Venice*, 35.

36 Cusick, *Francesca Caccini*, 28–35.

37 Ibid., 136.

38 Ibid., ch. 10.

39 Harness, *Echoes of Women's Voices*, 162–52.

40 Claude Dulong, 'From Conversation to Creation', in *A History of Women in the West. Vol. 3: Renaissance and Enlightenment Paradoxes*, ed. Natalie Zamon Davis and Arlette Farge (Cambridge: Belknap Press of Harvard University Press, 1993), 395–419; Catherine Gordon-Seifert, 'Precious Eroticism and Hidden Morality: Salon Culture and the Mid-Seventeenth-Century French Air', in Bonnie Blackburn and Laurie Stras (eds.), *Eroticism in Early Modern Music* (Farnham and Burlington: Ashgate, 2015), 227–60; and Patricia Howard, 'Quinault, Lully, and the Précieuses: Images of Women in Seventeenth-Century France', in Susan Cook and Judy S. Tsou, (eds.), *Cecilia Reclaimed: Feminist Perspectives on Gender and Music* (Urbana: University of Illinois Press, 1994), 70–89.

41 Catherine Cessac, *Elisabeth Jacquet de La Guerre: Une femme compositeur sous le règne de Louis XIV* (Arles: Actes Sud, 1995); and Cessac, 'Les jeux à l'honneur de la victoire d'Elisabeth Jacquet de La Guerre: premier opéra-ballet?' *Revue de Musicologie* 81/2 (1995), 235–47.

42 Wanda R. Griffiths, 'Jacquet de la Guerre's *Céphale et Procris*: Style and Drama', in Malcolm Cole and John Koegel (eds.), *Music in Performance and Society: Essays in Honor of Roland Jackson* (Warren: Harmonie Park Press, 1997), 251–68.

43 Robert M. Isherwood, *Music in the Service of the King: France in the Seventeenth Century* (Ithaca: Cornell University Press, 1973), 320–32; and Georgia Cowart, *The Triumph of Pleasure: Louis XIV and the Politics of Spectacle* (Chicago and London: The University of Chicago Press, 2008).

44 Julia Prest, *Theatre under Louis XIV: Cross-Casting and the Performance of Gender in Drama, Ballet and Opera* (New York: Palgrave MacMillan, 2006), 141–8.

45 Pierre Perrin, 'Lettre à l'Archevesque de Turin' in *Œuvres de poésie* (Paris: Estienne Loyson, 1661), 287. Quoted in Henry Prunières, *L'Opéra italien en France avant Lulli* (Paris: Librairie ancienne Honoré Champion, 1913), 267.

46 Sarah Nancy, *La voix féminine et le plaisir de l'écoute en France aux XVIIe et XVIIIe siècles* (Paris: Classiques Garnier, 2012), 97–143.

47 Julie Anne Sadie, '*Musiciennes* of the Ancien Régime', in Jane M. Bowers and Judith Tick (eds.), *Women Making Music: The Western Art Tradition 1150–1950* (Urbana: University of Illinois Press, 1987), 191–223; Lisandro Abadie, 'Anne de La Barre (1628–1688): Biographie d'une chanteuse de cour', *Revue de Musicologie* 94/1 (2008), 5–44; and Catherine Massip, *La vie des musiciens de Paris au temps de Mazarin (1643–1661): Essai d'étude sociale* (Paris: Picard 1976).

48 Abadie, 'Anne de La Barre', 21–4.

49 See Thomas Leconte, 'La Musique de la Chambre du roi au temps de Marin Marais', in Benoît Dratwicki (ed.), *Marin Marais: violiste à l'Opéra* (Centre de Musique Baroque de Versailles: Établissement public du musée et du domaine national de Versailles, 2006), 73–84: 81.

50 Jean-Laurent Le Cerf de la Viéville, *Comparaison de la musique italienne et de la musique françoise* (Brussels: François Foppens, 1704–1706; rpt. Geneva: Minkoff, 1972), part 1, 11–12.

51 '... le plus parfait modéle pour la déclamation, qui ait apparu sur le Théâtre; ... Quoiqu'elle fut d'une taille médiocre, fort brune, & d'une figure très-commune hors du Théâtre, aux yeux près, qu'elle avoit grands; pleins de feu & capables d'exprimer toutes les passions, elle effaçoit toutes les plus belles Actrices & les mieux faites quand elle étoit au Théâtre...' Évrard Titon du Tillet, *Suite du Parnasse françois, jusqu'en 1743. Et de quelques autres Piéces qui ont rapport à ce Monument* (Paris: J. B. Coignard fils, 1743), 790–1.

52 François Raguenet, *Paralele des Italiens et des François, en ce qui regarde la musique et les opéra* (Paris: Jean Moreau, 1702; rpt. Geneva, Minkoff), 97.

53 François Raguenet, *A Comparison between the French and Italian Musick and Operas. Translated from the French; With some Remarks; To which is added A Critical Discourse upon Opera's in England, and a Means proposed for their Improvement* (London: William Lewis, 1709), 45–6.

54 *La musique du diable ou le Mercure Galant dévalisé* (Paris: Robert le Turc, 1711). See Ilias Chrissochoidis, 'La Musique du Diable (1711): An Obscure Specimen of Fantastic Literature Throws Light on the Elusive Opera Diva Marie-Louise Desmatins (fl. 1682–1708)', *Society for Eighteenth-Century Music Newsletter* 11 (2007), 7–9.

55 Quoted and translated in Chrissochoidis, 'La Musique du Diable', 8.

56 François Couperin explicitly refers to Fanchon Moreau in the rondeau 'La tendre Fanchon' from the Cinquième Ordre of the *Pièces de clavecin*, and 'La femme entre deux draps' (the woman between two sheets; canon for three voices).

57 François and Claude Parfaict, *Dictionnaire des théâtres de Paris, contenant toutes les piéces qui ont été représentées jusqu'à présent sur les différens Théâtres François, & sur celui de l'Académie Royale de musique*, 7 vols. (Paris: Lambert, 1756; rpt. Geneva: Slatkine, 1967), vol. 3, 351.

58 Catherine Kintzler, *Poétique de l'opéra français de Corneille à Rousseau*, 2nd edn. (Paris: Minerve, 2005).

59 Nancy, *La voix féminine*, 217–60.

60 Reinhard Strohm, 'Italian Operisti North of the Alps' in *The Eighteenth-Century Diaspora of Italian Musicians*, ed. Reinhard Strohm (Turnhout: Brepols, 2001), 1–59.

61 Janet K. Page, 'Sirens on the Danube: Giulia Masotti and Women Singers at the Imperial Court', *JSCM* 17/1 (2011), http://sscm-jscm.org/jscm-issues/

volume-17-no-1/sirens-on-the-danube-giulia-masotti-and-women-singers-at-the-imperial-court/.

62　The Bodleian Library in Oxford houses the only known copy of Cavalli's *Erismena*. On this acquisition made in 2008, see David Stuart and Greg Skidmore, 'Cavalli's *Erismena*', *EM* 38/3 (2010), 482–3. Michael Burden edited the score and libretto of the English version in the critical edition of the work, *L'Erismena: dramma per musica (Venice, 1655/56): With Scores of the Original Italian Version and a Contemporary English Version*, ed. Beth L. Glixon, Nicola Badolato, Jonathan E. Glixon, and Michael Burden (Kassel: Bärenreiter, [2018]).

63　See William John Lawrence, 'The French Opera in London: A Riddle of 1686', *The Times Literary Supplement* 1782 (28 March 1936), 268, and Andrew R. Walkling, *Masque and Opera in England, 1656–1688* (New York: Routledge, 2017), 303–4.

64　Lowell Lingren, 'Critiques of Opera in London, 1705–1719', in *Il melodramma italiano in Italia e in Germania nell'età barocca*, ed. Alberto Colzani (Como: AMIS, 1993), 145–65.

65　Suzanne Aspden, 'L'Epine, Francesca Margherita de (d. 1746), Singer' in *Oxford Dictionary of National Biography*, www.oxforddnb.com/view/article/8828.

66　Charles Burney, *A General History of Music: From the Earliest Ages to the Present Period*, ed. Frank Mercer, 2 vols. (London: G. T. Foulis, 1935), vol. 2, 670–1.

67　She was referred to as 'Greber's pegg.' Her name L'Epine means *thorn* in French.

68　In 1704, L'Epine's rivalry with the first English prima donna, the soprano Catherine Tofts, reached its peak when a servant of the latter threw oranges at L'Epine during a performance. The underpinnings of this rivalry were politically motivated: in 1703–1704, subscription concerts organised by Tory grandees featured Margherite de L'Epine, while the Whigs had their own 'Subscription Musick' featuring Tofts. See Olive Baldwin and Thelma Wilson, 'The Subscription Musick of 1703–04', *MT* 153/1921 (2012), 29–44.

8 | Dance and Ballet

REBECCA HARRIS-WARRICK

Dance and opera had a much closer relationship in the seventeenth century than most histories of opera convey. It is well known that for the French dance was a fundamental part of the work, integrated into every act, but even across the rest of Europe audiences almost always watched dancing as part of an evening spent at the opera. What audiences saw varied considerably according to genre, time, and place; even in important operatic centres much remains to be learned about the intersections of opera and dance. Nowhere is it possible to fully perceive how dance functioned across an entire work, but there are a surprising number of surviving choreographies for individual dances, all from either the beginning or the end of the century. Moreover, enough accounts of dancing exist, some of them in libretti, to show that both action dances and dancing based on abstract floor patterns co-existed throughout the period. By the end of the century the technique of dance was expressed via terminology in French – a vocabulary still used in classical ballet – but local traditions helped define national and even regional styles that impacted operatic practices.

Pre-Operatic Practices in Italy

Early court operas absorbed practices from the *intermedio* tradition, which included dance. In fact, several of the genres of court entertainments, such as *ballo*, *balletto*, *mascherata*, or *festa*, either allude to or imply dancing in their very names. The particularly well-documented festivities for the wedding of Ferdinando de' Medici and Christine of Lorraine in Florence in 1589 were far from the only instances of interspersing *intermedi* between the acts of a play but were probably the most splendid – and exceptional, because most of the music survives.[1] The play in question, *La pellegrina* by Girolamo Bargagli, had six spectacularly staged *intermedi*, two of them embellished with dancing. The texts were written by several eminent poets, including Giovanni de' Bardi and Ottavio Rinuccini, and the music was composed primarily by Cristofano Malvezzi and Luca Marenzio, with additional contributions by Bardi, Giulio Caccini, Jacopo Peri, Antonio

Archilei, and Emilio de' Cavalieri, the latter of whom supervised the performance of the music. In the third *intermedio*, pastoral dances by nymphs and shepherds are interrupted by the arrival of a monster, who is vanquished by four expert dancing masters (one of them performing as Apollo). One eyewitness account reveals the mimetic nature of the movement:

In the meantime, the dancers approached the animal, jumped around this animal with great agility, fought with the same, finally pierced the same, so that it fell to the ground, twisting this way and that, and fell dead with a great clatter, back into the hole out of which it had emerged. Thereafter, the dancers performed yet another dance of joy, [and they] exited from the place [stage] again.[2]

The sixth *intermedio* had a much grander and more ceremonial character: its twenty-seven dancers, sixty singers, supernumeraries, and twenty-five instrumentalists brought the evening to a spectacular conclusion in a paean to the newly married couple. Remarkably, Cavalieri's choreography for the concluding dance of this *intermedio* survives; set to his own chorus 'O che nuovo miracolo', it is transmitted in the ninth partbook of Malvezzi's 1691 publication of the music, in lengthy instructions accompanied by two diagrams.[3]

The music alternates sections in duple and triple metre, switching between five-voice chorus, doubled by instruments, and trios for three sopranos (probably representing the three Graces); all of the sections were danced. Whereas ambiguities arise in reconstructing this choreography,[4] its general outlines can be discerned: of the twenty-seven dancers, seven (four women and three men) were featured; the floorplan positions the twenty group dancers in an upstage arc, with the soloists either in the centre of the arc or downstage in a smaller arc; much of the choreography alternates figures for the men and for the women, with all seven sometimes dancing simultaneously; the remaining twenty dancers join in toward the end. This dance is based on abstract and symmetrical figures, in distinction to the mimed dancing of the fourth *intermedio*.

The steps prescribed by Cavalieri (*seguito scorso, continenze, capriole, tempi di gagliarda*, etc.) are familiar from the large dance treatises by Fabritio Caroso – *Il ballarino* (Venice, 1581) and *Nobiltà di dame* (Venice, 1600) – and Cesare Negri, whose *Le Gratie d'amore* (Milan, 1602) was revised as *Nuove inventioni di balli* in 1604. Moreover, Negri's treatise provides two additional choreographies from *intermedi*, ones performed in Milan during the late sixteenth century. The 'Brando per otto', which followed the last act of the eclogue in five acts, *Arminia* by

Giambattista Visconte (Milan, 1599), was attributed to four nymphs and four shepherds who danced across seven musical sections. In Negri's treatise, one of these is labelled a 'gagliarda'; others appear to include a pavana, saltarello, and alemana.[5]

Court Opera in Early Seventeenth-Century Italy

The works we now identify as the earliest operas, starting with *La Dafne* (Rinuccini, Peri; Florence, 1598), were created by many of the same people who had contributed to *intermedi* and other musical entertainments, most notably Rinuccini, Bardi, Peri, Caccini, and Cavalieri. These early works incorporated similar dance practices, in which dancing was strongly associated with pastoral characters and featured in choruses, especially, but not exclusively, those that ended the entire opera. Even Cavalieri's *Rappresentatione di Anima, et di Corpo* incorporated dancing, notwithstanding its allegorical subject and performance in a church (the Chiesa Nuova in Rome, February 1600). Moreover, in the preface to his published score, Cavalieri even underlines the contributions dances make to this and similar works, noting that they 'truly enliven these plays, as, in fact, has been judged by all the spectators'.[6] Cavalieri distinguishes between dances that are 'unusual' ('fuori dell'uso commune'), such as battles, and 'formal dance' ('ballo formato'), by which he means ones organised around abstract patterns. He recommends that the concluding dance be 'sung and also played by the same persons who dance, with good occasion, holding the instruments in their hands'.[7] This general advice is, however, modified later in the introduction, where instructions given for the strophic chorus, 'Chiostri altissimi, e stellati', that concludes the work imply two groups of dancers: mixed couples who perform during the sung portions and four *maestri* (that is, highly trained male dancers) who dance the ritornelli in a more technically advanced manner, 'without singing'. For both sections, the description names some of the steps to be performed:

The dancing begins with a *riverenza* and *continenza*, and then other slow steps follow, the couples interweaving and passing with dignity. The ritornellos are performed by four people who dance exquisitely with leaps and capers, and without singing And so in all the strophes [of the chorus] always vary the dance, and the four masters who are dancing should vary them, one time doing a gagliard, then a canario, and then a corrente, which go very well with the ritornellos. If the stage is not large enough for four dancers, two at least should be used. The dance should be choreographed by the very best master that can be found.[8]

As the separate identification of the *maestri* suggests, the singing chorus and the dancers associated with it were not necessarily the same people; contemporary evidence suggests the co-existence of both singing-dancers and dancing-dancers. Peri's *Euridice*, performed in Florence later the same year, also ends with a strophic chorus, labelled a *ballo*, which shows the same alternation: the entire chorus sings and dances during the strophes, while the ritornelli are 'danced by two soloists from the chorus'. Both Cavalieri's and Peri's concluding complexes end with a choral strophe that must have been danced as well as sung.[9]

The score to Monteverdi's *Orfeo* (Mantua, 1607) refers to one piece as a *balletto* – the chorus 'Lasciati i monti' in Act I. Like several dances from earlier works, this one takes place within a pastoral realm and, structurally, consists of a strophic chorus with an instrumental ritornello; its first verse and ritornello are repeated later in the act, just before 'Vieni Imeneo'. The other clear dance comes at the end of the opera, where a strophic chorus is followed by a moresca – a dance that some recent commentators have interpreted as a remnant from the ending of the opera found in the libretto, where Orfeo is killed by Bacchantes. At least one other piece seems a likely candidate for dancing – Orfeo's strophic song, 'Vi ricorda o boschi ombrosi' in Act II; both the song and its ritornello feature an alternating hemiola pattern found in other triple-metre Italian dances from the period.

Francesca Caccini's *La liberazione di Ruggiero, dall'isola d'Alcina* (Ferdinando Saracinelli, Florence, 1625), called a *balletto* in its sources, uses dancing by the sorceress Alcina's female followers as an enhancement to the seductive attractions in Alcina's enchanted gardens; this is but one instance among many in operatic history of dancing being used as seduction by women of questionable motives. Toward the end of the work, Alcina's followers join with Ruggiero's knights to celebrate his liberation; the whole is followed by a horse ballet.[10]

Opera in Venice

When opera became a public spectacle in Venice in 1637, dance remained one of its components. Ground-breaking work by Irene Alm has allowed us to see how extensive dance was in Venetian opera, and how, as the anonymous librettist for Monteverdi's *Le nozze d'Enea con Lavinia* (Venice, 1641) put it, the *balli* should be 'derived in some way from the plot'.[11] One key figure, dancer and choreographer Giovan Battista Balbi (fl. 1636–1654), was involved from the start, and had already been mentioned in the libretto for the first opera produced there, *L'Andromeda* (Benedetto Ferrari, Francesco Manelli; 1637). Balbi's *Le nozze di Teti e di Peleo* (1639), with music composed by Francesco Cavalli, has a particularly large number of dances – some vocal, some instrumental – across all three of its acts. In one lengthy scene (whose music is extant), 'Bacco and Sileno praise the virtues of wine, and the choruses [fauns and Bacchantes] dance to their melody.'[12] Although subsequent operas by Cavalli and his contemporaries did not approach this degree of sumptuousness, there are indications in more libretti than not that dance was part of the performance: Alm has documented the presence of *balli* in 297 of the 346 operas performed in Venice up until 1700.[13]

Whereas the strength of the pastoral tradition meant that nymphs, dryads, shepherds, and fauns remained numerous among the dancing populations, dancers also embodied animals, soldiers, sailors, supernatural beings (demons, spirits, phantoms), comic pages or servants, gardeners, hunters, mad people, and exotic foreigners (Turks, Moors, Spaniards, etc.; see Figure 8.1). In *La Calisto* (Giovanni Faustini, Cavalli; Venice, 1651),

Figure 8.1 Conclusion of the *ballo* for the Turks, with dancing bears, as it was performed in Paris in 1645. Engraving by Valerio Spada, in *Balletti d'invenzione nella Finta Pazza di Giovanbattista Balbi* (n.p., c. 1658).
By permission of Bibliothèque Nationale de France, Paris

four bears come out of the forest and dance at the end of Act I (foreshadowing the heroine's transformation into the Great Bear constellation at the end of the opera), and at the end of Act II dancing nymphs with arrows come to the aid of Linfea, who is the object of unwanted sexual attentions by a young satyr and his dancing followers.[14]

No choreographies survive for any Venetian opera, although occasionally libretti provide tantalising glimpses of the dancers' movements. As with the *intermedi*, some of the dance pieces seem abstract, whereas others mime actions: for instance, a battle or an emotional state such as madness. In *Mutio Scevola* (Nicolò Minato, Cavalli; Venice, 1665) there is a *ballo* for eight statues who leave their pedestals surrounding a statue of Janus, dance while throwing flames from their mouths, then return to their places. Other stage descriptions call for the dancers to leap and spin, whereas calmer group dances might move in graceful curves, as in the following description from Adriano Morselli's libretto to *Falaride tiranno d'Agrigento* (Giovanni Battista Bassini, 1684): 'The *ballo* circles through the porticos ... . The dance circles around and they exit from the porticos.'[15] With the exception of Balbi, choreographers are rarely named in libretti and individual dancers not at all. As for the music, whereas a great deal more dance music survives than has generally been recognised, a significant proportion of it has been lost. Its absence from many of the Venetian opera scores has often been taken to mean that the composer of the vocal music did not write the dances, but Alm argues that the evidence does not support drawing such a categorical conclusion, especially in the face of scores such as *Le nozze di Teti e di Peleo* (Orazio Persiani, Cavalli; Venice, 1638/9), where the dance music is so interwoven into its surroundings that it must be by Cavalli. She argues further that practices from later periods or from other cities should not be read backwards into mid-seventeenth-century Venice.[16]

Dances could be set either to instrumental pieces or to vocal ones, most usually choruses. The earlier practice of choruses whose members both sang and danced appears to have given way to greater separation in the functions of the performers; it appears that in Venice, perhaps even as early as *Le nozze di Teti e di Peleo*, the singers and dancers were different people. Whereas some solo songs or duets may also have been danced, there are clear instances, such as in Cavalli's *Gli amori d'Apollo e di Dafne* (Francesco Busenello, Venice, 1640) that a song by Dafne (not danced) alternates with a chorus (danced; Act I scene 4); even when the bodies were different, the association between dancers and a singing chorus remained. The instrumental dances tended to be sectional, in two or three repeatable strains, often with irregular phrase lengths. As the century progressed, the proportion of dances in binary construction increased. Instrumental dances, whatever their form, rarely have generic designations, notwithstanding the few identified as 'giga', 'corrente', 'ciaccona', and the like. More often they are identified by the characters dancing, such as the 'Ballo d'Eunichi' in the 1663 Venetian performances from Antonio Cesti's *La Dori* (Giovanni Filippo Apolloni; Innsbruck, Hof-Saales, 1657) or the 'Ballo de Paggi e de Pazzi' from Carlo Pallavicino's *Diocletiano* (Matteo Noris, 1675) – titles suggesting that characterisation was key to the movement style.

As Venetian opera became more and more an art of solo singing, the number of choruses declined. Dancing, however, retained its place inside the opera – largely via instrumentally accompanied scenes at the ends of Acts I and II; these were connected to the plot, however loosely, although the connections grew more tenuous as time went on. Celebratory choruses that included dancing, generally found at the ends of acts or of the entire work, never entirely disappeared.

Opera in France

When Italian opera made intermittent appearances at the French court, under the patronage and encouragement of the Italian-born prime minister, Cardinal Mazarin, and the regent, Anne of Austria (widow of Louis XIII), the operas adhered to mid-century Venetian practices. Balbi drew upon his own experiences in Venice and Florence in choreographing the dances for two of the operas in Paris: in 1645, Francesco Sacrati's *La finta pazza* (Giulio Strozzi, Venice, 1641) and in 1647 the creation of Luigi Rossi's *Orfeo* at the Palais-Royal, both of which integrated the dances. Balbi later published eighteen designs for *La finta pazza* (see Figure 7.1). A vivid description of Balbi's ballets in Paris was written by Olivier Lefèvre d'Ormesson, who attended a performance of *La Découverte d'Achille par les Grecs* (1645) that contained three ballets: one for monkeys, another for ostriches and dwarves, and one for parrots and Ethiopians.[17]

In Rossi's *Orfeo*, on the other hand, the dances are mostly pastoral; in Act II, for example, a joyous *sarabanda* danced by twenty-four dryads sets up the shocking reversal when Euridice is bitten by a viper. But by the time Mazarin induced Cavalli to come to Paris in order to celebrate with due pomp the marriage of Louis XIV to Spanish Princess Maria Theresa, the composition of the dance music had been put into the hands of a local – the young Jean-Baptiste Lully – who, by birth, was Italian. Cavalli's first opera for Paris, the 1660 *Xerse* (Minato, Venice, 1654), modified one of his Venetian works to suit French tastes: it was still sung in Italian by Italian singers but acquired a prologue honouring the union of the two countries; three acts became five; and six ballets, performed by French dancers, were inserted between the acts. *Xerse* was fully professional as to both the dancers and the singers, but *Ercole amante* (Francesco Buti, Paris, 1662), Cavalli's new commission for the wedding celebrations, still carried vestiges of the *ballet de cour*, in that members of the royal family and the upper aristocracy danced alongside professional dancing masters in the purely instrumental ballets that ended the prologue and each of the five acts. The king himself, who was an excellent and enthusiastic dancer, performed four roles (the House of France, Pluton, Mars, and the Sun), his bride one (the House of Austria).

Lully absorbed much from Cavalli, but when, in 1672, he opened the Académie Royale de Musique (the Paris Opéra), he chose to integrate dancing inside each of the five acts of every opera, not to relegate it to between them. In his new model, the plot was carried primarily by the singers, but the divertissements were dramatically and thematically connected to their surroundings, and the dancing was interleaved with vocal music.[18] This integration has more structural relationship to the comedy-ballets Lully had earlier developed with Molière – in which danced divertissements are part of the plot – than it does to his court ballets, which were constructed around a series of instrumental entrées interspersed with occasional vocal numbers.

During his lifetime Lully had a monopoly on composing opera in France; his creative team included librettist Philippe Quinault (1635–1688) and dancer Pierre Beauchamps (1631–1705), who had served as choreographer for the king's *ballets de cour*. Quinault was responsible for structuring the divertissements into the opera, although Lully must have been the one to design their inner workings. Whereas in dialogue scenes Lully's musical language is restrained, featuring a kind of heightened speech that operates in something akin to real time, divertissements call attention to their own musicality: 'Chantons, chantons, faisons entendre / Nos chansons jusques dans les cieux' ('Let us sing, let us make our songs be heard all the way up to the heavens'), sings Apollon toward the end of *Alceste* (Quinault, Paris, 1674). Such an invitation allowed for long choruses, strophic songs, and instrumental dances using the full resources of the orchestra; time relaxes and music takes precedence over words. In order to conform to French principles of theatrical verisimilitude, the character types who appear in divertissements are either defined as beings who by their very nature express themselves through dance and song – Arcadian nymphs and shepherds, demons in the Underworld, and so forth – or, if they are ordinary mortals, find themselves in situations, such as wedding celebrations, that make dancing plausible.

Lully's divertissements serve to expand the world of the opera beyond the main characters to the societies that surround them. One of their functions is to uncover power relationships among individual characters: a hero such as Renaud in *Armide* (Quinault, Paris, 1686), who is acted upon during divertissements but does not control a single one of them, is revealed as weak. Often the anonymous characters in divertissements represent words or actions that the principals cannot or will not express for themselves: Cadmus arranges a divertissement as a subterfuge for communicating with the captive Hermione; the goddess Cybèle cannot bring herself to admit her love to Atys, so she sends dreams. Such reciprocities between the main characters and the worlds they inhabit are a fundamental feature of the operatic style that Quinault and Lully created together.

The members of the dance troupe, like all their colleagues, were salaried employees of the Académie Royale de Musique. Their numbers are not known for Lully's era, but in 1704 there were eleven men and ten women. As a practical matter, the functions of singing and dancing were supplied by different people; libretti show that a chorus consisted of group characters, 'some of whom sing, the others of whom dance'. In other words, every role inside a divertissement is assigned two sets of bodies, although the number of singers and dancers need not be equal. The members of the singing chorus generally stood around the perimeter of the stage, leaving the downstage area free for the solo singers and the dancers, who entered and left the space as appropriate. Quinault's libretti scrupulously distinguish between male and female roles (e.g., Bergers and Bergères), even though all of the dancers were men until 1681. Even after four women joined the troupe, starting with the ballet *Le Triomphe de l'Amour* (Isaac de Benserade, Quinault; Saint-Germain-en-Laye, 1681), men still danced some female roles. Their training prepared them to dance in many different styles, and their versatility can be seen in the role assignments shown in libretti; ballet remained a male-dominated art until well into the eighteenth century. Nonetheless, it is clear that the availability of women to dance on the stage changed the character of the divertissements Lully and Quinault wrote into their operas.

The internal structures of Lully's divertissements are enormously varied, but almost all of them reveal close connections between instrumental and vocal music.[19] Often a chorus or an instrumental march brings all the group characters on stage, to be followed by dance-songs, other choruses, and instrumental dances – almost never more than two of the latter in a row. Generic dance types – bourrée, menuet, sarabande, and so on – account for approximately one-third of the dances in any opera. Many more are called 'entrées' or 'airs' followed by the name of the characters performing them, a musical choice in line with contemporary theorists such as Michel de Pure, who wrote that 'the first and most essential beauty of an air de ballet is appropriateness – that is, the correct relation that the air must have to the thing represented'.[20] Dance pieces are either musically related to adjacent vocal pieces (this accounts for approximately two-thirds of them) or, if they are musically independent, are in close proximity to vocal pieces to which they have dramatic connections. Strophic dance-songs, which can be for solo voice, duet, or chorus, are usually performed in the following order: instrumental dance, the first strophe of the song, a repeat of the instrumental dance, and the second strophe. This means that the audience receives the visual sign before the texted one, since the norm was for the dancers to stop moving during the singing, even when the vocal music was identical to their dance. Choruses could sometimes be danced, if their texts invited movement or if they occurred at the end of a celebratory divertissement, but not solo songs, no matter how danceable the music. Thanks to the integrated structures that Lully and Quinault designed, dance in his operas is presented not as an interruption or as a parenthesis within the action, but as part of a natural continuum that incorporates multiple modes of expression.

During the 1680s three systems of dance notation came into existence in France.[21] The best known among them was developed by Beauchamps but exploited commercially by Raoul Anger Feuillet, author of the 106-page book *Chorégraphie* and a choreographer in his own right. Although *Chorégraphie* was not published until 1700, the sophistication of the system and the enormous movement vocabulary it records demonstrate that this style of dance had existed for many years. Moreover, a number of basic stylistic principles – not to mention dance terms – have been handed down over the generations as part of the technique of classical ballet. Beauchamps-Feuillet notation preserves over 350 individual choreographies, among which may be found forty-seven that originated on the stage of the Paris Opéra. Figure 8.2, for example, representing a choreography by Guillaume Pécour for two *divinités infernales*, can be dated to the revival of *Persée* in 1710. All of this group post-dates Lully's lifetime and was choreographed between 1690 and 1713 by Pécour,

Figure 8.2 Guillaume Pécour, 'Entrée for two men danced by Messieurs Marcel and Gaudrau in [Lully's] *Persée*'. Michel Gaudrau, *Nouveau recüeil de dance de bal et celle de ballet* (Paris: Chez le Sieur Gaudrau et Pierre Ribou, [1715]), 91.
By permission of Bibliothèque Nationale de France, Paris

Beauchamps's successor as ballet master at the Académie Royale de Musique.[22] These choreographies, all of them for one or two dancers, show that the dancing space is oriented around an invisible axis running from front to back through the centre of the stage; when one couple dances, whether same sex or mixed, the two dancers do the same steps and patterns in mirror image. Even in group dances, the patterns are symmetrical (see Figure 8.3).

After Lully's death in 1687, Beauchamps retired, yet the templates they had established for constructing divertissements remained in place, even in the new genre of opera-ballet, which was introduced in 1697 by André Campra's *L'Europe galante*. The lean Lullian divertissement only gradually

Figure 8.3 Jean Berain, a symmetrical grouping of six couples dancing with a soloist. Ink drawing, s.d., c. 1700.
By permission of Stockholm, Nationalmuseum (Photo: Cecilia Heisser, Nationalmuseum)

put on more weight through the addition of more instrumental dances and elaborate ariettes. The introduction of contemporary Italian themes onto the stage of the Opéra, which reached its apogee with Campra's *Les Fêtes vénitiennes* (1710), expanded the range of dancing roles and allowed the dancing body to become a site for humour, via characters borrowed from the *commedia dell'arte*. But the dance styles, however comic, remained French; it was not until 1739 when the first Italian dancers made guest appearances at the Opéra that the more athletic Italian dance style began to make serious inroads in Paris.

Operatic Dancing outside of Italy and France

Opera houses outside of Italy and France often borrowed musical and choreographic practices from one or both of the dominant styles, either by importing works, composers, or performers, or through imitation, generally tempered by local practices. Opera in Italian had the greater geographic spread but did not necessarily include Italian dance practices. In fact, France exported dancers and choreographers, and, to a lesser degree, composers of dance music; it was not rare for French-style divertissements to be taken up into diverse types of opera.

German-Speaking Areas

The court operas performed upon occasion before the advent of public opera houses tended to adopt Italian models, although the same German courts might perform *ballets de cour* and not infrequently employ French dancing masters. Jacques Rodier and his son François choreographed both ballets and operas at the court in Munich; another major French dancer, Jean-Pierre Dubreuil, worked there later. The most sumptuous court opera, however – Cesti's *Il pomo d'oro* (Vienna, 1668), commissioned for the wedding of Leopold I and Margherita of Spain – not only had an Italian librettist and Italian composer, it had an Italian choreographer, Santo Ventura; only the stylistically mixed ballet music was local, composed by Johann Heinrich Schmelzer, who between 1665 and 1680 supplied ballet music for most of the theatrical works at the Habsburg court. A ballet connected to the plot ended each of the five acts.

The public opera house that opened in Hamburg in 1678 presented most of its operas in German, whether they were original to Hamburg or translations, although Lully's *Acis et Galatée* was performed in French in 1689. (It was performed again in 1695, this time in German; six operas by Agostino Steffani were presented in German translation between 1696 and 1699). Johann Georg Conradi's *Die schöne und getreue Ariadne* (1691) adopted both Venetian and French dance practices: the end of the first act unexpectedly ushers ribald scissor-sharpeners onto the stage, whereas Act III features an integrated divertissement for the singing and dancing followers of Bacchus, and the opera ends with a passacaille, both instrumental and vocal, followed by a celebratory chorus. Subsequent operas performed in Hamburg by composers such as Reinhard Keiser, the young Handel, and Telemann reveal a similar mixture of styles that leans towards Italy in the vocal music and France for the overture and the dances, although the stylistic boundaries are porous.

Another measure of the penetration of French dance styles into Germany is the large number of books published there on the topic – no fewer than nine between 1703 and 1717.[23] Most of these concentrate on ballroom dancing, but *Die neueste Art zur galanten und theatralischen Tantz-Kunst* (Frankfurt, 1711), written by the French dancer Louis Bonin, who had moved to Iena after a career at the Paris Opéra, focuses primarily on theatrical styles.

The Low Countries

Operas performed were initially French, riding in part on the wave of émigré Huguenot musicians and printers from France. The first two operas performed in Antwerp, both in 1682, were Lully's *Bellérophon* and *Proserpine*. The company was, however, very small and included only four dancers.[24] In The Hague the first opera performed was Lully's *Armide* (1701); *Atys*, *Thésée*, and Campra's *L'Europe galante* were next in line. One of this troupe's most highly remunerated employees was Pierre de La Montagne, who was imported from Paris. His duties required him to train the dancers, to choreograph, and to dance; the operatic divertissements he oversaw appear to have been performed in full.[25]

Sweden

Despite a few scattered attempts to import Italian opera, it was not until 1699 – when the Francophile Swedish architect Nicodemus Tessin the

Younger promoted the formation of a troupe of French actors to come to Stockholm – that dancing in a semi-operatic context can be documented. At first the troupe, headed by Claude de Rosidor and including twelve actors, four singers, and four dancers, mostly performed comedy-ballets by Molière, plus a few operatic extracts by Lully. In 1701, however, the troupe mounted what has come to be called the *Ballet de Narva*, a 'Ballet meslé de chants héroïques', with a text in French by Charles Louis Sevigny, in honour of King Charles XII's victory at Narva over the Russians. The vocal music was composed by Anders von Düben the Younger, but the dance pieces and the final chorus were borrowed from the pastorale *Le Désespoir de Tircis* by Jean Desfontaines, with two additional dances from Lully's *Cadmus et Hermione*.[26] By 1706 all of the members of Rosidor's troupe had departed, and opera did not become firmly established in Sweden until well into the eighteenth century.

Spain

The plays written by Lope de Vega for public theatres and, later, by Pedro Calderón de la Barca for the court, were punctuated by music and dance, although the instrumental music rarely survives. Two operas were written in 1660–1661 for the wedding of the Infanta María Teresa with Louis XIV of France: *La púrpura de la rosa* (text by Calderón, music by Juan Hidalgo, lost) and *Celos aun del aire matan* (text by Calderón, music by Hidalgo).[27] The stage directions in the latter do not explicitly call for dancing, but the *loa* (prologue) that probably existed at the time could well have incorporated dances.[28] Although no other fully sung operas were composed in Spain during the seventeenth century, zarzuelas and other theatrical genres continued to incorporate dances such as jácaras, seguidillas, zarabandas, and chaconas.

England

When English theatres reopened after Charles II returned from exile in France, the musical entertainments put on between the acts of plays included dancing among the songs and acrobatics. Sometimes dances were integrated into the plot – in a scene of celebration, for instance – but most were individual set pieces that had little or no connection with their surroundings. Intermittent visits to London by dancers from the Paris Opéra kept English audiences aware of French styles.[29] The earliest operas – for example, John Blow's *Venus and Adonis* (c. 1683) and Purcell's *Dido and Aeneas* (1689) – followed Lullian models in incorporating dances into the storyline; *Dido and Aeneas*, short as it is, calls for no fewer than ten. All the dances appear in scenes involving the chorus, such as 'Fear no danger to ensue' in Act I, where the libretto says 'Dance this Cho.', or the Sailors' Dance at the start of Act III, which precedes a musically related song by a solo sailor that the chorus joins. The duet in Act I sung by Belinda and the Second Woman, 'Fear no danger to ensue', may also have been performed instrumentally, in alternation with the chorus, by simply leaving out the choral parts: not only is it in binary form but it adopts the rhythm of a seventeenth-century French minuet step ♩ ♩ 𝅗𝅥 │ 𝅗𝅥 ♩ │.[30] The opera closed with a dance by Cupids mourning the death of Dido, although the music for it, as for some of the other dances, does not survive.

Purcell's four semi-operas (1690–1695), performed publicly by the Theatre Royal company, also drew upon conventions established by Lully in constructing the masques performed between acts; the Frost Scene in *King Arthur*, for example, uses the same musical figure to evoke shivering as do Lully's Trembleurs in *Isis*. On the other hand, some of the dances Purcell inserted into his scores – such as country dances and hornpipes – are purely English. The semi-operas were choreographed by Jo. Priest (Josias or Joseph, who may have been the same person[31]), but none of his choreographies survive. Handel's first opera in London, *Rinaldo* (1710), has a single danced scene, and dancing is found intermittently in other operas; in some later works, such as *Alcina* (1725), Handel took advantage of the visiting French dancers to build in elaborate ballet sequences.[32] That the dancing technique and style were French can be seen by the frequent performances by French and English dancers together, the two almost simultaneous translations into English of Feuillet's *Chorégraphie* (by Siris and Weaver, both in 1706), the numerous choreographies in Feuillet notation published in England, and the French dance types that appeared on the English stage (minuets, rigaudons, sarabandes, chaconnes, etc.).[33]

* * *

By the end of the seventeenth century, French dance practices had penetrated even into Italy, albeit unevenly. Some Venetian operas dating from the 1680s and 1690s incorporate minuets, bourrées (borea), or rigaudons, and composers such as Carlo Francesco Pollarolo sometimes structured divertissements in a French manner, with instrumental dances related to and interwoven with solo songs and choruses.[34] However, these tendencies were in the minority; more and more the danced sequences were independent, done as *intermezzi* after Acts I and II of a three-act opera; by the time Metastasian *opera seria* arrived, the transformation was complete.[35] But even as French and Italian approaches to the relationship between dance and opera grew farther apart, the technical bases of dancing grew closer. The dearth of choreographic sources from the middle of the seventeenth century in both Italy and France makes tracking actual dance practices almost impossible, but it is clear that by the early eighteenth century French and Italian dancing shared a common technique whose lingua franca was French.

One important testimonial is Gregorio Lambranzi's *Neue und curieuse theatralische Tantz-Schul* (Nuremberg, 1716), an illustrated book of theatrical – mostly comic – dances in the Italian style, which uses French names when it mentions steps, as can be seen in Figure 8.4: 'Scapino dances alone, executing, among other *pas*, his *ballonnés*, *chassés*, *contretemps*, and

Figure 8.4 Gregorio Lambranzi, *Neue und curieuse theatralische Tantz-Schul* (Nuremberg, 1716), book I, plate 34. Private collection

[pas de] rigaudon, with his arms twisted from side to side. The air is played at will.' Yet Lambranzi's book also underscores differences between the two styles that transcended the steps: Italian athleticism that contrasted with French refinement, the greater latitude given to comic dancing and to mime in Italy, and greater allowance in Italy for choreographic improvisation.[36] When Italian dancers first appeared at the Paris Opéra in 1739, they created a sensation; their appearances were but one step in a process of greater hybridisation of the two styles.

Notes

1 Daniel P. Walker (ed.), *Musique des Intermèdes de 'La Pellegrina'* (Paris: Éditions du Centre National de la Recherche Scientifique, 1963).

2 Barthold von Gadenstedt, cited in Nina Treadwell, *Music and Wonder at the Medici Court: The 1589 Interludes for La pellegrina* (Bloomington: Indiana University Press, 2008), 107. According to Treadwell, 105, the music for this dance appears to be lost.

3 Reproduced in Walker, *Musique des intermèdes*, lvi–lviii. The tune for this chorus became something of a 'standard' under the name 'Ballo del gran duca', and was used as the basis for variation sets by harpsichordists and lutenists. The same tune was chosen by Cesare Caroso for the ballroom dance 'Laura suave.'

4 See Jennifer Nevile, 'Cavalieri's Theatrical Ballo "O che nuovo miracolo": A Reconstruction', *Dance Chronicle* 21/3 (1998), 353–88: 361–86; and Treadwell, *Music and Wonder*, 171–3.

5 See Yvonne Kendall, 'Theatre, Dance and Music in Late Cinquecento Milan', *EM* 32/1 (2004), 74–95; 88. For another theatrical choreography from the period, see Kathryn Bosi, 'Leone Tolosa and "Martel d'amore": A "balletto della duchessa" Discovered', *Recercare* 17 (2005): 5–70. This forty-five-minute *balletto* was danced in Ferrara in 1582 by eight court ladies dressed as nymphs and shepherds.

6 'A' lettori (To the readers)' in *Rappresentatione di Anima, e di Corpo (1600): Emilio de' Cavalieri*, ed. Murray C. Bradshaw (Middleton: American Institute of Musicology, 2007), 6–7. Bradshaw presents the original Italian and the translation on facing pages.

7 Cavalieri, 'A' lettori', in *Rappresentatione*, 6–7.

8 Ibid., 8–11. These named steps and examples of the dance-types can be found in the treatises of Caroso and Negri, mentioned on p. 133.

9 Ancient Greek writers such as Plato identify dances to both instrumental and choral accompaniment. Their writings were mined by seventeenth-century theorists such as Giovanni Battista Doni (*Trattato della musica scenica*, 1624,

in his *Lyra barberina* αμΦιχορδος [*amphichordos*], ed. Anton Francesco Gori, 2 vols. [Florence: Stamperia Imperiale, 1763, vol. 2; rpt. Bologna: Forni, 1974]) and the anonymous author of *Il corago* (c. 1630); see Irene Alm, 'Humanism and Theatrical Dance in Early Opera', *Musica Disciplina* 49 (1995), 79–93.

10 See Suzanne Cusick's reading of this gynocentric work in her *Francesca Caccini at the Medici Court* (Chicago and London: The University of Chicago Press, 2009), chs. 9 and 10.

11 This section is based upon the work of the late Irene Alm, in particular 'Winged Feet and Mute Eloquence: Dance in Seventeenth-Century Venetian Opera', *COJ* 15/3 (2003), 216–80, which represents a condensed version of her unpublished Ph.D. dissertation, 'Theatrical Dance in Venetian Opera' (University of California, Los Angeles, 1993). See also other writings of hers mentioned in the *COJ* article.

12 See the music for a pastoral dance sequence from this opera in Alm, 'Winged Feet', example 9, 266–8.

13 Alm, 'Winged Feet', 274. Monteverdi's *L'incoronazione di Poppea* is not among them: neither the libretto nor the score calls for dancing.

14 See Wendy Heller's interpretation of these two scenes in 'Dancing Desire on the Venetian Stage', *COJ* 15/3 (2003), 281–95: 290–5.

15 Alm, 'Winged Feet', 234.

16 Ibid., 225–6.

17 *Journal d'Olivier Lefèvre d'Ormesson*, Wednesday 27 December 1645, quoted in Henry Prunières, *Le Ballet de cour en France avant Benserade et Lully, suivi du ballet de 'La Délivrance de Renaud' de Pierre Guédron* (Paris, H. Laurens, 1914), 75–6.

18 This discussion of French operatic divertissements derives from my *Dance and Drama in French Baroque Opera: A History* (Cambridge: Cambridge University Press, 2016).

19 For several examples of Lully's divertissement architecture, see Harris-Warrick, *Dance and Drama*, 60–9.

20 Michel de Pure, *Idée des spectacles anciens et nouveaux* (Paris, 1668), 260, as cited in Harris-Warrick, *Dance and Drama*, 130.

21 On the development of dance notation, see Rebecca Harris-Warrick and Carol G. Marsh, *Musical Theatre at the Court of Louis XIV: Le Mariage de la Grosse Cathos* (Cambridge: Cambridge University Press, 1994), 82–92.

22 For a contextualisation of each of the operatic choreographies, see appendix 3 in Harris-Warrick, *Dance and Drama*, online under 'Resources.'

23 Stephanie Schroedter, 'The French Art of Dancing as Described in the German Dance Instruction Manuals of the Early 18th Century', in Stephanie Schroedter, Marie-Thérèse Mourey, and Giles Bennett (eds.), *Barocktanz im Zeichen französisch-deutschen Kulturtransfers* (Hildesheim: Olms, 2008), 412–72: 412–15.

24 Timothy De Paepe, 'French Opera in Print and on Stage in Antwerp: Three Generations of Antwerp Book Publishers and Their Opera Librettos (1682–1714)', *JSCM* 15/1 (2009), par. 2.7, https://sscm-jscm.org/v15/no1/depaepe.html.

25 Rebekah Ahrendt, 'A Huguenot Impresario in the Dutch Republic', in Michel Schuijer and Jed Wentz (eds.), *European Drama and Performance Studies: Dance and the Dutch Republic* (Paris: Classiques Garnier, 2015), 17–36: 18–21, and Ahrendt, personal communication.

26 For the history and contents of the ballet, see Maria Schildt, 'Hedwig Eleonora and Music at the Swedish Court, 1654–1726', in Kristoffer Neville and Lisa Skogh (eds.), *Queen Hedwig Eleonora and the Arts: Court Culture in Seventeenth-Century Northern Europe* (London: Routledge, 2017), 179–89. In July 2018 the *Ballet de Narva* was reconstructed and choreographed by Karin Modigh, with musical direction by Dan Laurin, at the Vadstena Academy (Sweden).

27 Calderón's libretto for *La púrpura de la rosa* was also set to music in Lima, Peru, in 1701 by Tomás de Torrejón y Velasco; its music survives: see Tomás de Torrejón y Velasco, Juan Hidalgo, and Pedro Calderón de la Barca, *La púrpura de la rosa*, ed. Louise K. Stein (Madrid: ICCMU and SGAE, 1999).

28 Juan Hidalgo and Pedro Calderón de la Barca, *Celos aun del aire matan*, ed. Louise K. Stein (Middleton: A-R Editions, 2014), 271 (appendix 1).

29 Jennifer Thorp, 'Dance in the London Theaters c. 1700–1750' in Jennifer Nevile (ed.), *Dance, Spectacle, and the Body Politick 1250–1750* (Bloomington: Indiana University Press, 2008), 136–52.

30 See Harris-Warrick and Marsh, *Musical Theatre at the Court of Louis XIV*, 115–16.

31 Jennifer Thorp, 'Dance in Late 17th-Century London: Priestly Muddles', *EM* 26/2 (1998), 198–212.

32 Sarah McCleave, *Dance in Handel's London Operas* (Rochester: University of Rochester Press, 2013).

33 Carol G. Marsh, 'French Court Dance in England, 1700–1740: A Study of the Sources' (Ph.D. dissertation, City University of New York, 1985).

34 Alm, 'Winged Feet', 229.

35 Kathleen Kuzmick Hansell, 'Theatrical Ballet and Italian Opera', in Lorenzo Bianconi and Giorgio Pestelli (eds.), *Opera on Stage. The History of Italian Opera, vol. 5* (Chicago and London: The University of Chicago Press, 2002), 177–308: 186–7. See also my 'Ballet', in *The Cambridge Companion to Eighteenth-Century Opera*, ed. Anthony R. DelDonna and Pierpaolo Polzonetti (Cambridge: Cambridge University Press, 2009), 99–111.

36 For more about Lambranzi, see Hansell, 'Theatrical Ballet', in Bianconi and Pestelli (eds.), *Opera on Stage*, vol. 5, 187–9.

9 | Staging Opera in the Seventeenth Century

ROGER SAVAGE

Opera, 'as every school boy knows', started life in the 1590s; and we might well suppose that such a novel phenomenon would cry out for entirely new techniques of staging. But in this we would be wrong. Most of the elements which fused to create opera as a form were already present in other musical and dramatic modes in the later sixteenth century, and that was the case, too, when it came to putting the form on stage.

Precedents and Continuities

To begin with, opera's most obvious theatrical requirement was the singer-actor. This wasn't a species that had to be created in 1598. There were already professional singers who made movement, gesture, and facial expression important parts of their projection of the solo songs they performed: for instance, the talented anonymous Italian lady who, coming to the front of the stage during a musical episode in *Alidoro*, Gabriele Bombasi's spoken tragedy of 1568, 'altered the expression in her face and eyes, and her gestures and movements, to accord with the changes in meaning of the words she sang'.[1] And among the professional actors whose usual stage-medium was speech, there were some who could act and sing simultaneously, not least those practising that thriving late sixteenth-century form, the *commedia dell'arte*, which, though it was mainly spoken, often included song. As it happened, versatility of this sort saved the situation when it came to the première of Ottavio Rinuccini and Claudio Monteverdi's opera *Arianna* (Mantua, 1608). Some weeks before, there had been a big casting crisis through the death of the opera's leading lady, but a noted actress from a *commedia* troupe, Virginia Ramponi ('la Florinda', 1583–1629/30), was able to step in to play and sing the heroine, and seems to have done it very well.[2]

The staging of choruses also grew out of pre-operatic theatrical activity. A couple of late sixteenth-century dates and places exemplify this: 1585 at Vicenza and 1589 at Florence. The ambitious production of a modern Italian translation of Sophocles' *Oedipus the King*, which opened Andrea

Palladio's remarkable, still-standing Teatro Olimpico at Vicenza in 1585, was in the main spoken, but it included musical settings by Andrea Gabrieli of four of the Theban Elders' choric odes, and these were sung and acted in character by a well-drilled chorus of fifteen. Then in 1589, six sung and staged 'interludes' or *intermedii* on the theme of harmony – musical, social, cosmic – were placed between and around the acts of Girolamo Bargagli's spoken comedy, *La Pellegrina,* during the lavish celebrations of the wedding of Ferdinando de' Medici and Christina of Lorraine at the theatre of the Medici in Florence. A versatile singing chorus played a range of parts in the six interludes: the inhabitants of a Greek island, the denizens of Hades, sundry sea-nymphs and pirates, the 'company of heaven', and so on. It would have been a short and simple step from that – via the singing huntsmen, cupids, zodiac-signs, and such of the highly *intermedio*-inflected Florentine opera of Gabriello Chiabrera and Giulio Caccini, *Il Rapimento di Cefalo* (1600) – to the choric fishermen and soldiers in *Arianna.*

As with performers, so with décor. Libretti in opera's first decade called for stage spectacle in the form of scene-changes (e.g., from a rural landscape to the Underworld and back) and special effects (e.g., a god descending from the heavens to sort out a fraught situation); but this didn't involve the invention of a new technology, rather the adoption of aspects of a tradition. By 1598 the Renaissance fascination with geometric perspective had for several decades been an important impulse behind the development of three-dimensional scenic arrangements in Italian court theatres, supplying apt backings for comedy (modern streets cunningly evoked), for 'satyric' drama (woodland glades), and for tragedy (vistas of classical city architecture, as can be seen at the Teatro Olimpico at Vicenza). Though only a few metres deep, these backings gave the illusion of much deeper space through the foreshortening of their perspectives, which looked particularly convincing when viewed from the prince's or duke's or cardinal's seat at the centre of the auditorium. At first it had been a case of one setting per show, but as the sixteenth century wore on, ways were found to change the scene during the performance in full view of the audience and seemingly without the intervention of human hands (bringing the curtain down to cover a scene-change didn't come in till centuries later).

This was first done by installing *periaktoi* (from the Greek, 'periaktos', turning on a centre): big rotatable triangular columns with elements of three different scenes painted on their three faces, placed symmetrically at the sides of the stage and complemented with a backdrop or a bigger central *periaktos.* By simultaneously rotating these 'triangles' and changing the backdrop, the whole scene would seem to change – from a town, say, to a forest, and then to a garden. The practical need to hide the backstage functionaries operating the *periaktoi* was one of the things that led to the installation of a 'proscenium' arch downstage of them (with the stage itself continuing in front of the arch as a forestage). And once you had created that kind of picture frame, you could put roped 'flying' devices behind it: devices developed and elaborated from those which had earlier been used for angels and other celestials in church dramas but which might now fly in a pagan god, an allegorical personage, or a consort of singers perched on a wood-and-canvas cloud. Upstage of the arch you could also install theatrical machinery that would simulate ocean waves – perhaps with mobile boats (on invisible wheels) or creatures rising through stage-traps from the deeps – or even perhaps suggest the flaming gulf of Hades itself. So the way was open, once the operatic time was ripe, for the hero of Alessandro Striggio and Monteverdi's *Favola d'Orfeo* at Mantua in 1607 to journey (per a scene-change) to the Underworld, cross the River Styx in Charon's ferry, meet the King and Queen of the Shades in their palace, return to the fields of Thrace, and finally be led up to the heavens by his vertically mobile father Apollo.

The 1589 interlude-sequence in *La Pellegrina* with its versatile chorus (and its many spectacular scenic effects, too) was devised and designed by the Florentine poet Giovanni de' Bardi and scenographer Bernardo Buontalenti (Bernardo delle Girandole, c. 1531–1608). The pair went on to supervise a large part of its practical preparation and rehearsal, but the grand duke eventually put his recently appointed controller of arts and entertainments, Emilio de' Cavalieri, above them in the hierarchy of control. On the spine of the new controller's account-book for the show it is described as 'la commedia diretta da Emilio de' Cavalieri': a nice marker of the arrival in secular theatre of a 'director'.[3] This idea of some kind of supervisor or organiser for an elaborate theatre-piece can be traced back to the religious drama of the Middle Ages and High Renaissance.

There are records of the activities of such figures in connection with some of the age's big annual open-air Passion Plays (the versatile Renward Cysat, for instance, who was the controlling 'regent' of the play at Lucerne in the 1580s and 1590s); and the function moved into secular theatre not only in Medici Florence but in other north Italian cities too. At Mantua the highly professional Leone de' Sommi Portaleone was for decades the hands-on controller of drama at the Gonzaga court and around 1565 wrote a guide to theatrical practice, his *Quattro Dialoghi di Rappresentazioni Sceniche (Four Dialogues on Scenic Representation)*.[4] Then there was

Angelo Ingegneri, a man of the theatre known to be 'capable of such things', [5] who was put in charge of the rehearsals of the already mentioned Italian translation of Sophocles' *Oedipus* (Vicenza, 1585), later publishing a little book about staging that made special reference to the Vicenzan show: *Della Poesia Rappresentativa e del Modo di Rappresentare le Favole Sceniche* (*On Dramatic Poetry and the Ways of Performing Stage-Plays*, Ferrara, 1598).[6] In all, then, there would have been nothing strange or particularly novel about an expert in theatre arts in the line of Sommi, Ingegneri, and Cavalieri taking responsibility for the overall smooth running of one of the new operas in the years that followed – 'directing' them, that is to say. In fact, Cavalieri himself did pretty much that. A decade after his work on the *Pellegrina* interludes in Florence, he was central to the *Rappresentatione di Anima, et di Corpo* (the quasi-operatic Roman oratorio *The Play of the Soul and the Body*, 1600), not only composing the music for it but being involved with its première production and writing some memoranda on the staging of 'the present work, or others like it', which are added to his colleague Alessandro Guidotti's introduction to the published score.[7]

Court Opera: Mantua, Florence, Rome

This is not to say that in the earliest decades of opera such a director-figure was always considered necessary. True, there were people who cared deeply that up-market court and college shows (operas among them) should be done to the best of everyone's abilities and who felt that this could only be achieved if there was a controller with a distinct job-description: a figure who might sometimes take the Latin name of *choragus* in Jesuit college theatricals (where Latin was the norm) or *corago* in Italian-speaking court circles. But there were also situations when the librettist and composer of a new opera along with the whole theatrical team – singer-actors and dancers, chorus and instrumentalists, choreographer, scene-designer and the special-effects people responsible for 'props', lighting and stage-machinery – were able to collaborate harmoniously without the need for a specially appointed co-ordinator or dictatorial regent.

As it happens, we have illuminating documents from the period that reflect both ways of arranging things. In Mantua in 1608 there was a new opera on the Daphne myth for which Marco da Gagliano made a fresh setting of Rinuccini's 1598 *Dafne* libretto, slightly revised. It seems to have been a happily cooperative production, and one so successful that the composer included a description of how it had been staged in the preface to the score, with the recommendation that, if it were to be performed again, it might well be done in much the same way. About twenty years later an anonymous gentleman, almost certainly at the Medici court in Florence (possibly Pierfrancesco Rinuccini, son of the pioneering librettist), wrote a treatise, not published at the time, on the proper staging of operas and other court shows with a well-informed expert in overall charge. He called it (after the expert) *Il Corago, o vero alcune osservazioni per metter bene in scena le composizioni drammatiche*. The printed *Dafne* preface and the *Corago* manuscript complement each other nicely and give us a good view of operatic staging in the early years.[8]

Both writers are concerned that their principal performers should *act* properly while never forgetting that everything they do has to mesh with the music. It's interesting to find in that connection that a question still asked today about operatic acting was already being asked in *Il Corago*: 'whether one should cast a tolerable musician who is a perfect actor or an excellent musician with little or no talent for acting'.[9] Though aware that musical connoisseurs might demur, the author feels that audiences as a whole prefer good actors who can sing tolerably, pointing out that this needn't wholly exclude fine singers with small acting talent, since they can be given roles involving stage-machines (heavenly chariots, floating clouds, and such) which will, so to speak, do their moving for them. The competent singer-actors permitted by the *corago* to tread the stage-proper are recommended to follow the rules of ordinary spoken acting – at this period quite a presentational, rhetorical affair – but urged to supplement them with some precepts specific to opera. For example, they should normally stand still while singing, only moving about during instrumental ritornelli, though they might break this rule when the music is 'specially meant to convey motion'.[10] They should keep their gestures quite slow, since sung words don't move as quickly as spoken ones. And it would be best if they didn't gesture violently (except when playing infernal gods) – best, too, if, when singing in dialogue with other characters, they only turned half-way towards them, since turning further might render their words inaudible to the audience.

Gagliano in his 1608 *Dafne* preface has similar feelings about singer-actors delivering their performances clearly and visibly out to the audience and integrating the vocal with the gestural. He stresses that physical movement should correspond both to the music's emotional contour and to its actual beat. As an example, he gives a detailed, almost step-by-step, account of how the character of Ovid in the opera's prologue should move while delivering it. He should make his entrance 'at the fifteenth or twentieth measure' of the prologue,

taking care to regulate his steps to the sound of the orchestra. . . . Above all, his singing and gestures should be full of majesty, more or less in accordance with the loftiness of the music. He must take care that every gesture and step follow the beat of the music and singing. When the first four lines are finished, let him take a breath, walking two or three steps during the ritornello, always observing the beat.[11]

Gagliano also suggests groupings of characters on stage that will make the action easy to 'read' – solo singers, for instance, should keep several paces clear of the chorus – and recommends careful rehearsal of difficult scenes involving pairs of characters, especially the energetic dumb-show encounter at the start of *Dafne* between Apollo and the writhing, fire-breathing Python: 'The fight', he says, 'shall be in time with the music.'[12] He's equally keen that roles requiring more subtle skills should be carefully cast and is eager to praise the young castrato Antonio Brandi, 'a most exquisite contralto', who brought great verbal and gestural expressiveness to the role of the opera's messenger-figure. Indeed, he seems to have considered 'Il Brandino' the star of the show – an early example of the star-making that would become a permanent characteristic of opera.

Gagliano is just as concerned with the deportment of the chorus of nymphs and shepherds (about seventeen of them at the première, though the number might vary at a revival, depending on the capacity of the stage). The choristers should, he thinks, be focused, alert, and well synchronised, though they should not have the regimented look of a dance-troupe. Most of the time they should form a half-moon, backing the principal singers, visibly responding with gesture and facial expression to the prevailing emotion, kneeling at appropriate moments, rising in good order, and accompanying sung choral numbers with group movements to left, to right, and back again to upstage centre (which suggests that the dancing master in 1608 had been looking at accounts of choric movements in ancient Greek tragedy). The blend of psychological realism and courtly formality that is characteristic of seventeenth-century opera is nicely reflected in Gagliano's view that, even when vividly 'imitating flight and terror', the chorus should never turn their backs impolitely on the distinguished audience.[13] *Il Corago*'s author agrees; it's something that a good *corago* would ensure, as he would that the chorus's gestures are unanimous and their 'processings and interlacings' telling. (One way of guaranteeing that choristers end up in the right stage-positions after such complicated movements, he suggests, is 'to make marks on the stage floor' that they can steer by – much as Ingegneri fifty years before had used the coloured marbles patterned on the floor at Vicenza as markers for his *Oedipus* chorus).[14]

It's likely that the stage for a court opera in the early seventeenth century would need to be set up especially for the event. That done – *Il Corago* advises at length on this – a lot of care was called for to ensure the show's technical smooth running. For instance, both the *Dafne* preface and *Il Corago* are at pains to secure optimum placing for the instrumentalists. The convention that would later be established of a band settled permanently in an orchestra-pit just in front of the stage didn't apply at the time. Instruments and their players, largely hidden, could be located before or behind or above the action as seemed best for any particular situation – Monteverdi went to some lengths to get this matter right when he made a professional visit to Parma in 1627.[15] *Il Corago*, in a chapter on the rival claims of strings and winds to be the best support for sung drama, stresses that careful placing of either group is essential to achieving good vocal–instrumental balance and ensuring that there are clear lines of communication between players and singers during the performance. (For instance, putting an *organo di legno* in the *wrong* place in the wings would not only risk impeding the *periaktoi* and the work of the stage-machinists but might also mean that the organist, having 'the inconvenience of not being able to see or hear the actors well, would be constrained to adopt a [regular] beat [*sarà forza cantar a battuta*], which is something considered improper for the recitative style'.[16] Gagliano is keen on this too, and he's eager to explain a related special effect when his Apollo seems to be playing his lyre exquisitely during his lines in praise of the metamorphosed Daphne, though the sound is actually coming from a consort of viols placed just out of sight behind the scenery.

Rather surprisingly, Gagliano doesn't feel called on to praise the designer of that scenery, but maybe this is because the opera was done against a single pastoral set which had already been used for earlier shows. *Il Corago*, on the other hand, is full of praise for one scenographer, Bernardo Buontalenti, he of the *Pellegrina* interludes back in 1589. Though dead for about twenty years by 1630, the treatise reveres him as the father-figure of the whole fashion for changeable perspective-scenes, stressing that proper management of such scenery is one of the two most important responsibilities of a *corago* (the other being instruction in acting). It discusses the means of maximising illusion in scene-painting and scene-changing, along with effective techniques of illumination with candles and oil lamps, the provision of apt but rich costumes for the cast (peasant roles included: this is court opera after all), and the use of a stage curtain at the very beginning and end of the show. Machines that fly singer-actors down from above are another special concern: their safety (check it regularly), their smooth operation (soap the ropes and pulleys frequently), and the speed of their descents and ascents (keep these slow when a performer is actually singing on one of them).

Records from other north Italian princely courts and from the establishments of equally princely cardinals in Rome reveal similar activities and concerns.[17] We learn that staging an opera was something that consumed time and ingenuity, though the preparation time could vary widely: about five months were set aside for rehearsals of the Mantuan *Arianna* after the singers had learned their parts, but a mere forty-four days covered the writing, composing, preparing, and rehearsing of a 'favola in musica', the Roman *Aretusa* (Ottavio Corsini and Filippo Vitali) in 1620. Records of that *Aretusa* and of Monteverdi's *Orfeo* give us glimpses of the care that was taken to recruit properly talented singer-actors and of the appreciation that such people received if they came up to expectation. And away from the soloists and chorus, we see groups of anonymous 'extras', the non-singing *comparse*, being put through their paces effectively. The conflict between the Romans and the Huns in *La Regina Sant'Orsola* (Andrea Salvadori, Gagliano; Florence, 1624) is an instance. The engraving in Figure 9.1, made for the libretto of the 1625 revival by Alfonso Parigi (son of the show's designer), shows the battle, staged by the dancing master Agniolo Ricci, raging beneath the walls of Cologne: the Temple of Mars to the left, the Romans defending the city walls to the right. Equally elaborate crowd-work is evident in the remarkable scene of a country fair, the 'Fiera di Farfa', designed by one of the greatest artists of the Roman Baroque, the sculptor and architect Gian Lorenzo Bernini, and staged in Rome as an interlude for the 1639 version of the opera *L'Egisto, ovvero, Chi soffre speri* (Giulio Rospigliosi, Virgilio Mazzocchi, and Marco Marazzoli; first performance 1637). This featured street-cries, popular songs, dancing, duelling, and a bevy of *comparse* energetically enjoying all the fun of the fair – the whole rounded off with an impressive sunset.[18]

The backstage wizards who devised scenic devices in connection with such spectacles could be singled out for praise: for instance, the architect Francesco Guitti (1605–c. 1645), who worked in Ferrara, Parma, and Rome, and whose 'excellence in inventing, setting up and controlling

Figure 9.1 Andrea Salvadori and Marco da Gagliano, *La regina Sant'Orsola* (Florence, 1624), Act II: the battle, staged by Agniolo Ricci. Engraving by Alfonso Parigi, from the libretto printed for the 1625 revival.
By permission of the Getty Research Institute, Research Library, Los Angeles

machines and theatrical effects', a contemporary said, 'was attested by universal amazement and applause'.[19] Sometimes even the composer was amazed at what his backstage colleagues had done, as at the Roman staging of Rospigliosi and Stefano Landi's *Sant'Alessio* in the 1630s. (Figure 9.2 represents the final scene of the 1634 version: a 'tragic street', possibly designed by Pietro da Cortona, with Religion singing Saint Alexis' praises as the Virtues dance and a host of heavenly musicians descends on two cloud-machines). 'What shall I say', Landi enthused,

of the scenic apparatus? The first appearance of the new Rome, the flight of the angel through the clouds [and] the appearance in the sky of [the Spirit of] Religion were all works of ingenuity and machines, but they rivalled nature herself. The scene was most cunningly wrought: the visions of Heaven and Hell were marvellous; the changes of the wings and the perspective were ever more beautiful.[20]

Things went best when the stage-hands were properly trained; thus Nicola Sabbattini in his *Pratica di Fabricar Scene e Machine ne' Teatri* of 1638 says that the scene-shifters should be 'familiar with sound and time cues, so that during the playing of the music, they cause the [scenic] frames to be run to their positions all at one time'.[21]

Figure 9.2 Giulio Rospigliosi and Stefano Landi, *Il Sant'Alessio* (Rome, 1631), final scene of the 1634 version. Engraving by François Collignon, from *Il S. Alessio: dramma musicale: dall eminentissimo, et reverendissimo signore card. Barberino* (Rome: Paolo Masotti, 1634).
By permission of the Beinecke Rare Book and Manuscript Library, Yale University

As several of these instances have shown, some of the liveliest operatic action in the middle decades of the century took place in Counter-Reformation Rome. Interest in staging there was apparent in the highest circles, both of the Church and of the community of talented artists who served it, especially if they were in the sphere of the powerful Barberini family. The prime instance of ecclesiastical involvement was the copious librettist Rospigliosi, who would be elevated to the Chair of St. Peter as Pope Clement IX in 1667, but he seems earlier to have been very closely involved with the staging of his sophisticated yet highly moral operas.

Extensive records survive of the circumstances of their productions at the Palazzo Barberini, the most revealing perhaps being the marginalia in one manuscript of *Dal Male il Bene*, the libretto he had written with his nephew Giacomo in 1654. The notes indicate scenic locations, itemise props (right down to a couple of candle-holders and a broom), cue scene-changes, refer to sound-effects, and make clear which of the numbered routes for getting on and off the stage the performers should use for particular entrances and exits.[22] If that document embodies the minute concerns with staging of a highly placed librettist, an entry in the diary of the English traveller John Evelyn for 19 November 1644 illustrates the breadth of the operatic interests of the great Bernini:

a little before my Comming to the Citty, [he] gave a Publique Opera (for so they call those Shews of that kind) where in he painted the Seanes, cut the Statues, invented the Engines, composed the Musique, writ the Comedy & built the Theater all himselfe.[23]

Add to that the information from Filippo Baldinucci's life of Bernini that at the rehearsals of his theatre pieces, he 'would himself take all the parts to teach the others how to play them', and you have an omnicompetent centraliser of opera who out-Wagners Wagner at the Bayreuth of the 1870s.[24]

Public Opera: Venice, Paris, London, Naples

Such stories of Bernini in Rome may have improved a little in the telling, but we can take Evelyn's account of the operatic Venice of the 1640s at face value, as he was there to see things for himself. He was witnessing the momentous innovation of opera given not at court as part of the munificence and magnificence of a prince but as a commercial proposition open to all – all anyway who could afford the price of admission. Court opera, of course, didn't come to an end, and among the vivid accounts of its staging in the decades after the 1640s there are several which stress the numbers of *comparse* in stately retinues, energetic armies, and the like that rich courts could display, and the grandiose sets that they could display them in. The shop-window example was *Il Pomo d'oro* of Francesco Sbarra and Antonio Cesti, given at the Viennese court in 1668 on the empress's birthday, with its fifty named characters, its twenty-three sumptuous sets by the architect Ludovico Burnacini, and an action which found room for a fiery flying dragon, a collapsing temple, a pair of elephants drafted into siege-work, and more besides.

The focus, however, was now on public opera, and Evelyn had an eye for its practicalities when he saw the *Ercole in Lidia* of Maiolino Bisaccioni and Giovanni Rovetta in Venice at the Teatro Novissimo in Ascension Week 1645 (the year of its première):

That night ... we went to the Opera, which are comedies and other plays represented in Recitative Music by the most excellent Musitians vocal & Instrumental, together with variety of Sceanes painted & contrived with no lesse art of Perspective, and Machines, for flying in the aire, & other wonderfull motions. So taken together it is doubtlesse one of the most magnificent & expensefull diversions the Wit of Man can invent: The historie was *Hercules* in Lydia, the Seanes chang'd 13 times. [Among] the famous Voices [was] *Anna Rencia*, a Roman, & reputed the best treble of Women; but there was an *Eunuch*, that in my opinion surpass'd her, also a *Genoveze* that sang an incomparable Base.[25]

Although several aspects of Venetian staging were seamless continuations of Roman and north Italian courtly practice, Evelyn here points up three things which were different and which would in time become important over the whole of operatic Europe. The first is the (to us) simple concept of 'going to the opera', which implies a choice of performances to see – 'comedies and other plays represented in recitative music' – and, if we are lucky, a choice of opera houses to see them in. In the first five years of public opera, four such houses came into existence in Venice, the city having invented the purpose-designed (or at least purpose-adapted) public building devoted to the staging of operatic performances under the management of an impresario who had to think carefully about investments and returns when providing these 'expensefull diversions' for a paying audience.

Establishing an influential precedent, the auditoria of these Venetian houses tended to be U-shaped, centring on a crowded 'pit' for in-the-main male spectators (who might stand for the whole show or perhaps pay to sit on benches), surrounded on three sides by balconies or galleries generally divided into 'boxes': an arrangement deriving from earlier Venetian theatres for the *commedia dell'arte*. Renting a box – sometimes even buying one – implied social stature, though the view from it of the scene-stage behind the proscenium arch could be so bad that a production might sometimes have to be modified out of consideration for such box-holding gentlefolk as wanted to watch the action. Thus Aurelio Aureli reports an emendation to his 1659 libretto for *La Costanza di Rosmonda* (music by Giovanni Battista Volpe [Rovettino, c. 1620–1691]) which meant that one singer-actress's delivery of an important monologue would be moved from its rightful place (on a balcony that was part of the scenery) to the stage floor, 'in order to make her visible to the eyes of everyone, especially those seated in the boxes'.[26]

Evelyn's counting the thirteen changes of scene in *Ercole in Lidia* is a second revealing point. Though it seems that in some places the older triangular *periaktoi*-method of scenic display and transformation was still in use in the mid-seventeenth century, from the 1610s and 1620s onwards it was being widely replaced – partly under the influence of the architect and designer Giovanni Battista Aleotti – by the new-fangled 'wing-flats' (with matching 'borders' above): sets of two-dimensional, perspective-painted and profiled units which were set up in grooves to the right and left of the stage behind the proscenium arch so as to complement and frame a backdrop. These were capable of being drawn back – and the backdrop raised – to reveal another set immediately behind them, thereby changing the scene in a few seconds from, say, a meadow to a city street. In the early years, simultaneously drawing back such a set of perhaps eight flats – four each side – was decidedly labour-intensive; but the scenographer and machinist Giacomo Torelli (1608–1678), active in Venice in the late 1630s and early 1640s before moving influentially to Paris, hit on a system related to naval rope-work whereby all the flats in a set were attached to a single counter-weighted capstan-drum beneath the stage, which could be operated by one man. 'The artifice of this device is amazing', a contemporary wrote; 'a fifteen-year-old boy can work it by himself!'[27]

Torelli was closely connected with the Teatro Novissimo that Evelyn visited, and he may well have had a hand in designing the numerous easily changed scenes the diarist saw in *Ercole*. Henceforward for many decades, no self-respecting Continental opera house would be without a scene-changing system somewhat in the Torelli style and a collection of Torellian perspective-scenes that could be used for a wide range of shows: a city street or two perhaps, some rooms of state, a dungeon, a temple, an army camp, a cave, a seashore, a wilderness, an arbour, or a grove. Figure 9.3, for instance, shows a design by Torelli for Niccolò Bartolini and Francesco Sacrati's *Venere gelosa* (Venice, Teatro Novissimo, 1643): a woodland scene on the island of Naxos (tree-flats with city backdrop) with the goddess Flora appearing in a machine above, supported by Zephyrs.

Within and in front of these scenes, lit by candles and oil-lamps, which also lit the auditorium during the performance, were the singer-actors – which brings us to the third significant element in Evelyn's account of the Novissimo: his concern to rank-order the voices he heard in Rovetta's opera and his noting the star-status of Anna Renzi (c. 1620–d. after 1661). Singer-actors, as much as or more than libretto, music, or décor, were becoming a principal operatic talking point in Venice, and la Renzi could be rated as the first big star of public opera. Indeed, in 1644, the year before Evelyn's visit, she had been the subject of the first operatic fan-book, the librettist Giulio Strozzi's *Glorie della Signora Anna Renzi Romana*. Strozzi celebrates his heroine's compound of intellect, imagination, and memory; her versatility; her powers of character-observation; her ability to

Figure 9.3 Niccolò Bartolini and Francesco Sacrati, *Venere gelosa* (Venice, 1643). Anonymous engraving from a libretto published in 1644 to accompany a revival of the opera.
By permission of University of Michigan Library (Special Collections Research Center), Ann Arbor

'transform herself completely into the person she represents' – and her voice.[28] Voices were at a premium. A French visitor to Venice in the 1670s, Alexandre-Toussaint Limojon de Saint-Didier, describes the gentlemen who 'bend themselves out of their Boxes, crying *Ah cara!* [. . .] expressing after this manner the Raptures of Pleasure which those divine Voices cause to them', along with the gondoliers in the pit whose earthier acclamations 'are not always within the bounds of Modesty'.[29]

The surviving documentation of the financing and management of operatic houses and companies in seventeenth-century Venice is considerable, but very little of it has to do with staging in the sense of training and rehearsing particular casts or making decisions about particular décors. This may be in part because a figure like the courtly *corago* could have no place in the busy commercial environment of the new impresarios; in part because opera singers and backstage technicians were becoming more experienced, so needing less and less documented instruction; and in part because the librettists were themselves quite often impresarios – there are several known instances in mid-century Venice – and so could include a director-like function as part of their daily work in the theatre without there being any call to put that fact on record. Giovanni Faustini, for instance, the author of eleven libretti for Francesco Cavalli, was at one time or another impresario at three different Venetian houses.[30] Even a librettist with no *impresa* or other opera house job might include in his word-book so many details of moves, asides, and emotional states, along with details of scenery, props, and machine-effects, that almost all the staging-information needed for the rehearsal of his opera was there in the printed text, and the cast and crew needed no further guidance. Thus Matteo Noris's (d. 1714) libretto for *Totila*, his fate-of-the-Roman-Empire piece staged in Venice in 1677 to a score by Giovanni Legrenzi, has stage-directions (called in Italian 'didascalie') galore, covering movement ('*Attempting to leave, Desbo is waylaid by Publicola*' [Act III scene 15]), mental states ('*Longing to kiss Marcia*' [Act II scene 16]), and scenic spectacle ('*A storm breaks out*' [Act II scene 8]; '*Slaves drag from a distance a huge gold-covered elephant*' [Act I scene 17]).

Across the Alps to the northwest, however, a powerful director – a near-dictator indeed – was alive and well and working in Paris, Saint-Germain-en-Laye, and Versailles: Jean Baptiste Lully (1632–1687). When French opera truly got under way in the early 1670s with his *Cadmus et Hermione* and *Alceste*, it was formed by combining things imported from Italy (continuous music, a narrative conducted entirely in song) with something that had been characteristically north-European for generations: an enthusiasm for dramatic dance, fanciful costumes, and spectacular sets in allegorically themed court entertainments. In the earlier years of the century, the French manifestation of this enthusiasm, the *ballet de cour*, had had a tradition of determined directors: sometimes the aristocratic devisers of the ballets themselves and sometimes their subaltern *maîtres de l'ordre* – gentlemen who worked closely with dancing masters, costume and mask designers, and latterly set designers to produce a successful show. Regarding such a *maître*'s responsibilities – involving not only such preparatory matters but also stage-managing 'on the night' as well – there is a lively chapter in a little treatise of 1641 by one M. de Saint Hubert, *La Manière de Composer et Faire Réussir les Ballets*. Ballets 'mastered' in that way may have flowed the more easily into the early development of operatic *tragédie en musique* because the new form's creative organiser had been born Giovanni Battista Lulli in Florence in 1632: almost certainly the place, and very close to the time, of our treatise on the idea of a *corago*.

Along with his Florentine background and his contracting into the *ballet de cour* tradition, Lully had a third reason for taking a dictatorial approach to the staging of his works: the direct responsibility he had from

Figure 9.4 Philippe Quinault and Jean-Baptiste Lully, *Alceste*, Versailles, fête de 1674, 4 juillet. Engraving by Jean Le Pautre.
By permission of Bibliothèque Nationale de France, département de la musique, Paris

1672 onward to the absolutist *grand monarque* Louis XIV for making a success of a uniquely French style of opera. (Figure 9.4, an engraving by Jean Le Pautre, shows an open-air, scenery-less performance of Philippe Quinault and Lully's *Alceste* as staged on 4 July 1674 at Versailles before the king some months after the opera's indoor première in Paris. Having defied the Fury Alecto, the hero Hercules, right of the central group, is claiming Alceste from the King and Queen of the Underworld, who stand on either side of her). Things went on the more swimmingly for Lully because he was working at a time when the procedures and achievements of French spoken and danced theatre were of a remarkably high standard, and when gifted theatre-artists – librettists like Quinault (bap. 1635–1688), designers like Jean Berain (1640–1711), choreographers like Pierre Beauchamps (1631–1705) – were available for co-option or conscription. Further, before he began his operatic career, Lully had collaborated on *comédie-ballets* with the great playwright, actor, and company manager Molière (Jean-Baptiste Poquelin, bap. 1622–1673), perhaps studying the method of rehearsal by instruction, demonstration, and energetic, sharp-tongued good humour that Molière sketches in his rehearsal-play of 1663, *L'Impromptu de Versailles*. Beyond that he could recommend to his leading ladies that they study the art of the heroines in Jean Racine's newly written spoken tragedies. With all this in the background, Lully was able to be a highly effective autocrat. In 1705, eighteen years after his death, his admirer the critic Jean Laurent Le Cerf de la Viéville recalled that the brilliant Florentine had 'an extraordinary talent for everything connected with things theatrical'. Lully, he said, knew as well how to have an opera performed and how to govern

its performers as he did how to compose one. From the moment a singer, male or female, fell into his hands, he applied himself to their training with marvellous affection. He himself taught them to make an entrance, to walk on stage, to achieve grace in gesture and movement. ... Eventually the rehearsals came. To these he only admitted essential people (the librettist, the machinist etc.), [so] he had the liberty to instruct and correct his actors and actresses. ... When he needed to, he would set about dancing before his dancers so that they could the better understand his ideas.[31]

Across the English Channel, there's a finely farcical demonstration of how such shows of omnicompetence do *not* work if the would-be autocrat has neither the personality nor the skills to bring them off. It's in the Duke of Buckingham's burlesque comedy *The Rehearsal,* staged in London in 1671 around the time of the first stirrings of what would become the characteristically English form of 'semi-opera'. Buckingham's Mr Bayes – probably a satiric amalgam of the poet-dramatists William Davenant and John Dryden – is a thoroughgoing coxcomb who has written a grotesque hybrid of a 'heroic' play which features songs (including a 'battel in *Recitativo*'), much scenic spectacle, and dances to music of his own composition 'apted for the business'. But the poor performers can't understand it in rehearsal; Mr Bayes' attempts at explanation only make matters worse; his music resists being danced to ('Sir, 'tis impossible to do any thing in time, to this Tune'); and when he tries practical demonstration, he 'puts 'em out with teaching 'em', at one point tripping and falling flat on his face when attempting to show off a particular move ('Ah, gadsookers, I have broke my Nose').

But more accomplished stagings could be expected in England when towards the end of the century the actor–manager Thomas Betterton was in charge of the fairly rare manifestations of public opera in London.[32] They were mainly works in the 'semi-operatic' mode that combined spoken dialogue with very extensive and picturesque masque-like sung and danced passages, music often by Henry Purcell (1658 or 1659–1695) and choreography by Josias Priest (c. 1645–bur. 3 January, 1735). Where their special scenic effects are concerned, these formed something of a *summa* of the

Baroque tradition. Thus one can see the surfacing from the stage-ocean of Britannia's island in the last act of *King Arthur* (Dryden and Purcell; London, 1691) as reflecting the surfacing of the pearl-rich island of beautiful princesses in the first *intermède* of Molière's *Les Amants magnifiques* of 1670 (its music by Lully) and that of the American coral reef in the Amerigo Vespucci interlude of the Florentine multi-media show *Il Giudizio di Paride* of 1608[33] – which itself derives technically from the thrusting-up of the Mountain of the Wood Nymphs in the second *intermedio* of *La Pellegrina* in 1589. And the scene of the sun rising after the mistakes of the night in the Shakespeare-Betterton-Purcell *Fairy Queen* (London, 1692) – Purcell writes a big orchestral 'sonata' for it – recalls the sunset Bernini had devised for the 'Fieri di Farfa' in *Chi Soffre Speri* at Rome in 1639, which itself could be traced back to the radiant dawn that had come up at the beginning of *La Pellegrina*'s final *intermedio* fifty years before.

Late in the same decade as *King Arthur* and *The Fairy Queen*, but a thousand miles away in the Kingdom of the Two Sicilies, the Naples-based Andrea Perrucci wrote his *Dell'Arte Rappresentativa* (1699), stressing the desirability of someone who will take care and pains to monitor the preparation and performance of spoken-scripted plays and *commedia dell'arte* improvisations, and of operas as well. This *corago* – Perrucci reverts to the word – will act as construction-supervisor, troubleshooter, props master, stage manager, and general cast co-ordinator: a central figure who 'guides, plans and trains, for [. . .] in this sort of business it is better to go for a monarchy than a republic'.[34] And it is doubtless this *corago* who will insist on Perrucci's behalf that the singer-actors in his operas should act just as well as speaking actors do and who will ensure that there are no occasions for confusion among – let alone collisions between – performers over entrances and exits. His recommendation for avoiding such things is the posting of a list behind the proscenium arch detailing who comes on, who goes off, and when they do it at entrances numbered 1–6 or lettered A–F, though for opera he also suggests another way of ensuring good stage-traffic, one clearly in line with growing practice in *opera seria* where the 'exit aria' was concerned: a matter of entering the scene as far upstage and exiting as far downstage as possible.[35]

Meanwhile, opera in Paris and at Louis XIV's court was coping with the aftermath of Lully's death in 1687. His royally authorised monopolies over *tragédie en musique* and the long shadow they threw forward helped to ensure that the staging of French opera, like its composition, stayed broadly Lullian for years to come. Significantly, when the structure, management, and running of his Académie Royale de Musique at the Palais-Royal theatre were overhauled and rationalised by two royal ordinances in 1713 and 1714,[36] the company was required to keep a production of a Lully opera permanently 'in readiness' in case it was needed, and also to appoint two Syndics responsible to the company's court-connected Inspector General. One of these was 'the official responsible for theatrical control' (*le syndic chargé de la régie du théâtre*). He was to see to artistic planning and casting (along with the composer, if contactable) and to oversee all rehearsals and performances, during which everyone connected to the production – front-of-house, onstage, and back-stage – was answerable to him.

Lully's ghost would have been pleased, as it would have been by the continuing didactic influence of the singer-actors he had trained, the fiery-eyed Marie Le Rochois (c. 1658–1728) especially, who had created the role of the lovelorn sorceress in his *Armide* and held audiences breathless with it. However high the style of her performances, there was clearly a level of close psychological identification involved in their preparation. The story is told of her instructing a younger singer in the correct approach to role-play in lyric tragedies like *Armide* and asking her at one point what *she* would do if, like the character she was playing, she were abandoned by the man she passionately adored. 'Get another one', said the pupil. 'In that case, mademoiselle, we are both wasting our time', said Le Rochois and ended the lesson abruptly.[37] It was an involvement with the role in hand which would doubtless have appealed to Renzi, creator of Ottavia in *L'Incoronazione di Poppea* (Giovanni Francesco Busenello, Claudio Monteverdi; Venice, 1643), and to Ramponi, whose performance as the despairing Ariadne at Mantua in 1608 had, in Marco da Gagliano's words, 'visibly moved the whole theatre to tears'.

Notes

1 Anonymous report on Gabriele Bombasi's *Alidoro*, quoted in Nino Pirrotta and Elena Povoledo, *Music and Theatre from Poliziano to Monteverdi*, trans. Karen Eales (Cambridge: Cambridge University Press, 1982), 202.

2 Roger Savage, 'Meetings on Naxos', in Judith Chaffee and Olly Crick (eds.), *The Routledge Companion to Commedia dell'Arte* (London: Routledge, 2015), 268–75: 268–70.

3 '*Commedia diretta*': Aby Warburg, *The Renewal of Pagan Antiquity* (Los Angeles: Getty Research Institute, 1999), 393 note 29. In fact, the actual term 'director' was not much used in the seventeenth century, though it is, e.g.,

applied to a certain Lodovico Lenzi at Rome in 1668: see Margaret Murata, *Operas for the Papal Court, 1631–1668* (Ann Arbor: UMI Research Press, 1981), 211, note 30. For 'direction' and 'production' in early opera, see the relevant sections of Lorenzo Bianconi and Giorgio Pestelli (eds.), *The History of Italian Opera*, vols. 4 and 5: respectively *Opera Production and Its Resources*, trans. Lydia G. Cochrane (Chicago and London: University of Chicago Press, 1998), and *Opera on Stage*, trans. Kate Singleton (Chicago and London: University of Chicago Press, 2002).

4 Leone de' Sommi, *Quattro dialoghi in materia di rappresentazioni sceniche*, ed. Ferruccio Marotti (Milan: Il Polifilo, 1968).

5 Alois M. Nagler, *A Source Book in Theatrical History* (New York: Dover, 1959), 84.

6 Angelo Ingegneri, *Della Poesia Rappresentativa e del Modo di Rappresentare le Favole Sceniche*, ed. Maria Lisa Doglio (Ferrara: Edizioni Panini, 1989).

7 Preface from *Rappresentazione di Anima, et di Corpo*, in Carol MacClintock (ed.), *Readings in the History of Music in Performance* (Bloomington and London: Indiana University Press, 1979), 183–7: 183.

8 For the *Dafne* preface in translation, see ibid., 187–94. For the edition of the manuscript of *Il Corago*, see Paolo Fabbri and Angelo Pompilio (eds.), *Il corago, o vero alcune osservazioni per metter bene in scena le composizioni drammatiche* (Florence: Olschki, 1983). Four chapters are translated with commentary in Roger Savage and Matteo Sansone, '*Il Corago* and the Staging of Early Opera: Four Chapters from an Anonymous Treatise *circa* 1630', *EM* 17/4 (1989), 494–511, and four (only one of them overlapping with the Savage-Sansone selection) in Oliver Strunk (ed.), *Source Readings in Music History*, rev. ed. Leo Treitler (New York: Norton, 1998), vol. 4: *The Baroque Era*, ed. Margaret Murata, 629–33.

9 Fabbri and Pompilio (eds.), *Il Corago*, ch. 15; Savage and Sansone, '*Il Corago*', 501.

10 Fabbri and Pompilio (eds.), *Il Corago*, ch. 15; Savage and Sansone, '*Il Corago*', 500.

11 MacClintock, *Readings*, 190.

12 Ibid., 192.

13 Ibid., 191.

14 Fabbri and Pompilio (eds.), *Il Corago*, ch. 17; Savage and Sansone, '*Il Corago*', 503–4.

15 Irving Lavin, 'On the Unity of the Arts and the Early Baroque Opera House', in Barbara Wisch and Susan Scott Munshower (eds.), '*All the World's a Stage*': *Art and Pageantry in the Renaissance and Baroque*, Part 2: *Theatrical Spectacle and Spectacular Theater* (University Park: Department of Art History, The Pennsylvania State University, 1990), 518–79: 524.

16 Fabbri and Pompilio (eds.), *Il corago*, ch. 13. In the Italian original text, 'cantar a battuta' seems to be musicians' jargon meaning to perform in strict tempo and/or with someone manually indicating the beat.

17 For a case-study, see Massimo Ossi, *'Dalle Macchine … la Maraviglia*: Bernardo Buontalenti's *Il Rapimento di Cefalo* at the Medici Theater in 1600', in Mark A. Radice (ed.), *Opera in Context* (Portland: Amadeus, 1998), 15–35.

18 Frederick Hammond, *Music and Spectacle in Baroque Rome: Barberini Patronage under Urban VIII* (New Haven: Yale University Press, 1994), 236–9.

19 Murata, *Operas for the Papal Court*, 251.

20 David Kimbell, *Italian Opera* (Cambridge: Cambridge University Press, 1991), 101.

21 Barnard Hewitt (ed.), *The Renaissance Stage: Documents of Serlio, Sabbattini and Furttenbach* (Coral Gables: University of Miami Press, 1968), 102–3.

22 Murata, *Operas for the Papal Court*, 54–7.

23 *The Diary of John Evelyn: Now First Printed in Full from the Manuscripts Belonging to Mr. John Evelyn*, ed. Esmond Samuel de Beer, 6 vols. (Oxford: Clarendon Press, 2000), vol. 2, 261.

24 Cesare D'Onofrio (ed.), *Bernini: Fontana di Trevi* (Rome: Staderini, 1963), 106.

25 *The Diary of John Evelyn*, June 1645, vol. 2, 449–50.

26 Ellen Rosand, *Opera in Seventeenth-Century Venice: The Creation of a Genre* (Berkeley, Los Angeles, and London: University of California Press, 1991), 209.

27 Per Bjurström, *Giacomo Torelli and Baroque Stage Design* (Stockholm: Almqvist, 1961), 109.

28 Rosand, *Opera in Seventeenth-Century Venice*, 228–35.

29 Nagler, *A Source Book*, 264.

30 On the impresarii and their various responsibilities – including writing libretti – see Beth L. Glixon and Jonathan E. Glixon, *Inventing the Business of Opera: The Impresario and His World in Seventeenth-Century Venice* (Oxford and New York: Oxford University Press, 2006).

31 Jean-Louis Le Cerf de la Viéville, *Comparaison de la musique italienne et de la musique françoise, où, en examinant en détail les avantages des Spectacles, & le mérite des Compositeurs des deux nations, on montre quelles sont les vrayes beautez de la Musique* (Brussels: François Foppens, 1704–1706; rpt. Geneva: Minkoff, 1972), part 2, 226–8.

32 See Judith Milhous, 'The Multimedia Spectacular on the Restoration Stage', in Shirley Strum Kenny (ed.), *British Theatre and the Other Arts 1660–1800* (Washington, DC: Folger Shakespeare Library, 1984), 41–66.

33 Roger Savage, 'Sea Spectacles on Dry Land: The 1580s to the 1690s', in Margaret Shewring and Linda Briggs (eds.), *Waterborne Pageants and Festivities in the Renaissance. Essays in Honour of J. R. Mulryne* (Farnham, Burlington: Ashgate, 2013), 359–71: 359–63, 368–9.

34 Andrea Perrucci, *Dell'Arte Rappresentativa*, ed. Anton Giulio Bragaglia (Florence: Sansoni, 1961), 143.
35 Ibid., 139–40, 143.
36 Caroline Wood and Graham Sadler, *French Baroque Opera: A Reader* (Aldershot: Ashgate, 2000), 11–13.
37 Ibid., 132.

National Traditions (outside Italy)

LAURA NAUDEIX

Introduced in Paris in the middle of the seventeenth century, Italian opera took a long time to conquer French audiences. The genre of the spoken tragedy, represented by the works of Pierre Corneille and Jean Racine, had brought French theatre since the 1640s to a point of perfection: the notion of a play being sung throughout was thus met with much scepticism. French desire for cultural hegemony also resisted opera, which was perceived as an Italian import. The fate of this genre was also complicated at the political level: Cardinal Mazarin's attempt to impose opera in France did not sit well in the hostile climate generated by the Fronde (1648–1653), during which time several members of Parliament and high-ranking nobles vehemently opposed strengthening the absolute monarchy. While Italian influence was considerable in the artistic domain, it was progressively restricted to theatrical architecture, machinery, and décors, all aspects that would nevertheless become paramount for the development of 'pièces à machines', that is, spectacular theatrical plays mostly performed on private stages – princely residences, the king's palaces – and in Parisian public theatres.

As in other European countries, French opera arose from the development of the *divertissement de cour* in combination with the new expectations of urban audiences, who wanted to enjoy in public theatres the performances usually restricted to the court – thus, the significant imprint left by the *ballet de cour* on French opera, in which dance is an essential ingredient. All these factors explain the fairly late year – 1671 – of the first public performance of a French opera, *Pomone,* on a libretto by Pierre Perrin (c. 1620–1675) with music by Robert Cambert (c. 1628–1677). Founded by Perrin and Alexandre de Rieux, Marquis de Sourdéac, in 1669, the Académie d'Opéra (renamed in 1671 Académie Royale de Musique) promptly institutionalised French opera through the suppression of all foreign influences, securing for many decades to come the preservation of a specific French model.

The *Ballet de Cour*

During the first half of the seventeenth century, the 'ballet participatif' (participatory ballet) – today known as *ballet de cour* – was the prevalent divertissement at the court. It was meant to entertain courtiers, members of the royal family, and the king himself, and offered them the possibility of participating. The practice of hiring commoners as professional dancers and having them mingle on stage with members of the court began in 1630. However, the final *grand ballet* danced at the end of these spectacles was restricted to courtiers only.[1]

Dance – in addition to fencing and horse ballet – was part of the formal education of young French aristocrats. The young king had daily lessons with his *maître à danser* (dance master). During the seventeenth century, dance played an essential social and artistic role in court life, not only during the increasingly codified great balls but also during exceptional performances that would usually take place during the carnival season.[2]

The origins of the *ballet de cour* go back to court festivities and divertissements: prime examples are those ordered by Queen Catherine de' Medici at the end of the sixteenth century.[3] In keeping with the legacy of masquerades and large-scale political ballets of the Renaissance, these ballets were conceived by the intendants of princely houses, or, when motivated by less prestigious demands, improvised by the courtiers themselves.[4] The content of most of these seventeenth-century spectacles is known to us through their libretti, which remain nevertheless without much detail.[5] Only the most important or monumental ballets were preserved thanks to commemorative publications in connection with their political agenda.[6]

Historically, a ballet consisted of a succession of very brief danced sequences called *entrées* (entrances). When the number of *entrées* was extensive, the ballet was divided into *parties* (parts). These *parties* were sometimes unified by a single subject (for instance, the *Ballet Royal de la Nuit*). Generally, however, variety and surprise were favoured. As a collective enterprise, the ballet nevertheless had one author responsible for the general *dessein* (design) – that is to say, the subject and organisation of the plot. The responsibility for the music and for the poetic text was delegated to others. In parallel with printed occasional poems lauding patrons, printed programmes or booklets detailed the *dessein*, with an explanation of the décors and the characters. Later, these booklets would also give the text of the narrations sung by the chorus and the soloists, as well as the 'verses for the characters', in either a laudatory tone or a comic vein. These printed materials fulfilled a social function that was much appreciated by the audience, who would attempt during performances to identify the masked dancers.

The composers of the *Chambre du Roi* (the king's chamber) provided different types of music according to their own specialties: the dancer and composer Louis de Mollier (c. 1615–1688) composed ballet music, Jean de

Cambefort (c. 1605–1661) *récits*, and so on. These scores usually required an ensemble of lutes, violins, or flutes; choirs set for four or five voices; and solo parts. A group of dancers could also include musicians: the leader could sing, often accompanying himself while surrounded by other musicians. In 1673, the French writer Charles Sorel praised the lute, as 'there is grace when holding it and pinching [its strings]', stressing that 'one can dance and walk' while playing.[7]

Some ballets were organised around a single plot: *Le Ballet comique de la Reine* (1581) is about Ulysses being freed by the gods from Circe. Other ballets were based on Italian epics: *Le Ballet de Monseigneur le duc de Vandosme ou Ballet d'Alcine* (1610), *Le Ballet de la délivrance de Renaud* (1617),[8] and *Le Grand Ballet du Roi sur l'aventure de Tancrède en la Forêt enchantée* (René Bordier, 1619). Most of the music for these three ballets is attributed to Pierre Guédron (1564–d. 1619–1620). Other ballets were thematic: *Le Ballet des Fées des Forêts de Saint-Germain* (1625) or *Le Grand Bal de la Douairière de Billebahaut* (Bordier, Antoine Boësset; 1626). Ballets with a laudatory purpose alternated with more informal divertissements and masquerades: some of them – those related to the carnival season – were grotesque, and their performances were often lengthy.

One such work is the allegorical *Ballet Royal de la Nuit* (Clément, Cambefort, Mollier, Jean-Baptiste Boësset [1614–1685], Michel Lambert [c. 1610–1696]), which celebrated the end of the Fronde conflicts in 1653: it included no less than forty-three *entrées*, among which was *Ballet en Ballet* and two short ballets in several acts each: *Les Nopces de Thétis* and the *Comédie muëtte d'Amphitrion*. In 1654, *Le nozze di Peleo e di Theti* or *Les Noces de Pélée et de Thétis* (Francesco Buti, Carlo Caproli [1615/20–1692/5]) was commissioned by Mazarin after the Fronde as an 'Italian comedy in music, mixed with a ballet on the same subject, danced by His Majesty'. The opera is augmented by some ten *entrées* chosen by François de Beauvilliers, Duke of Saint-Aignan, Premier Gentilhomme de la Chambre du Roi, and set to music by court musicians. The king and his family participated in these danced *entrées*, in the company of the young Giambattista Lulli.[9]

Les Amants magnifiques, the divertissement created by Molière and Lully for the carnival in 1670, is sometimes considered to be the last participatory ballet: it is made up of two small poetic and musical units, bookending a *comédie-ballet*. Each of them is organised around the figure of the king as Neptune (first *intermède*) and Apollo ('Les Jeux Pythiens'). The king, however, did not dance.[10]

The *ballet de cour* is emblematic of the popularity of dance within the court and, more broadly, among the French aristocracy. This explains why the 1669 status of the newly formed institution, the Académie Royale d'Opéra, allowed the nobility to participate in operas, whether as dancers or as singers, without endangering their privileged social rank. The situation was slightly different outside the court: although four courtiers took part in the première of the first opera performed at the Académie Royale de Musique – *Les Fêtes de l'Amour et de Bacchus* (1673), a medley of court *intermèdes* reused by Lully[11] – over the years, the separation on stage between amateur dancers (courtiers) and professional ones became increasingly marked. Participatory dance persisted only within colleges, especially those of the Jesuits: pupils who played in Latin tragedies would also dance on stage during *intermèdes*, often mingling with professional dancers.[12]

Having taken the reins of the Académie Royale de Musique, Lully attached to it a professional 'corps de ballet' (which included several members of the Académie Royale de Danse that had been created in 1660) and a permanent *maître de ballet*.[13] During the academy's first decades, professional female dancers, such as the celebrated Mlle Verpré, performed at the court; they were dismissed during the 1670s but continued to be hired by the Académie Royale de Musique.[14] For the Parisian performance of the ballet *Le Triomphe de l'Amour* (Philippe Quinault, Lully; Palais-Royal, 6 May 1681), Lully hired new professional female dancers to replace the female courtiers who had created those roles earlier in the year at the court (Saint-Germain-en-Laye, 21 January). From that point on, female dancers came to be among the most celebrated performers of the Académie Royale de Musique's company.

Italian Opera in Paris

At the beginning of the seventeenth century, the strengthening of the absolute monarchy was affirmed, justified by the divine-right theory of kingship. Cardinal de Richelieu, Chief Minister of Louis XIII, displayed his artistic patronage through the creation of the Académie Française (1635), the protection of authors, and the development of theatre. Designed on the Italian model by the architect Jacques Lemercier, Richelieu's own theatre was built in his Palais Cardinal (later Palais-Royal) and inaugurated in January 1641 with a ballet, *La Prospérité des armes de la France* (Jean Desmarets de Saint-Sorlin, François de Chancy, Mollier, Michel Verpré), which he had himself commissioned.[15] It is in this context that Jules Mazarin (Giulio Raimondo Mazarini, 1602–1661) arrived in Paris in December 1643 as the Pope's extraordinary nuncio. Richelieu designated

Mazarin to succeed him as Chief Minister to the king. Pursuing Richelieu's politics of state interventionism in artistic life, but also seeking to strengthen the ties between France and the Papal states, Mazarin emulated the example of the Barberini family in Rome, who had been among the most important patrons and mentors of his youth.[16]

In order to foster spectacles in the Roman style, Mazarin, beginning in 1641, invited the composers Marco Marazzoli (c. 1602–1662), Mario Savioni (1606–1685), and Caproli, as well as Italian singers, to the French court.[17] The presence of an Italian itinerant company, the Febiarmonici, is documented for the year 1644.[18] During the autumn, other musicians arrived at the court, answering the French invitation: the singer Anna Francesca Costa ('la Checca'; fl. 1640–1654), the castrato Atto Melani (1626–1714), and his brother, the composer and singer Jacopo Melani (1623–1676), were sent by the Médici. The castrato Marc'Antonio Pasqualini (1614–1691) was sent by the Pope; and the tenor Venanzio Leopardi (as Venanzio d'Este), at the service of Cardinal Colonna, was called to Paris by the Duke of Modena. One of the greatest singers of her time, Leonora Baroni (1611–1670), accompanied by her husband, arrived at the French court in 1644 on the invitation, mediated by Mazarin, of Anne of Austria, the queen regent of France. They all participated in the première of Luigi Rossi's *Orfeo* at the Palais-Royal in 1647 (more on this later). After that, the company was disbanded, but the habit of bringing Italian musicians to the French court had begun. After the end of the Fronde conflicts, the famous Roman singer Anna Bergerotti arrived in Paris in 1655.

The first attempt to perform musical plays occurred in February 1645 at the Louvre. This was probably an allegorical play, staging the ties between France and Rome: the 'dramma per musica' *Il Giudizio della ragione tra la Beltà e l'Affetto* (Buti, Marazzoli or Marco dell'Arpa; Rome, 1643).[19] Complemented with ballets by Giambattista Balbi, *La Finta pazza* (Giulio Strozzi, Francesco Sacrati; Venice, 1641) was performed a few times in December 1645 at the Petit-Bourbon in the presence of the queen regent and the young Louis XIV, with machines and stage sets by Giacomo Torelli, who had been sent expressly to Paris by his patron, the Duke of Parma.[20] According to a contemporary review from the *Gazette de France,* the audience was as much dazzled by the music and poetry as by Torelli's décors, his machines, and 'admirable changes of scenery, so far unknown in France'.[21]

In February 1646 at the Palais-Royal, several performances were given of the opera *Egisto, ovvero, Chi soffre speri* (1637), originally written for the

Barberini theatre in Rome on a libretto by Giulio Rospigliosi (1600–1669) with music by Virgilio Mazzocchi (1597–1646) and Marazzoli.[22] An Italian traveller, Giambattista Barducci, noted the success which greeted the Italian 'manner of singing'.[23] But, apart from this, the concert version did not meet with much enthusiasm: on Fat Tuesday (13 February 1646), 'only the King, the Queen, the cardinal [Mazarin], and the inner circle of the Court' attended. In her memoirs, Françoise de Motteville, the *première femme de chambre* of Anne of Austria (Louis XIV's mother) lamented the fact that 'we were only twenty or thirty people in this place, and we thought that we would die of boredom and cold there. Entertainments of this sort require company, and solitude isn't in keeping with the theater.'[24] Such reactions may have discouraged performances of Monteverdi's *L'Incoronazione di Poppea* (Venice, 1643) that had been planned 'only with beautiful costumes'.[25] But Mazarin prepared a brilliant première: in June 1646, he brought Rossi, the Roman composer in the service of the Barberinis, to Paris. The machinery of the Palais-Royal was renovated with the help of the French painter and architect Charles Errard in order to accommodate Torelli's stage settings. Beginning on 2 March 1647, Rossi's opera *Orfeo* (Buti) was performed eight times as *Le Mariage d'Orphée et d'Euridice, tragi-comédie en musique et vers italiens, avec changement de théâtre et autres inventions jusqu'alors inconnus en France*, with machines by Torelli and ballets by Balbi – the music of which was mostly composed by French court musicians.[26]

Once again, the queen regent and Louis XIV attended these performances. The *Gazette de France* praises the décors and machines, notably those of Apollo, noting that the spectators did not know 'what to admire most' between 'the variety of scenes, the diverse ornaments of the theater, and the novelty of the machines', or 'the grace and the voice of those who recited'.[27] The expressive quality of the music remained nevertheless the main object of admiration. While pointing out that a part of the audience was bored due to their ignorance of the Italian language, a reviewer from the *Gazette de France* stresses that the music 'could express no less than the verses all the affects of those who did recite these'.[28] Nevertheless, this lavish *Orfeo* became the target of attacks by the Frondeurs against Mazarin.

Triumph of the Machine

Private companies followed this vogue for the spectacular. Considered since 1644 the most beautiful public theatre in Paris, the Théâtre du

Marais reopened in 1647; it accommodated theatrical machines designed by Georges Buffequin and staged monumental plays with musical accompaniment. At around the same time, in 1648, Mazarin commissioned Corneille and Charles Coypeau d'Assoucy (1605–1679), the former lute master of Louis XIII, to create a mythological tragedy mixed with music that could reuse the machines from Rossi's *Orfeo*. *Andromède* was finally premièred in February 1650 at the Petit-Bourbon, after some delay caused by the illness of the child king, then by the Fronde. Composed of four airs, a dialogue in music, and nine choruses, *Andromède* was favourably received and served to strengthen the association between music, machines, and mythology. Thus, opera made its way into the French public through the importation of Italian décors and the insertion of ballets in the French manner, as in Caproli's *Le Nozze di Peleo e di Theti* featuring Torelli's machines. Some French singers appeared for the first time among a cohort dominated by their Italian peers.

This period saw the French monarchy reaffirming its authority: the victory over the Fronde was followed in 1659 by the signing of the Treaty of the Pyrénées. The termination of the long war between France and Spain (1635–1659) culminated in a reconciliatory gesture, the wedding of Louis XIV and the Infanta Maria Theresa of Spain. Festivities lasted for three years: Italian opera was prominently featured. Francesco Cavalli, who travelled from Venice to Paris in the spring of 1660, was commissioned to compose an opera for the occasion, adapted to the greatest indoor theatre ever constructed in France, the *salle des machines* at the Tuileries, commissioned in 1659 to Gaspare Vigarani, who was employed by the Duke of Modena. As the construction was still in progress, a new performance of Cavalli's *Xerse* (Venice, 1655) took place in November 1660 with six 'entrées de ballet' set to music by Lully. The young violinist, who had been admitted as musician to the court in 1652, quickly became extremely popular, first as a dancer and then as a comic pantomime in his own ballets, which featured operatic dialogues (sung by the company of Italian singers) in combination with French *récits* (*L'Amor malato*, 1657; *Ballet royal de l'Impatience*, 1661). Lully staged a competition between the two styles in his *Ballet de la Raillerie* (1659).

Finally completed after the Fronde, Mazarin's new theatre was inaugurated on 7 February 1662, after his death in March 1661. Cavalli's opera *Ercole amante* (Buti) was premièred there, augmented with eighteen *entrées de ballet* composed by Lully, in which members of the court and the royal family participated. The cast comprised two French singers, Hilaire Dupuis and Anne de la Barre, and an Italian company led by Bergerotti.

The audience was impressed by the imposing size of the décors: the *Gazette de France* noted that the machine in the final scene could carry 'as many men as the Trojan horse'.[29] Italian guests were more critical. Barducci praised the ballet, the magnificent décors, the costumes, and the machines, but he lamented that the music, which should have been the main 'reason for the celebration, is entirely lost in the middle of the racket' caused by the greater part of the audience, who did not understand the libretto.[30] The Venetian ambassador, Giovanni Grimani, attributed this failure to the theatre's poor acoustics.[31]

The Franco-Italian experiment of *Ercole amante* was abandoned, but the influence of using such vast frescoes in combination with machines remained paramount for the inception of a specifically French form oriented towards the spectacular. Yet the issue of language remained to be addressed, since the majority of French audiences did not understand Italian. This explains the parallel development of the *pastorale en musique*, a work not only of much smaller proportions but also one that offered the possibility for conveying the passions of the libretto with a typically French musical language.

Return to the *Pastorale en Musique*

Such smaller dramatic works sung throughout appeared from the middle of the century: the pastoral comedy *Les Charmes de Félicie, tirés de la Diane de Montemayor* (Jacques Pousset de Montauban, Cambefort; Hôtel de Bourgogne, 1654) and *Le Triomphe de l'Amour sur des bergers et bergères*, a pastorale in one act (Charles Beys, Michel de la Guerre, music lost; concert version performed on 21 January 1655; slightly revised staged version on 26 March 1657). In his preface to the pastorale *La Muette ingratte* (concert version, 1658–1659), Cambert referred to his desire to 'introduc[e] plays in music as has been done in Italy':

I began in 1658 to compose an elegy for three different voices in a type of dialogue, as are heard in concerts, and this elegy is entitled *La Muette ingratte*. M. Perrin, having heard this piece which was successful and did not become tiresome – even though it lasted, with symphonies and solos, a good three-quarters of an hour – became inspired to compose a little pastoral.[32]

Cambert and Perrin collaborated again with the *Pastorale d'Issy* (music lost), which premièred in early April 1659 in a private context and was subsequently given, with success, at the court. According to Ménestrier, the work was an attempt to introduce more recitative into French music and render it 'capable of expressing the most pathetic feelings without losing any of its words'.[33] Going back stylistically to earlier court divertissements, if not to narrative models from the beginning of the century, these works failed to rival the tragedies that had been blossoming on the Parisian stage for more than twenty years. Perrin decided to set to music a serious play, *La Mort d'Adonis* (Antoine Boësset, music lost), which was performed at the 'petit coucher' of the king in 1661. This, as well as a comic play – *Ariane ou le mariage de Bacchus* (Cambert, rehearsed in public, music lost) – met Perrin's main purpose, which was to prove that 'it is possible to succeed in all dramatic genres'.[34]

Comédies Mêlées

Today referred to as *comédies-ballets*, *comédies mêlées* (mixed comedies), which featured songs or musical and danced *intermèdes* that had been first performed at the court and then in Parisian theatres, began to be incorporated into pastoral plays. Considered the first *comédie-ballet*, *Les Fâcheux* (Molière, Pierre Beauchamps; July 1661) was given as part of a lavish series of celebrations in honour of Louis XIV organised by Nicolas Fouquet, the Surintendant of Finances, in his own residence, the castle of Vaux-le-Vicomte. Since the dancers had to change their costumes between the different *entrées*, Molière decided to insert comic scenes within the danced divertissement. In public theatres, the practice of mixing spoken scenes and musical or danced sequences had started to gain momentum, with an increasing number of plays integrating musical scenes. For instance, *Le Bourgeois gentilhomme*, a *comédie-ballet* by Molière and Lully first performed at the court in October 1670 and then at the Palais-Royal in November, is a comic play that incorporates *intermèdes*, the most celebrated of which are 'La cérémonie turque' (The Turkish Ceremony), conceived and performed by Lully himself in the manner of his own ballets, and 'Le Ballet des Nations', which evokes different European countries and was inspired by the *Ballet royal de Flore* (Lully, 1669).

The Turning Point: 1671

By the end of the 1660s, the various options available for musical performance, whether at the court or in the city, were ready to converge and fully realise the union of ballet, court entertainment, and plays with machines. Commissioned for the reopening of the *salle des machines* at the Tuileries Palace, *Psyché*, a tragedy in *vers mêlés* (poetry composed of lines featuring different metres) with five musical and danced divertissements, premièred on 17 January 1671. Conceived by Molière, partly versified by Corneille and Quinault (the latter for the sung parts), and choreographed by Beauchamps, *Psyché* was inspired by *Andromède*. Its mythological subject justified the use of machines, exemplifying the monumental proportions assumed by the divertissement during Louis XIV's reign – nevertheless, spectators were particularly sensitive to the suffering of a young girl confronted by the gods' wrath.

Among *Psyché*'s highlights, 'La plainte italienne' – a scene imitating the Italian *lamento* – and the final scene – a wedding celebration in the heavens – incorporate both the opulent old tradition of the Florentine divertissement and the French *ballet de cour*. In a letter relating the event, the Marquis of Saint-Maurice, ambassador of the court of Savoy, counted no less than seventy 'maîtres à danser' and more than three hundred violinists, 'all lavishly dressed', the singers and musicians suspended by machines, and producing 'the most beautiful symphony in the world, with violins, theorbos, lutes, harpsichords, oboes, flutes, trumpets and cymbals'.[35]

In the meantime, a royal privilege dated 28 June 1669 granted to Perrin the authorisation to establish 'Royal Academies of Opera, or representations in music in French, on the model of those from Italy'. On 3 March 1671, *Pomone*, his pastorale in five acts, was performed in Paris (Jeu de Paume de la Bouteille; the music by Cambert is mainly lost, except for the overture, Act I, and part of Act II). Presented as an 'opera or representation in music', it featured machines built by the Marquis of Sourdéac (who became, later in December, one of the business managers of Perrin's Académies d'Opéra, with the financier Laurent Bersac, Sieur de Champeron). Entirely sung, its half-pastoral, half-mythological plot narrates in a rather comic vein the loves of Vertumne, the god of the seasons, and Pomone, the goddess of fruitful abundance. *Pomone* was performed continually over the course of seven to eight months (146 performances), making this work the greatest triumph of its century.

Like *Psyché*, *Pomone* offered all the necessary ingredients for the *tragédie en musique*. It was performed on the Parisian stage at considerable expense, financed by individuals but under the strict control of the royal authority; fully sung and in five acts, it featured dances and machines – the opulence of which recalled the court divertissement – and a prologue praising the king as the protector of the 'Académie Royale des Opéras'.[36] Nevertheless, the libretto, obviously comic, was generally considered weak and ridiculous, comparing unfavourably with Lullian opera, which, with the help of the librettist Quinault, tended more toward the dignity of *Psyché*.

In the wake of *Pomone*'s success, Molière's company invested generously in a series of new performances of *Psyché* at his own theatre, the Palais-Royal. The machines were repaired and readjusted for new effects; new musicians, dancers, singers, and acrobats were hired. The intention was clearly to attain a pomp comparable to that of court performances, but also to reaffirm the prestige of the *comédies mêlées* in response to the triumph of opera. Molière's attempt was successful, as is shown by the public reception of these new performances of *Psyché*, as would later be the case for the comedy *Le Malade Imaginaire* (Molière, 1673), the mythological tragedy *Circé* (Thomas Corneille, 1675), and, in 1682, Pierre Corneille's *Andromède* – all three plays with scores composed by Marc-Antoine Charpentier (1643–1704).[37] This success can also explain the aggressiveness with which Lully, as leader of the Académie Royale de Musique, defended his privileges against other Parisian stages.

Lully and the New Académie Royale de Musique

Lully arrived in Paris in 1646 as Giambattista Lulli. In 1653, he became composer of the king's instrumental music. He succeeded Cambefort in 1661 as 'Surintendant de musique et compositeur de la musique de chambre du Roi'. From his first *ballet de cour*, *Le Ballet du temps* (Benserade, 1654), through *Psyché*, Lully gradually established his control over the royal divertissements. Begun in 1664, Molière and Lully's fruitful teamwork (*Le Mariage forcé*) lasted until 1671: the causes of their rupture were the success of *Psyché* and, above all, Molière's decision to restage the work, most likely without Lully's permission. In addition, the success of *Pomone* led the king to encourage other composers: in November 1671, *Les Amours de Diane et d'Endymion* (Henry Guichard) on a score by Jean Granoulhiet (Grenouillet) de la Sablières (1627–c. 1700) was performed in Versailles, then repeated with ballets in February 1672 at Fontainebleau with the title *Le Triomphe de l'Amour*.[38] In Paris, Sourdéac and Champeron presented another pastorale, *Les Peines et les Plaisirs de l'Amour* (Gabriel Gilbert, Cambert). Hoping to maintain control over virtually every musical production given on Parisian stages, Lully bought Perrin's privilege and received a new patent in March 1672 from the king, which gave a quasi-monopoly to the brand-new Académie Royale de Musique. The Académie could from then on exercise complete control over the amount of music in any given performance as well as the number of musicians. For instance, shortly after the première of Molière's *Le Malade imaginaire*, Lully stipulated on 30 April 1673 that the orchestra, which had already been dramatically reduced, would number no more than two singers and six violinists – the usual configuration for musical entr'actes in spoken theatre. Protests from other theatres helped to loosen some of these rigid rules, but the Académie kept the privilege for performances that were entirely sung. After Lully's death, the privilege authorised his successors to trade with private managers willing to open opera houses in the provinces: Lyons in 1687; Rouen in 1688; Aix-en Provence, Marseilles, and Montpellier in 1689; cities in Brittany, Bordeaux, and Toulouse in 1690; Toul, Metz, and Verdun, and other cities in the French Lorraine in 1699.[39]

The very first première at the Académie Royale de Musique was Quinault and Lully's *Cadmus et Hermione*, a *tragédie en musique* on a mythological plot based on Ovid (Jeu de paume de Béquet, 27 April 1673). It was received with great success, and the king attended the performance. Following Molière's death in February 1673, Lully was granted royal permission to move the opera house to the Palais-Royal, a venue which had up to that point been occupied by Molière's company and the Italian comedians. The Palais-Royal could accommodate up to 1300 persons, out of which 700 could be seated in the loges. Although Lully seemed to have wanted at the beginning of his tenure at the Académie to attract a wide audience, the price of admission remained in general much higher than that for spoken theatre.[40]

After *Cadmus* and the exceptional performance of *Alceste* at Versailles on 4 July 1674 (see Figure 8.4), almost all of Lully's operas were first performed at the court in Saint-Germain-en-Laye.[41] The king financed the décors and rehearsals, as well as the exceptional honoraria for his protégé, who usually composed one opera per year, in January, at the beginning of the carnival season: *Alceste, ou le Triomphe d'Alcide* (1674), *Thésée* (1675), *Atys* (1676), *Isis* (1677), *Proserpine* (1680), *Persée* (1682), *Phaëton* (1683), *Amadis* (1684), and *Roland* (1685) were all composed on Quinault's libretti. Lully also wrote two operas on libretti by Thomas Corneille and Bernard Le Bouyer de Fontenelle: *Psyché* in 1678 – the score of which reuses the *intermèdes* Lully had composed for Molière's *Psyché* in 1671 – and, in 1679, *Bellérophon*.

Lully's masterwork, *Armide* (Quinault, 1686), was received with unprecedented enthusiasm even though it was not performed at court due to the king's developing disinterest in opera. A contemporary spectator described the theatre as filled over its maximum capacity and 'so profusely overcrowded that one could not understand the quantity of people who attended'.[42] In the title-role, Marthe Le Rochois eclipsed all the other actresses of the Académie Royale. Her imprint on the role lasted until the second half of the eighteenth century, especially in the most celebrated scene, Armide's monologue, 'Enfin, il est en ma puissance' (Act V scene 2):

In what rapture weren't we . . . to see her, dagger in hand, ready to pierce the heart of Renaud, asleep on a bed of grass! Fury animated her; love had just seized her heart; both agitated her alternately; pity and tenderness succeeded them in the end; and love remained victorious. Such beautiful and truthful attitudes! How many different movements and expressions in her eyes and her face, during this monologue.[43]

This long soliloquy offered singers the possibility of showcasing their vocal and acting talents, and expressing theatrical passions. Until the eighteenth century, Armide's monologue remained the most emblematic piece in the operatic French repertoire.

Following Lully's death in March 1687, his son-in-law Jean-Nicolas de Francine (1662–1735) became the director of the Académie Royale de Musique until 1704. In 1714, the Académie required that all of Lully's operas be inscribed in the repertoire of the theatre. The predominance of Lully's works had already cast a considerable shadow over those of other composers. *David et Jonathas*, Charpentier's first *tragédie en musique*, was performed in 1688 at the Jesuit college Louis-le-Grand: its acts were performed as *intermèdes* for a Latin tragedy, *Saul* (François de Paule Bretonneau). Yet Charpentier would have to wait until after Lully's death for his opera *Médée* (Thomas Corneille, 1693) to be brought to the stage of the Académie Royale de Musique. Judged exceedingly difficult, it was poorly received.[44] The composer Henri Desmarets (1661–1741) had more success the same year with *Didon* (Louise-Geneviève Gillot de Saintonge).[45]

Francine was able to rely on the works of other composers: Lully's secretary Pascal Collasse (1649–1709) composed the successful *Thétis et Pélée* (Fontenelle, 1689), which would then be performed over the course of seventy-six years at the Académie Royale. Another major success was *Alcyone* (Antoine Houdar de Lamotte, 1706) by Marin Marais (1656–1728). Himself a musician of the orchestra of the Académie, Marais solidified the Lullian legacy in Paris before the arrival of a second generation of composers whose works had first been noticed at the court. Such was the case for André Cardinal Destouches (1679–1742) and André Campra (1660–1741), who enjoyed their first successes with ballets and opéras-ballets.[46] Nevertheless, the genre that continued to bring artistic recognition was the *tragédie en musique.*

Tragédie en Musique

Lully's favourite librettist, Philippe Quinault (1635–1688), was renowned not only as a librettist but also as a playwright – he authored several spoken tragedies and plays in a lighter vein.[47] His double competence served French opera well. The product of a synthesis between diverse forms of court entertainments, it adopted as its referential frame the paradigmatic genre of tragedy.[48]

A paramount requirement of French classical aesthetics was to adapt the theatrical representation to the concepts of *vraisemblance* (verisimilitude) and *bienséance* (decorum, implying a general sense of suitability and plausibility).[49] The fictional plot must adequately observe moral standards and answer to the cultural expectations of the audience. Yet music poses a major problem with regard to verisimilitude, as it creates a distance between the object and its imitation – an issue that was also discussed in Italian opera. The recourse to themes defined as *galant* and *merveilleux* (marvellous), encompassing mythological and supernatural worlds and beings, helped to reduce this distance.

Machines were justified by the presence of supernatural characters and their otherworldly powers, increasing the theatrical illusion – thus, magicians and gods fill the universe of the *tragédie en musique.*[50] As Charles Perrault put it, *tragédie en musique* is justified because it belongs to an 'opposed species' to comedy, which 'only accepts the *vraisemblable* [verisimilitude]'. On the other hand, *tragédie en musique* can accommodate 'extraordinary and supernatural events, and this is what operas and plays with machines are about, while the tragedy stands in the middle, mixing the marvellous with the *vraisemblable*'.[51]

Other commentators pointed to the issue of characters who sing instead of speak. Saint-Evremond criticised the prosaism of specific scenes: for instance, a master asking his valet to run errands, dictating military orders through song, singing while 'killing by sword and spear', and so forth.[52] Opera should solve this difficulty by adopting mostly 'gallant' subjects. Saint-Evremond's argument is that some passions and actions are better rendered through song than others, as they harm neither the *bienséance* nor the reason: 'tender and painful passions are naturally expressed through some sort of song'.[53] Thus one must exclude 'cold' passions such as ambition or political reasoning. Pierre Perrin criticised Italian operas for being exceedingly narrative, lacking in passion and lyricism – thus the widespread French criticism of Italian operas based on historical figures such as Nero or Alexander the Great. These characters were deemed generally 'unfit to song': these operas are rather 'recited comedies' characterised by 'lengthy intrigues, cold and serious reasonings, as they would happen in a spoken play'.[54] As late as 1741, Mably declared that tragic heroes, usually cold and sententious with their 'feelings often locked deep down in their heart', are unfit as operatic characters.[55] All is then better in the marvellous universe of French opera: its characters, because completely imaginary, are also more apt to express themselves through song.

The relatively late surge of opera in France can be explained by a general distrust of the efficacy of music for conveying dramatic interactions and by issues surrounding the intelligibility – or absence thereof – of sung lyrics. With his deep knowledge of court tastes, Lully was perfectly aware of the expectations of French audiences in terms of vocal style. *Psyché* was not entirely sung, while *Pomone* presented a succession of airs: the invention of French opera had to wait for Lully's achievement, in which musical scenes would be coordinated with the help of the recitative. By offering a vocal style that could render all the nuances of affect, whether in monologues or dialogues, Lullian recitative became the most remarkable response to these constraints.[56]

Tragédies en musique were built on a hybrid succession of musical sequences: recitative scenes;[57] 'airs sérieux' or 'petits airs' – that is, short lyrical airs intertwined within scenes; longer *récits* for soliloquies imitated from spoken theatre that often privilege the narration of hallucinations, dreams, or laments;[58] and symphonies – that is, instrumental pieces, often with a descriptive purpose. The 'chansons' – dances and choruses inspired by the former tradition of *comédies mêlées*, and usually the most alien to the dramatic fabric – were gathered within scenes to provide poetic coherence. These scenes were used to represent ceremonies (religious rituals, weddings, sacrifices); popular or pastoral celebrations, including supernatural manifestations of otherworldly creatures; magical rites; infernal demons; allegorical representations of passions; and so on – in short, any type of situation in which music is diegetically or aesthetically justified.[59]

The spectacular dimensions of the *tragédie en musique* reveal its princely origins. Furetière's *Dictionnaire universel* (1690) defines opera as a 'public spectacle, a magnificently staged representation of some dramatic work, the verses of which are sung and are accompanied by a great symphony, dances, ballets with costumes, lavish decors and surprising machines'.[60]

Alongside dances and choruses, the presence of machines first required musical preludes, then descriptive symphonies: for instance, the evocation of spectres in Lully's *Amadis*, the unleashing of demons in Charpentier's *Médée*, the tempests in Collasse's *Thétis et Pélée*, and Marin Marais' *Alcyone*.[61]

While Lully enjoyed mixing comic characters with pathetic heroes, the comic became increasingly proscribed in the *tragédie en musique*. By the end of the seventeenth century, the genre had become perfectly well defined, its dramaturgy remarkably stable until the last decades of the eighteenth century.

A 'Ballet Moderne'

By the end of the 1680s, as Louis XIV was losing interest in the *tragédie en musique*, his son, Louis de Bourbon, the Grand Dauphin (1661–1711), became the new arbiter of taste at the court.[62] This led to the return of older forms of entertainment: in 1681, for the Grand Dauphin's wedding, the *ballet de cour Le triomphe de l'amour* was performed in Saint-Germain-en-Laye. In 1685, the prince commissioned a ballet from Lully, *Le Temple de la Paix* (Quinault; Fontainebleau), and, in the following year, the pastorale *Acis et Galatée* (Jean Galbert de Campistron; Château d'Anet). Court residences began to offer representations of 'petits opéras' (small operas), works of smaller dimensions, often on a pastoral theme.[63] Such works met with great success in Paris, including *Issé*, a *pastorale héroïque* in three acts (Antoine Houdar de La Motte and Destouches; Fontainebleau, 1697), which was presented in the capital in 1708.

These shifts also explain the necessity to better define the genre of *tragédie en musique* at a time when the Académie Royale de Musique was struggling with recurrent financial issues. This led the institution to rationalise its offerings: on the one hand, tragedies reinforcing the spectacular and the pathetic, especially at the beginning of the eighteenth century, and, on the other, the development of a new genre, the modern ballet, today referred to as *opéra-ballet*. Intended to alternate with *tragédies en musique* and to fill the slower summer season, the *opéra-ballet* favoured lighter themes. It also attempted to bring to the Parisian stage the distinctive spirit of courtly festivities.

In 1695, the ballet in three acts *Les Amours de Momus* (Duché de Vancy, Desmarets) paved the way to comedies in music, such as *Le Carnaval et la Folie* (La Motte, Destouches, 1703). Similarly, separated acts or ballet *entrées*, each focused on an independent plot, could be connected through a common theme that had been previously developed in the prologue. This strategy was profitable to the permanent company of singers and dancers: they could fully showcase their talents while offering Parisian audiences a wider range of musical styles.[64] Prime instances of these *opéra-ballets* are *Les Saisons* (Jean Pic, Collasse, 1695), which was followed by the triumph of *L'Europe galante* (La Motte, Campra, 1697). In 1754, Louis de Cahusac gave a well-known definition of the genre in which the hierarchy between action and divertissement seems reversed: compared to the five acts of the *tragédie en musique*, 'a vast composition, as those by Raphael and Michelangelo', *opéras-ballets* feature 'several different acts, each representing a single action mixed with divertissements, song and dance. These are pretty Watteaus, witty miniatures that require all the precision of the design, the graces of the brushstroke, and the whole brilliance of the color.'[65]

This taste for lightness goes hand in hand with the revival of the Italian influence, now present inside and outside the court, from the entourage of the Grand Dauphin to Italophile circles in Paris.[66] Several Italian composers were settled in Paris at that time: Paolo Lorenzani (1640–1713) beginning in 1678; Theobaldo di Gatti (c. 1650–1727) beginning in c. 1675; and later, around 1705, Jean-Baptiste Stuck [Stück] (Battistin, or Batistin, 1680–1755). Lorenzani received two commissions: the pastorale *Nicandro e Fileno* (Fontainebleau, 1681) followed by an opera in the Venetian style, *Orontée* (Chantilly, 1688), modelled after Cesti's *Orontea* (1649). Fashionable divertissements granted a substantial space to an Italian imaginary world, as in Campra's *L'Europe galante*: one of its acts, entitled 'L'Italie', brings Italian music to the stage of the Académie Royale. Campra's subsequent works, *Le Carnaval de Venise* (Jean-François Regnard, 1699) and *Les Fêtes vénitiennes* (Antoine Danchet, 1710), evoke the famous entertainments of the Republic.[67] The Italian style is primarily noticeable in the vocal writing, allowing for the increased virtuosity that would soon launch the swift success of the French cantata.[68]

This Italian vogue explains the controversy provoked by the publication in 1702 of François Raguenet's text, *Parallèle des Italiens et des Français en ce qui regarde la musique et les opéras*. Essentially praising Italian music and its musicians, this argument motivated Jean-Laurent Le Cerf de Viéville to publish his *Comparaison de la musique italienne et de la musique française* (1704), a text considered to be the first to discuss the 'goût français' in music, defining the *tragédie en musique* versus Italian opera and its aesthetic impact on contemporary audiences.[69]

Beginnings of the Opéra-comique

The comic musical style had been traditionally associated with Italian culture since the end of the sixteenth century. It gained ground at the beginning of the eighteenth century at the Académie Royale de Musique as well as on other stages, affecting the specialisation of theatres that had been carefully decreed by the king at the end of the seventeenth century. In 1680, the reunion of the spoken theatre companies gave birth to the Comédie-Française, which continued to perform comedies featuring divertissements with musical scores composed from 1692–1693 by Nicolas Racot de Grandval (1676–1753) and Jean-Claude Gillier (1667–1737).[70] On the other hand, the Comédie-Italienne granted a larger place to music: two-thirds of the plays, including the *canevas* plays printed in the anthology *Le Théâtre italien* first published in 1694 by Evariste Gherardi, contain sung airs – serenades, burlesque ceremonies, drinking songs, masquerades, and so forth.[71]

Following the creation of the Académie Royale de Musique, competition between the different theatres increased: it would lead at the beginning of the eighteenth century to a real war between the different stages. A much favoured tactic was to ridicule the taste for opera. Saint-Évremond's *Les Opéras* (around 1676) portrays a young mad girl only able to express herself through song: the theme reappears in the first original play to be staged at the Comédie-Française, *Les Fous divertissants* (Raymond Poisson, 1680), in which passages from Lully's *tragédies en musique Proserpine* and *Bellérophon* are quoted. Dancourt satirises victims of the opera craze in *Angélique et Médor* (1685) and in *Renaud et Armide* (1686). These latter three plays have a score by Charpentier.[72]

While these practices were a blow to the Lullian hegemony, they also took advantage of the popularity of his works.[73] The Comédie-Italienne transposes the intrigues into a lighter setting by presenting comic characters dealing with trivial matters. They sing tragic laments on original music (by Angelo Constantini, known as Mezzetin), but also 'vaudevilles' – that is, well-known tunes or famous operatic airs, the lyrics of which are altered following the example of the *canevas*.[74] *L'Opéra de campagne* by poet and musician Charles Rivière Dufresny transports Quinault's and Lully's *Armide* to a rustic farm: Renaud's air 'Plus j'observe ces lieux' (Act II scene 3), in which he is lulled to sleep, is parodied by Arlequin, who sings in praise of a roasting spit.

Eventually, such practices led to full-blown parodies that tweaked the plots of *tragédies en musique* staged at the Académie Royale de Musique, and, in so doing, opened the path to the genre of the *opéra-comique*.[75] Following the expulsion of Italian actors from Paris in 1697, the Parisian fairs (the Foire Saint-Laurent and the Foire Saint-Germain) attempted to take their place. The Académie Royale responded by banning the use of song in works performed at such fair theatres; similarly, the Comédie-Française forbade them to use speech. The fair theatres were obliged to come up with imaginative alternatives to compensate for the loss of spoken and sung dialogues: they required that the audience sing well-known operatic airs ('timbres') and vaudevilles.[76] This type of interaction between the public and the actors was itself viewed as desirable by the Académie Royale, since its audience enjoyed singing along with the actors, especially during the divertissements. Attending a performance of Campra's *L'Europe galante* in 1698, the English physician Martin Lister could thus marvel at the large audience and at the 'great numbers of the nobility that come daily to [the operas], and some that can sing them all'.[77] This in turn explained the enduring success of the fair theatres where this practice continued, even after they had regained the right to use song and speech.

Eventually, after strenuous negotiations between the Académie Royale and the fair theatres, two directors of the latter, Charles Alard and the widow Maurice (Jeanne Godefroy), obtained in 1709 the authorisation to hire singers and dancers, and to change the décors, the sole condition being that they would not present plays with continuous musical accompaniment.[78] The convention signed later in December 1714 marked the birth of the *opéra-comique*, perpetuating in its own terms the legacy and specificities of the French *tragédie en musique*.

Translated from the French by Jacqueline Waeber and Laura Williams

Notes

1 Henry Prunières, *Le Ballet de cour en France avant Benserade et Lully, suivi du ballet de 'La Délivrance de Renaud' de Pierre Guédron* (Paris: H. Laurens, 1914), 178; Margaret M. McGowan, *L'Art du ballet de cour en France: 1581–1643* (Paris: Editions du CNRS, 1978).

2 Mark Franko, *Dance as Text: Ideologies of the Baroque Body* (New York: Oxford University Press, 1993); Sarah R. Cohen, *Art, Dance, and the Body in French Culture of the Ancien Régime* (New York and Cambridge: Cambridge University Press, 2000).

3 Frances A. Yates, *The Valois Tapestries* (London: Routledge & Kegan Paul, 1959).

4 See Margaret M. McGowan, *Dance in Renaissance: European Fashion, French Obsession* (New Haven: Yale University Press, 2008).

5 A large compilation of these libretti can be found in Paul Lacroix, *Ballets et mascarades de cour de Henri III à Louis XIV (1581–1652)*, 6 vols. (Geneva: J. Gay et fils, 1868–1870).

6 Laura Naudeix, 'Qui est l'auteur d'un ballet de cour? du *Paradis d'amour* (1572) aux *Fâcheux* (1662)', in Sabine Chaouche, Estelle Doudet, and Olivier Spina (eds.), *European Drama and Performance Studies. Écrire pour la scène (XVe– XVIIIe siècle)* (Paris: Garnier, 2017), 97–113.

7 Charles Sorel, *De la prudence ou des bonnes reigles de la vie* (Paris, 1673), quoted in Laura Naudeix, 'La "mélodie harmonieuse des cieux": musiciens visibles ou cachés dans le ballet français du XVIIe siècle', in Bénédicte Louvat-Molozay and Xavier Bisaro (eds.), *Les Sons du théâtre, Angleterre et France (XVIe–XVIIIe siècle). Éléments d'une histoire de l'écoute* (Rennes: Presses Universitaires de Rennes, 2013), 73–84.

8 *La Délivrance de Renaud: Ballet dansé par Louis XIII en 1617. Ballet danced by Louis XIII in 1617*, ed. Greer Garden (Turnhout: Brepols, 2010).

9 Margaret M. McGowan, 'Échanges entre le ballet de cour et le théâtre au milieu du XVIIᵉ siècle', in Irène Mamczarz (ed.), *Les Premiers opéras en Europe et les formes dramatiques apparentées* (Paris: Klincksieck, 1992), 153–69.

10 Laura Naudeix (ed.), *Molière à la cour. Les Amants magnifiques en 1670* (Rennes: Presses Universitaires de Rennes, 2020).

11 Nathalie Lecomte, *Entre cours et jardins d'illusion. Le ballet en Europe 1515–1715* (Pantin: Centre national de la danse, 2014), 317.

12 Judith Rock, *Terpsichore at Louis-le-Grand: Baroque Dance on a Jesuit Stage in Paris* (Saint Louis: Institute of Jesuit Sources, 1996).

13 Lecomte, *Entre cours et jardins d'illusion*, 419. See also Ariane Ducrot, 'Lully créateur de troupe', *XVIIᵉ Siècle*, 98–9 (1973), 91–107.

14 Julia Prest, *Theatre under Louis XIV: Cross-Casting and the Performance of Gender in Drama, Ballet and Opera* (New York: Palgrave MacMillan, 2006).

15 Joseph Bergin, *Cardinal Richelieu: Power and the Pursuit of Wealth* (New Haven: Yale University Press, 1985); Hugh Gaston Hall, *Richelieu's Desmarets and the Century of Louis XIV* (Oxford: Clarendon Press, 1990).

16 David J. Sturdy, *Richelieu and Mazarin: A Study in Statesmanship* (Basingstoke and New York: Palgrave Macmillan, 2004).

17 See Barbara Nestola, *Les Italiens à la Cour de France: de Marie de Médicis au Régent Philippe d'Orléans* (Versailles: CMBV, 2004), 11–45.

18 Lorenzo Bianconi and Thomas Walker, 'Dalla *Finta Pazza* alla *Veremonda*. Storie di Febiarmonici', *RIM* 10 (1975), 379–454.

19 See Neal Zaslaw, 'The first opera in Paris: a study in the politics of art', in John Hajdu Heyer (ed.), *Jean-Baptiste Lully and the Music of the French Baroque. Essays in Honor of James R. Anthony* (Cambridge: Cambridge University Press, 1989), 7–23.

20 Margaret Murata, 'Why the First Opera Given in Paris Wasn't Roman', *COJ* 7/2 (1995), 87–105.

21 Quoted in Henry Prunières, *L'Opéra italien en France avant Lully* (Paris: Librairie ancienne Honoré Champion, 1913), 74–5.

22 Barbara Nestola, 'L'*Egisto* fantasma di Cavalli: nuova luce sulla rappresentazione parigina dell'*Egisto ovvero Chi soffre speri* di Mazzocchi e Marazzoli (1646)', *Recercare* 19/1–2 (2007), 125–46.

23 Quoted in Nicola Michelassi, '*La finta pazza*: un dramma incognito in giro per l'Europa', in Davide Conrieri (ed.), *Gli Incogniti e l'Europa* (Bologna: I libri di Emil, 2011), 145–208: 188.

24 Quoted and translated in Zaslaw, 'The first opera in Paris', 22.

25 Stefano Costa to Cornelio Bentivoglio, 3 January 1647, quoted in Dinko Fabris, 'Relazioni musicali tra Venezia e Parigi da *Orfeo* a *Xerse*: il ruolo dei Bentivoglio', *I Musicisti veneziani e italiani a Parigi (1640–1670)* (Venice: Venetian Centre for Baroque Music, 2014), 6–15, www.vcbm.it/public/research_attachments/I_musicisti_veneziani_e_italiani_a_ Parigi_-_Atti_della_giornata_di_studio.pdf (accessed 1 July 2019). See also Ellen Rosand, *Monteverdi's Last Operas. A Venetian Trilogy* (Berkeley, Los Angeles, and London: University of California Press, 2007), 126.

26 Prunières, *L'Opéra italien*, 127; see also Michael Klaper, 'New Light on the History of L'*Orfeo* (Buti-Rossi)', in Alessandro Di Profio and Damien Colas (eds.), *D'une scène à l'autre: l'opéra italien en Europe*, 2 vols. (Liège: Mardaga, 2008), vol. 1, 27–40.

27 Quoted in James R. Anthony, *French Baroque Music: From Beaujoyeulx to Rameau*, rev. edn. (Portland: Amadeus Press, 1997), p. 75.

28 *Gazette de France*, 8 March 1647, quoted in Prunières, *L'Opéra italien*, 110 and 109, note 1.

29 *Gazette de France*, 1662, quoted in Prunières, *L'Opéra italien*, 170–1.

30 Prunières, *L'Opéra italien*, 302.

31 See Nestola, *Les Italiens à la Cour de France*, 27.

32 John S. Powell, *Music and Theatre in France, 1600–1680* (Oxford: Oxford University Press, 2000), 43, note 86.

33 Claude-François Ménestrier, *Des Représentations en musique anciennes et modernes* (Paris: René Guignard, 1681), 208–9.

34 Pierre Perrin, c. 1666, quoted in Louis E. Auld, *The Lyric of Pierre Perrin, Founder of the French Opera*, 3 vols. (Henryville: Institute of Medieval Music, 1986), vol. 3, xiv.

35 Quoted by John S. Powell, Introduction to *Psyché*, in Jean-Baptiste Lully, *Œuvres complètes. Série II. Comédies-ballets et autres divertissements*, vol. 6, ed. John S. Powell, Herbert Schneider, Laura Naudeix (Hildesheim, Zürich, New York: G. Olms, 2007), 6.

36 See Robert M. Isherwood, *Music in the Service of the King: France in the XVIIth Century* (Ithaca: Cornell University Press, 1973); Manuel Couvreur, *Jean-Baptiste Lully: musique et dramaturgie au service du prince* (Brussels: M. Vokar, 1992); Geoffrey V. Burgess, *Ritual in the* Tragédie en musique *from*

Lully's Cadmus et Hermione *(1673) to* Rameau's Zoroastre *(1749)* (Ph.D. dissertation, Cornell University, 1998).

37 On the performance and reception of these plays, see *The Demise of the Machine Play*, vol. 3 of Jan Clarke, *The Guénégaud Theatre in Paris (1673–1680)*, 3 vols. (Lewiston, Queenston, and Lampeter: Edwin Mellen, 2007).

38 Jérôme de La Gorce, *Jean-Baptiste Lully* (Paris: Fayard, 2002), 179.

39 Jérôme de La Gorce, *L'Opéra à Paris au temps de Louis XIV* (Paris: Desjonquères, 1992), 88–9; La Gorce, 'Une Académie de musique en province au temps du Roi-Soleil: l'Opéra de Rouen', in Marc Honegger and Christian Meyer (eds.), *La musique et le rite sacré et profane, vol. 1: Tables rondes; vol. 2: Communications libres. Actes du 13. Congrès de la Société Internationale de Musicologie Strasbourg, 29 août–3 septembre 1982*, vol. 2 (Strasbourg: Association de Publication près les Universités de Strasbourg: 1986), 465–96; La Gorce, 'Recherches sur les débuts de l'opéra de Metz: privilèges, répertoires et troupes (1699–1732)', in Yves Ferraton (ed.), *Itinéraires musicaux en Lorraine, sources, événements, compositeurs* (Langres: D. Guéniot, 2002), 41–58.

40 La Gorce, *L'Opéra à Paris au temps de Louis XIV*, 37–9.

41 Thierry Boucher, 'Un haut lieu de l'Opéra de Lully. La salle de spectacles du château de Saint-Germain-en-Laye', in Herbert Schneider and Jérôme de La Gorce (eds.), *Jean-Baptiste Lully: Actes du colloque/ Kongressbericht: Saint-Germain-en-Laye – Heidelberg 1987* (Laaber: Laaber-Verlag, 1990) 457–67: La Gorce, *L'Opéra à Paris au temps de Louis XIV*, 54–5.

42 Letter by Sainte-Frique, 22 February 1686, quoted in La Gorce, *Jean-Baptiste Lully*, 330.

43 Évrard Titon du Tillet, *Le Parnasse français* (Paris: J.-B. Coignard, 1732), 791–2.

44 Catherine Cessac, *Marc-Antoine Charpentier*, 2nd edn. (Paris: Fayard, 2004).

45 Desmarets has been the object of one important collection of essays: Jean Duron and Yves Ferraton (eds.), *Henry Desmarets (1661–1741). Exils d'un musicien dans l'Europe du Grand siècle* (Sprimont: CMBV-Mardaga, 1999).

46 See the essays in Catherine Cessac (ed.), *Itinéraires d'André Campra, 1660–1744 : d'Aix à Versailles, de l'Église à l'Opéra* (Wavre: CMBV-Mardaga, 2012).

47 Buford Norman, *Touched by the Graces: The Libretti of Philippe Quinault in the Context of French Classicism* (Birmingham: Summa Publications, 2001); Norman, 'Le rôle de Quinault dans la création de l'opéra français', in Jean Duron (ed.), *'Cadmus & Hermione' (1673) de Jean-Baptiste Lully et Philippe Quinault: livret, études et commentaires* (Wavre: Mardaga, 2008), 71–95.

48 Laura Naudeix, *Dramaturgie de la tragédie en musique (1673–1764)* (Paris: H. Champion, 2004), 33–119.

49 Catherine Kintzler, *Poétique de l'opéra français de Corneille à Rousseau*, 2nd edn. (Paris: Minerve, 2005); Downing A. Thomas, *Aesthetics of Opera in the Ancien régime, 1647–1785* (Cambridge: Cambridge University Press, 2002).

50 Bénédicte Louvat-Molozay, *Théâtre et musique. Dramaturgie de l'insertion musicale dans le théâtre français (1550–1680)* (Paris: H. Champion, 2002), 365–400.

51 Charles Perrault, *Critique de l'Opera ou Examen de la tragédie intitulée Alceste ou le Triomphe d'Alcide*, modern edition published in Philippe Quinault, *Alceste, suivi de la Querelle d'Alceste: Anciens et modernes avant 1680*, ed. Buford Norman, William Brooks, Jeanne Morgan Zarucchi (Geneva: Droz, 1994), 99.

52 Charles de Saint-Évremond, *Sur les Opera*, in René Ternois (ed.), *Œuvres en prose*, ed. René Ternois, 4 vols. (Paris: Société des Textes français modernes, Librairie M. Didier, 1962–1969) 1966, vol. 3, 151.

53 Ibid., 153.

54 Pierre Perrin, 'Avant-propos', in *Argument des scènes de Pomone* (Paris: Lemercier, 1671), 15.

55 Gabriel Bonnot de Mably, *Lettres à Madame la Marquise de P*** sur l'opéra* (Paris: Didot, 1741), 48.

56 Lois Rosow, 'The Metrical Notation of Lully's Recitative', in Schneider and La Gorce (eds.), *Jean-Baptiste Lully*, 405–22.

57 Herbert Schneider, 'Strukturen der Szenen und Akte in Lullys Opera', in Schneider and La Gorce (eds.), *Jean-Baptiste Lully*, 77–98.

58 Naudeix, *Dramaturgie de la tragédie en musique*, 450–63; Naudeix, 'Le jeu du chanteur dans l'esthétique spectaculaire de l'opéra lulliste', in Jacqueline Waeber (ed.), *Musique et Geste en France de Lully à la Révolution* (Bern: Peter Lang, 2009), 43–54.

59 Naudeix, *Dramaturgie de la tragédie en musique*, 320–405; Rebecca Harris-Warrick, *Dance and Drama in French Baroque Opera: A History* (Cambridge: Cambridge University Press, 2016), notably ch. 8, 'Dance and Ballet'.

60 Antoine Furetière, *Dictionnaire universel*, 3 vols. (La Haye and Rotterdam: chez Arnout & Reinier Leers, 1690), vol. 2, np.

61 Caroline Wood, 'Orchestra and Spectacle in the Tragédie en musique, 1673–1715: Oracle, Sommeil and Tempête', *Proceedings of the Royal Musical Association* 108 (1981–1982), 25–46, and also her *Music and Drama in the Tragédies en musique, 1673–1715* (New York, and London: Garland, 1996).

62 See Georgia Cowart, *The Triumph of Pleasure: Louis XIV and the Politics of Spectacle* (Chicago: University of Chicago Press, 2008), especially ch. 4, 'Tragic Interlude. Reversals at the Paris Opéra, 1671–1697'.

63 Nathalie Berton-Blivet, *Le Petit Opéra (1668–1723). Aux marges de la cantate et de l'opéra* (Ph.D., Université de Tours, 1996).

64 Jérôme de La Gorce, 'L'Académie royale de Musique en 1704, d'après des documents inédits conservés dans les archives notariales', *Revue de musicologie* 65/2 (1979), 160–91.

65 Louis de Cahusac, *La Danse ancienne et moderne ou Traité historique de la danse*, ed. Nathalie Lecomte, Laura Naudeix, and Jean-Noël Laurenti (Paris: Desjonquères/Centre National Supérieur de la Danse, 2004), 219.

66 Don Fader, 'The "Cabale du Dauphin," Campra, and Italian Comedy: The Courtly Politics of French Musical Patronage around 1700', *ML* 86/3 (2005), 380–413.

67 Rebecca Harris-Warrick, 'Staging Venice', *COJ* 15/3 (2003), 297–316.

68 See David Tunley, *The Eighteenth-Century French Cantata*, 2nd edn. (Oxford: Clarendon Pres, 1997), especially ch. 3, 'Stylistic Traits in French and Italian Vocal Music of the Baroque', which goes back to specific features of seventeenth-century vocal music in both geographic areas.

69 François Raguenet, *Parallèle des Italiens et des Français en ce qui regarde la musique et les opéras*, and *Défense du Parallèle* (1702–1705), Jean-Laurent Le Cerf de Viéville, *Comparaison de la musique italienne et de la musique française*, (1704 et 1706), in *La Première Querelle de la musique italienne (1702–1706)*, ed. Laura Naudeix (Paris: Classiques Garnier, 2018); Georgia Cowart, *The Origins of Modern Musical Criticism: French and Italian Music 1600–1750* (Ann Arbor: UMI Research Press, 1981), especially her ch. 3, 'The Quarrel between Raguenet and Le Cerf'.

70 Maurice Barthélémy, 'L'opéra-comique des origines à la Querelle des Bouffons', in Philippe Vendrix (ed.), *L'Opéra comique en France au XVIIIe siècle* (Liège: Mardaga, 1992), 9–78: 18–20.

71 Three years after the banishment of the Italian comedians by the king in 1697, Gherardi published an expanded collection: *Le Théâtre italien de Gherardi, ou, Le Recueil général de toutes les comédies & scènes françaises jouées par les comédiens italiens du roi, pendant tout le temps qu'ils ont été au service*, 6 vols. (Paris: Jean-Bapt. Cusson et Pierre Witte, 1700).

72 John Powell, 'The Opera Parodies of Florent Carton Dancourt', *COJ* 13/2 (2001), 87–114.

73 Judith le Blanc, *Avatars d'opéras: parodies et circulation des airs chantés sur les scènes parisiennes* (Paris: Classiques Garnier, 2014).

74 François Moureau, 'Lully en visite chez Arlequin: parodies italiennes avant 1697', in Schneider and La Gorce (eds.), *Jean-Baptiste Lully*, 235–50, and 'Parties et parodies musicales à la Comédie-Française sous Louis XIV', *Revue d'Histoire du Théâtre* 57 (2005), 227–42.

75 See David Trott, 'Réflexions sur les conditions de la parodie d'opéra en France entre 1669 et 1752', in Letizia Cagiano Norci and Delia Gambelli (eds.), *Le Théâtre en musique et son double (1600–1762)* (Paris: H. Champion, 2005), 105–19; Pauline Beaucé, *Parodies d'opéra au siècle des Lumières: évolution d'un genre comique* (Rennes: Presses Universitaires de Rennes, 2013); Pauline Beaucé and Françoise Rubellin (eds.), *Parodier l'opéra: pratiques, formes, enjeux* (Montpellier: Éditions Espaces 34, 2015).

76 Monique Rollin, 'Les œuvres de Lully transcrites pour le luth', in Schneider and La Gorce (eds.), *Jean-Baptiste Lully*, 483–94; Herbert Schneider, *Das Vaudeville: Funktionen eines multimedialen Phänomens* (Hildesheim, Zürich, and New York: G. Olms, 1996); Schneider (ed.), *Timbre und Vaudeville: zur Geschichte und Problematik einer populären Gattung im 17. und 18. Jahrhundert* (Hildesheim, Zürich, and New York: G. Olms, 1999); Judith le Blanc and Herbert Schneider (eds.), *Pratiques du timbre et de la parodie d'opéra en Europe: XVIe–XIXe siècles* (Hildesheim, Zürich, and New York: G. Olms, 2014).

77 Martin Lister, *A Journey to Paris in the Year 1698* (London: Jacob Tonson, 1699), 174.

78 Hedy Law, 'Orphée at the Forains. Silencing and Silences in Old Régime France', in Kirsten Gibson and Ian Biddle (eds.), *Cultural Histories of Noise, Sound and Listening in Europe, 1300–1918* (Abingdon and New York: Routledge, 2017), 111–26.

11   Song and Declamation in French Opera

JACQUELINE WAEBER

The French versus Italian Problem

In his *Memoirs*, the Italian playwright Carlo Goldoni describes the performance of a French opera he attended in Paris at the Académie Royale de Musique in 1763. There is much to admire in this unnamed work, from the technical ability of the dancers to the sumptuous décors, machines, and costumes. But soon, all this spectacle wears him out:

I patiently waited for the airs, in the expectation that I should at least be amused with the music. The dancers made their appearance, and I imagined the act finished, but heard not a single air. I spoke of this to my neighbor, who laughed at me, and assured me that we had had six in the different scenes which I had heard. "What!" said I, "I am not deaf; the instruments never ceased accompanying the voices, sometimes more loudly, and sometimes more slowly than usual, but I took the whole for recitative . . . Everything was beautiful, everything was grand, everything was magnificent, except for the music . . . It is a paradise for the eyes, and a hell for the ears.[1]

This passage has often been quoted to pinpoint the strangeness of French opera, even its absurdity, at least when judged alongside the expectations of eighteenth-century audiences to whom *opera seria* provided the normative model. At the time of Goldoni's description, the *tragédie en musique* had been weakened by the vogue for opéra-comique and by the absence of a leading composer: Rameau had died in 1764, and his most recent *tragédie en musique, Zoroastre*, had been premièred in 1749.[2]

Goldoni perceived French opera primarily as a visual spectacle – the privileged place of ballet and the use of machines had been an essential feature of the *tragédie en musique* since its inception. His description sheds light on the clichés attached to French opera that had existed since the time of Lully. Goldoni's argument implies that the French conception of song is problematic, at least for Italian(ate) ears. That Goldoni refers to the French vocal style as nothing other than 'récitatif' was not an isolated claim at that time. Discussions about the relevant merits and flaws of French and Italian vocal styles had been going on since the birth of opera in France. These had

240

culminated with the *Querelle des Bouffons* (end 1752–1754) and were provoked when the Académie Royale de Musique invited Felice Bambini's Italian company to perform a series of *intermezzi comici*, among which was Pergolesi's *La Serva padrona*.[3]

The confrontation on the Parisian stage between the *tragédie en musique* and the repertoire of Italian comic opera triggered the polemical discussions of the *Querelle*, but this was also much more than the collision of two antagonistic conceptions of vocality as exhibited by French and Italian opera. The *Querelle* was the culmination of tensions that had accompanied the *tragédie en musique* since its inception, including the question of its attachment to the tradition of French *tragédie classique*, the spoken classical tragedy. Moreover, the *Querelle* led to radical reconsiderations regarding the musicality of French versus Italian – a debate that had been brewing throughout the seventeenth century, well before the publication of Jean-Jacques Rousseau's *Lettre sur la musique française* in November 1753.

Prior to the eighteenth century, the development of the *tragédie en musique* and other related dramatic genres, such as the opéra-ballet, provided secure outlets for French musicians and their librettists. The absence of real competition with the Italian operatic model helped them promote and preserve their own style. Still, to speak of a complete French rejection of Italian music and its lyric style would be excessive. Since the early seventeenth century, the fashion of 'Italianisme' had been encouraged by the presence at the court of the Marquise de Rambouillet, who was of Roman origin, and the marriage of Henry IV of France with Maria de' Medici in 1600.

Certainly, the French did not come naturally to opera, at least when we conflate the term 'opera' with the Italian *dramma per musica*. Understanding the complex history of the assimilation of Italian opera by the French stage cannot neglect the importance of non-musical factors, such as the political relationships between the kingdom of France and several powerful Italian states. Various attempts to graft the Italian operatic model on the French tradition of court entertainment ended with the advent of the *tragédie en musique*, which was inaugurated with Jean-Baptiste Lully and Philippe Quinault's *Cadmus et Hermione* (1673), a genre intended more as a departure from the Italian opera than a reappropriation of it. After Lully's death (1687) and throughout the eighteenth century (that is, until Gluck arrived in Paris in 1773), French opera continued to be contrasted with the Italian model. This was primarily due to the centralised system implemented through royal institutions that ruled the arts: it remained crucial for France, home to the second major operatic tradition in Europe, to preserve its own paradigmatic model.

The Persistence of the *Tragédie Classique* in the *Tragédie en Musique*

Other factors were paramount for explaining the physiognomy of French opera and its antithetical perception of Italian opera. Assessing the emergence of the French model for opera must first consider the ground on which this model originated: the classical tragedy, France's most illustrious theatrical tradition. The *tragédie en musique* was organically tied to theoretical and aesthetic conceptions that defined the genre of spoken tragedy, itself a reaction against the dramatic excesses of the sixteenth-century humanist tragedy. The blossoming of French tragedy was encouraged by improvements to Parisian theatrical locations – such as the reopening in 1644 of the renovated Théâtre du Marais – which better equipped them for the display of spectacular stage settings and machines. Another crucial factor was the emergence of a new generation of playwrights, among whom were the genre's two most prominent figures, Pierre Corneille (1606–1684) and Jean Racine (1639–1699).

French classical tragedy is defined by a series of paradigmatic features: division into five acts and a plot taken from Classical antiquity – be it history or mythology, as shown in Racine's plays – or from ancient or early history (for instance, Corneille's *Le Cid*). The genre also excluded lowly characters, privileging instead aristocratic, regal figures. This can be understood as an extension of the rule of *bienséance* (decorum), which prohibited the representation on stage of actions involving physical violence or death. Moreover, anything tending towards an excessive eroticisation of the body or any other physical activity that would have been deemed trivial was banned.

All these aspects transited easily from spoken tragedy to *tragédie en musique*. However, the crux of the problem originated with the adjunction of music and its entanglement in the requirements of the art of declamation expected for the performance of spoken tragedy. 'Musicalising' or not the spoken model of tragedy had been a consubstantial debate in the history of French opera since its inception. At the end of the seventeenth century, the *tragédie en musique* was a prominent topic among the debates propelled by the *Querelle des Anciens et des Modernes*. The writer Charles Perrault keenly defended the new genre of French opera, demonstrating its validity against the arguments in favour of the Ancients in his *Critique de l'opéra, ou Examen de la tragédie intitulée Alceste* (1674). This opened an enduring tradition of controversies that traversed the entire eighteenth century—the *Querelle des Lullistes et des Ramistes* (ignited by Rameau's first *tragédie en musique, Hippolyte et Aricie*, premièred in 1733), the *Querelle des Bouffons*, and the *Querelle des Gluckistes et des Piccinnistes* (1775–1779).

It would be a mistake to imply that the French resisted the novelty of opera because they were 'less musical' than Italians. The model of the *tragédie en musique*, a consequence of French misgivings regarding Italian opera, was embedded in a paradigmatic conception of lyric poetry. Thus theatrical declamation was perceived as being as musical as it was poetic. To summarise the arguments of French contemporary commentators opposed to opera, why would the French need tragedies set to music when their art of theatrical declamation was already *musical*?

The Reign of the Alexandrine

The French strongly believed in the musicality of their poetic language, which could be revealed by an adequate observation of accents, quantity, and rules of versification. As Claude Jamain puts it, 'to bring back song to the spoken text had always been the natural inclination of [French] classicism', an attitude viewed as antithetical to the vocalic sensibility of Italian opera.[4]

Lyric poetry of that period relied to a great extent on the *alexandrin*, or alexandrine verse. Popularised during the sixteenth century by the poets Pierre Ronsard and Joachim du Bellay, the alexandrine remained until the nineteenth century the main verse in French poetry. The alexandrine line consists of twelve syllables and is divided by two hemistichs of equal length, separated by a caesura falling after the sixth syllable. When ending on a masculine rhyme, that is to say, any syllable ending with a consonant (as in the words *sommeil, fracas, vainqueur, soupir*, etc.), the alexandrine counts exactly twelve syllables. When the ending rhyme is feminine, it counts twelve syllables, plus a final one, the mute "e" (as in *heure, larmes, venge, soupire*, etc.). Both alexandrine lines given here, from Armide's famous monologue in Quinault's *tragédie en musique, Armide* (Lully, 1686), respectively end with a masculine and a feminine rhyme:

Ce fa-tal en-ne-mi, ce su-per-be vain-<u>queur</u>.
1 2 3 4 5 6 | 1 2 3 4 5   6   (12)

A-che-vons, je fré-mis; ven-geons-nous, je sou-<u>pi-re</u>.
1 2 3   4 5 6 | 1   2 3 4 5 6 (+1)   (12+)

In the first line, the caesura of the first hemistich is marked by the tonic accent on 'ennemi' and in the second on 'frémis'. A defining prosodic feature of the classical alexandrine is to echo the caesura on the accented sixth syllable by the syllable of the final rhyme. To this can be added the possibility of other accents within each hemistich. For instance, in the line, 'Achevons, je frémis; vengeons-nous, je soupire', the natural rules of French prosody, aided by punctuation and, as indicated here, by the accent falling on the underlined syllables, tend to create within each hemistich an anapestic rhythm (BBL), a frequent one in the French language.

This tendency to create the repetition of rhythmic patterns, added to the length of the alexandrine line, encouraged a restrained declamation that was viewed as ideally suited to the solemn genre of tragedy. But the alexandrine was also frequent in comedies, as, for instance, in Molière's plays *Les Femmes savantes* or *Tartuffe*. Indeed, the declamation of tragedy was defined by a 'general *tempo* characterized by a certain slowness',[5] what Grimarest had already praised in 1707, stating that the proper use of the French language is to be spoken aloud 'in a grave and noble manner'.[6]

These declamatory standards and their poetic style were maintained in the *tragédie en musique*. While a libretto may give less prominence to the alexandrine by mixing it more frequently with other lines, such as octosyllables and decasyllables, the musical setting also tends to enhance the slowness of prosody, at this tempo creating something akin to a magnifying glass effect. In his *Réflexions critiques sur la poésie et la peinture* (1719), Jean-Baptiste Dubos evoked the art of French opera singers as 'the art of declamation proper for the realization of a recitation *slowed down by song*'.[7]

If theatrical declamation possessed an inherently musical quality, attempting to outline its rhythm and melodic inflexions through musical notation was the obvious task of the musician. By the end of the seventeenth century, the most emblematic example was the one provided by the actress Marie Champmeslé (1642–1698). As one contemporary commentator put it, 'the delivery of the actors is a kind of song, and you would well admit that La Champmeslé would not please us so much, had her voice been less agreeable'.[8] After La Champmeslé's death, Le Cerf de la Viéville gave a slightly modified retelling of this anecdote in his *Comparaison de la musique italienne, et de la musique françoise* (1704), according to which Lully was said to have fashioned many of his recitatives on La Champmeslé's declamation, an enduring tale that continued to be perpetuated well after the eighteenth century.[9]

What appeared to be a porous line between declamation and song was in France an ongoing issue made all the more significant by the rise of the *tragédie en musique.* But this trope originated before the late seventeenth century and culminated by the end of the sixteenth century with the experiments of the Pléiade, an academy founded in 1570 by the poet Jean Antoine de Baïf. Using the technique of *vers mesurés à l'antique*, Baïf attempted to recover the Greco-Latin poetic metre by following French rules of prosodic quantity.[10] Baïf and his circle were influential among French composers of the early seventeenth century, who adopted the style of the *musique mesurée à l'antique* in which the melody must adhere as much as possible to the scansion of the verses. Understanding the style of *musique mesurée* is essential to understanding both the melodic style of the French *air de cour* – which would later be incorporated into ballets and *tragédies en musique* – and the characteristic style of French musical recitative.

The *Air de Cour* and the Italian Model of Monody

In seventeenth-century French vocal music, the most important genre was the *air de cour*, which developed by the end of the sixteenth century. The expression 'air de cour' appeared in 1571 in the first printed collection of these pieces, which indicates that the form was originally meant for the entertainment of the king and court. Aided by the large number of airs available in collections published by royal printers, it quickly gained popularity beyond those venues.

The *air de cour* could be either polyphonic (mostly four to five voices) or monodic with a lute accompaniment, as shown in the compositions of Pierre Guédron (1564–around 1619–1620). As its popularity grew, the *air de cour* made its way into the *ballet de cour,* where it often had an introductory function by appearing at the beginning of an *entrée*, usually in a monodic form with lute accompaniment. Guédron himself, as well as Antoine Boësset (1586–1643), composed several airs for these staged works: both composers had a major impact on the incorporation of the *air de cour* into the *ballet de cour*.

It would be tempting to view the *air de cour* as the French equivalent to the new genre of the monody, as heralded by Caccini's *Nuove Musiche* (1602). Yet, the treatment of prosody and rhythm and the musical setting of the *air de cour* continued to be indebted to the French tradition of *musique mesurée,* with its musical accompaniment carefully supporting the standard accents and syllable counts. The vocal range, usually within one octave, tended to be much narrower than that of the Italian monody. Vocal ornamentation was also much less common, the emphasis being instead on the syllabic setting of the text.

The French did not judge the Italian monody by hearsay only: Caccini came to the French court in 1604 at the invitation of Henry IV. In comparing the two styles, contemporary commentators noted that French song appeared much more restrained than the Italian monody, a feature that could be construed as a flaw or, by those who disliked the excesses of the Italian manner, a quality. In his *Harmonie universelle* (1636), Marin Mersenne pondered the respective merits of French and Italian song: he described the Italians as 'more vehement than us when it comes to expressing the strongest passions of anger with their accents, especially when they sing their verses on the theatre to imitate the staged music of the Ancients'.[11]

As shown by his correspondence with Caccini, Mersenne had a good knowledge of the *Nuove Musiche* and the Italian manner of ornamentation. He adopted a compromise position, since he was aware of the negative perception that French musicians had of the Italian penchant to embellish melody with extended melismas, 'exclamations and accents'.[12] French singers rejected this manner, as it smacked too much of the genres of tragedy and comedy. Mersenne offered that it would be entirely possible to find a middle ground by softening these Italian 'excesses' of ornamentation and adapting them to the idiosyncratic 'French sweetness'.[13]

Mersenne also stressed the novelty of the Italian *stile recitativo*: he mentioned 'Giacomo [sic] Peri' as the one who 'had started to introduce in 1600, in Florence, during the wedding of the Queen Mother, the manner of reciting Music verses on the theatre'.[14] Mersenne's description suggested the superiority of the Italians, at least when it came to their capacity for representing 'as much as they can the passions and the affections of the soul and the mind, for instance, anger, fury, spite, rage, heartbreaks . . . with such an uncanny violence, that one thinks they are being affected by the very affections they represent through their song'. French singers, on the other hand, remained in a state of 'perpetual sweetness' that accomplished little else besides 'flattering the ears'. More importantly, such sweetness lacked 'energy', which Mersenne used in the sense of *enargeia*, the rhetorical manner of offering listeners a description so vivid that they seem to experience it.[15]

For Mersenne these differences seemed more of degree than of kind: limited by its 'sweet' nature, French music was considered improper for the display of violent passions. Mersenne invited French musicians to unbridle their style – advice he may have gotten from his correspondence with

Giovanni Battista Doni, who recommended that French musicians take 'the opportunity to perfect [their musical style] and change it. . . . I am assured that if your princes would go to the expense, and time permitted it, this would succeed enormously.'[16] A similar argument was offered by the French musician Pierre Maugars, who spent time in Rome during the 1620s and considered the manner of the Italian song 'more animated, ornamented' than that of the French, exhorting his countrymen to travel to Italy and free themselves of the rigidity of their rules.[17]

Yet the comparison between French and Italian was unfair, as it took place at a time before the French had devised their own operatic genre. Epitomised by the *air de cour* that originated outside the world of the stage, the French vocal style was not entirely comparable to the Italian monody nor to the *stile recitativo* motivated by the expression of passions consubstantial to the *dramma per musica*. To this must be added the weight of French tragedy, which provided a normative model not only for the dramaturgy of opera but also for the varieties of its vocal style of delivery as first shaped by Lully and Quinault.

French recitative was theoretically rooted in the theatrical and musical practices of the Ancients – another point of comparison with the Italian tradition. The argument was clearly articulated in Dubos's influential treatise *Réflexions critiques sur la poésie et la peinture*. Originally published in 1719, Dubos' text was augmented by a third part in the new edition of 1733. Entitled 'Dissertation sur les représentations théâtrales des Anciens', this new part scrutinises the conception of music and declamation among the Ancients. Dubos defines the art of declamation as primarily an art of *melopeia*, a Greek term referring to the art of composing the modulation, thus melody. If melody belongs as much to 'music' as it does to the oratory of the Ancients, one can push the syllogism further by affirming that this oratory is a sort of music. Of course, when reading Dubos today we should ask ourselves what the term 'music' meant to him and his contemporaries, for whom the minimal separation between music and declamation was being constantly renegotiated. Dubos warns his readers that the art of *melopeia* should not be considered 'music' (in its modern sense); the musical art of the Ancients should be viewed as the crafting of an instrumental accompaniment to sustain tragic declamation.

This is why Dubos argues that 'the Ancients had a composed declamation that was written in notes, without being a musical song [*chant musical*]'.[18] Granted, in several instances he describes this declamation as 'musical', implying a double meaning to the term. The beauty of *melopeia* or declamation, which can be described in musical terms, is a consequence of the poetic art. On the other hand, the beauty of music, as in the instrumental accompaniment to a tragic declamation, results from the principles of harmony.[19]

In any case, Dubos does not denigrate the art of declamation in comparison to the art of music: they were complementary in ancient tragedies. This is what he finds to have gone awry in modern operas, that is, those departing from the Lullian norm:

Let's admit that we do not fully understand how music could ever be considered as being part of the tragedy, so to speak; if there is anything in the world that seems alien and contrary to a tragic action, it is song, which is, whether the inventors of tragédies en musique like it or not, poetry as ridiculous as it is new.... Because operas are, if I may say so, the grotesques of poetry.[20]

The French mistrust of Italian vocality lies essentially in the potential of the latter to supplant the virtues of French theatrical declamation, which they viewed as the most appropriate medium for the rendering of passions in their tragedies.

Experiencing the first Italian operas performed in Paris and at the court, the French perceived in Italian song a problematic mixture in which music appears as an *added* element to the text, endangering the primacy of the latter. Operatic vocality, for the French, should be a sublimation of declamation without ever becoming full song, and as such it runs the risk of detaching itself from its original textual substratum. The typical French concern for textual intelligibility is anchored in the necessity of finding as close a correspondence as possible between music and text – its syntax and prosodic qualities. The recitative is then viewed as the privileged vocal locus of the *tragédie en musique* – the pièce de résistance of the operatic spectacle – as long it does not become full song and lose its ties to the theatrical model of declamation (hence the enduring fame of the apocryphal anecdote on Lully modelling his recitative on La Champmeslé's declamation).

Récit and Air as Paradigmatic Categories

The vocal style of the *tragédie en musique* is divided into two categories, known as 'récit' and 'air' in late seventeenth-century terminology. The first referred to a syllabic, recitative-like manner, and the second to a more tuneful style.[21] In practice, however, the categories could overlap: the delivery of the *récit* could take the character of an air, while the air could also be referred to as a *récit* – this can be seen in scores and other sources. In its common usage, 'air' refers to a closed form, most frequently a vocal piece following the model of the *air de cour*, with which it also shares its brevity, especially when compared to the Italian aria. 'Air' could also be the name given to an instrumental piece (sometimes the instrumental adaptation of an *air de cour*), one often used for a specific dance in a ballet or a divertissement: for instance an *air de ballet* or, more specifically, a dance related to its performance (e.g., *air pour les matelots*, etc.). Whether instrumental or vocal, the air is defined by its recurrent melodic pattern and its regular metre, which is often matched with a dance rhythm: the 1694 edition of *Dictionnaire de l'Académie française* defines the air as 'a succession of agreeable tones that make a *regular* song'.[22]

'Récit' has a more varied meaning. When translating it as 'recitative', one should keep in mind that its original French meaning is 'narration', a relation of some action that occurred. The *Dictionnaire de Furetière* (1690) gives two entries for the term: 'narration' and 'what is sung by a solo voice and especially by a dessus. A beautiful music should be intermixed with récits and choirs'.[23] The 1694 edition of the *Dictionnaire de l'Académie française* gives only one entry but addresses both meanings. As a musical term, a *récit* is 'what is sung by a solo voice, and that begins a ballet, an opera, or another divertissement by exposing its subject' and as 'everything sung by a solo voice detached from a great choir of music'.[24] Tellingly, neither definition elaborates on its musical peculiarities, except to mention that it is sung by a solo voice. What prevails is a rhetorical conception of the *récit* and its function to reveal and develop the tenets of the plot, or the 'sujet', to use the seventeenth-century French term.

The musical texture of a *récit* requires a *basse continue* written in a harmonic language generally simpler than the Italian recitative (all these features of Lullian opera were going to change dramatically in Rameau's works, leading many of his contemporaries to label his musical style exceedingly Italianate during the *Querelle des Lullistes et des Ramistes*). The French *récit* is easy to notice in a score, due to the changes of time signature and alternations between binary and ternary measures. Since the intention is to follow and emphasise the poetic rhythm of the lines by marking their caesuras and tonic accents, the *récit* is devoid of any regular beat, a feature that highlights the legacy of *musique mesurée*.

We tend nowadays to call this French recitative 'unmeasured recitative'. It was paradigmatic of the style idealised by the Lullian model of sung declamation, but its metrical idiosyncrasies were not systematically observed. Here, establishing a parallel with the Italian practice can be helpful to a certain point. (Italian) recitative is routinely viewed as the primary vehicle for dialogue and for conveying information. As for the aria, it should focus on a more effusive exploration of one or two affects, which is why an Italian libretto easily reveals which verses are intended for the aria: they tend to be shorter than those for the recitative and are gathered in more compact strophes. For that reason, the aria is often said to create a pause in the dramatic unfolding of the action. To this must be added the case of impassioned monologues signalling extreme displays of passion (e.g., mad scenes). These would often be carried by the *recitativo accompagnato*, that is, a recitative with a more complex instrumental accompaniment, usually strings reinforcing the continuo. While this division of labour is mostly typical of eighteenth-century *opera seria*, it was already well under way by the end of the seventeenth century.

The function of the recitative in late seventeenth-century French opera could also be used both for conveying information and for rendering climactic moments of passion: but these different degrees of expression did not seem much to alter the style of the recitative itself, when compared with the Italian simple recitative and its accompanied counterpart. A typical instance of such a climactic use of the unmeasured recitative is Armide's celebrated scene in Lully's eponymous opera (1686; Act II scene 5). An extended monologue, the scene starts with an instrumental ritornello introducing Armide's unmeasured recitative, 'Enfin, il est en ma puissance', followed by a brief conclusion on a strophe of six lines (starting on 'Venez, venez, secondez mes désirs'). This conclusion is itself introduced by another instrumental ritornello on a $\frac{3}{4}$ time signature, the melody of which is repeated twice in the vocal part. Departing from the preceding unmeasured recitative, this conclusion is written entirely in the $\frac{3}{4}$ time signature: the new ternary measure and its recurrent melodic pattern lend the passage the aura of an air. Yet, it would be a stretch to suppose, just by looking at the disposition and length of verses in a French libretto as compared to those of an Italian libretto, that this is where the closed form of an air should take place. Here, the dramatic emphasis of the entire monologue is carried by the unmeasured recitative, not by the concluding and much shorter air-like section.

During and after Lully's time, it was this section in unmeasured recitative ('Enfin, il est en ma puissance') that was regarded as the climax of the scene. Its fame as a model of impassioned monologue continued throughout the eighteenth century.[25] An Italian conception along the lines of *opera seria* would have predicted the contrary: a rather brief recitative, possibly with an accompanied recitative in the middle to emphasise Armide's trouble (starting at 'Quel trouble me saisit'). Then, as the climax of the scene, Armide's 'aria' ('Venez, secondez mes désirs').

This scene typically uses the unmeasured recitative in contradistinction to another type of *récit* in which the time signature remains unchanged, as in an air (here the section 'Venez, secondez mes désirs'). This second type of recitative is usually referred to as a 'measured recitative' (*récit* or *récitatif mesuré*). However, these expressions (*récit/récitatif mesuré* and *non mesuré*) were anachronistic during Lully's time and at least during the first half of the eighteenth century. Pierre Estève may have been the first to distinguish both categories of recitative by coining the expressions '*récitatif simple*' and '*récitatif mesuré*' in his book *L'Esprit des beaux-arts* published in 1753. *Récitatif simple*, a French translation of the Italian *recitativo semplice*, was used by Estève to mean unmeasured recitative.[26] Rousseau later followed with his own definition of *récitatif mesuré* in his *Dictionnaire de musique* (1768). His article is essentially a critique of this expression, which he finds to be a contradiction in terms. Understanding recitative as an Italian conception, Rousseau rejects the possibility of a recitative being measured, which is to him an absurdity belonging to French opera: 'any recitative where one can feel any other measure than the one of the poetic lines is not a recitative anymore'.[27]

The distinction between the two terms only began to be fully realised after the 1750s: for instance, the definition 'récit' in the first edition of the *Dictionnaire de l'Académie* (1694; quoted earlier) remains unchanged in the 1762 edition, except for this added sentence at the very end of the article: 'The récits are not subjected to the measure like the airs.'[28] By the middle of the eighteenth century the need to differentiate 'récit' from 'air' owes much to the growing knowledge among French audiences of Italian recitative and aria: 'récit' became increasingly synonymous with recitative in its Italian sense, finally and definitively differentiating itself from 'air'. Before the *Querelle des Bouffons*, Rousseau, Rousseau defined 'air' in Diderot and d'Alembert's *Encyclopédie* as the name given to 'any pieces of *measured music* [*morceaux de musique mesurés*] so that they can be distinguished from the recitative which isn't; and generally we call air any piece of music, be it vocal or instrumental, that has its beginning and its ending'.[29]

Before the introduction of these eighteenth-century lexical terms, French opera generally used the term 'récit' indiscriminately, no matter whether the recitative was unmeasured or measured. This creates another layer of complication: the presence of these terms in engraved scores and writings was far from systematic, making it hard to establish any fixed meaning. Certainly, an unmeasured recitative with its changing time signatures cannot be confused with an air, but the demarcation is murkier between an air and a measured recitative. The recurrent melodic and rhythmic patterns generated by a regular metre, often matched with a dance rhythm, would potentially make any *récit mesuré* lean towards the air category.

While not a paradigmatic rule, the appearance of a passage written in measured recitative following or preceding an unmeasured recitative is motivated by rhetorical emphasis: affirming a truth or a maxim, asserting a claim or a conclusive sentence. These passages can be woven within the unmeasured recitative in a manner not dissimilar to the Italian practice of embedding a *mezz'aria* within a recitative.[30] When they reach a certain length that allows for the repetition of periods in order to generate a sense of form, these passages could be construed as airs, all the more so when they offer a clear sense of closure.[31] Among these frequent forms is one that James R. Anthony has labelled an 'extended binary configuration', an ABB′ structure often built on a poetic quatrain: its first two lines constitute the section A, the last two lines the section B. These two lines in B are also repeated musically, only with minor alterations to the melodic and rhythmic outline. This extended binary configuration was quite common in seventeenth-century arias in operas and cantatas by Italian composers such as Giacomo Carissimi, Marco Marazzoli, and Luigi Rossi.[32] Lully may have been familiar early in his career with this extended binary form: a probable first exposure could have been the performance of Rossi's *Orfeo* in Paris in 1647 when Lully was fifteen years old. Lully's frequent use of this form in his dramatic music contributed to its popularity among French composers in the subsequent generation, especially André Campra, who often relied on it in his opéras-ballets.[33]

In any case, these sections perform a structural role that clarifies the architecture of a scene. Act I scene 3 of Quinault and Lully's *tragédie en musique, Atys* (Saint-Germain-en-Laye, 1676) counts six sections, the first and the last being the ritournelle ('Allons, allons, accourez tous, / Cybèle va descendre'). The first section presents a first statement of the ritournelle, sung by Sangaride and Doris, followed by a *récit mesuré* ('Que dans nos concerts les plus doux') leading to the second statement of the ritournelle, now sung by Sangaride, Doris, Atys, and Idas. The final (sixth) statement of the ritournelle, sung by Atys and Idas, occurs at the conclusion of the scene. Between these two framing points, a dialogue between Sangaride and Atys takes place. But this exchange is itself subdivided into four sections, three of them written in *récitatif mesuré* (see Table 11.1).

Table 11.1 Distribution of *récits* in Quinault and Lully's *Atys*, Act I, sc. 3

1	*Sangaride, Doris:* Allons, allons, accourez tous, Cybèle va descendre.	RITOURNELLE **2** (mm. 1–12)
	Sangaride: Que dans nos concerts les plus doux, Son nom sacré se fasse entendre.	*MR $\frac{3}{2}$ (mm. 13–27)
	Atys: Sur l'Univers entier son pouvoir doit s'étendre.	
	Sangaride: Les Dieux suivent ses lois, et craignent son courroux.	
	Atys, Sangaride, Idas, Doris: Quels honneurs! Quels respects ne doit-on point lui rendre? Allons, allons, accourez tous, Cybèle va descendre.	RITOURNELLE **2** (mm. 36–48)
2	*Sangaride:* Ecoutons les oiseaux de ces bois d'alentour, Ils remplissent leurs chants d'une douceur nouvelle: On dirait que dans ce beau jour Ils ne parlent que de Cybèle.	**UMR mm. 49–81
	Atys: Si vous les écoutez, ils parleront d'amour. Un Roi redoutable, Amoureux, aimable, Va devenir votre époux; Tout parle d'amour pour vous.	
	Sangaride: Il est vrai, je triomphe, et j'aime ma victoire. Quand l'amour fait régner, est-il un plus grand bien? Pour vous, Atys, vous n'aimez rien, Et vous en faites gloire.	
3	*Atys:* L'Amour fait trop verser de pleurs; Souvent ses douceurs sont mortelles: Il ne faut regarder les belles, Que comme on voit d'aimables fleurs. J'aime les roses nouvelles, J'aime à les voir s'embellir; Sans leurs épines cruelles, J'aimerais à les cueillir.	MR [Air] **3** mm. 82–116

Table 11.1 (*cont.*)

4	*Sangaride:*	MR **3** mm. 117–40
	Quand le péril est agréable,	
	Le moyen de s'en alarmer?	
	Est-ce un grand mal de trop aimer	
	Ce que l'on trouve aimable?	
5	Peut-on être insensible aux plus charmants appâts?	mm. 141–8 (descending tetrachord)
	Atys:	
	Non, vous ne me connaissez pas.	
	Je me défends d'aimer autant qu'il m'est possible.	
	Si j'aimais, un jour, par malheur,	MR [Air] **3** mm. 149–85
	Je connais bien mon cœur,	
	Il serait trop sensible.	
	Mais il faut que chacun s'assemble près de vous,	
	Cybèle pourrait nous surprendre.	UMR 186–9
6	*Atys & Idas:*	mm. 190–end
	Allons, allons, accourez tous,	RITOURNELLE **2**
	Cybèle va descendre.	

*MR: measured recitative
**UMR: unmeasured recitative

Translation:
Sangaride, Doris:
Come, come, all come,
Cybele is descending.

Sangaride:
May in our sweetest concerts
Her holy name be heard.

Atys:
May her power extend on the entire universe.

Sangaride:
The Gods follow her laws, and fear her wrath.

Atys, Sangaride, Idas, Doris:
What honours! What tributes should we not render her?
Come, come, all come,
Cybele is descending.

Sangaride:
Listen to the birds in these woods,
They fill their song with a new sweetness:

It seems that on this beautiful day
They only speak of Cybele.

Atys:
If you listen to them, they will speak of love.

A feared King,
Amorous, gentle,
Will become your husband;
Everything speaks of love to you.

Sangaride:
Indeed, I triumph and enjoy my victory.
When love rules, is there any greater good?
As for you, Atys, you love nothing,
And you take pride in this.

Atys:
Love causes too many tears to be shed;
Often his joys are deadly:
One should only admire beauty,
The way one looks at lovely flowers.

I love the new born roses,
I love to see them grow beautiful,
Without their cruel thorns,
I would like to gather them.

Sangaride:
When danger is pleasant,
Is there any reason to be alarmed?
Is it evil to love too much
What one finds agreeable?

Can one be insensible to the most beguiling charms?

Atys:
No, you don't know me.

I forbid myself to love as much as possible;
If I should love, unfortunately, one day,
I know well my heart,
It would be too much hurt.

But let's everyone come gather around you:
Cybele could take us by surprise.

Atys & Idas:
Come, come, all come,
Cybele is descending.

Section 2, a dialogue between Sangaride and Atys, starts with an unmeasured recitative ('Ecoutons les oiseaux de ces bois d'alentour'). The changes of time signature are rather infrequent; compare this with the first part of Armide's monologue, where the changes of metre happen more frequently. Yet the declamatory style in this scene from *Atys* is aptly suited for this exchange between two characters who have not admitted their love for each other. Instead, they both continue to feign an amicable indifference.

What follows (Section 3), 'L'Amour fait trop verser de pleurs', sung by Atys on the time signature 3, presents features similar to those of an air. The libretto consists of two quatrains, the first in octosyllables (*rimes embrassées*: ABBA), the second in heptasyllables (*rimes croisées*: CDCD). The melody of both quatrains and the *basse continue* evoke the rhythm of a minuet. The whole setting creates a sense of closure characteristic of an air, with the repetition of the two last lines of the second quatrain ('Sans leurs épines cruelles, / J'aimerais à les cueillir'). The repetition is neither textual nor symmetrical (the first occurrence is longer due to the repetition of 'J'aimerais') but saves for the fourth line the cadential gesture V–I in G. After this, Sangaride sings one quatrain (Section 4: 'Quand le péril est agréable') in the same time signature. Here as well the *récit mesuré* takes on an air-like allure, with the exact repetition of the melodic line on the two last lines of the quatrain: 'Est-ce un grand mal de trop aimer / Ce que l'on trouve aimable?'

Before the conclusive return of the ritournelle, the second to the last section, also in *récit mesuré*, leans even more clearly towards an air (Section 5; see Example 11.1). It is introduced by two lines: first an alexandrine sung by Sangaride ('Peut-on être insensible aux plus charmants appâts?'), then an octosyllable sung by Atys ('Non, vous ne me connaissez pas': mm. 147–9). The continuo accompanies each line with a descending tetrachord, introducing a new section consisting of a quatrain.

The first line, an alexandrine ('Je me défends d'aimer autant qu'il m'est possible'), is also the longest: it is accompanied by three occurrences of the descending tetrachord (mm. 150–62). The second, third, and fourth lines (respectively an octosyllable, followed by two hexasyllables) are accompanied by three occurrences of the tetrachord, with repetition of the fourth hexasyllable, ending on the cadence V–I in G (mm. 163–74). The group consisting of these three last lines is repeated once more (as in a BB'

Example 11.1 Jean-Baptiste Lully, *Atys, Tragedie mise en musique* (Paris: Christophe Ballard, 1689), Act I, sc. 3, Sangaride and Atys, mm. 142–90

pattern) with the repetition of the final fourth verse and the cadential ending on G (mm. 175–86). The transition from this air to the conclusion (the final occurrence of the ritournelle 'Allons, accourez tous') is rendered by four measures written in unmeasured recitative and sung by Atys (mm. 187–90).

As Robert Fajon observed, 'when repetitions occur in the literary or musical text, one enters into récitatif mesuré'.[34] But the difficulty is to assess when a *récit mesuré* morphs into an air. The truth is that it remains difficult to establish according to the standards of the Lullian operatic model a clear-cut distinction between *récit mesuré* and an air, especially when considering these terms through purely musical means. A better angle would be to focus on the rhetorical intentions of the libretto, and consider how these motivate the musical articulations of the scene and how they determine the most adequate style to adopt.

This scene from *Atys*, as with many others from the same repertoire, is not by any means an undifferentiated flow of recitative: it reveals subtle articulations throughout the exchanges between Sangaride and Atys, here framed by the symmetrical structure provided by the ritournelle.[35] After Lully's death, long scenes in French operas perpetuated this model. Spectators more familiar with the language of Italian opera may have missed these articulations –as Goldoni obviously did. The full reappraisal of this technique and its merging with the binary recitative–aria of the *opera seria* would become an essential tool for the revitalisation of opera propelled by the reforms led by Christoph Willibald Gluck during the 1770s.

Notes

1 Carlo Goldoni, *Memoirs*, trans. John Black, with an essay by William D. Howells (Boston: James R. Osgood and Company, 1877), 363–4; slightly emended.

2 Rameau's last *tragédie en musique*, *Les Boréades*, was rehearsed in 1763 but never performed before his death. After *Zoroastre*, other dramatic works performed at the Paris Opéra were his actes de ballet *La Guirlande ou les fleurs enchantées* (1751) and *Anacréon* (1757), the pastoral héroïque *Acanthe et Céphise* (1751) and the comédie lyrique *Les Paladins* (1760).

3 On the *Querelle des Bouffons* and the comparison between Italian and French styles, see David Charlton, 'Genre and Form in French Opera', in Anthony R. DelDonna and Pierpaolo Polzonetti (eds.), *The Cambridge Companion to Eighteenth-Century Opera* (Cambridge: Cambridge University Press, 2009), 155–83.

4 Claude Jamain, *L'imaginaire de la musique au siècle des Lumières* (Paris: H. Champion, 2003), 28.

5 Jean Mesnard, 'La Musicalité du texte dans la tragédie classique', in Irène Mamczarcz (ed.), *Les premiers opéras en Europe et les formes dramatiques apparentées* (Paris: Klincksieck, 1992), 117–32: 123; emphasis in the original.

6 Jean-Léonor Le Gallois de Grimarest, *Traité du recitatif dans la lecture, dans l'action publique, dans la declamation, et dans le chant. Avec un Traité des Accens, de la Quantité, & de la Ponctuation* (Paris: Jacques Le Fevre et Pierre Ribou, 1707), 82–3.

7 Jean-Baptiste Dubos, *Réflexions critiques sur la poësie et la peinture*. 2 vols. (Paris: chez Jean Mariette, 1719), vol. 1, Section 41, 'Of simple recitation & declamation', 397; my emphasis. In the 1719 edition, Dubos did not name the singers but he had in mind Marthe Le Rochois, who was then explicitly referred to in the second edition of 1733. In this passage, Dubos also mentions that this quality is more frequently found among female as compared to male singers, due to their 'most sudden sensibility' to which they are more readily prone than men, and to 'the greater suppleness of their heart'. See Dubos, *Réflexions critiques sur la poësie et la peinture. Nouvelle édition revue, corrigée & considérablement augmentée*, 3 vols. (Paris: Pierre-Jean Mariette, 1733), vol. 1, 416.

8 In *Entretiens galans. La mode, La musique, Le jeu, Les louanges*, 2 vols. (Paris: chez Jean Ribou, 1681), vol. 1, 90. La Champmeslé's Parisian career started at the Théâtre du Marais; later, in 1680, she became a member of the newly born Comédie-Française. Many of Racine's leading female roles were written for her, including Phèdre in the eponymous play from 1677.

9 Jean-Louis Le Cerf de la Viéville, *Comparaison de la musique italienne et de la musique françoise, où, en examinant en détail les avantages des Spectacles, & le mérite des Compositeurs des deux nations, on montre quelles sont les vrayes beautez de la Musique* (Brussels: François Foppens, 1704–1706; rpt. Geneva: Minkoff, 1972), part 2, 149. In 1986, Claude V. Palisca was already questioning this 'myth' of La Champmeslé's declamation as a model for Lully, noting that Le Cerf was born in 1674; see Claude V. Palisca, 'The Recitative of Lully's Alceste: French Declamation or Italian Melody?' in Claude V. Palisca, *Studies in the History of Italian Music and Music Theory* (Oxford: Clarendon Press, 1994), 491–507: 497–8. In the absence of any fact reported in Lully's lifetime that would prove the veracity of this anecdote and thus the deconstruction of said myth, see Manuel Couvreur, 'Le récitatif lullyste et le modèle de la Comédie-Française', *Entre théâtre et musique: récitatifs en Europe aux XVIIe et XVIIIe siècles. Cahiers d'histoire culturelle* 6 (1999), 33–45.

10 See notably Jean Vignes, 'Brève histoire du vers mesuré français au XVIe siècle', *Albineana, Cahiers d'Aubigné* 17 (2005), 15–43; Barbara E. Bullock, 'Quantitative Verse in a Quantity-Insensitive Language: Baïf's vers mesurés', *Journal of French Language Studies* 7/1 (1997), 23–45. For an in-depth analysis

of the 'musique mesurée' in Baïf's collection of poems *Le Printans* set to music by Claude Lejeune, see Pierre Bonniffet, *Un ballet démasqué. L'union de la musique au verbe dans 'Le printans' de Jean-Antoine de Baïf et Claude Lejeune* (Paris, Geneva: Champion-Slatkine, 1988).

11 Marin Mersenne, *Harmonie universelle*, part 2 (Paris: Pierre Ballard, 1637), Livre Sixième: 'De L'Art de bien chanter', Seconde Partie, Proposition XV, 371.

12 Marin Mersenne, *Harmonie universelle*, part 1 (Paris: Sebastien Cramoisy, 1636), 'Traitez de la voix et des chants', Livre 1 'De la voix'.

13 Mersenne, *Harmonie universelle*, part 2, Livre Sixième: 'De L'Art de bien chanter', Seconde Partie, Proposition VI, 357.

14 Mersenne implicitly refers to *L'Euridice*, ibid.

15 Ibid., 356.

16 Doni to Mersenne, *Correspondence*, quoted in Georgia Cowart, *The Origins of Modern Musical Criticism: French and Italian Music 1600–1750* (Ann Arbor, MI: UMI Research Press, 1981), 10–11.

17 For a useful overview of these arguments, see Cowart, *The Origins of Modern Musical Criticism*, especially 5–16.

18 Dubos, *Réflexions critiques*, 1733, vol. 3, Section V, 100. This argument runs throughout the entire Section IV as well ('De l'Art ou de la Musique Poëtique. De la Mélopée. Qu'il y avoit une Mélopée qui n'étoit pas un chant musical, quoiqu'elle s'écrivît en notes'), 54–83.

19 Ibid., 1733, 88.

20 Ibid., 1733, 92.

21 *Récit* can, of course, be rendered by the English 'recitative', as long as one does not have an Italian understanding of the latter. The term 'récitatif' also occurs in late seventeenth-century France, but it can refer to declamation in spoken theatre – see, for instance, Grimarest's *Traité du recitatif*.

22 *Dictionnaire de l'Académie française*, 2 vols. (Paris: chez la veuve de Jean Baptiste Coignard, 1694), vol. 1, 25; my emphasis. The 1762 edition of the *Dictionnaire* provides the same definition except for the expression 'air de cour' that has been suppressed. *Dictionnaire de l'Académie française*, 2 vols. (Paris: chez la Vve Brunet, 4th edn. 1762), vol. 1, 47.

23 *Dictionnaire de Furetière*, 3 vols. (La Haye and Rotterdam: chez Arnout & Reinier Leers, 1690), vol. 3, 326.

24 'Récit', in *Dictionnaire de l'Académie française*, 1694, vol. 2, 380.

25 Jean-Jacques Rousseau famously criticised Armide's monologue in the final section of his *Letter on French Music* (1753) by using Lully's setting to demonstrate the impossibility for the French to have a music of their own. It provoked the wrath of the musicians of the Académie Royale de Musique and launched the final and most heated episode of the *Querelle des Bouffons*.

26 Palisca, 'The Recitative of Lully's Alceste', 492.

27 Jean-Jacques Rousseau, *Dictionnaire de musique*, ed. Jean-Jacques Eigeldinger, in Jean-Jacques Rousseau *Œuvres complètes. V. Écrits sur la musique, la langue*

et le théâtre, ed. Bernard Gagnebin, Marcel Raymond, et al. (Paris: Gallimard, 1995), 'Récitatif mesuré', 1012. Rousseau criticises the use of a single time signature in the *récit mesuré*, yet this is also the case in Italian recitative, as it only uses the common time. In the latter, the time signature is purely conventional, as it does not affect the prosody (see his entry 'Récitatif', 1009).

28 'Récit', in *Dictionnaire de l'Académie française*, 1762, 553.

29 'Air', in Denis Diderot and Jean Le Rond d'Alembert (eds.), *Encyclopédie ou Dictionnaire raisonné des sciences, des arts et des métiers, par une Société de Gens de lettres*, 17 vols. (Paris: Briasson; Neuchâtel: Samuel Faulche; Amsterdam: Marc-Michel Rey, 1751–1772), vol. 1 (1751); my emphasis.

30 See Palisca, 'The Recitative of Lully's Alceste', 493.

31 Paul-Marie Masson defined the air as a closed form, in his *L'Opéra de Rameau* (Paris: H. Laurens, 1930), 202–3. For a discussion of this structural aspect within the recitative sections, see Charles Dill, 'Eighteenth-Century Models of French Recitative', *JRMA* 120/2 (1995), 232–50: 234–5.

32 James R. Anthony, 'Lully's Airs. French or Italian?', *The Musical Times* 128/1729 (1987), 126–9: 127.

33 Ibid., 129.

34 Robert Fajon, *L'Opéra à Paris du Roi Soleil à Louis le Bien-Aimé* (Geneva: Slatkine, 1984), 35, quoted and translated in Dill, 'Eighteenth-Century Models of French Recitative', 235.

35 See, for instance, Lois Rosow, 'Lully's Musical Architecture: Act IV of *Persée*', *JSCM* 10/1 (2004), https://sscm-jscm.org/v10/no1/rosow.html.

12 | Opera in England

AMANDA EUBANKS WINKLER

How might we define English opera in the seventeenth century? Whole books have been written on this topic, and because of the variable terminology with which seventeenth-century writers labelled their works ('opera', 'dramatick opera', 'masque', 'comedy', 'tragedy'), it is unlikely that absolute clarity will ever be had.[1] Indeed, the English had a capacious and fluid notion of what constituted opera during the seventeenth century, and we should adjust our overly narrow definitions if we are to understand English opera as people in the seventeenth century did: as a genre that sometimes was fully sung, but, more often than not, included spoken dialogue.[2]

Although the English were not enamoured of fully sung opera, they had a long tradition of pairing drama with music and dance – elements that would become the building blocks of English opera. Elizabethan and Jacobean plays included instrumental music cues for entrances and exits and underscoring to accompany stage action, and vocal music was required in a range of conventionalised circumstances.[3] Servants sing to their masters and mistresses, the inebriated sing drinking songs, and supernatural creatures or characters hoping to summon supernatural forces through ritual also sing. Fools, passionate lovers, melancholics, and mad people lapse into song as well, musico-dramatic signifiers of their instability.[4] Dances also played a role during this early period – many of Shakespeare's comedies end with them (for example, *As You Like It*), but dancing was included in the darkest tragedies (*Romeo and Juliet*) and even in histories (*Henry VIII*).[5]

Thus, from quite early on, the English had developed conventional situations for music-making in their drama. Over time, these musical scenes expanded: in a sense, the transition from play to opera was a change of degree, not kind. The transformation of Shakespeare's *Macbeth* into an increasingly musical play exemplifies this trend. When it premièred in 1606, the witches probably had no music. At some point in its early performance history, material from Thomas Middleton's *The Witch* (1615–1616), a play with substantial music, was interpolated into the Scottish play.[6] After the Restoration it was adapted and changed even further – music became central to its popularity and success.

Court Masques

The court masque – a genre that was populated by allegorical characters and combined spoken text, songs, and choruses; dances; and lavish scenic effects – was codified during the Jacobean and Caroline eras, and its form would have a profound influence on the development of English opera. Playwright Ben Jonson (1572–1637) and designer Inigo Jones (c. 1573–1652), created the template for the court masque during the reign of James I. It began with an antimasque, which included unruly, disruptive, and/or low-class characters, usually played by professionals. After declaiming, sometimes singing, and often dancing in grotesque ways (as indicated by the rapidly shifting metres found in this music), these characters would be banished from the stage by the noble characters of the main masque, portrayed by a mix of professionals and aristocrats, sometimes even including the queen herself. Although the aristocrats generally left the singing and acting to the professionals, they were keen dancers, and during the lengthy revels at the end of the evening they demonstrated their terpsichorean prowess.[7] The dances for the main masque were more rhythmically regular, and some used French dance types. Indeed, the influence of the French *ballet de cour* upon the English court masque was considerable and would only increase with the ascension of Charles I and his French wife, Henrietta Maria, to the throne in 1625.[8]

The composer Nicholas Lanier (bap. 1588–1666) made considerable innovations to the vocal music for the court masque, but we must bear in mind that his experiments with musical declamation were conducted and encouraged by a small group of elites rather than in response to a widespread public thirst for recitative or Italianate opera. Lanier's 'Bring away this sacred tree' from Thomas Campion's *Somerset Masque* (1613) is one of the earliest examples of what Ian Spink calls a 'declamatory ayre' – the vocal line matches the scansion of the text and is set to a chordal accompaniment.[9] Ben Jonson claims in his *Works* (1640) that *The Vision of Delight* (1617) and *Lovers Made Men* (1617) both included music in 'stylo recitativo'. *Lovers Made Men* was particularly remarkable, for the '*whole Masque was sung (after the Italian manner) Stylo recitativo by Master Nicholas Lanier*'.[10] Scholars have cast doubt upon these claims, believing that Lanier probably would not have composed recitative until after his visits to Italy in 1625 and 1628.[11] Whatever the case, Lanier's 1617 settings do not survive; the first extant example of English recitative is his *Hero and Leander* (1628 or later), although all the sources date to after 1660, so it is impossible to know when he actually composed it.[12]

Operatic Experiments during the Civil War and Interregnum

The court masque and plays with music for the public stage were the primary forms of dramatic music until the closure of the public theatres in 1642 and the dissolution of the court musical establishment due to the Civil War, which culminated in the regicide of Charles I in 1649. Despite these disruptions, music and theatre did not completely founder during this difficult period. Oliver Cromwell believed the public theatre to be a hotbed of inequity, but he was not entirely opposed to musical entertainments, and some who had served the previous regime, such as James Shirley and William Davenant, found opportunity in adversity. Shirley wrote the masque *Cupid and Death* in honour of the visit of the Portuguese ambassador on 26 March 1653, potentially suggesting state sponsorship. The first version featured music by Christopher Gibbons (bap. 1615–1676); his score seems to have been revised by Matthew Locke (1621/3–1677) for a 1659 revival at Leicester Fields.[13] Musically, *Cupid and Death* is an important forerunner to the dramatick operas (i.e., plays with substantial musical scenes, dancing, instrumental music, and spectacle) of Matthew Locke and Henry Purcell (1659–1695).[14] Locke's expressive and florid recitative for the 1659 performance paves the way for Purcell's later experiments, as does his use of choral responses. Indeed, *Cupid and Death* is an important intermediary between the Caroline court masque and the Restoration musical forms to come.[15] It has an 'entry' structure, a holdover from the English court masque as well as the French *ballet de cour*, spoken dialogue, songs, choruses, dances, and scenic spectacle (i.e., Mercury 'descending upon a Cloud').[16] The division of labour found in *Cupid and Death* – main characters tend not to sing – also becomes the norm, with a few exceptions, in dramatick opera.

Locke's music for the 1659 *Cupid and Death* revival may provide a window into an earlier Commonwealth experiment whose music has been lost.[17] In September 1656 Davenant, a Royalist who had written Caroline court masques, penned the libretto for *The Siege of Rhodes*, the first fully sung English opera. The score to *The Siege of Rhodes* was a collaborative affair, written by Henry Cooke (c. 1615–1672; the organiser, who composed entries two and three), Henry Lawes (bap. 1596–1662; first and fifth entries), Locke (fourth entry), Charles Coleman (d. 1664; instrumental music), and George Hudson (d. 1672; instrumental music). The versification of the libretto indicates that much of the work would have been sung in recitative, and the chorus played a significant role (as it did in *Cupid and Death*), appearing at the end of each scene. Also, like *Cupid and Death*,

Davenant's opera was organised according to 'entries'. Scenic display, in this case supplied by Jones's protégé John Webb, was also tremendously important. Davenant continued his operatic experiments with *The Cruelty of the Spaniards in Peru* (1658) and *The History of Sir Francis Drake* (1659), although the precise nature of these entertainments is unclear, as most of the music has been lost. After the Restoration, Davenant appears to have given up on fully sung opera, opting instead for the hybrid approach found in *Cupid and Death*.[18]

Various Approaches: Music and/or Drama

After the Restoration, Charles II sought to emulate the elaborate entertainments he had enjoyed in exile at the court of Louis XIV, although he did not have the financial resources to fully support his ambitions. Nevertheless, he restored the court musical establishment, and for many years there was a free flow of personnel between the public stage and the court.[19] Locke and John Banister (1624/5–1679), two of the primary composers for Charles's Twenty-Four Violins, the instrumental ensemble at court modelled on Louis XIV's group, composed much of the music for the public theatres during this period, because this ensemble was working regularly in the theatres by the king's command.[20] The two patent companies – Davenant's Duke's Company and Thomas Killigrew's King's Company – benefitted substantially from this arrangement. Killigrew's company mounted a series of highly musical plays, including Sir Robert Howard and John Dryden's *The Indian Queen* (1664) with music by Banister.[21] Davenant's company was granted the rights to some of Shakespeare's plays by the king, and he reshaped the work of the Bard to suit new tastes, significantly expanding the role of music in two of Shakespeare's plays: *Macbeth* (1663 or 1664) and *The Tempest*, co-written with John Dryden (1667). [22]

The structure in Davenant's revisions of Shakespeare affected English operatic conventions going forward. In fact, they are very similar to what John Dryden would call 'dramatick opera', as they combine spoken text with songs, choruses, and dance. For instance, in Act II scene 5 of Davenant's *Macbeth*, non-singing characters (the Macduffs) encounter the witches singing and dancing. Also, the witches speak and sing in *Macbeth*, serving as intermediaries between the two modes of discourse: a convention we will see with other characters in English dramatick operas of the 1670s and onwards.[23] Dryden and Davenant's adaptation of *The Tempest* functions in a similar way, expanding upon the music in Shakespeare and adding new opportunities for singing that correspond with established conventions. The playwrights amplify Ariel's singing role, including a new 'echo song' for Ariel and Ferdinand, 'Go thy way';[24] and they add a supernatural musical extravaganza, a 'Masque of Devils', which serves a similar musico-dramatic purpose as the witches' scene in Act II scene 5 in *Macbeth*.[25]

The 1670s saw the further expansion of these operatic impulses. In 1670 the actor and theatre manager Thomas Betterton (1635–1710) visited France to learn more about Continental practices, and in 1671 the Duke's company moved into the new Dorset Garden Theatre, which was equipped with machinery.[26] Henceforth, English opera became increasingly indebted to French models and incorporated more special effects.[27] The prompter John Downes recalls a revival of *The Tempest* at Dorset Garden from 1674:

having all New in it; as Scenes, Machines; particularly, one Scene Painted and *Myriads* of *Ariel* Spirits; and another flying away, with a Table Furnisht out with Fruits, Sweet meats and all sorts of Viands; just when Duke *Trinculo* and his Companions, were going to Dinner; all things perform'd in it so Admirably well, that not any succeeding Opera got more Money.[28]

This *Tempest* was probably revised by Thomas Shadwell (1640 or 1641–1692) and includes songs by Banister, Pelham Humfrey (1647/8–1674), Pietro Reggio (bap. 1632–1685), and James Hart (1647–1718); instrumental music by Locke and possibly Robert Smith;[29] and dances by Giovanni Battista Draghi (c. 1640–1708) (lost). *The Tempest* is also notable for its integration of instrumental music into the dramatic action, with Locke's 'Curtain Tune' being a prime exemplar. In his self-published score he incorporates detailed performance instructions (i.e., soft, louder by degrees, violent, etc.) and this, coupled with running semiquaver and demisemiquaver passages and tortured chromaticism, evokes the flying spirits, sinking ship, blustery winds, and stormy waters described in the opening stage direction of the play (see Example 12.1). In other cases, integration of music and drama is less of a priority. For instance, Humfrey's Act V 'Masque of Neptune' is only tangentially connected to the main plot: Prospero calls forth the entertainment to 'make amends' for his misdeeds. We should not presume, though, that masques of this kind were deficient or lacking somehow. These episodes had their own internal logic and were very successful in a dramaturgical sense, as music (instrumental and vocal), dance, and elaborate spectacle worked syncretically to provoke awe and wonder in both the onstage and offstage audience.[30]

Example 12.1 Matthew Locke, *The English opera, or, The vocal musick in Psyche: with the instrumental therein intermix'd: to which is adjoyned the instrumental musick in The tempest* (London: Printed by T. Radcliff and N. Thompson for the author, 1675), 'Curtain Tune', from *The Tempest*, 68

Psyche, also with a text by Shadwell (adapted from Lully, Molière, Pierre Corneille, and Philippe Quinault's *tragédie-ballet, Psyché*; 1671) and music by Locke, was presented the following year (1675), and its score, along with the instrumental music from *The Tempest*, was disseminated by Locke in his aforementioned self-published score, *THE ENGLISH OPERA, OR, The Vocal Musick IN PSYCHE* (1675).[31] In Locke's lively introduction to the volume he makes the case that *Psyche*, is, in fact, a proper opera, for it possesses all the elements of its Italian counterpart: '*splendid Scenes and Machines*', as well as varied '*kinds of Musick as the Subject requires*'. He finishes by stating:

And therefore it [Psyche] *may justly wear the Title* [of opera], *though all the Tragedy be not in Musick: for the Author prudently consider'd, that though* Italy *was, and is the great Academy of the World for that Science and way of Entertainment,* England *is not: and therefore mixt it with interlocutions, as more proper to our* Genius.[32]

Locke's approach to music and drama – along with the operatic Shakespearean experiments of the 1660s and 1670s – provides a template for the ways in which music, drama, and spectacle could work together on the public stage. In some cases, encapsulated entertainments are presented for onstage auditors, and, in others, music and drama flow seamlessly into each other, in part because one of the main characters, Venus, sings and speaks. Locke also composed a light-hearted drinking song and chorus for Vulcan, Cyclops, and their followers. The combination of the comic with the tragic carries over into later English opera, probably by commercial design.[33]

Psyche, like *The Tempest*, had a multi-national production team behind it. Locke, an English composer, provided the bulk of the music, but the Italian Draghi wrote the instrumental music while *the most famous Master of* France, *Monsieur St. Andrée'* made the dances.[34] These collaborations were facilitated by the influx of musicians from the Continent, a result of Charles's musical tastes and his wife's need for musicians to staff her Catholic Chapel.[35] Other immigrants, such as the Italian Reggio and the librettist and playwright Peter Motteux (1663–1718), a Huguenot refugee, came in the 1660s, 1670s, and 1680s, quickly finding opportunity in the theatre of their adopted land.

French and English Opera

Royal occasions seem to have prompted some of these operatic performances in the public theatre: Betterton may have commissioned *Psyche* in 1673 for the marriage of the Duke of York (later James II) and Mary of Modena. It is puzzling that it was not performed until 1675, but the delay may have been caused by music politics at court. In 1673 Robert Cambert

(c. 1628–1677) – the composer of the first French opera, *Pomone* (1671) – arrived in England with some French musicians.[36] Early in 1674 he presented the *Ballet et musique pour le divertissement du roy de la Grande-Bretagne* in celebration of the Duke of York and Mary of Modena's marriage. French music, at least temporarily, had supplanted Locke's 'English Opera'. On 30 March, Charles inaugurated a French-style 'Royall Academy of Musick' with a revised version of Cambert's fully sung 'opera', *Ariane, ou Le marriage de Bacchus*, presented at Drury Lane with additional music supplied by French-trained Catalan composer Louis Grabu (fl. 1665–1694).[37]

Although Cambert's efforts were not well received, Charles's Francophilia deeply affected the few court-based entertainments from this period that survive, even if the king balanced his love of French music with the judicious employment of English composers. About some entertainments with music produced at court, such as *Rare en tout* (1677), performed for Charles II's birthday, little is known beyond the composer: Jacques [James] Paisible (c. 1656–1721), a French wind player who had come to England with Cambert, provided the score.[38] However, there is copious documentary evidence about John Crowne's *Calisto* (1675). Almost all of the music is by Nicholas Staggins (d. 1700), Master of the King's Music, who succeeded Grabu in the post (the Catholic Grabu may have run afoul of the Test Act of 1673, which, although applied inconsistently, required all those at court to take an oath of loyalty to the Church of England).[39] *Calisto*, like *Cupid and Death* in 1653, is called a 'masque' on the title page and has some elements in common with the older English court masque, including amateur performers, in this case the royal princesses, Anne and Mary; the Duke of Monmouth; and other courtiers.[40] *Calisto* was deeply influenced by the *comédie-ballet* and features a French overture, an allegorical prologue, which, like the prologue of *Ariane*, features a female singer as the River Thames, and danced entries for different sets of characters (gypsies, satyrs, Basques, etc.), a French feature that had been taken up in earlier English court masques and Shirley's and Davenant's operatic experiments of the 1650s.[41] With the exception of the sung allegorical prologue, in *Calisto*, the musical episodes take place at the end of each act. Integration of music and drama is not a high priority. Perhaps this separation was born of necessity; it meant that the youthful performers could practice the musical and dramatic components separately. Indeed, this lack of integration, sometimes seen on the public stage, might have served a practical purpose: to expedite the rehearsal process.[42]

Through-Composed Operas and Masques of the 1680s

Determined to enjoy French-style opera at home, in the summer of 1683 Charles II sent Betterton to Paris to commission Jean-Baptiste Lully and his Académie Royale de Musique to produce a *tragédie en musique*. Betterton was unsuccessful in his quest, and so he brought back Grabu, who since 1679 had been living in exile in Paris, 'to represent something at least like an Opera in England for his Majestyes diversion'.[43] Dryden, who had collaborated with Davenant on the adaptation of *The Tempest*, and Grabu began work on what would become *Albion and Albanius*, an opera to be performed at Dorset Garden. Dryden's planned opera originally had a through-composed allegorical prologue in the same vein as *Calisto*'s, followed by an English-style opera with spoken dialogue, spectacle, dance, and music for soloists and chorus. By August 1684, possibly because the king preferred French-style opera, Dryden had altered his project; the English opera would later be revised and performed as *King Arthur* (1691).[44] He expanded the allegorical prologue into a three-act opera, *Albion and Albanius*, which addressed the key moments of Charles's reign.[45] It was completed in 1684 but was shelved because of the unexpected death of Charles in February 1685. Dryden and Grabu worked to accommodate the new political reality, and the opera was finally performed at Dorset Garden in early June, although the run was cut short because Charles's illegitimate son, the Protestant Duke of Monmouth, attempted to seize the throne from the Catholic James II.

Dryden's preface to the printed libretto reveals that the battle between French and English music was hardly settled: 'some *English* Musicians, and their Scholars' had objected to Dryden's collaboration with Grabu, because the 'imputation of being a *French-man*' was enough to prejudice them.[46] Although Grabu was actually Catalan, he was French by training, and not surprisingly his musical idiom is entirely French.[47] Grabu set the recitative sections of *Albion and Albanius* accordingly, incorporating frequent changes from duple to triple metre that are typical of the French *récit mesuré* – a technique not generally used by English composers. In some cases Grabu's score incorporates French conventions that would become anglicised, in particular, the use of dance as a structural device in opera. Most impressive in this regard is his lengthy C major chaconne at the end of the second act, 'Ye nymphs, the charge is royal', which is admirable for its variety of instrumental and vocal writing.[48]

In 1683, the same year that Betterton departed for France, a native English entertainment was being planned at court. This too would be a through-composed work, but on a mythological topic – *Venus and Adonis*. One of the earliest manuscripts describes it as 'A Masque for ye entertainment of ye King',[49] and circumstantial evidence indicates that it was performed on 19 February 1683.[50] It may have been associated with Staggins and John Blow's petition in April 1683 to 'erect' an 'Academy or Opera of Musick', a possible response to the failed academy associated with Cambert or to the prospect of Grabu's return to England.[51] Based on stylistic evidence, James Winn has posited that the librettist may have been Anne Kingsmill, a lady-in-waiting to Mary of Modena, the Duke of York's second wife.[52] The cast included Mary (Moll) Davis, the king's former mistress, as Venus, and their illegitimate daughter, Lady Mary Tudor, as Cupid.

Blow's masque possesses some features seen in previous entertainments: a mythological topic and French-inspired music (a French overture, danced 'entries', including a 'Sarabrand' [*sic*] for the Graces, and a chaconne ground), pervasive use of the chorus, a mixture of comedy with tragedy, and a style of florid recitative adapted from Locke.[53] In other respects *Venus and Adonis* was unusual. Musically, the most notable difference between *Venus and Adonis* and the English-style operas of the 1660s and 1670s was that it was through-composed – Blow was the first English composer to attempt such a thing since the Interregnum. With its comments directed to dissolute courtiers in the prologue ('At court I find constant and true / Only an aged lord or two') and its satirical Act II spelling lesson ('M-E-R-C-E-N-A-R-Y'), the libretto has the quality of a private conversation among a small coterie. *Venus and Adonis* did eventually find a broader audience, most notably at Josias Priest's boarding school for girls at Chelsea, where, as noted by John Verney on his souvenir libretto (GB-Cu Sel.2.123 [6]), it was presented on 17 April 1684.[54]

Dido and Aeneas, performed sometime in the late 1680s, is a similar work to Blow's *Venus and Adonis*. The only surviving seventeenth-century documentation about this work is a printed libretto from a performance at Priest's school (GB-Lcm D144), Thomas D'Urfey's epilogue issued in *New Poems* (1690), and the song 'Ah! Belinda' in *Orpheus Britannicus*, book 1 (1698).[55] After the discovery of Verney's annotated libretto from the school performance of *Venus and Adonis*, many wondered if *Dido* also had its genesis at court, and Bruce Wood and Andrew Pinnock argued for a first performance date shortly after *Venus and Adonis*.[56] More recently, Bryan White discovered a 'Letter from Aleppo' in which a factor of the Levant Company, Rowland Sherman, writes to his friend in London, the merchant James Pigott, and requests that he ask 'Harry' to prick down the C minor overture to 'the mask he made for Preists [*sic*] Ball'. White's remarkable discovery has, once again, called into question the date and location of *Dido*'s first performance.[57]

Musically, *Dido* incorporates some of the same French components as *Venus and Adonis*, with its French overture, incorporation of solos with choral responses, and its French-style dances, whose rhythms infiltrate the vocal music, most famously in 'Fear no danger', a rondeau duet with chorus.[58] *Dido* also includes influences beyond the French, including the English court masque (the antimasque-influenced music and dances for the Sorceress and her band of witches) and Italian-style opera, particularly in the two ground bass laments for Dido, 'Ah, Belinda' and 'When I am laid in earth'. Purcell chooses his ground basses carefully – the oscillating figure in Dido's 'Ah, Belinda' perfectly encapsulates the Queen's indecision – and the descending tetrachord – an 'emblem of lament' in Venetian opera – is used to great dramatic effect in Dido's 'When I am laid in earth'.[59]

Purcell's Dramatick Operas

Purcell's engagement with theatre music only increased after 1690, as he sought new sources of income due to the reduction of the court musical establishment under William III and Mary.[60] In 1682 the rival King's and Duke's companies had combined into the United Company, so competition had been eliminated, at least for the time being. From 1690 to his premature death in 1695, Purcell composed a remarkable amount of theatre music, including a series of dramatick operas: *Dioclesian* (1690), *King Arthur* (1691), *The Fairy-Queen* (1692, 1693), and *The Indian Queen* (1695). Continuing earlier practises, most of these dramatick operas were adaptations of earlier works.

The driving force behind these dramatick operas was a by-now familiar figure: Thomas Betterton. Betterton had played both sides of the fence in the 1660s–1680s, during which time he was involved in through-composed operas in the French style (*Albion and Albanius*) and English-style opera, works that combined spoken text with song.[61] In the 1690s, he took on the role of adaptor as well. His first attempt was John Fletcher and Philip Massinger's tragicomedy *The Prophetess* (1622), which he transformed into the dramatick opera *The Prophetess: Or, The History of Dioclesian*.

Betterton expanded pre-existing musical moments and added music in conventional places (for instance 'What shall I do to show how much I love her', which Purcell set as a beautiful minuet, performed in Act III as

Maximinian gazes longingly upon Aurelia).[62] The prophetess Delphia instigates many other musical episodes in the opera, using her supernatural abilities to call forth songs, dance, and spectacle. *Dioclesian* also continues the dramatick opera tradition (cf. 'The Masque for Neptune' in *The Tempest*) of having a spectacular entertainment in Act V with a tenuous connection to the plot, in this case a pastoral interlude that concludes with an extended chaconne, 'Triumph victorious Love', a possible response to Grabu's chaconne in *Albion and Albanius*.[63] There are also scenes of ceremonial praise and ritualised rejoicing, such as Act IV's 'Sound, Fame, thy Brazen Trumpet sound' in response to Dioclesian's military victory.

Dioclesian contained beautiful and varied music (the pastoral masque at the end particularly struck the fancy of audiences well into the early eighteenth century),[64] but Purcell's next dramatick opera, *King Arthur*, performed by the United Company at Dorset Garden, had a newly written text by the experienced Dryden, and as a result this work achieves an unprecedented integration of music and drama. Employing a strategy found in previous dramatick operas, Dryden included intermediaries between the world of speech and song: the *Tempest* had Ariel, *Psyche* had Venus, and *King Arthur* has the spirits Grimbald and Philidel.

King Arthur incorporates scenic spectacle and dance, as well as stock musical scenes: a sung ritual, a drinking song, a rejoicing song after victory in battle, pastoral entertainments, and a spectacular Act V masque with little connection to the plot. But in other respects, Purcell's music forges new ground. 'Hither this way' in Act II expands upon a dramatic situation seen in the famous action duet 'Go thy way' from Davenant and Dryden's *Tempest*, where Ariel lures Ferdinand into following him. Philidel and his spirit followers coax Arthur and his men to take the correct path, and Purcell responds to Dryden's evocative textual cues with vivid text painting: the jagged descending line on 'down you fall, a furlong sinking' being a prime example (see Example 12.2). Grimbald gamely echoes the airy sprites, but it is to no avail. As Grimbald explains, 'I had a Voice in Heav'n, ere Sulph'rous Steams / Had damp'd it to a hoarseness'. He does not give up, but his air 'Let not a moonborn elf', with its awkward rhythms and high tessitura, renders his attempt ungainly and ridiculous (see Example 12.3). When the competing spirits chime in with a reprise of 'Hither this way', it is all too clear that Philidel and his band will triumph.[65]

In the less fully integrated scenes, Purcell also provides music of remarkable invention and variety. The famous Act III Frost Scene, particularly the song for the Cold Genius, is a prime example. Although Purcell may have taken the idea of using wavy lines to signify shivering from Lully's *Isis*

Example 12.2 Henry Purcell, *King Arthur*, ed. Dennis D. Arundell [1928], rev edn. Margaret Laurie (London: Novello, 1971), Philidel, 'Hither this way' (excerpt), mm. 26–9.

(1677), the adventurous chromaticism of the Cold Genius's 'What pow'r art thou?' has very little do with the French idiom;[66] it is an extension of the musical language of Locke and Blow.[67] And the Act V masque has everything from the rollicking comedy of 'Your hay it is mow'd' to the sublime minuet song for Venus, 'Fairest Isle'.

With *The Fairy-Queen* of the following year, the anonymous adapter, possibly Betterton, returned to Shakespeare for inspiration. This time the adapter chose *A Midsummer Night's Dream* for treatment, but instead of expanding scenes that were musical in the original play, as other revisers had done with *Macbeth* and *The Tempest*, he often ignored these opportunities, adding scenes entirely of his own invention. Still, many of these interpolated entertainments tick similar dramaturgical boxes to those we

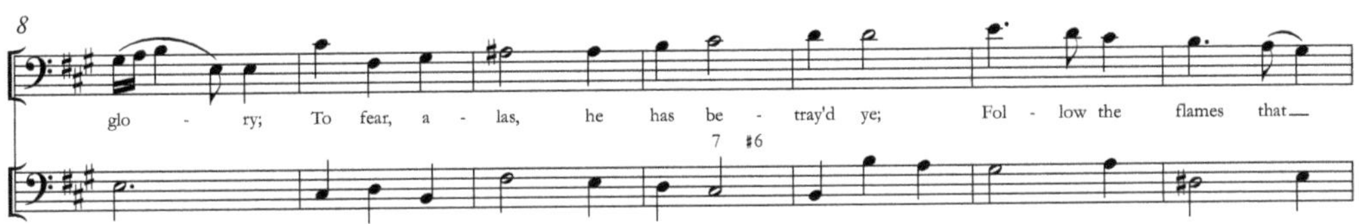

Example 12.3 Henry Purcell, *King Arthur*, Grimbald, 'Let Not a Moonborn Elf', mm. 1–25.

have seen before – not surprisingly most of the music is instigated by the fairies, and these scenes are presented in the style of masques: self-contained entertainments directed toward a specific onstage spectator (or spectators). Only the Act II masque has a direct musical analogue in Shakespearean drama; it takes the place of Shakespeare's lullaby 'Ye spotted snakes', as Titania's fairies first entertain their queen and then present an allegorical masque of Night, Mystery, Secrecy, and Sleep designed to induce slumber.[68]

Despite the considerable beauties of Purcell's music, the opera did not turn a significant profit. It was revived almost immediately in 1693, but the state of the musical and textual sources is such that we cannot conclusively know what alterations were made for the 1693 production. The most substantial musical difference between the 1692 and 1693 quartos is the inclusion in the latter of a comical scene of a Drunken Poet tormented by fairies. It is unclear if this was a late revision to the 1692 production that did not make it into the 1692 quarto, or if it was newly written for the 1693 production.[69]

Purcell wrote one final dramatick opera before his untimely death in 1695, an adaptation of an earlier play, Dryden and Howard's *The Indian Queen* (1664).[70] He died before he completed the Act V masque, which was set by his brother or cousin, Daniel Purcell (c. 1664 or later–1717). This dramatick opera was performed by very young performers, as most of the veteran actors, including Betterton and actress-singer Anne Bracegirdle (1671–1748), had left to establish a rival theatre at Lincoln's Inn Fields.[71] This means that Betterton was probably not involved with the adaptation, although a document survives from the patentees of the Theatre Royal asking Betterton to undertake the task; Price has suggested that Dryden may have done the adaptation himself.[72] Despite the difficult circumstances, Henry Purcell wrote sublime music, most notably for an incantation scene in Act III in which the eponymous Indian queen Zempoalla consults the magician Ismeron regarding her fate. The bass singer Richard Leveridge (1670–1758) performed the role of the sorcerer Ismeron, and his ominous and chromatic G minor recitative 'You twice ten hundred deities' and air 'By the croaking of the toad' are justifiably famous; the latter imitates hopping with dotted rhythms and includes some very thorny harmonies, including a rare augmented sixth chord on the word 'unwilling'.[73]

1695 and Beyond

Although Purcell died in 1695, English opera did not die with him. Post-Purcellian dramatick opera took two tracks: one in which music and drama were consistently integrated, and one in which musico-dramatic cohesion was not as pressing a concern. During the theatre season of 1698–9, two competing visions of dramatick opera went head-to-head. The theatre at Lincoln's Inn Fields offered John Dennis's *Rinaldo and Armida*, with a score by John Eccles (c. 1668–1735) in 1698.[74] Although it has some elements in common with Lully's *Armide*, Dennis's text, like that of *King Arthur*, was newly written. Dennis makes clear in his preface to *The Musical Entertainments in the Tragedy of Rinaldo and Armida* (1699) that he is deeply interested in providing a rational, coherent entertainment in which music, even the act tunes, play a part in the drama. In 1699 Christopher Rich's company at the rival theatre at Drury Lane presented their own dramatick opera, Motteux's adaptation of Fletcher's *The Island Princess* (ca. 1621).[75] *The Island Princess* was a collaborative affair, with music provided by Jeremiah Clarke (c. 1674–1707), Leveridge (the Ismeron of *The Indian Queen*), and Daniel Purcell, as well as Robert King (c. 1660–c. 1726), Thomas Morgan (fl. 1691–9), and William Williams (1765–1701).[76] *The Island Princess* was a massive success; only the 1674 version of *The Tempest* was revived more often in the first few decades of the eighteenth century.[77] Although the music in Acts II, III, and IV works in conjunction with the plot (particularly the 'Enthusiastick Song' written by Leveridge for his own performance as a superannuated Brahmin), elsewhere the music's connection with the drama is tenuous (the Act IV rustic dialogue and the Act V 'The Four Seasons or Love in every Age').[78]

The other predominant operatic form, the through-composed miniature, was transferred to the public stage, interpolated into otherwise spoken plays, or used as an afterpiece. Most of these miniatures were given at Lincoln's Inn Fields; as Robert Hume observes, these through-composed works, which prioritise musical pleasures over scenic display, were 'what an under-capitalised company in a minimal theater could afford'.[79] Frequently called 'masques' on their title pages, these works are akin to *Venus and Adonis* and *Dido and Aeneas* – other small-scale operatic works on an intimate scale. Notable examples include Eccles and Gottfried [Godfrey] Finger's (c. 1660–1730) setting of Motteux's *The Loves of Mars and Venus* (1696); Daniel Purcell and Finger's setting of Dryden's *The Secular Masque* (1700); Eccles's setting of Motteux's *Acis and Galatea* (1701); and William Congreve's (1670–1729) *The Judgment of Paris* (1701) – set by Eccles, Daniel Purcell, John Weldon (1676–1736), and Finger as part of a 'song contest' to encourage music.[80]

Around the turn of the century, native English composers also began to compose full-length, fully sung operas in an attempt to compete with the fashionable Italian opera. In these works, one sees the continuation of older English and French traditions together with an increased engagement with the Italian style. They include Eccles and Congreve's unstaged *Semele* (1706) and Thomas Clayton's (1673–1725) *Rosamond* (1707; libretto by

Joseph Addison, [1672–1719]), performed at Drury Lane. *Semele* fell afoul of the tumultuous theatre politics of the time, and the failure of *Rosamond* in March 1707 did not help to make the case that audiences craved fully sung English opera.[81]

Conclusions

So why did full-length, through-composed opera in English fail to take hold? Lurking behind such a question is the modern assumption that through-composed opera is superior to opera with spoken dialogue, a sentiment not shared by the majority in seventeenth-century England. It was not until the 1690s that through-composed works were successfully performed on the public stage, and usually only as afterpieces or inter-polations into spoken plays, as was famously the case with the masques cited above or Purcell's *Dido and Aeneas*, inserted into Charles Gildon's 1700 adaptation of *Measure for Measure*. Clearly, the English preferred their opera with spoken dialogue – an expansion of the aesthetic found in earlier seventeenth-century plays as well as the court masque. Although some contemporaries bemoaned their compatriots' lack of appetite for fully sung English opera or critiqued the lack of dramatic coherence in drama-tick operas, most audience members seem to have had no such qualms. Dramatick operas by Purcell and others were performed well into the eighteenth century and beyond, demonstrating the genre's longstanding popularity. As Motteux opined in *The Gentleman's Journal*: 'Other Nations bestow the name Opera only on such Plays whereof every word is sung … experience hath taught us that our English genius will not rellish that perpetual Singing.'[82]

Notes

1 For a lucid description of the genre problem, see Robert D. Hume, 'The Politics of Opera in Late Seventeenth-Century London', *COJ* 10/1 (1998), 15–43. Andrew R. Walkling also grapples with the issue in his books, *Masque and Opera in England, 1656–1688* (New York: Routledge, 2017) and *English Dramatick Opera, 1661–1706* (London: Routledge, 2019).

2 For a study of English opera libretti that demonstrates this point, see Eugene Haun, *But Hark! More Harmony: The Libretti of Restoration Opera in English* (Ypsilanti: Eastern Michigan University Press, 1971).

3 On music in Shakespeare see Ross W. Duffin, *Shakespeare's Songbook* (New York: W. W. Norton & Company, 2004), and David Lindley, *Shakespeare and*

Music (London: Thompson Learning, 2006). Linda Austern has studied the place of music in non-Shakespearean drama: *Music in English Children's Drama of the Later Renaissance* (Philadelphia: Gordon and Breach, 1992). See also Ross W. Duffin, *Some Other Note: The Lost Songs of English Renaissance Comedy* (New York: Oxford University Press, 2018).

4 On some of these conventions, see Amanda Eubanks Winkler, *O Let Us Howle Some Heavy Note: Music for Witches, the Melancholic, and the Mad on the Seventeenth-Century English Stage* (Bloomington: Indiana University Press, 2006).

5 Lindley, *Shakespeare and Music*, 128–40. For a recent study of theatrical dancing, but particularly the jig, see Roger Clegg and Lucie Skeaping, *Singing Simpkin and Other Bawdy Jigs: Musical Comedy on the Shakespearean Stage; Scripts, Music and Context* (Exeter: University of Exeter Press, 2014).

6 Eubanks Winkler, *O Let Us Howle*, 32–5.

7 For a lucid description of the genre, Jones's costume sketches, and editions of the extant masque texts, see Stephen Orgel and Roy Strong, *Inigo Jones: The Theatre of the Stuart Court Masque*, 2 vols. (London: Sotheby Parke Bernet; Berkeley: University of California Press, 1973). See also Peter Walls's analysis of the genre in his *Music in the English Courtly Masque, 1604–1640* (Oxford: Clarendon Press, 1996).

8 Walls, *English Courtly Masque*, 221–59.

9 Ian Spink, *English Song: Dowland to Purcell*, 2nd edn. (New York: Taplinger Publishing Company, 1986), 44–5; Walls, *English Courtly Masque*, 51–4.

10 Ben Jonson, *The Workes of Benjamin Jonson*, 2 vols. (London: Printed for Richard Meighen, 1640 [*recte* 1641]), vol. 1, 10.

11 For a summary of this argument, see Walls, *English Courtly Masque*, 87. Among the sceptics are Emslie McDonald, 'Nicholas Lanier's Innovations in English Song', *ML* 41/1 (1960), 13–27, and Vincent Duckles, 'English Song and the Challenge of Italian Monody', in Vincent Duckles and Franklin B. Zimmerman (eds.), *Words to Music: Papers on English Seventeenth-Century Song* (Los Angeles: The William Andrew Clark Memorial Library, 1967), 3–42.

12 For a discussion of the music see also Spink, *English Song*, 103–4.

13 This, the only extant version of the music, survives in Locke's autograph 'short score' manuscript, GB-Lbl Add 17799: Locke calls it a 'Morall representation'. The later printed copy of the libretto labels it a 'private entertainment', while the 1653 edition calls it a 'masque'.

14 Many scholars prefer to use the term 'dramatick opera', the genre designation used by John Dryden on the title page to *King Arthur*, rather than 'semi-opera', which implies these works are something less than 'real' opera.

15 The grand dance at the end as well as the antimasque style of some of the entries also ties the work to older court masque practices.

16 This stage direction appears in both imprints of the masque (1653 and 1659).

17 James Winn makes the same observation in 'Heroic Song: A Proposal for a Revised History of English Theater and Opera, 1656–1711', *ECS* 30/2 (1996/1997), 113–37: 116–17. Richard Flecknoe also experimented with opera during the same period (*Ariadne Deserted by Theseus* [1654] and *The Mariage of Oceanus and Brittania* [1659]), but the music for these entertainments has been lost, and it does not appear that either was performed; see Haun, *Hark! More Harmony*, 24–49.

18 On Davenant's operas during the 1650s, see Haun, *But Hark! More Harmony*, 50–95; Andrew Pinnock and Bruce Wood, 'A Mangled Chime: The Accidental Death of the Opera Libretto in Civil War England', *EM* 36/2 (2008), 265–84; Winn, 'Heroic Song', 114–22; and Walkling, *Masque and Opera*, ch. 4. *Sir Francis Drake* was through-composed and included recitative.

19 As described by Peter Holman, *Four and Twenty Fiddlers: The Violin at the English Court 1540–1690*, rev. edn. (Oxford: Clarendon Press, 1995), 331–55.

20 Ibid., 336.

21 For a list of plays with music from 1660–1669, see ibid., 356–8. For an overview of Restoration-era musical conventions, see Curtis Price, *Music in the Restoration Theatre: With a Catalogue of Instrumental Music in the Plays, 1665–1713* (Ann Arbor: UMI Research Press, 1979).

22 Christopher Spencer (ed.), *Five Restoration Adaptations of Shakespeare* (Urbana: University of Illinois Press, 1965), 1.

23 For an edition of the surviving music by Matthew Locke, John Eccles, and Richard Leveridge from three different productions and a description of the sources, see Amanda Eubanks Winkler (ed.), *Music for Macbeth* (Middleton: A-R Editions, 2004).

24 On 'Go thy way' see Amanda Eubanks Winkler, 'A Thousand Voices: Performing Ariel', in Dympna Callaghan (ed.), *A Feminist Companion to Shakespeare*, 2nd edn. (Chichester: John Wiley & Sons, 2016), 520–38: 536.

25 The 'Masque of Devils' is included in Dryden and Davenant's texts; a setting of this survives by Pelham Humfrey, although it is unclear whether he composed it for the 1667 production or the 1674. For an overview of *The Tempest* music see Roger Covell, 'Seventeenth-Century Music for The Tempest', *Studies in Music* 2 (1968): 43–65 and Matthew Locke, *Dramatic Music*, ed. Michael Tilmouth, *Musica Britannica*, vol. 51 (London: Stainer and Bell, 1986). Humfrey's setting of 'Where the bee sucks' probably belongs to the 1674 Dorset Garden revival, as the printed copy in *Ariels Songs* indicates that it was sung in a machine.

26 On Dorset Garden see Robert D. Hume, 'The Nature of the Dorset Garden Theatre', *Theatre Notebook* 36/3 (1982), 99–109; Judith Milhous, 'The Multimedia Spectacular on the Restoration Stage', in Shirley Strum Kenny (ed.), *British Theatre and the Other Arts 1660–1800* (Washington, DC: Folger Shakespeare Library, 1984), 41–66; Frans and Julia Muller, 'Purcell's *Dioclesian* on the Dorset Garden Stage', in Michael Burden (ed.), *Performing the Music of*

Henry Purcell (Oxford: Clarendon Press, 1996), 232–42; and Mark A. Radice, 'Sites for Music in Purcell's Dorset Garden Theatre', *MQ* 81/3 (1997), 430–48.

27 Rebecca Herissone draws a similar conclusion in 'Playford, Purcell, and the Functions of Music Publishing in Restoration England', *JAMS* 63/2 (2010), 243–90: 273.

28 John Downes, *Roscius Anglicanus,* ed. Judith Milhous and Robert D. Hume (London: The Society for Theatre Research, 1987), 73–4.

29 Holman, *Four and Twenty Fiddlers*, 338.

30 This follows an argument I make in a recent article, where I show how dramatick opera's constituent parts work together in performance: 'The Intermedial Dramaturgy of Dramatick Opera: Understanding Genre through Performance', *Restoration: Studies in English Literary Culture, 1660–1700* 42/2 (2018), 13–38.

31 On this adaptation, see Murray Lefkowitz, 'Shadwell and Locke's *Psyche*: The French Connection', *PRMA* 106 (1979–1980), 42–55.

32 All quotations from Matthew Locke, *The English opera, or, The vocal musick in Psyche with the instrumental therein intermix'd : to which is adjoyned the instrumental musick in The tempest* (London: Printed by T. Ratcliff and N. Thompson for the author, 1675), unpaginated preface.

33 Shadwell indicates that a variety of genres were included to appeal to diverse audience tastes; see Thomas Shadwell, *Psyche: A Tragedy* (London: Printed by T. N. for Henry Herringman, 1675), unpaginated preface.

34 Ibid., unpaginated preface. This 'Master of France' was Adrien Merger de Saint-André.

35 Draghi had come to England as part of a vocal consort lead by Vincenzo Albrici that arrived in London to establish an opera company in 1663; Holman, 'Draghi, Giovanni Battista', *Grove Music Online*. Charles also had a group of French musicians; Holman, *Four and Twenty Fiddlers*, 290–1 as well as Italians; Margaret Mabbett, 'Italian Musicians in Restoration England (1660–90)', *ML* 67/3 (1986), 237–47. See also Peter Leech, 'Musicians in the Catholic Chapel of Catherine of Braganza, 1662–92', *EM* 29/4 (2001), 570–87. For a general overview of foreign musicians at court, see William John Lawrence, 'Foreign Singers and Musicians at the Court of Charles II', *MQ* 9/2 (1923), 217–22; Jack A. Westrup, 'Foreign Musicians in Stuart England', *MQ* 27/1 (1941), 79–89; and Walkling, *Masque and Opera*, ch. 5.

36 Holman, *Four and Twenty Fiddlers*, 343; John Buttrey, 'New Light on Robert Cambert, and His *Ballet et Musique*', *EM* 23/2 (1995), 198–220.

37 On this opera and the Royal Academy, see Pierre Danchin, 'The Foundation of the Royal Academy of Music in 1674 and Pierre Perrin's *Ariane*', *Theatre Survey* 25/1 (1984), 55–67, and Christina Bashford, 'Perrin and Cambert's *Ariane, ou Le Mariage de Bacchus* Re-Examined', *ML* 72/1 (1991), 1–26. For a comprehensive assessment of Grabu's career, see Andrew R. Walkling, 'The

Ups and Downs of Louis Grabu', *Royal Musical Association Research Chronicle* 48/1 (2017), 1–64.

38 David Lasocki, 'Paisible [Peasable], James [Paisible, Jacques]', *Grove Music Online*.

39 Peter Holman, 'Grabu [Grabeu, Grabue, Grabut, Grebus], Luis [Louis, Lewis]', *Grove Music Online*; and Walkling, 'The Ups and Downs of Louis Grabu', 14–16.

40 Much is known about the rehearsals, expenditures, and performance of this masque; see Eleanore Boswell, *The Restoration Court Stage (1660–1702)* (Cambridge: Harvard University Press, 1932), 175–227 and the relevant appendices; Walkling, 'Masque and Politics at the Restoration Court: John Crowne's *Calisto*', *EM* 24/1 (1996), 27–62; Holman, *Four and Twenty Fiddlers*, 366–71; and James Anderson Winn, *Queen Anne: Patroness of Arts* (New York: Oxford University Press, 2014), 1–41.

41 On the French influence on *Calisto* see Walkling, 'Masque and Politics at the Restoration Court', 51–2; Winn makes the observation about the connection between *Ariane* and *Calisto* in *Queen Anne*, 20.

42 In the public theatres, dialogue rehearsals were held in the morning, and music rehearsals to learn songs and dances were held in the evening; Tiffany Stern, *Rehearsal from Shakespeare to Sheridan* (Oxford: Clarendon Press, 2000), 166.

43 Quotation from a letter from Lord Preston to the Duke of York, 22 September 1683; Royal Commission on Historical Manuscripts, *Seventh Report of the Royal Commission on Historical Manuscripts. Part 1. Report and Appendix* (London: Printed by Eyre and Spottiswoode for H.M.S.O., 1879), appendix, 288a, 290a; John Dryden, *The Works of John Dryden*, ed. Earl Roy Miner and George R. Guffey, vol. 15. *Plays: Albion and Albanius, Don Sebastian, Amphitryon*, ed. Earl R. Miner, George R. Guffey, and Franklin B. Zimmerman (Berkeley, Los Angeles, and London: University of California Press, 1976), 341.

44 Curtis Price, *Henry Purcell and the London Stage* (Cambridge: Cambridge University Press, 1984), 265–70, and Bryan White's introduction to Louis Grabu, *Albion and Albanius*, ed. Bryan White, The Purcell Society Edition Companion Series, vol. 1 (London: Stainer & Bell, 2007).

45 For an interpretation, see Paul Hammond, 'Dryden's *Albion and Albanius*: The Apotheosis of Charles II', in David Lindley (ed.), *The Court Masque* (Manchester: Manchester University Press, 1984), 169–83.

46 Dryden, *The Works of John Dryden*, vol. 15, 8.

47 On this, see Bryan White, 'Grabu's *Albion and Albanius* and the Operas of Lully: "...acquainted with all the performance of the French Opera's,"' *EM* 30/3 (2002), 410–27.

48 Ibid., 421–2.

49 GB-Lbl Add MS 22100, fol. 123v.

50 Bruce Wood suggests this date, as court records indicate that there was a major event involving music and dance; *Venus and Adonis*, ed. Wood, The Purcell Society Edition Companion Series, vol. 2 (London: Stainer & Bell, 2008), xiii.

51 Herissone connects this 'Academy' with Grabu's anticipated return in 'Playford, Purcell, and the Functions of Music Publishing', 274. The petition is reproduced in Bruce Wood and Andrew Pinnock, '"Unscarr'd by Turning Times"? The Dating of Purcell's *Dido and Aeneas*', *EM* 20/3 (1992), 372–90: 387. Walkling believes this was a proposed space, a music room for opera, *Masque and Opera*, 130–1.

52 James A. Winn, '"A Versifying Maid of Honour": Anne Finch and the Libretto for *Venus and Adonis*', *The Review of English Studies* 59/238 (2008), 67–85. Andrew Pinnock has recently extended Winn's argument, suggesting that another lady-in-waiting to Mary of Modena, Anne Killigrew, also helped to shape the libretto; 'The Rival Maids: Anne Killigrew, Anne Kingsmill and the Making of the Court Masque *Venus and Adonis* (Music by John Blow)', *EM* 46/4 (2018), 631–52.

53 For a discussion of the score, see Holman, *Four and Twenty Fiddlers*, 371–5; on the sources for the opera, see Wood's introduction to *Venus and Adonis*.

54 Richard Luckett, 'A New Source for "Venus and Adonis,"' *MT* 130/1752 (1989), 76–9.

55 The publication date of *New Poems* was 1690, but, as John Buttrey notes, it actually appeared in November 1689; 'Dating Purcell's *Dido and Aeneas*', *PRMA* 94 (1967–1968), 51–62.

56 Wood and Pinnock, 'Unscarred by Turning Times?', 372–90. For summary of the debate and citations to articles, see Bryan White, 'Letter from Aleppo: Dating the Chelsea School Performance of *Dido and Aeneas*', *EM* 37/3 (2009), 417–28: 417 and notes 1 and 7.

57 A transcription of the letter and partial facsimile appears in White's 'A Letter from Aleppo', 419–20, but see also his full article for further information about Sherman, Pigott, and Priest's school.

58 Cf. 'In these sweet groves' from *Venus and Adonis*. On the French models, see Martin Adams, *Henry Purcell: The Origins and Development of His Musical Style* (Cambridge: Cambridge University Press, 1995), 57. Some of Purcell's dances also have precedents in Locke's music for *The Tempest* and *Psyche*: see 57–8.

59 See Price, *Henry Purcell and the London Stage*, 247, 258–9, and Eubanks Winkler, chs. 2–4 of *O Let Us Howle*.

60 This occurred in May 1690; see Holman, *Four and Twenty Fiddlers*, 431–5.

61 Richard Luckett observes that 'dramatick opera was Bettertonian opera'; 'Exotick but Rational Entertainments: The English Dramatick Operas', in Marie Axton and Raymond Williams (eds.), *English Drama: Forms and Development: Essays in Honour of Muriel Clara Bradbrook* (Cambridge: Cambridge University Press, 1977), 123–41: 133. For an overview of some of the dramaturgical issues presented by Purcell's dramatick operas, see Michael

Burden, 'Aspects of Purcell's Operas', in Michael Burden (ed.), *Henry Purcell's Operas: The Complete Texts* (Oxford: Oxford University Press, 2000), 3–27.

62 Price suggests that this song was replaced by 'When first I saw the bright Aurelia's eyes' when the dramatick opera was revived three years later; *Henry Purcell*, 278.

63 Ibid., 286.

64 Ibid., 282. Purcell also published his full score; Herissone has examined the self-publication of opera scores in part as a manifestation of ongoing debates over opera aesthetics; see 'Playford, Purcell, and the Functions of Music Publishing.'

65 Price, *Henry Purcell*, 301–2; Rodney Farnsworth, '"Hither, This Way": A Rhetorical-Musical Analysis of a Scene from Purcell's *King Arthur*', *MQ* 74/1 (1990), 83–97; and Eubanks Winkler, 'Sexless Spirits?: Gender Ideology and Dryden's Musical Magic', *MQ* 93/2 (2010), 297–328: 308–12.

66 On the connection to *Isis*, see Jack A. Westrup, *Purcell*, rev. edn. (London: Dent & Sons, 1980), 134. For a discussion of how the wavy lines might be performed, see Lionel Sawkins, '*Trembleurs* and Cold People: How Should They Shiver?' in Burden (ed.), *Performing the Music of Henry Purcell*, 243–64.

67 Price, *Henry Purcell*, 305.

68 On this adaptation's relationship to Shakespeare see Roger Savage, 'The Shakespeare–Purcell *Fairy Queen*: A Defence and Recommendation', *EM* 1/1 (1973), 200–22. Michael Burden has discovered a letter that indicates that Titania and Oberon were played by children of about eight or nine years of age, which may have caused 'the rigid division between spoken and sung sections.' See Burden, 'Casting Issues in the Original Production of Purcell's Opera "The Fairy Queen,"' *ML* 84/4 (2003), 596–607, especially 607. Children had also been used in *Dioclesian* and later *The Island Princess*: see 606, note 52.

69 On the *The Fairy-Queen* sources see Rebecca Herissone, *Musical Creativity in Restoration England* (Cambridge: Cambridge University Press, 2013), 137–145, and Bruce Wood and Andrew Pinnock, '*The Fairy Queen*: A Fresh Look at the Issues', *EM* 21/1 (1993), 44–62.

70 On the adaptation, see Andrew Pinnock, 'Play into Opera: Purcell's *The Indian Queen*', *EM* 18/1 (1990), 3–21.

71 For a discussion of what led to the rupture, see Judith Milhous, *Thomas Betterton and the Management of Lincoln's Inn Fields, 1695–1708* (Carbondale and Edwardsville: Southern Illinois University Press, 1979), 51–79.

72 GB-Lna LC 7/3; see also Milhous, *Thomas Betterton*, 230–46. The abridged play and the music survive in GB-Lbl Add MS 31449. The same music copyist produced the 1699 adaptation of *The Island Princess* (GB-Lbl Add MS 15318) and other sources associated with Drury Lane; Price postulates that these scores were prepared by one of the Theatre Royal's copyists, *Henry Purcell*, 131, and for Price's theory on the adaptor, 126. For more on the sources and scribes see

Margaret Laurie and Andrew Pinnock's introduction to their edition of *The Indian Queen*, The Works of Henry Purcell, vol. 19 (London: Novello, 1994).

73 Ismeron's text is carried over from the 1664 playtext; the incantation 'Ye twice ten hundred deities' was printed in italics but no stage direction indicates it was sung; Price, *Henry Purcell*, 135, and for a musical analysis, 136. See also Steven E. Plank, '"And Now About the Cauldron Sing": Music and the Supernatural on the Restoration Stage', *EM* 18/3 (1990), 392–407.

74 For a modern edition of the music and text, see John Eccles, *Rinaldo and Armida*, ed. Steven Plank (Middleton: A-R Editions, 2011).

75 Already *The Island Princess* had been adapted twice after the Restoration, once by an anonymous adapter in 1668 and again in 1687 by Nahum Tate.

76 On the *Rinaldo and Armida* and *The Island Princess* see Kathryn Lowerre, *Music and Musicians on the London Stage, 1695–1705* (Farnham: Ashgate, 2009), 230–2, and Lowerre, 'Dramatick Opera and Theatrical Reform: Dennis's *Rinaldo and Armida* and Motteux's *The Island Princess*', *Theatre Notebook* 59/1 (2005), 23–40. See also the introduction by Curtis Price and Robert Hume, in the facsimile edn. *The Island Princess: British Library Add. MS 15318, a Semi-Opera*, ed. Curtis Price and Robert Hume, Music for London Entertainment 1660–1800, series C, English Opera and Masque, vol. 2 (Tunbridge Wells: R. Macnutt, 1985).

77 Price, 'Island Princess, The', *Grove Music Online*.

78 For an analysis of the 'Enthusiastick Song', see Eubanks Winkler, 'Enthusiasm and its Discontents: Religion, Prophecy, and Madness in the Music for *Sophonisba* and *The Island Princess*', *JM* 23/2 (2006): 317–30.

79 Hume, 'The Politics of Opera', 21. *The Secular Masque*, however, was performed at Drury Lane; see Lowerre, *Music and Musicians*, 257–8.

80 On Motteux's contribution to the genre see Lucyle Hook, 'Motteux and the Classical Masque', in Shirley Strum Kenny (ed.), *British Theatre and the Other Arts, 1660–1800* (Washington, DC: Folger Shakespeare Library, 1984), 105–15. On this song contest, see Eubanks Winkler, '"O Ravishing Delight": The Politics of Pleasure in *The Judgment of Paris*', *COJ* 15/1 (2003), 15–31, and three essays on Congreve's masque in Kathryn Lowerre (ed.), *The Lively Arts of the London Stage, 1675–1725* (Farnham: Ashgate, 2014): Olive Baldwin and Thelma Wilson, 'The Singers of *The Judgment of Paris*', 11–26; Robert Rawson, 'Harmonia Anglicana or Why Finger Failed in The Prize Musick', 27–46, and Matthew Roberson, 'The 'Prize Musick' of 1701. A Reinvestigation of the Stage Issue', 47–60. On the continuation of this genre into the eighteenth century see Michael Burden, 'The Independent Masque 1700–1800: A Catalogue', *Royal Musical Association Research Chronicle* 28/1 (1995), 59–159.

81 For a discussion of the tumultuous theatre scene during this period, see Price, *Music in the Restoration Theatre*, 111–34.

82 Peter Motteux, *Gentleman's Journal* (January 1691–1692), quoted in Lowerre, *Music and Musicians on the London Stage*, 89.

13 | The Development of Opera in the German Countries

MICHAEL MAUL

Statistical Analysis

The beginnings of German-language opera can only be sketched loosely based on available sources. Our knowledge of its early history depends on 'dates without visual aids'[1] and 'words without songs', that is, mentions of performances and dates in more-or-less reliable archives, chronicles, and bibliographies,[2] as well as mute libretti, which ultimately only hint at how the first opera-like works in German sounded and were performed onstage. The musical losses must be considerable. According to cautious estimates, in the twenty-four known sites of operatic performance in Protestant-Lutheran regions in northern, central, and southern Germany, about 230 works were performed in the seventeenth century alone.[3]

When reconstructing the beginnings of German-language opera, we must turn to speculation since the pieces that survive only as libretti raise at least as many questions as they seem to answer. Often, it cannot even be determined with certainty whether a certain multi-act libretto was actually intended as a 'stage action entirely to be sung' – Werner Braun's definition for 'German Baroque Opera'[4] – or simply as a spoken play interspersed with songs.

Early History

Early efforts towards *Singspiele* occurred in Protestant regions. Here, in the wake of Luther's Bible translation, new worship practices, educational curricula, and ultimately the flourishing language societies – especially 'The Fruitbearing Society' (*Die fruchtbringende Gesellschaft*) founded by Prince Ludwig of Anhalt-Köthen – the mother tongue was musically elevated to an art form. In contrast, in German Catholic lands, the language of early opera was Italian (just as Latin remained the language of church music), and the leading composers were 'imported' from Italy at great expense.

The earliest documentation for performances of Italian opera in German-speaking areas is comparatively precise, though fraught with some uncertainties. These performances significantly predated German opera, and took place close to the birth of the genre and in Catholic regions, especially the Court of Marcus Sitticus, Prince-Archbishop of Salzburg. Here, during carnival in 1614, an anonymous *Orfeo* was performed in a newly constructed theatre. Two years earlier, the singer Francesco Rasi (1574–1621), who premièred Monteverdi's *Orfeo* (Mantua, 1607), had given the prince-archbishop a number of musical items, possibly including a score of Monteverdi's work; the conjecture arises that this setting may actually have been performed in Salzburg.[5] Additional (Catholic) German courts that had become centres of Italian opera by 1680 include the Imperial Court in Vienna, Regensburg (in connection with the *Reichstag*), Innsbruck, and Munich.[6] These stages were almost exclusively supplied with Italian composers. An exception was the Electoral Court of Munich. Here, the Saxon-born Hofkapellmeister Johann Caspar Kerll (1627–1693) – educated in Vienna with Froberger and with Carissimi in Rome – wrote at least nine Italian operas between 1657 and 1672; the music has been lost.

The Torgau *Dafne*, 1627

The printed libretto for the 'Tragicomoedia von der Dafne' is generally counted as the oldest surviving document related to German-language opera. According to information provided by the title page, Martin Opitz's libretto (based on Ottavio Rinuccini's *Dafne*, 1598) is said to have been brought 'musically to the stage' in 1627 in Torgau by the Dresden Hofkapellmeister Heinrich Schütz in honour of the marriage of the Saxon elector's eldest daughter to the Landgrave of Hesse-Kassel. However, Wolfram Steude has plausibly argued that the scanty contemporary statements on *Dafne*'s structure (from court diaries and other archival documents) point rather to the form of a *Singspiel* or spoken play, and therefore a work containing limited individual musical scenes.[7] This is especially plausible because the characterisation of the piece as the first German opera apparently stems from the Leipzig professor of philosophy Johann Christoph Gottsched (1700–1766). Gottsched, who had access only to the libretto, may have concluded from the collaboration between the 'Father of German poetry' (Opitz) and the 'Father of modern German music' (Schütz) that an epoch-making piece of theatre must have been performed in Torgau at that time. Admittedly, *Dafne* did not take the most prominent position among the stage works performed in conjunction with the wedding. And the libretto seems decidedly untheatrical. In any case, there is hardly room for the expressive recitative-like style that Schütz himself would later call 'style oratorio' in the title of his *Kleinen Geistlichen Konzert* 'Eile mich, Gott, zu erretten' SWV282 (Leipzig, 1636). As late as 1633, Schütz noted in a letter that the Italian manner in which 'a spoken comedy of many voices could be translated and brought to the stage to be sung ... to my knowledge (in the way I conceive it) is still completely unknown in Germany', and thus established a relatively lagging state of development.[8]

It is possible that Schütz initiated a type of opera project that was 'still completely unknown' in Germany when he composed music 'in an Italian manner' for the ballet *Orpheus und Eurydice* (libretto by August Buchner) in 1638 on the occasion of another electoral wedding.[9]

The Nuremberg *Seelewig*, 1644

The earliest preserved music for an entirely sung German-language theatrical piece is for the *Geistliche Waldgedicht* [German counterpart to *Favola boscareccia*] *oder Freudenspiel, genant Seelewig* by the well-travelled Nuremberg patrician Georg Philipp Harsdörffer (libretto; 1607–1658) and the local organist and town piper Sigmund Theophil Staden (1607–1655).[10] In 1644, Harsdörffer founded the 'Order of the Commendable Shepherds and Flowers on the Pegnitz' (*Löblichen Hirten- und Blumenorden an der Pegnitz*: in short, the 'Pegnitz Flower Order') on the model of the Italian academies. The stated purpose for founding this language society was the cultivation and improvement of German language and poetry. This was reason enough for Harsdörffer to publish eight volumes of so-called 'Spoken Plays for Women' (*Frawen-Zimmer Gespräch-Spiele*) during the 1640s. At the end of the fourth volume of the anthology (publ. 1644) is the music for the *Geistlichen Waldgedicht* that Staden – according to the title – had 'set' to Music 'in the Italian way of singing'. The plot and form of *Seelewig* point to much older Italian models, especially Emilio de' Cavalieri's *La Rappresentazione di Anima, et di Corpo* (Rome, 1600), although Harsdörffer's nymph, who must decide between heavenly and earthly joys, is called Seelewig rather than Anima. Her adversary is Trügewaldt (*trügen*: 'to deceive'), a cloven-hoofed satyr, who over the course of three acts tries in vain to lure her to ruin, with all kinds of cunning and some outside assistance. Only the prologue, in which

'Music or Singing' enters the scene, is reminiscent of Monteverdi and his *Orfeo*. Otherwise, *Seelewig* is far from Monteverdi's principles of *seconda pratica*, especially in its musical language. Staden's music and Harsdörffers's text follow a rather pedagogical, instructive approach, even in the instrumentation: strings and flutes for the nymph, shawms for the shepherd; Trügewald supported by trombones and bassoons; and a theorbo playing continuo. Italian recitative seems foreign to these Nuremberg authors. Protagonists speak almost exclusively in strophic form, whether in solo songs or in strophic dialogue. In both genres, the music remains much closer to the contemporary German lied (as practiced by Heinrich Albert and Andreas Hammerschmidt) than to Schütz's 'style oratorio'; phrases in true recitative are the exception, and grand laments are entirely absent. What is operatic is that the print of Harsdörffer's 'Liederspiel' contains eleven stage engravings. The 'Art of Painting' (*Mahlkunst*) even appears onstage in the epilogue, and, in the accompanying conversation, the ideal stage is described as an 'often-changing scene' in the form of a 'round disc', which is 'painted with perspective' and 'can be rotated'.[11]

Whether, by whom, and how *Seelewig* may have been performed in Nürnberg remains unknown. In any case, in 1654 in Wolfenbüttel, a good 300 kilometres away, a performance of *Seelewig* has been documented in honor of the seventy-fifth birthday of Duke August, brought about by his music-loving wife Sophie Elisabeth von Braunschweig-Lüneburg, who was a composer herself.

The Newly Discovered *Pastorello musicale* in Königsberg, 1663

The oldest surviving German-language opera manuscript dates from 1663: the *Pastorello musicale* (title on the partial autograph score) or the *Verliebte Schäffer-Spiel*[12] (title on the printed text) by Königsberg Hofkapellmeister Johann Sebastiani (1622–1683),[13] which was performed in the presence of the Great Elector to mark the wedding of Count Gerhard von Dönhoff with the step-daughter of the influential Prussian Oberregimentsrat and Landeshofmeister Johann Ernst von Wallenrodt, Anna Beata von Goldstein (1644–1675).

The libretto is by Johann Röling (1634–1680), who succeeded Simon Dachs as Professor of Poetry at the University of Königsberg in 1660. Even if the piece is dressed in the trappings of a pastoral opera, it is actually a satire of the genre. The plot involves Thyrsis, a foreigner, who has since his youth read and internalised novels, pastoral plays, and Ovid's *Metamorphoses*.

Believing all of this literary and mythological material to be true, he decides to go out into the pastoral world in hopes of encountering 'pastoral desire and transformation'.[14] Immediately after arriving in the supposed pastoral world – a courtly society that takes great pleasure in the confused 'intruder' – he falls in love with the beautiful Chrysille. For five acts, the amused company enjoys putting on a series of traditional bucolic scenes, arranged into episodes, for the naïve foreigner. However, these behavioural patterns are used as the basis for parody, in order to take the various models of pastoral literature down exaggerated new paths from the burlesque to the satirical. In the first act, Chrysille becomes a false Echo; in the following act, Thyrsis refuses to fight with a rival suitor bearing a rapier – in his literary pastoral world, the only suitable instrument for a duel is the shepherd's staff. Eventually, Thyrsis is rejected by Chrysille, flees in tears, falls into a hollow tree stump, and believes himself, like Daphne, to have been transformed into a tree. Goddesses of the forest dance around him, greeting him as one of their own. The absurd story ends with joy all around.

Röling's text is based on a specific model: Thomas Corneille's pastoral play *Le Berger Extravagant* (publ. 1653), itself a stage adaptation of the French novel of the same name by Charles Sorel. Here, Don Quixote is 'translated into the bucolic'. Andreas Gryphius had already engaged with Corneille's play in 1660, with his 'satyric comedy' *Der Schwärmende Schäfer* (expanded edition Breslau, 1660).

Sebastiani's score encompasses eighteen scenes in five acts. Recitative predominates in the approximately 2,000 measures, which otherwise include only seven strophic sections: five arias (some with ritornelli), as well as opening and closing choruses. The recitative is formulaic, primarily 'babbling' eighth-notes strung together syllabically in even metres. Sebastiani only sparingly uses effects such as melismas to illustrate the text, changes to triple metre, or the repetition of words and phrases. Nevertheless, his recitative follows certain formal principles and is not without charm. It falls into two types – one more songlike and one more freely structured – and one type often leads fluidly into the other; the songlike recitative resembles the style of the arias, which have ritornelli and a tendency towards symmetry and clear divisions akin to Adam Krieger's contemporary lieder. In addition, clear echoes of Francesco Cavalli's canzonetta style of the 1640s can be heard, appearing also in many of Sebastiani's surviving occasional songs[15] – born in Thüringen, Sebastiani is thought to have travelled to Italy before arriving in Königsberg (1650).[16]

What the *Pastorello musicale* is missing musically are distinctively dramatic passages and a large number of arias and instrumental sections, which, if they were present, would make it easier to designate the *Pastorello musicale* an opera. Nevertheless, such reservations are subject to a misunderstanding. The apparent defects of the piece are less a matter of Sebastiani's conception or any potential step backwards in the development of German theatrical music than of the principles of its genre: Sebastiani's *Pastorello* is a pastoral opera, whose charm lies in its humour. Röling did not provide models for expressive monodies, and Corneille even less so. The libretto did not even designate a 'lamento'. Sebastiani created an instrumental one (end of Act II). In any case, Sebastiani convincingly set the conversational text in a natural manner, that is by following speech declamation and avoiding 'dead pauses' in the music. The 'singing recitative' differentiates the piece, sometimes fundamentally, from the later German-language operas of the 1680s and 1690s.[17] Presumably, Sebastiani was not alone in his treatment of recitative, and so the opera could be viewed as representative of all lost German operas from around 1660. At least, this *Pastorello musicale* provides the first proof of Johann Mattheson's claim that German opera was originally – and thus surely before 1680 – sung 'in time, as our Arioso is now'.[18]

Königsberg was certainly not a focal point for the development of German-language opera, and neither was Sebastiani an innovator in theatrical music. The value of his *Pastorello musicale* lies in the uniqueness of its transmission. It is hardly possible to estimate the extent to which various courts with mid-century operatic activity may have developed forms that were more clearly aligned (and analogous to developments in Protestant church music) with the truly dramatic examples coming from Venice or Rome.

Italians Compose Operas in Dresden

Among Protestant lands, the Dresden Hofkapelle held an exceptional position, even before the elector converted to Catholicism (1697, in order to become King of Poland). In the middle of the seventeenth century, the court was largely staffed by Italians, a situation that led to the formation of two competing ensembles in 1666: a mostly Italian 'first choir' for official court music, and a 'small German music' (*Kleine deutsche Musik*) primarily for Protestant worship services.[19]

Likewise, it was an Italian who opened a new chapter of opera history in Dresden: Giovanni Andrea Bontempi (1625–1705) of Piegaro near Perugia, a pupil of Virgilio Mazzocchi, and apparently the first castrato employed in Protestant Germany. After entering into the elector's service as a singer and composer in 1650, his duties soon expanded in theatrical directions: in 1657 he became Vice-Kapellmeister, and in 1664 the architect, machine-master, and inspector of the new comedy theatre. A correspondingly large number of documents exist for *Singballette* performed under his watch. Bontempi's first opera for Dresden was a first-rate representational product: in honour of the marriage of the daughter of Elector Johann Georg II, Erdmuthe Sophie, to the Margrave of Brandenburg-Bayreuth in 1662, he composed *Il Paride*, the first Italian opera performed in Dresden. It would remain representative for posterity as well, as not only the text but also the score was published, a practically unique occurrence north of the Alps.

The libretto, apparently also by Bontempi, embellishes Paris's famous judgement in the goddesses' contest for the apple and concludes with the arrival of Paris and Helena in Troy. In part, it follows Giacomo Badoaro's *Il ritorno d'Ulisse in patria*. In the preface to the print edition, Bontempi designates the piece – appropriately for the occasion – as an 'Erotopaegnion Musicum', that is, a 'play of love, set in music'. Despite a relatively linear narrative style, it demanded a lot of attention from the Dresden *Festgesellschaft*: fourteen singers play thirty-one roles, acting out the story of a love triangle. All of the entertainment that Venetian opera can offer is present here: the stuttering Ancrocco, a constantly quarrelling servant couple, and of course some cross-dressing confusion. In short, 'all these scenes run one to the next like a string of pearls', without, however, 'getting entangled in a knot of intrigue'.[20]

Bontempi's music offers pronounced declamatory recitatives, with arias mostly in triple time; strophic and cyclical arias stand side-by-side on equal footing. There are also large scenes in which Bontempi artfully combines arioso and recitative sections. What is surprising about the score, however, is that the most dramatic notes are found in the scenes of the comic servant figures – causing, so to speak, 'dramatic' strain on the laughing muscles.

In 1667, the new Komödienhaus am Taschenberg designed by Wolf Caspar von Klengel was dedicated with a performance of the opera *Il Teseo* (music by Pietro Andrea Ziani). In 1671, Bontempi ventured for the first time to write a German-language opera, *Musicalisches Schauspiel von der Dafne*, which was written together with his Kapellmeister colleague, Marco Giuseppe Peranda. It is impossible to differentiate their styles. In comparison with *Paride*, a stronger emphasis on strophic arias with instrumental ritornelli is noticeable, which might come from the large number of scenes involving the peasant world.[21] The libretto is based on Opitz's earlier text, but in more contemporary clothing: the traditional plot is enriched with additional gods, shepherds, and elements from the world of Venetian opera. For example, the anonymous librettist freely adapted servant-scenes in distinctively lower-class language and with ribald lines, such as when the peasant Urban asks, 'Did the devil screw us over' ('Hat der Teufel uns beschissen?'), or when conversation turns to the 'damned whore'.

The score was clearly tailored to the capability of the Dresden Hofkapelle, especially regarding the figure of the hunter. The fact that he usually stands alone on the stage and his part is rather more virtuosic than the others points to Johann Jäger, then a singer in the German Kapelle in Dresden. Mattheson reports that Jäger far surpassed the Italian bass whom the elector had engaged for the Hofkapelle, so as to keep up with the emperor in Vienna – 'not only with his voice, but also with his clean manner'; Jäger 'lay in wait for the cadenzas of the castrati, which they stretched out; when these had passed, Jäger came along and sang his wonderful *passagi*, much better than those'.[22]

The following year, the same pair of authors brought another German opera to the stage: *Jupiter und Jo*, of which only the libretto has survived.

Upon the death of Elector Johann Georg II (22 August 1680), the tender sprout of German-language opera withered at the Dresden court. His successor, Johann Georg III, preferred Italian operas, which he procured, together with staff, directly from the source (Venice), namely the successful opera composer and *maestro di coro* of the Ospedale degli incurabili, Carlo Pallavicino (ca. 1630–1688). After having served as Vice-Kapellmeister (1662–1672) and succeeding Schütz as Kapellmeister (1672) in Dresden, he was called back to the court as Prefect of chamber and court music in 1687 with the goal of establishing Italian court opera. Immediately after his arrival, the opera *Gerusalemme liberata* (Giulio Cesare Corradi, after Tasso) was premièred, in parallel with Venice, based on one of the greatest texts of Italian literature. The opera centres around the pagan sorceress Armida, who converts to Christianity for the love of Rinaldo. In parallel, the duel of Tancredi and Clorinda is told with a kind of happy ending: Clorinda appears to Tancredi in a dream and confesses her love. In comparison with Bontempi's work, Pallavicino's music was a quantum leap ahead: the score is characterised by three-part da capo arias and a marked virtuosity.

Together with his son Stefano (1672–1742), who became Court Poet when he was hardly sixteen, Pallavicino probably began his last opera project in 1687: *Antiope*. Left incomplete upon Pallavicino's death on 29 January 1688, the work was eventually completed by the newly arrived Vice-Kapellmeister Nikolaus Adam Strungk (1640–1700) and premiered in February 1689. From the surviving copy of the manuscript, it is impossible to determine who wrote which sections, an indication that Strungk persuasively attempted to imitate Pallavicino's style.

In the years after Pallavicino's death, opera culture in Dresden seems to have lost its lustre at times. This is not least because a main figure, namely Strungk (who had been a pioneer of Baroque opera in Hamburg) regularly brought German-language operas to the stage for the elector elsewhere within the electorate: during the fairs, in the civic opera house on the Brühl in Leipzig.

Opera Tradition in Smaller Central German Courts, 1660–1700: Highlights in Halle and Weißenfels

A rich courtly opera tradition developed in the 1660s and 1670s at smaller courts, especially in central Germany.[23] However, research relies exclusively on silent witnesses: printed libretti and here and there other archival material related to performance. Focal points were the ducal courts of Gotha, Halle, and Weißenfels.

Opera in Halle is tied to Duke Augustus (1614–1680), son of the Saxon Elector Johann Georg I, who lived in this city as Administrator of the Archbishopric of Magdeburg – since the Peace of Westphalia, under the toleration of the House of Brandenburg, to whom the archbishopric was to fall after the duke's death. The artistically minded duke, who became president of the Fruchtbringenden Gesellschaft in 1667, invested remarkable resources in the cultural life of the court. He had a comedy theatre built, whose budget was at times on a par with those of Dresden and Gotha. His Hofkapelle had approximately twenty members, including some singers who later achieved fame on the stages of Weißenfels and Hamburg. Printed libretti and archival materials from Halle between 1658 and 1679, often in connection with festivities and honorary days in the ducal house, document productions of well over twenty stage works: libretto titles call them 'Sing-Spiele' with ballets and 'Trauer- und Freudenspiele', although it is often not clear whether the latter were sung through, or were rather plays with individual songs and entr'acte music.[24] Subjects run the gamut from the biblical and bucolic to the antique and medieval, with texts that are often remarkably substantial and, in many cases, have a moral undertone. The libretti use various forms. Within one piece, such as the fest-opera in honor of a princely marriage in 1669, *Liebe krönt Eintract, oder erworbene Prinzessin Mösien*, long passages evidently in recitative style stand alongside closed ensemble scenes (canzonettas, madrigals?) or strophic arias and antiphonal conversations.

The primary librettist for opera in Halle was probably – most printed libretti do not list an author – the local councillor and privy secretary David Elias Heidenreich (1638–1688), who was also the secretary for the Fruchtbringenden Gesellschaft. In addition, he made a contribution to church music history: his volume *Geistlichen Oden* (1665), with texts for all Sundays and festival days with a mixture of biblical dicta and freely written strophic arias, represents the birth of the so-called concerto-aria cantata.[25] Initially, Philipp Stolle, the director of court music, seems to have been responsible for the music of the operas in Halle, but, from 1660, Schütz's pupil David Pohle (1624–1695, Kapellmeister from 1661) took over. However, Pohle left the court over a dispute in 1679, after the duke had engaged as his deputy a student of Rosenmüller, Johann Philipp Krieger (1649–1725), who had matured as a composer in Venice and Rome. From his new home in Merseburg, Pohle then seems to have supplied the Gotha court with several pieces made in the 'Halle model' in the 1680s: opera apparently flourished here in the 1680s and 1690s under Dukes Friedrich I and II and Kapellmeister Wolfgang Michael Mylius.[26]

Meanwhile, Krieger was an opera composer primarily in Weißenfels. After the death of Duke August of Halle (1680), his son Johann Adolf I continued the tradition of rich and ambitious opera activity. In the time before his death in 1697, records can be traced for over thirty opera productions in the 'Schau-Platz' in the Neu-Augustusburg, and both of his sons continued the tradition with equal enthusiasm despite the small duchy's precarious economic situation until the 1720s.[27] Most of the scores (all of which have been lost) were by Krieger and were performed by what was, considering the size of the duchy, a relatively large and capable Hofkapelle with additional paid guest musicians. The topics vary widely. Some of the mostly anonymous libretti are slavish translations of famous Italian texts and are entirely up-to-date. Identifiable librettists include Paul Thymich (Thiemich or Thiemick; 1656–1694), teacher at the Leipzig Thomasschule and husband of a celebrated opera singer, Anna Catherina, and the young preacher Erdmann Neumeister (1671–1756). Both were deeply influenced by contemporary *opera seria*, and Neumeister soon transferred its basic elements – the alternation of recitative and da capo arias – into other genres. First for Krieger and the court at Weißenfels, and shortly thereafter for the entire generation of young musicians around Telemann and Bach, Neumeister developed the poetic form of the church 'cantata' around 1700, which he conceived of as looking like 'nothing other … than a section from an opera, composed of *stylo recitativo* and arias'.[28] Two printed collections include musical material from the early Weißenfels court operas, with 'selected arias' from seven 'Sing-Spiele', published in 1690 and 1692. The approximately 200 pieces remain largely in the tradition of the German strophic lied with primarily syllabic declamation and instrumental ritornelli; traces of his Italian musical education can be found most clearly in the bass ostinato aria 'Einsamkeit, du Qual der Herzen' (from the opera *Die ausgesöhnte Eifersucht oder Cephalus und Procris*, 1689).

Agostino Steffani: Catalyst for German Opera and Political Opera in Catholic Courts in Munich, Hanover, and Düsseldorf

The centres of Italian opera in Catholic Germany in the late seventeenth century were Munich, Hanover, and Düsseldorf.[29] Opera in these three courts is inextricably linked with the name of Agostino Steffani, the 'key figure for the establishment of Italian culture in Germany' and a 'clever transmitter of new musical ideas to the next generation'.[30] Born in Castelfranco near Venice in 1654, he came to the court of Ferdinand Maria, the Bavarian elector in Munich, at age twelve. Steffani was a choirboy and composition student of Kerll. Under Elector Maximilian Emanuel II (Ferdinand Maria's successor), Steffani began his career as a diplomat and opera composer – and quickly excelled in both fields. Ordained as a priest in 1680, he had written at least six operas for Munich by 1688: *Marco Aurelio, Solone, Audacia e rispetto, Servio Tullio, Alarico il Baltha*, and *Niobe, Regina di Tebe*. The last two are based on texts by Luigi Orlandi, while the earlier libretti are by Ventura Terzago. Like his career, Steffani's operas were increasingly political. His Munich operas are all allegories about the elector; they honor the ideal ruler.

Steffani first met his next employer, Duke Ernst August of Hanover, in 1683 while conducting diplomatic inquiries into the possibility of a marriage between the duke's daughter Sophia Charlotte and the Bavarian elector (she eventually married into the Prussian royal family as the wife of King Frederick I). However, Steffani's primary diplomatic assignment in the Hanover Court was to help Ernst August to become elector, which eventually occurred in 1692. Musical life in the Hanover court had been dominated by Italian forces. Following Duke Johann Friedrich's conversion to Catholicism (r. 1665–1679), Kapellmeister Antonio Sartorio (1630–1680) and eight Italian singers provided Catholic church music during the 1670s. Ernst August, who re-introduced Lutheranism, entirely reshaped his Hofkapelle along the lines of Lully, dismissing singers and instrumentalists and replacing them with many French musicians. There began an entirely brilliant period in Hanover musical theatre, initially in the castle theatre (1678), and then from 1689 in the new, larger castle theatre built by Tommaso Giusti (stage machinery by Johann Oswald Harms). Contemporaries called it 'the best in all of Europe' due to 'both the painting and the furnishings'.[31]

Steffani composed multiple Italian operas for these stages, beginning with the highly political *Henrico Leone* (Ortensio Mauro, 1689). The piece treats the history of the heroic Hanoverian Duke Heinrich (called Henry the Lion) – Frederick Barbarossa's powerful rival – and thus indirectly supports Ernst August's claim to the throne.[32] Steffani's remaining seven operas for Hanover were also used for court propaganda, especially as his work for the Welfs increasingly focused on diplomatic service; in 1695, he moved to Brussels as a Hanoverian envoy.

Finally, in 1703, Steffani arrived in Düsseldorf in the service of Palatine Elector Johann Wilhelm, now as a secret councillor, soon to be President of the Palatinate and rector of the University of Heidelberg. His operas composed for the court of Düsseldorf remained political: with his last opera, *Tassilone* (Stefano Pallavicino, 1709), he celebrated the success of his employer in having taken the Upper Palatinate from the Prince-Elector of Bavaria; the libretto reflects the contemporary political situation rather clearly. Meanwhile, in the same year, Steffani returned to Hanover, now as Vicar Apostolic – a result of his excellent relations with Pope Innocent XI. His main task was the re-catholicisation of Protestant northern Germany; he spent the rest of his life in diplomatic service (d. 1728 in Frankfurt).

Steffani's operas, mostly preserved, are musically varied. His colourful arias offer imaginative da capo and dal segno forms. Their instrumentation is often more French than Italian; he often uses five-part strings, establishes the oboe in the opera orchestra, and composes arias for obbligato bassoon, cello, and even lute. The chalumeau is used in his Düsseldorf operas, even within recitative.

Niobe, Steffani's last Munich opera, is surely his most musically important piece from his time at the Bavarian court. Steffani created some enthralling, vividly composed scenes on the tragic story of the Queen of Thebes: to punish her, the gods kill her children, and in her pain she transforms into a stone. One example is the singing of Niobe's husband, Amphion, in the first act of the opera (Act I scene 13), when he, the inventor of the lyre, stages the harmony of the spheres and transforms them into enchanting sounds. Steffani writes a da capo aria ('Sfere amiche') over an ostinato bass in running quarter notes, over which viols and flutes unfurl in a colourful and polyphonic manner typical of his style. Thus, the ostinato represents order on the one hand, and, on the other, the everlasting oscillation of the spheres. Unlike the tonally stable A section (in B-flat major), the B section takes a harmonious journey through seven sometimes remote keys (from D minor through C minor, E-flat major, G minor, and A-flat major back to C minor and E-flat major) – surely a reference to the seven planetary orbits.[33]

A remarkable fusion of Italian and French elements is to be found in Steffani's works, some of which made the leap from courtly stages to the commercial Hamburg stage. Here, they offered the north German generation of Johann Sigismund Kusser (1660–1727), Georg Caspar Schürmann (1672/3–1751), Reinhard Keiser (1674–1739), Handel, and Telemann both a benchmark and a model, which played a not insignificant role in the shaping of their own operatic styles.

Opera Focal Point: Wolfenbüttel/Braunschweig

French and Italian opera came together in the court of Braunschweig-Wolfenbüttel starting in the 1680s. Numerous German-language opera-like structures have already been documented between 1657 and 1663.[34] Surviving printed libretti are mostly by the artistically minded Prince Anton Ulrich (1633–1714), a life-long author who hardly missed a literary or poetic genre from the historical novel and the opera libretto all the way to the religious song. The composer of these early operas was apparently the Schütz pupil Johann Jakob Löwe of Eisenach (1629–1703), who was Kapellmeister in Wolfenbüttel from 1655 to 1663.

After Anton Ulrich had come to know and appreciate Italian opera in Venice in the early 1680s, operatic activity was renewed in Wolfenbüttel in the mid-1680s, now with a notably European perspective and under the leadership of new Kapellmeister Johann Theile (1646–1724), a pioneer of the Gänsemarkt Opera. For a few years starting in 1685, French operas (mostly Lully) and Italian operas (mostly Venetian) were performed in colourful alternation in the original language in the Wolfenbüttel court theatre (built in 1688) or in the summer palace Salzdahlum.

In 1690 in the neighbouring trade-fair town of Braunschweig, Ulrich renovated the town hall on the Hagenmarkt as an opera house. Operas were performed during trade fairs (during carnival) for members of the Wolfenbüttel court, invited nobles, and also a ticket-buying general public.

Unlike the performances in Wolfenbüttel, the Braunschweig operas were primarily sung in German. The texts were mostly by court poet Friedrich Christian Bressand, with music by the newly arrived Kapellmeister Kusser, and later (from 1695) by Kapellmeisters Keiser and Schürmann; the operas were closely connected with the Hamburg stage, in terms of both content and personnel. The Italian works heard in Wolfenbüttel were generally imports, with the exception of a few by Clemente Monari (c. ? 1660–d. ? after 1728), who was engaged as the court 'Maestro di Capella di Camera' in 1692.

Public Opera Houses in Hamburg and Leipzig, and Their Protagonists

In Germany, opera was relatively slow to move from the closed walls of elite courtly society out into the public. It first became 'public' and commercial on 2 January 1678, when the first public opera house opened its doors on the Gänsemarkt in Hamburg; it operated for sixty years before ending in bankruptcy. 'Public' refers primarily to the form of organisation: a standing opera house unattached to a court, whose performances were open to anyone who could buy a ticket, and led by bourgeois figures who ran the theatre at their own financial risk. This development is also a striking episode in music history because these public opera houses (Braunschweig in 1690 – though that house was de facto financed and run by the duke – and Leipzig in 1693) provided the playground for a thoroughly original operatic development in Germany, which was initially entirely in the German language.

However, one should approach very cautiously the tempting conclusion that this situation of opera in a public context was the spark for the development of German national opera. Although the repertoire in the first two decades of 'public' and commercial opera in Protestant Germany consisted almost entirely of German-language works written by German composers and poets, the libretti and music were both European, that is, under Italian and French influence. Even in 1677 when seeking permission for the first opera in Hamburg, Theile (who would soon join the opera's permanent staff) expressly requested permission to 'present a few musical operas in the Italian style'.

Many of the figures on, behind, and in front of the stage who influenced developments beginning in 1693 at the Gänsemarkt Opera in Hamburg and the Leipzig Opera moved in courtly circles. A contemporary witness at the dedication of the Hamburg Opera remarked sceptically: 'It seemed that

Hamburg, with so many merchants and intermediaries, [was] unsuited to opera.'[35] And it was no coincidence that Mattheson emphasised in 1728: 'The performance of opera contradicts the disposition of the residents; to sum it up, operas are more for kings and princes than for merchants and traders.'[36]

The impulse to found an opera house in Hamburg began with a regent: Christian Albrecht of Schleswig-Gottorf, a deposed duke who had ceded his small state to the Danish king in 1675 and lived in exile in Hamburg. It was the jurist Gerhard Schott (1641–1702), an artistically minded patrician and member of the Hamburg Council beginning in 1693, who put these plans into action; at first he partnered with financiers Johann Adam Reincken (1643–1722; organist at St Catherine's Church) and Hamburg Mayor Peter Lütkens (der Jüngere), and then served as sole owner and director from 1685, solving several staff and economic crises during this time, and leading the operation until his death.[37] Such crises arose, not least because the house and the genre faced a great deal of public criticism early on, especially from religious figures. The initial attempt to establish the cathedral refectory as a performance site was denied by religious authorities. Thus, Schott and his backers had to commission the Italian master-builder Girolamo Sartorio to build a new freestanding house on the Gänsemarkt: a wooden building with a twenty-eight-foot-deep stage, four stories of loges (for the well-off public), as well as a gallery and a parterre; the house accommodated about 2,000 spectators.[38] The completed house evidently offered performances three or even sometimes four times per week, with a variable repertory. By 1700, ninety-five different pieces had been staged.[39]

The house opened in January 1678 with Theile's *Orontes* (librettist unknown). It seems as if the singers first performed *Der erschaffene, gefallene und aufgerichtete Mensch* (libretto by Christian Richter, music likely by Theile), an opera about Adam and Eve.[40] Against the background of fermenting hostility on the part of the clergy, this was probably a conciliatory gesture. The prophylactic effect failed, however, because, although the subjects of the Hamburg operas in the following years were often of biblical origin, the critics did not hold back. Many pastors preached against opera and the opera house from the pulpit, as well as in polemical pamphlets, calling opera a hotbed of sin – the so-called 'theological dispute' (*Theologenstreit*) on the suitability of the genre produced all sorts of printed texts over the next three decades and quickly grew beyond Hamburg itself, as supporters and opponents attacked each other in heated debates.[41] Certainly, there were a few theologians who sided with the supporters of opera, above all Heinrich Elmenhorst (1632–1704), deacon at St Catherine's Church in Hamburg. He offered his opponents the written defence titled 'Dramatologia … Report on Operas' in 1688. Elmenhorst knew what he was talking about: he was one of the central librettists in the first phase of the Gänsemarkt Opera.

In Leipzig, the situation was different. In 1692, the Elector of Saxony in Dresden granted the request of his Kapellmeister Strungk for a privilege allowing him the exclusive right to perform operas (at his own cost) in the trade city of Leipzig during the three annual trade fairs; for each of the three-week fairs, fifteen performances were envisioned.[42] The granting of the privilege was also self-serving, in a double sense. On the one hand, the regent and the illustrious fair attendees no longer wanted to be entertained nightly by traveling theatrical troupes alone but also by the increasingly popular genre of opera. On the other hand, Strungk's opera enterprise was also meant to be a kind of training centre for aspiring musical elites. The privilege has a visionary scope: 'His Electoral Highness has graciously considered how the study of music would be increasingly cultivated, attracting foreign lovers of this science, and He would have a seminary in His lands, and would be able to fill the empty chapel- and chamber-musician posts.'

The purpose did not overreach: all subsequently famous musicians who studied at the Leipzig University during the twenty-seven-year run of the public opera (until the opera company's bankruptcy in 1720) were involved with the opera house and acquired their first recognition there, among them Telemann, Johann Friedrich Fasch (1688–1758), Johann Georg Pisendel, and Gottfried Heinrich Stölzel (1690–1740). However, the house received this youthful/student character only after Strungk's death (d. 1700), when his five daughters (singers themselves, one even a librettist) took over the direction of the opera company and soon fell into chronic financial need due to internal family disputes.

Strungk's initial plan to renovate the old St Peter's Church (Alte Peterskirche; which had not been used as a house of God since the Reformation) as an opera house was evidently challenged by the supreme consistory. In the end, Strungk had to lease a back courtyard on the northeast end of the Brühl. Here, Girolamo Sartorio (who had already built the stage at the Gänsemarkt in Hamburg and who soon became a co-partner in the Leipzig stage because of Strungk's financial problems) built a large wooden opera house, with 125 loges on five levels. The building held its own in comparison with others. The Uffenbach brothers from Frankfurt commented after a visit to the Hamburg Opera House in 1710 that it was 'like the one in Braunschweig but somewhat bigger, though a good deal smaller and much more humble than the one in Leipzig, which surpasses both in daintiness, but the [other] theatres in both places are probably much larger than that in Leipzig'.[43]

Strungk brought most of his artists with him from Dresden or engaged them from other courts. During each fair, there was one new production, apparently always written by Strungk himself, although only the printed libretti to his works survive. The opening performance on 8 May 1693 was Strungk's *Alceste*, with a text by Thymich (based on Aurelio Aureli's *L'Antigona delusa*; Venice, 1660); Thymich's wife performed the role of Alcestis.

The subjects of Hamburg operas at the end of the seventeenth century were of various origins: often biblical at first, and then based on material from antique and medieval times. Occasionally, there were *Fortsetzungsopern* (sequels), such as *Cara Mustapha* (Johann Wolfgang Franck, 1686), *Die Verstöhrung Jerusalem* (Conradi, 1692), and *Störtebecker* (Keiser, 1701), each of which had two parts. A number of adapted Italian and French libretti have been documented, and even performances of German versions of Italian and French works: Lully's *Achille et Polyxène* (Paris 1687) was performed as *Die unglückliche Liebe des Achilles und der Polixena* in 1692 (rhymed translation by Christian Heinrich Postel, 1658–1705); and Agostino Steffani's *Orlando generoso* (Hanover 1691) ran as *Der grossmütige Roland* (German version by Gottlieb Fiedler) on several occasions between 1695 and 1735(!). The practice of mixing languages within a libretto that would become typical of German opera, especially the juxtaposition of German and Italian operas, first became established in Hamburg in 1703 (in *Claudius* by Barthold Feind and Keiser),[44] and was then taken up in Leipzig and Braunschweig.

Under Strungk, the first decade of opera in Leipzig was shaped by antique and mythological subjects. Dependence on Italian operas was even stronger than in Hamburg: of the twenty-nine operas performed between 1693 and 1702, at least half were based on Italian models, especially ones from Venice in the 1670s–1680s. The Italian libretti were often translated directly into German, with what might be called 'slavish fidelity' to the original.[45] The aria forms are correspondingly modern. Characteristic figures from *commedia dell'arte*, such as Hanswurst figures, were also eagerly adopted in Hamburg and Leipzig, providing humourous moments even in the most dramatic stories, and using parables and more-or-less slanted metaphors to bring philosophical wisdom and sometimes highly politically charged messages to the people. The political meaning and dimension of opera became especially evident in Hamburg under the direction of soon-to-be-councilman Schott. His stages were continually used for performances of so-called festival operas (*Festopern*) marking important political events or notable days related to important rulers.[46] To be sure, the subjects appearing onstage were primarily drawn from antiquity, and it was left to the viewer to make connections with present times. On one occasion, however, three years after the 1683 victory of the Imperial Army against the Turkish besiegers of Vienna, this practice was notably broken. The jurist and later major Lucas von Bostel wrote the libretto to *Cara Mustapha*, which was set by Franck (b. 1644) and performed in 1686. The opera tells the story of the siege of Vienna and the victory of the emperor over the Ottoman army; 'the false prophet of the Turks' Mohammed sings during the prologue. The foreword justifies the temporal proximity to the historical core of the plot. It claims it is entirely 'respectable' to perform a story in which 'many [of those who participated] are still alive', and refers to Jean Racine: the territorial distance from the original setting (a few hundred miles) would adequately mitigate the problem of temporal proximity. Naturally, in this opera there is a Hanswurst figure. He is the 'amusing servant' of the Grand Vizier, who sings in low German (*Plattdeutsch*) dialect, a popular method in Hamburg of symbolising low status.

While no musical sources have been preserved from the first decade of Leipzig Baroque opera (1693–1702), at least excerpts of pieces have survived from the beginnings of opera in Hamburg. Unfortunately, entire scores are hardly available from prior to 1700. Extant sources are often in the form of adaptations – mostly strophic arias in reduced versions – edited for use in the home or perhaps changed and modified for the public in printed collections.[47] Therefore, it is difficult to reconstruct and evaluate the musical structure of the first Hamburg operas from the early 1680s by composers Theile, Strungk (director of the Hamburg town band, 1679–1682) and Johann Philipp Förtsch (initially a tenor in Hamburg, and then from 1680 Kapellmeister in the court of the Duke of Gottorf). The printed arias from the operas *Orontes* (Theile, 1678) and *Die liebreiche, durch Tugend und Schönheit erhöhte Esther* (Strungk, 1680) are almost all strophic. They have predominantly songlike, dancelike characteristics and only occasionally contain melismas, coloratura, word repetition, or concertante passages.

A better evaluation is offered by the surviving material for the operas of Franck, the fourth and perhaps most important composer of the first decade at the Gänsemarkt Opera. Born in middle Franconia, Franck studied in Italy from 1668 to 1672, thereafter becoming 'Director of comedy' at the court of the Margrave of Ansbach, until he was forced to flee to Hamburg after committing a murder. Here, he created about fifteen operas through 1686 for the Gänsemarkt, and others for Ansbach.[48] His works were performed in Hamburg far into the 1690s, and several of his arias appeared in print. The score for his opera *Die drey Töchter Cecrops* has survived in Ansbach (premièred in Ansbach, evidently in spring 1686, followed by a shortened version in Hamburg).

In his score to *Cecrops*, Franck provides da capo arias as they were being developed in Italy just then by Legrenzi and Sartorio. In general, Franck's music shows that he had internalised the means and techniques of Venetian opera and musical drama during his stay in Italy and had incorporated them into his personal style; elements of French opera hardly appear in his music. Franck's recitative is fluid and interspersed with cantabile elements, and is reminiscent of Cavalli. His arias have contrasting middle sections. The use of tonality is also based on contrast – a well-planned harmonic structure is evident in *Cecrops*; the spectrum of Franck's arias ranges from B major to B-flat minor. During a break in performances in 1686/7 he left Hamburg; he is known to have been in London from 1790 and is said to have been murdered in Spain in 1710, allegedly because of his favour with the king.

Up until the arrival of Keiser, who in a sense opened the door to the eighteenth century in 1697 with *Adonis*, the 1690s were characterised by two artistic figures: Kusser and Johann Georg Conradi (d. 1699). Their works, along with Franck's, dominated the repertoire. In addition, the alto Jakob Kremberg (c. 1650–1715), who had come temporarily from Dresden as the commercial director appointed by Schott, also influenced the house's fortune at times; five years had been planned, but this episode ended after a year of fierce quarrels between Kusser, Kremberg, and Schott – and Schott returned to the helm.

Born in Preßburg and initially active at the courts of Baden-Baden and Ansbach, Kusser studied with Lully in Paris in the 1670s–1680s, where he internalised French styles of composition and playing. In 1690, he was given leadership of the newly founded Wolfenbüttel Opera. Here and in the public opera house in Braunschweig (which was financed by the duke), he wrote several works that raised his profile as he sparred with Italian music. Disputes with his librettist Friedrich Christian Bressand seem to have been the catalyst for his eventual move to Hamburg. Starting in 1694, his operas received great acclaim on the Gänsemarkt stage, though they were also associated with some internal disputes. Conradi, born in Oettingen in Bavaria, was Kapellmeister in Ansbach for a few years and can be documented as having held the same position at the Gänsemarkt Opera from 1690 to 1694. Kusser ascribed to him a 'hot temper'; at the same time, he is said to have been a superb orchestra leader and, according to Mattheson, introduced the modern Italian manner of singing in Hamburg. However, he left Hamburg soon, moving through the country with a travelling opera troupe. He was at the Stuttgart Court from 1698; in London in 1704; and, from 1707 until his death in 1727, 'Chappel-Master of Trinity College' in Dublin.[49] Several arias have survived from his Hamburg operas, including authorised prints with excerpts from *Erindo* (1694) and *Ariadne* (Braunschweig, 1692), as well as the recently discovered original performance materials for his Stuttgart opera *Adonis* (1700?).[50] Conradi's score to *Die schöne und getreue Ariadne* (1691) has been preserved.

Both works show that opera in Hamburg in the 1690s, and probably for the first time, offered a musically notable synthesis of French and Italian styles, and with forms that were rich in variation. Conradi's *Ariadne* contains charming arias modelled on French styles, which are not at all mere direct copies: for example, Ariadne's fantastic aria 'Auf, auf, erbostes Glücke' in the form of a large chaconne at the beginning of the second act, which consists of 201 measures supported by a 20-bar ground bass pattern. Conradi takes a similar approach in a large-scale ensemble near the end of the opera: a passacaille based on the familiar Italian bass line, in which the seven following arias seen in the printed text (for Venus, two Graces, and Bacchus) are linked together into a 313-bar through-composed structure, interspersed with ritornelli that include dancing. Conradi may have learned the idea from comparable models in contemporary French opera; however, one must look through many choruses and ballets from the Paris Court in order to find a comparable structure (also artfully shaped by librettist Postel), in which the boundaries between aria, chorus, and ballet blur to such an extent. Conradi's *Ariadne* must have become a box-office hit in its day; it was performed as late as the 1720s in a shortened version by Keiser, now enriched with a few Italian arias. In retrospect, Mattheson claimed that *Ariadne* had 'paid off very well, and received much applause'.[51] Also, Conradi's score must have been an important model for him: the great ciacona at the end of Mattheson's *Boris Goudenow* (Hamburg 1710) proves itself to be, in many respects, an imitation of Conradi's abovementioned passacaglia.

Italian and French aria types also appear on equal footing in Kusser's operas, and he arranged these in unusually colourful fashion. *Erindo* includes arias with obbligato parts for recorder, oboe, flute, 'tromba overo hautbois', long-necked lute ('colachono'), and violin, as well as pairs of oboes, bassoons, and flutes – this sort of variety was to be found in contemporary Italian opera. Arias without melody instruments often follow French dance types: bourrée, bransle de village, galliard, gavotte, menuet, and passepied. There are also arias patterned on Italian models, such as those with virtuoso basso continuo.

This plurality of styles is also a characteristic of the only surviving opera score from middle-German lands in the 1690s: Christian Ludwig Boxberg's *Sardanapalus*. To be sure, the piece came into being in 1698 on the occasion of a guest visit to the Ansbach Court, but its roots lie within the orbit of opera in Leipzig. Boxberg (1670–1729) had been a pupil, overlapping with Keiser, at the Thomasschule under Kantor Johann Schelle, and when the Leipzig Opera House opened, he sang in the performance of Strungk's *Alceste*. Boxberg learned the trade of the opera composer and librettist as a 'pupil of the famous Kapellmeister Strungk', for whom he provided a few libretti in subsequent years.[52] He first became noticed as a composer in Leipzig around 1700, before becoming the organist in Görlitz, a post he would hold for the rest of his life. It is very possible that his surviving score in Ansbach gives an idea of how the lost works by his teacher Strungk might have looked. The piece is written in three acts; after the French overture, continuo arias (often da capo) with string ritornelli predominate; arias with obbligato instruments are rather the exception. Contemporary Italian aria types provided models, which Boxberg adapted perfectly, just as he did the French dance types: for example, in the glittering ostinato aria 'Keine Qual soll mich erschrecken' (Act I scene 5), in which Belochus unfurls an extensive virtuoso da capo aria atop a rhythmically striking bass. His free-flowing singing could undoubtedly measure up to works by Giuseppe Torelli and Francesco Antonio Pistocchi, whom the young, artistically inclined Margrave Georg Friedrich of Ansbach had enticed, along with other Italian virtuosi, to his court by offering terrific salaries.[53]

What the few surviving scores and arias from Hamburg and Leipzig (respectively Ansbach) from the 1690s show is that, already before Keiser, Handel, and Telemann brought their music to the stage around the turn of the century, a remarkable synthesis of different European national styles had developed in German-language opera. In addition to features of German tradition, there are unmistakable echoes, imitations, and fusions of elements of French and Italian opera. It is quite possible that the genre of opera was one of the decisive gateways for the way German composers reacted to leading European national styles. At any rate, extant scores already paradigmatically reveal what Johann Joachim Quantz would, one generation later, call 'mixed taste', which he described as being characteristic of the German style.

Translated from the German by Kirsten Santos-Rutschman

Notes

1 Werner Braun, *Die Musik des 17. Jahrhunderts* (Laaber: Laaber-Verlag, 1981) 91.

2 See supporting documents in the following publications: Johann Christoph Gottsched, *Nöthiger Vorrath zur Geschichte der deutschen Dramatischen Dichtkunst…* 2 vols. (Leipzig: Teubner, 1757–1765; rpt. Hildesheim, New York: Olms, 1970); Renate Brockpähler, *Handbuch zur Geschichte der Barockoper in Deutschland* (Emsdetten: Lechte [1964]); Reinhart Meyer, *Bibliographia dramatica et dramaticorum: kommentierte Bibliographie der im ehemaligen Reichsgebiet gedruckten und gespielten Dramen des 18. Jahrhunderts nebst deren Bearbeitungen und Übersetzungen und ihrer Rezeption bis in die Gegenwart. Abteilung 2. Einzeltitel*, 4 vols. (Tübingen: Niemeyer, Berlin: De Gruyter, 1993–1994), vol. 1.

3 Werner Braun, *Vom Remter zum Gänsemarkt: aus der Frühgeschichte der alten Hamburger Oper (1677–1697)* (Saarbrücken: Saarbrücker Druckerei und Verlag, 1987), 94.

4 Ibid., 93–4.

5 See Warren Kirkendale, 'Zur Biographie des ersten Orfeo, Francesco Rasi', in Ludwig Finscher (ed.), *Claudio Monteverdi. Festschrift Reinhold Hammerstein zum 70. Geburtstag* (Laaber: Laaber-Verlag, 1986), 297–335, especially 312.

6 See the corresponding summaries in Brockpähler, *Handbuch*.

7 Wolfram Steude, 'Heinrich Schütz und die erste deutsche Oper', in Frank Heidelberger, Wolfgang Osthoff, and Reinhard Wiesend (eds.), *Von Isaac bis Bach. Studien zur älteren deutschen Musikgeschichte. Festschrift Martin Just zum 60. Geburtstag* (Kassel: Bärenreiter, 1991), 169–79. For further discussion, see Irmgard Scheitler, 'Martin Opitz und Heinrich Schütz: Dafne – ein Schauspiel', *Archiv für Musikwissenschaft* 68/3 (2011), 205–26.

8 Letter from Heinrich Schütz to the Elector of Saxony's office, Friedrich Lebzelter, dated 6 February 1633, quoted in Erich H. Müller, *Heinrich Schütz. Gesammelte Briefe und Schriften* (Regensburg: G. Bosse, 1931), 125ff.

9 See Silke Leopold, *Geschichte der Oper*, vol. 1: *Die Oper im 17. Jahrhundert* (Laaber: Laaber-Verlag, 2006), 276.

10 For more on *Seelewig* see Rolf Hasselbrink, 'Harsdörfer, Georg Philipp', in *MGG1*, vol. 5 (1956), col. 1737, and, with additional references, Andreas Waczkat, 'Simon Dachs Liederspiele und die Anfänge der deutschen Oper', in Axel E. Walter (ed.), *Simon Dach (1605-1659). Werk und Nachwirken* (Tübingen: Max Niemeyer Verlag, 2008), 321–36, especially 322ff.; see also

Irmgard Scheitler, 'Harsdörffer und die Musik', in Stefan Keppler-Tasaki and Ursula Kocher (eds.), *Georg Philipp Harsdörffers Universalität* (Berlin: De Gruyter, 2011), 213–36, especially 228, and Judith P. Aikin, 'Narcissus and Echo: A Mythological Subtext in Harsdörffer's Operatic Allegory *Seelewig* (1644)', *ML* 72/3 (1991), 359–71.

11 See Leopold, *Die Oper im 17. Jahrhundert*, 278–88.

12 Johann Sebastiani, *Pastorello musicale oder Verliebtes Schäferspiel*, ed. Michael Maul (Beeskow: Ortus Musikverlag, 2005). For more on the piece, see the introduction to Maul's volume, as well as Werner Braun, '"Preußisches" im Pastorello musicale von 1663', in Günther Walter (ed.), *Jahrbuch des Staatlichen Instituts für Musikforschung Preußischer Kulturbesitz. 2005* (Mainz: Schott Music, 2009), 115–23.

13 For biographical information on Sebastiani, see Michael Maul, 'Sebastiani, Johann', in *MGG2*, Personenteil, vol. 15 (2006), col. 492–4.

14 Synopsis in printed text for Act I scene 2.

15 See, for example, the aria 'Quel bel fior di giovanezza' from *Gli Amori d'Apollo e di Dafne* (1640, rpt. in Braun, *Die Musik des 17. Jahrhunderts*, 99ff).

16 Georg Christoph Pisanski, *Entwurf der preußischen Literärgeschichte*, vol. 2: *Mittlere Geschichte von der Ausbreitung gelehrter Kenntnisse in Preussen bis zum Anfange des 18. Jahrhunderts*, ed. Adolf Meckelburg (Königsberg: Hartung, 1853), 266.

17 See Meder, Franck, and Löhner's characterisation of recitative in Werner Braun, 'Johann Valentin Meders Opernexperiment in Reval 1680', in Uwe Haensel (ed.), *Beiträge zur Musikgeschichte Nordeuropas. Kurt Gudewill zum 65. Geburtstag* (Wolfenbüttel, Zürich: Mösele, 1978), 69–78, especially 75ff.

18 Johann Mattheson, *Der Vollkommene Capellmeister* (Hamburg: Christian Herold, 1739; rpt. Kassel: Bärenreiter, 1954), 78.

19 On the Dresden Hofkapelle and its opera performances, see Moritz Fürstenau, *Zur Geschichte der Musik und des Theaters am Hofe zu Dresden*, 2 vols. (Dresden: Kuntze, 1861–1862; rpt. Leipzig: Edition Peters, 1971), vol. 1: *Zur Geschichte der Musik und des Theaters am Hofe der Kurfürsten von Sachsen, Johann Georg II., Johann Georg III. und Johann Georg IV.*; Brockpähler, *Handbuch*, 130–7, and the article 'Dresden' by Wolfram Steude in *MGG2*, Sachteil, vol. 2 (1995), col. 1531–1534; see also Helen Watanabe-O'Kelly, *Court Culture in Dresden: From Renaissance to Baroque* (Houndmills, Basingstoke, and New York: Palgrave Macmillan, 2002), 34–6 and 189–92.

20 Leopold, *Die Oper im 17. Jahrhundert*, 296.

21 On the opera, see the summary in ibid., 294–8.

22 Johann Mattheson, *Grundlage einer Ehren-Pforte* (Hamburg: in Verlegung des Verfassers, 1740); rpt. Berlin: im Kommissionsverlag von Leo Liebmannssohn, 1910), 18.

23 See Erdmann Werner Böhme, *Die frühdeutsche Oper in Thüringen* (Stadtroda: Richter, 1931).

24 A good summary of opera activity in Halle is available in Brockpähler, *Handbuch*, 188–92. See also Walter Serauky, *Musikgeschichte der Stadt Halle*, 2 vols. (Halle: 1939; Hildesheim and New York: Olms, 1971), vol. 2, 1. Halbband: *Von Samuel Scheidt bis in die Zeit Georg Friedrich Händels und Johann Sebastian Bachs.*

25 David Elias Heidenreich, *Geistliche Oden auf die fürnehmsten Feste und alle Sonntage des gantzen Jahres* (*Halle* in Sachsen: Christoph Salfeld, 1665).

26 See Brockpähler, *Handbuch*, 170–7.

27 See ibid., 369–79, and Torsten Fuchs, *Studien zur Musikpflege in der Stadt Weißenfels und am Hofe der Herzöge von Sachsen-Weißenfels* (Lucca: Libreria Musicale Italiana, 1997).

28 Quotation from the preface to his collection, initially printed anonymously: *Geistliche Cantaten Uber alle Sonn-Fest- und Apostel-Tage, Zu einer, denen Herren Musicis sehr bequemen Kirchen-Music in ungezwungenen Teutschen Versen ausgefertiget. Anno 1702* (s.l. [Weißenfels?]: s.n., 1702). On this first cycle of cantatas by Neumeister see Ute Poetzsch-Seban, *Die Kirchenmusik von Georg Philipp Telemann und Erdmann Neumeister. Zur Geschichte der protestantischen Kirchenkantate in der ersten Hälfte des 18. Jahrhunderts* (Beeskow: Ortus Musikverlag, 2006).

29 On the opera performances, see Brockpähler, *Handbuch*, 138–46, 212–23 und 274–82. On Steffani, see Leopold, *Die Oper im 17. Jahrhundert*, 301–11, and the essays in Claudia Kaufold, Nicole K. Strohmann, and Colin Timms (eds.), *Agostino Steffani: europäischer Komponist, hannoverscher Diplomat und Bischof der Leibniz-Zeit / Hanoverian Diplomat and Bishop in the Age of Leibniz* (Göttingen: V&R Unipress, 2017).

30 Leopold, *Die Oper im 17. Jahrhundert*, 301ff.

31 Quoted in Axel Fischer's article 'Hannover' in *MGG2*, Sachteil, vol. 4 (1996), col. 28.

32 On Steffani's works for Hanover, see Candace Marles, 'Opera in Hannover: The German Synthesis of National Styles', in Corinna Herr, Herbert Seifert, Andreas Sommer-Mathis, and Reinhard Strohm (eds.), *Italian Opera in Central Europe 1614–1780*, 3 vols. (Berlin: Berliner Wissenschafts-Verlag, 2006–2008), vol. 2: *Italianità: Image and Practice*, 141–62.

33 See Leopold, *Die Oper im 17. Jahrhundert*, 303–5 (with musical examples).

34 Overview in Brockpähler, *Handbuch*, 88–9. For an extensive early history of opera in Wolfenbüttel/Braunschweig, see Gustav Friedrich Schmidt, *Neue Beiträge zur Geschichte der Musik und des Theaters am Herzoglichen Hofe zu Braunschweig-Wolfenbüttel. Ergänzungen und Berichtigungen zu Chrysanders Abhandlung ... Erste Folge. Chronologisches Verzeichnis der in Wolfenbüttel, Braunschweig, Salzthal, Bevern und Blankenburg aufgeführten Opern, Ballette und Schauspiele (Komödien) mit Musik bis zur Mitte des 18. Jahrhunderts* (Munich: Wilhelm Berntheisel, 1929), and Schmidt, *Die frühdeutsche Oper*

und die musikdramatische Kunst Georg Caspar Schürmanns, 2 vols. (Regensburg: Verlag Gustav Bosse, 1933–1934).

35 Quoted in Braun, *Vom Remter zum Gänsemarkt*, 17.

36 Johann Mattheson, *Der musicalische Patriot* (Hamburg: s.n., 1728; rpt. Leipzig: Zentralantiquariat der DDR; Kassel: Bärenreiter, 1975), 199.

37 See Joachim R. M. Wendt, *Materialien zur Geschichte der frühen Hamburger Oper*, vol. 1: *Eigentümer und Pächter* (Aurich: Wendt, 2002).

38 Specifications from Hans Joachim Marx, 'Geschichte der Hamburger Barockoper. Ein Forschungsbericht', in Constantin Floros, Hans Joachim Marx, and Peter Petersen (eds.), *Studien zur Barock Oper. Hamburger Jahrbuch für Musikwissenschaft*, vol. 3 (Hamburg: Verlag der Musikalienhandlung, 1978), 7–34.

39 See the surveys of repertoire in Mattheson, *Der musicalische Patriot*, 177–200, and in Hans Joachim Marx and Dorothea Schröder (eds.), *Die Hamburger Gänsemarkt-Oper. Katalog der Textbücher (1678–1748)* (Laaber: Laaber-Verlag, 1995); also Michael Maul, 'Die Gebrüder Uffenbach zu Besuch in der Gänsemarktoper – Bemerkungen zu einem altbekannten Reisebericht', in Hans Joachim Marx and Wolfgang Sandberger (eds.), *Göttinger Händel-Beiträge*, vol. 12 (Göttingen: Vandenhoeck & Ruprecht, 2008), 183–95.

40 For a thorough discussion on dating, performance location, and authorship, see Braun *Vom Remter zum Gänsemarkt*, 15–47.

41 See Marx, 'Geschichte der Hamburger Barockoper', 10–13. On the dispute in central Germany, see Gudrun Busch, 'Die Beer-Vockerodt-Kontroverse im Kontext der frühen mitteldeutschen Oper. Oder: Pietistische Opern-Kritik als Zeitzeichen', in Rainer Lächele (ed.), *Das Echo Halles: kulturelle Wirkungen des Pietismus* (Tübingen: Bibliotheca-Academica Verlag, 2001), 131–70.

42 On the Leipzig opera, see Michael Maul, *Barockoper in Leipzig (1693–1720)*, 2 vols. (Freiburg im Breisgau: Rombach, 2009).

43 Quotation from the travel diary, printed in ibid., vol. 1, 19.

44 Ibid., 786.

45 Norbert Dubowy characterises it as such in his comparison of the Leipzig opera *Agrippina* (1699, libretto by C. L. Boxberg) with its model by Matteo Noris (*Nerone fatto Cesare*, Venice, 1693); see Norbert Dubowy, 'Italienische Opern im mitteldeutschen Theater am Ende des 17. Jahrhunderts: Dresden und Leipzig', in Friedhelm Brusniak (ed.), *Barockes Musiktheater im mitteldeutschen Raum im 17. und 18. Jahrhundert. Arolser Beiträge zur Musikforschung* 2 (Cologne: Studio, 1994), 23–48.

46 See Dorothea Schröder, *Zeitgeschichte auf der Opernbühne: barockes Musiktheater in Hamburg im Dienst von Politik und Diplomatie (1690–1745)* (Göttingen: Vandenhoeck & Ruprecht, 1998), and Schröder, 'Baroque Opera, Politics and Ceremony in Hamburg', in Herr, Seifert, Sommer-Mathis, and Strohm, *Italian Opera in Central Europe*, vol. 1: *Institutions and Ceremonies*, ed. Melania Bucciarelli, Norbert Dubowy, and Reinhard Strohm, 193–202.

47 An overview of surviving sources that is largely still current is Walter Schulze, *Die Quellen der Hamburger Oper (1678–1738). Eine bibliographisch-statistische Studie zur Geschichte der ersten stehenden deutschen Oper* (Hamburg-Oldenburg: G. Stalling, 1938); see also Jürgen Neubacher, 'Drei wieder zugängliche Ariensammelbände als Quellen für das Repertoire der Hamburger Gänsemarkt-Oper', in Hans Joachim Marx (ed.), *Beiträge zur Musikgeschichte Hamburgs vom Mittelalter bis in die Neuzeit. Hamburger Jahrbuch für Musikwissenschaft*, vol. 18 (*Frankfurt am Main: Peter Lang*, 2001), 195–206.

48 For an extensive look at his work, see Braun, *Vom Remter zum Gänsemarkt*, and Johann Wolfgang Franck, *Hamburger Opernarien im szenischen Kontext: (Aeneas, 1680; Vespasian, 1681; Diocletian, 1682; Cara Mustapha, 1686)*, ed. Werner Braun (Saarbrücken: Saarbrücken Druckerei und Verlag, 1988). See also George J. Buelow, 'Hamburg Opera during Buxtehude's Lifetime: The Works of Johann Wolfgang Franck', in Paul Walker (ed.), *Church, Stage, Studio: Music and Its Contexts in Seventeenth-Century Germany* (Ann Arbor: UMI Research Press, 1990), 127–41.

49 On Kusser, see Samantha Owens, 'The Rise and Decline of Opera at the Württemberg Court, 1698–1733' in Herr, Seifert, Sommer-Mathis, and Strohm, *Italian Opera in Central Europe*, vol. 1, 103–7.

50 Johann Sigismund Kusser, *Adonis*, ed. Samantha Owens (Middleton: A-R Editions, 2009).

51 Mattheson, *Der musicalische Patriot*, 180.

52 See Maul, *Barockoper in Leipzig (1693–1720)*, vol. 1, 209.

53 See Brockpähler, *Handbuch*, 30–40, and Günther Schmidt, *Die Musik am Hofe der Markgrafen von Brandenburg-Ansbach* (Kassel: Bärenreiter, 1956).

14 | Opera in Spain and the Spanish Dominions in Italy and the Americas

LOUISE K. STEIN

Opera was produced only rarely in the otherwise vibrant theatrical culture of seventeenth-century Spain and her American dominions, though Italian operas and occasional Spanish ones became a mainstay of public life in the Spanish-held territories in Italy, especially Naples and Milan. At the royal court in Madrid and the principal administrative centres of the overseas colonies (Lima and Mexico), opera was inextricably bound to dynastic politics and constrained by conventions about the gender of onstage singers. Several other kinds of plays with music were produced at theatres both public and private, however, and commercial theatres known as *corrales* were among the busiest sites of musical performance and cultural transmission. Some 10,000 plays were performed in Madrid in the course of the seventeenth century, although only about 2,000 such texts have been preserved. The principal theatrical genre was the *comedia nueva*, a three-act play in poly-metric verse in which the tragic and the comic were mingled to recreate the natural balance of human existence with varying degrees of verisimilitude.

From the last decades of the sixteenth century, the Spanish royal court enjoyed spectacle plays with music; partly sung mythological semi-operas and mythological or pastoral zarzuelas were produced beginning in the 1650s. These hybrid genres called for more singing than did the standard *comedia*, although their incorporation of music was shaped by concerns about the power of musical expression and the ease with which different types of songs could mark the social status, intentions, or nature of the characters onstage.[1] The most definitive of the Spanish musical-theatrical conventions separated divine and mortal discourse, so that in the semi-operas and zarzuelas, the gods and goddesses generally sing in the heavens, speak to each other when they are on earth, and sing especially lyrical airs (*tonos* and *tonadas*) to influence the mortals. The mortal characters, who do not have supernatural power, also lack the power to sing in the same fashion as the gods. They converse in spoken declamation and sing appropriately mortal songs – common *romances*, *bailes*, or musical settings of well-known poems of the day – in verisimilar situations, just as do ordinary characters in the *comedias*. This necessary distance between gods and mortals both mirrored the rigid social hierarchy of the monarchy and conditioned the Spanish approach to musical theatre, including opera.[2]

The First Opera in Spanish

The first opera performed in Spain, *La Selva sin amor* (Filippo Piccinini and Bernardo Monanni [music lost]; poetic text by Félix Lope de Vega Carpio; Madrid, *salón grande* of the Alcázar, 1627), was put together by Florentine diplomats at the Madrid court of Philip IV who were hoping to gain some political advantage for the Medici while securing a lucrative position for the stage architect and artist Cosimo Lotti, who had been sent to Madrid from Florence. Lotti designed a series of remarkable visual effects for a short pastoral eclogue, with a prologue and seven scenes (some 700 lines) contributed by the esteemed dramatist Lope de Vega. Lope appears to have studied Florentine pastoral libretti by Ottavio Rinuccini that circulated in print; his Spanish libretto, *La selva sin amor*, is entirely in the Italian poetic metre suitable for recitative (lines of seven and eleven syllables), except for the short ensemble *coros* in the octosyllabic metre typical of Spanish song-texts. Because none of the Spanish court composers in this early part of Philip IV's reign were familiar with opera, or even the *cantar recitando* of Italian accompanied monody, the Florentine diplomats drafted Filippo Piccinini (d. 1648), the Bolognese lute player who was among the king's favourite chamber musicians, as their composer. Piccinini was reluctant, pointing out his dearth of experience with recitative and begging assistance from a secretary with the Tuscan delegation, an amateur musician named Bernardo Monanni. Indeed, letters to the grand duke's secretary in Florence describe the whole project as 'an embassy undertaking', hardly surprising since Monanni contributed music for the two longest scenes.

La selva sin amor was performed twice behind closed doors for the royal family in December 1627. A few years after its performance, Lope's text was published in an anthology of his work with a prefatory letter describing the performance. The dramatist reported that he felt 'rapture' at hearing his poetry in song, while Lotti's spectacular visual effects and fast changes of scene triumphed over all else. The opera did not arouse any other recorded praise or criticism. This experiment in fully sung opera after the model of the Florentine pastoral operas did not establish opera in Madrid.[3] Further, *La selva sin amor* seems also to have been Madrid's only seventeenth-century production of an opera by a non-Spanish composer.

The Marquis del Carpio and Partly Sung Productions

Spectacle plays with ensemble songs had become a feature of private celebrations for the royal family at royal palaces and during their sojourns at the country estates of high-ranking aristocrats such as the Duke of Lerma in the early seventeenth century. But opera did not grow from or evolve out of these. In contrast, the partly sung mythological plays, zarzuelas, and two fully sung operas produced at the royal court in the mid-seventeenth century were a direct response to the challenges that opera presented in the Spanish system of theatrical production. Partly sung entertainments were organised quite deliberately by a young aristocrat, Gaspar de Haro y Guzmán (1629–1687), known as the Marquis de Heliche (also Liche, Eliche, Licce) and later by his title as Marquis del Carpio (see Figure 14.1). Carpio was the son of Luis Méndez de Haro y Guzmán, Philip IV's *valido* or first minister, who played a decisive role in European politics as principal representative of the Spanish crown in the negotiations toward the Peace of the Pyrénées and the marriage of Louis

Figure 14.1 Gaspar de Haro y Guzmán (1629–1687), Marquis del Carpio. Pencil and ink drawing, unnamed artist, in *Mamotreto o Índice para la memoria y uso de Juan Vélez de León*, ms. c. 1683, E-Mn, MSS/7526, fol. 1r.
By permission of the Biblioteca Nacional de España

XIV to the Infanta María Teresa of Spain. At a relatively young age, Carpio inherited wealth, art, and a large and excellent library. He became the 'foremost private collector' of paintings in Europe in his time, if only for the quantity he possessed, and was a patron of contemporary artists.[4] He was a zealous producer of musical theatre whose creativity and organisational verve were recognised by his contemporaries, though his contributions to the history of opera in Madrid and Spanish Naples have sometimes been overlooked in modern scholarship.[5]

Carpio took charge of the royal court's entertainments at a crucial moment, c. 1650, after the reopening of Madrid's theatres following several years of national mourning for the deaths of Philip IV's first wife, Isabel (Elisabeth of France), in 1644, and his only male heir, Prince Baltasar Carlos, in 1646. Philip was married by proxy to his fourteen-year-old Austrian niece, Mariana, in 1647. Following her arrival in Madrid, Carpio spared no expense, entertaining her and supplying the court with all manner of diversion, from the nautical serenades performed by boatloads of musicians on the lake of the Buen Retiro, to staged performances of comedias, zarzuelas, and semi-operas at the several royal palaces, to the hunting parties on the grounds surrounding the Pardo and Zarzuela palaces that he arranged to invigorate the king. He supervised the renovation of the Coliseo theatre in the Buen Retiro palace and was an especially demanding producer of musical machine plays with daring effects, such as the semi-operas *La fiera, el rayo y la piedra* (1652) and *Fortunas de Andrómeda y Perseo* (1653) with text by the court dramatist Pedro Calderón de la Barca (1600–1681) and music most likely by Juan Hidalgo de Polanco (1614–1685). In the *loa* (prologue) to this work, the character of La Música outlines the most distinctive convention of the partly sung genre when she explains to Pintura (painting) that 'the deities that you introduce must have a different harmony in their voice than that of the mortals; for it is better that the gods do not speak as the mortals do.'[6] Songs for the zarzuelas and other partly sung plays, especially later ones such as *Los celos hacen estrellas* (Juan Vélez de Guevara, 1672), are scattered among an array of loose scores, performing parts, and anthologies, generally without notated instrumental parts beyond a bass line or minimal tablature for harp or guitar.[7] Many of the songs call for improvised embellishment; most are strophic (easier for the actress-singers to learn quickly) but contain both declamatory *coplas* and more lyrical, subjectively expressive *estribillos*. Players of harps and guitars composed, arranged, and directed theatrical music, but seem not to have worked from staff notation. Musicians of all types in the Spanish realms were famous as expert improvisers, but theatrical musicians in particular provided music quickly, with little rehearsal time.

Partly sung genres endured even beyond the lifetimes of those who collaborated during the formative decade of the 1650s, and zarzuelas first organised by Carpio were repeatedly revived after his departure from the court. Many practices established by Calderón and Hidalgo became standard, but a few sources from the final years of the seventeenth century evidence changes in attitude and procedure. Among them, *Destinos vencen finezas* (1699) – a zarzuela on the story of Dido and Aeneas, with poetry by Lorenzo de las Llamosas and music by Hidalgo's pupil, Juan de Navas (c. 1650–1719) – is the first printed score of a Spanish theatrical work and the first music issued by the new Imprenta de Música in Madrid.[8] This beautiful volume is innovative in several ways, most especially because it includes the spoken verse, in addition to what was sung, and instrumental parts beyond the bass. Navas's solo vocal pieces register the durability of Hidalgo's approach to setting the poetry, but notated parts for violins, 'viola de amor', viols, oboes, bassoon, and *clarines* reveal new practices at work. Tradition and modernity are fused in the final chorus of *Destinos vencen finezas*, 'Hagan la salva', an 'ocho con todos los instrumentos', calling for five groups above the basso continuo – two vocal choirs, parts for two *clarín* trumpets, an ensemble of violins, and a group of four oboes. Navas's vocal writing for the two choirs, one slightly higher than the other, is reminiscent of Hidalgo's in *Celos aun del aire matan* (libretto by Calderón; Madrid, Coliseo del Buen Retiro, 6 June 1661). Although it was partly sung, this was a royal 'fiesta' performed by a large cast (twenty roles) for the 6 November birthday of Carlos II in 1698 and organised by a ranking aristocrat, the Marquis de Laconi (Juan Francisco de Castellví y Dexart). It may be that Maria Anna of Neuburg, Carlos II's second wife, to whom the printed score is dedicated, encouraged changes in the court's theatrical music in the last years of the century. The pan-European musical taste of leading court aristocrats returning from their postings abroad was an essential catalyst for change,[9] coinciding with performances by or collaboration with foreign musicians brought to the Madrid court in the last decades of the seventeenth century.[10]

Fully Sung Opera for Royal Celebrations

Opera was reserved for the most significant court celebrations, though partly sung 'fiestas' were usually offered on royal birthdays and onomastic days at the royal court. The extensive rehearsals required for fully sung theatre taxed the system of theatrical production in Madrid, which depended on the rapid preparation of new plays for the public theatres. Singers from the acting companies normally were busy preparing almost daily performances in the *corrales* (singers from the Spanish royal chapel did not perform onstage). Yet Carpio chose to produce fully sung opera to showcase the court's elegance in its commemoration of two political and dynastic events of heightened importance, though musical theatre at the mid-century did not somehow 'evolve' toward fully sung opera, Italianate vocal styles, or Italianate approaches to setting Spanish texts. Well aware that the French were planning to produce an opera by Francesco Cavalli (1602–1676) and were building a new theatre to house it, Carpio commissioned two operas from Calderón and Hidalgo. In 1659–1661, these operas commemorated a long-desired treaty and the most important dynastic alliance of the century – the signing of the Peace of the Pyrénées, and the marriage of the Infanta María Teresa to Louis XIV of France. Note that the Spaniards did not import an opera (as the French did) or invite a foreign composer to Madrid. Hidalgo's score for the first of these operas, *La púrpura de la rosa* (probably 17 January 1660), has not been found, though a few pieces from it appear in other manuscript sources.[11] The surviving music for *La púrpura de la rosa*, composed or compiled in Lima (Peru) by the Spanish composer Tomás de Torrejón y Velasco (1644–1728) in 1701, includes music from Hidalgo's 1659–1660 setting (see 'La púrpura de la rosa in Madrid and Lima').[12] The second Hidalgo opera, the three-act *Celos aun del aire matan*, is the earliest extant Spanish opera for which a complete score is preserved.[13] The two manuscripts for *Celos*, together with the music for *La púrpura de la rosa* from Lima, and the music copied into the special presentation manuscript of *Fortunas de Andrómeda y Perseo,* are the only bound manuscript musical scores for individual theatrical works from the period.

The one-act *La púrpura de la rosa* explored the story of Venus and Adonis to celebrate the treaty between Spain and France (signed on 7 November 1659); some of it may well have been heard during the visit of the Marshal-Duke of Gramont in October 1659 when he visited Madrid to request the hand of María Teresa on behalf of Louis XIV. All of the roles except that of the comic *gracioso* Chato (most likely a tenor) and the figure of Desengaño (a baritone in the Lima manuscript) were sung by young female actress-singers. Hidalgo's three-act *Celos aun del aire matan* was the pendant to *La púrpura de la rosa* and drew a similar cast from two conjoined acting companies. Both operas pour forth with extraordinary lyricism and sound strikingly concordant, though tragic consequences unfold when amorous harmony is disturbed by neglect, jealousy, and vengeance.[14]

Carpio produced these operas before he had visited Italy or experienced opera of any kind in performance, though he learned about the genre from his correspondents in Italy. During the years in which the Roman librettist Giulio Rospigliosi (1600–1669; the future pope Clement IX) served as papal legate in Madrid (1644–1653), the Italian stage architect and engineer Baccio del Bianco (Luigi Baccio del Bianco 1604–1657) reported that Rospigliosi was eager to introduce recitative, but had made little progress because the Spaniards were sceptical about the effectiveness of 'speaking in song'.[15] In 1653 Hidalgo had experimented with a Spanish kind of recitative in *Fortunas de Andrómeda y Perseo*. A few years later, del Bianco, always opinionated concerning the pre-eminence of Italian music, even attempted, unsuccessfully, to teach Hidalgo to compose an Italianate lament for the nymph Canente, the female protagonist in the court pastoral *Pico y Canente* (text by Luis de Ulloa y Pereira) in 1656. Hidalgo found a more tuneful and concordant vehicle for declamation than mid-century Italian recitative, thus effectively inventing Spanish *recitado*. In *Celos aun del aire matan*, Hidalgo did not employ Italianate recitative; instead, together with *recitado*, soaring melodies caress the ear in the flowing musical textures of strophic *tonos* and persuasive declamatory *tonadas*.

Celos aun del aire matan in Madrid and Elsewhere

Celos is not only the first extant Spanish opera, but the most significant musical-theatrical work to survive from the vibrant culture of the Spanish *siglo de oro*. In *Celos*, Calderón and Hidalgo transformed the ancient myth of Cephalus and Procris, such that chastity is dethroned by the power of womanly desire. The date and site of performance for the première of *Celos aun del aire matan* have often been assumed to be December 1660 or January 1661 at the Alcázar palace, but this date may be ruled out due to the fact that three of the actress-singers listed in the opera's printed cast list (*reparto*) were in France entertaining María Teresa at this time (their company did not return to Madrid until April 1661).[16] As for the location, it is unlikely that Carpio would have chosen to present the opera at the Alcázar palace, where the most visually spectacular scenes would have been difficult to stage in the smaller space and with the limitations of the dismountable theatre. The Coliseo at the Buen Retiro, whose design he had supervised, is the site named in the libretto, and it was fully equipped with the necessary *tramoyas* (machines for stage effects). The likely date of the *Celos* première is 6 June 1661, when a 'fiesta grande' with stage machines was performed there after a dedicated period of rehearsals. A letter sent from Madrid by an Italian diplomat confirms that this *fiesta* was *Celos aun del aire matan*, stating 'the day before yesterday the performances began for the *opera in musica* called Procri in the large theatre of the Retiro.'[17] Performances of *Celos* for an enthusiastic public continued until the beginning of the feast of Corpus Christi. The opera was revived in Madrid in 1679, with the involvement of both Hidalgo and Calderón, and again in 1684 and 1697.

Both *La púrpura de la rosa* and *Celos aun del aire matan* received private and public performances in Madrid, and both can claim to have been heard in more diverse locations than most Italian operas of the age. *Celos* travelled beyond Madrid, at least as far as Naples, and probably to Vienna and Mexico, thanks to a web of political and dynastic relationships among Habsburg and Spanish representatives in far-flung diplomatic posts. The score of *Celos* was sent to Vienna, though it may not have been performed there. The Spanish court regularly sent plays and theatrical songs to Habsburg cousins (the presentation manuscript of *Fortunas de Andrómeda y Perseo* is just one example). *Celos* is mentioned several times in letters during the time that the Infanta Margarita was emperor Leopold I's consort.[18] The emperor requested the music of *Celos aun del aire matan* for Margarita probably because she had appreciated its Madrid première. The first Spanish play performed for her in Vienna was not *Celos*, however, but Calderón's play *Amado y aborrecido* instead, probably because the Spanish opera would have required more Spanish-speaking female actress-singers than were available at the imperial court.

Celos aun del aire matan served as an epithalamium for a very reluctant bride when it was performed in Naples in 1682 to honour an aristocratic marriage between the Roman Princess Lavinia Ludovisi and the Neapolitan Duke of Atri, from the Acquaviva d'Aragona family. This dynastic alliance was designed to fortify the Spanish cause and reinforce Spanish territorial claims in Italy. The bride's brother, Prince Giovanni Battista Ludovisi, produced the opera in his apartments within the Castel Nuovo.[19] The large audience that filled his theatre was delighted by the costumes, staging, and overall quality of the production. The opulent staging was rumoured to have cost 'an almost royal sum'. But the opera was 'otherwise not in the best taste because it was done with Spanish music, and, as a consequence, was tedious'. The strophic *tonos* and *tonadas* composed by Hidalgo just over twenty years earlier naturally sounded old-fashioned in Naples in early 1682, especially compared to the music of the opera that had just been presented by the viceroy for the queen mother's birthday in December 1681 – Alessandro Scarlatti's (1660–1725) *Gli equivoce nel sembiante*.

La púrpura de la rosa in Madrid and Lima

The performance history of *La púrpura de la rosa* shows just how closely this opera was associated with dynastic alliances, especially those between Spain and France. Its performances in January 1660 (apparently first at the Zarzuela palace and then at the Buen Retiro) were arranged to honour the Peace of the Pyrénées and the engagement between María Teresa and Louis XIV.[20] It was revived in Madrid to commemorate the announcement of the marriage by proxy between Carlos II and Marie-Louise d'Orléans in performances that began on 25 August 1679, following rehearsals that had commenced before 11 August, 'both mornings and afternoons' in spite of the heat.[21] Carlos II and his bride met near Burgos, on 19 November 1679, but the bride's public entry at Madrid was delayed due to the official mourning after the unexpected death of Prince Juan José de Austria on 17 September. Rehearsals for another revival of *La púrpura de la rosa* began on 6 January 1680, and the opera was performed on 18 January, the birthday of the Habsburg Archduchess Maria Antonia, following the new queen's formal entry on 13 January. These revivals, supervised by Calderón and Hidalgo, included a number of singers and musicians who had participated in the opera's 1660 première.[22] It is significant that this fully sung epithalamium on the overtly erotic mythological story of Venus and Adonis was performed by a nearly all-female cast to welcome the new queen, whereas a number of the spoken plays performed within the court's celebrations treated chivalric and heroic themes. *La púrpura de la rosa* was revived yet again at court in 1690 and 1694, presumably with Hidalgo's music (as was the case with revivals of a number of other plays).

It is remarkable that we know anything at all about opera in the American colonies governed by Spanish viceroys and their ecclesiastical counterparts, because the history of music in colonial Mexico and Latin America has so often focused on the implantation of the music of the Catholic Church, such that the musical 'history' of the colonies has been steered by this evangelising project.[23] Nevertheless Hispanic opera as shaped by Calderón and Hidalgo travelled to the Spanish territories at the behest of aristocrats with the political power and the financial resources to produce it.[24] *La púrpura de la rosa* was the first opera of the Americas, produced in December 1701 in Lima (Peru) for the eighteenth birthday and first year of the reign of the first Bourbon King of Spain, Philip V.[25] Philippe d'Anjou, grandson of Louis XIV, had been proclaimed King of Spain in Madrid on 24 November 1700. The Spanish-French alliance in this case was not a marriage, but the enthroning of a Bourbon king. Official accounts of the coronation and the local celebrations in many cities were published across the geography of the Spanish empire. The news reached Lima on 9 September 1701, and Lima's official commemoration took place on 5 October 1701, more than two months before the opera performances. The viceroy, Melchor Portocarrero y Lasso de la Vega, third Count of Monclova (1636–1705), was reported to have scheduled Lima's official acclamation without waiting for the official instructions to arrive; according to the published *relación*, he recognised the 'general and public joy' that the loyal citizens of Lima felt at such 'happy news'.[26] It was essential that the city project a positive description of its punctual acclamation.[27] *La púrpura de la rosa* was not part of the official acclamation, because the time-worn protocols for such demonstrations of fealty had been invented well before the invention of opera. Theatrical performances in Lima (at the public Coliseo and the viceroy's court) had been suspended during the period of mourning following the death of Carlos II, but the opera rehearsals as well as plans for the reopening of the public Coliseo apparently commenced with the news of Philip V's accession. Because so many female solo singers were called for, actresses from two of Lima's acting companies probably were recruited to perform together in 1701.

The manuscript of *La púrpura de la rosa* is the most extensive single collection of secular vocal music from colonial Peru.[28] Its title page characterises the opera as a 'representación música' and 'fiesta' composed or compiled by ('compuesta por') Tomás de Torrejón y Velasco (bap. 23 December 1644–1728), the Spanish-born chapel-master at Lima cathedral. The anonymous poetry of the opera's 1701 *loa* proclaims "¡Viva, Felipo, viva!", voicing Lima's symbolic reception of the new king in a brilliant chorus. Tunes from the Lima manuscript appear in Spanish sources with attribution to Hidalgo, so it likely contains at least some music from Hidalgo's now lost *La púrpura de la rosa* composed in 1659,[29] though it is unclear just how Hidalgo's opera (or sections of it) reached Peru. Both Torrejón and the Count of Monclova received letters and packages from Madrid, so either may have possessed music from *La púrpura de la rosa* before 1701. Torrejón had lived most of his adult life in Peru after travelling there in 1667 at the age of twenty-two as a gentleman of the chamber in the large retinue of the tenth Count of Lemos when that grandee was appointed nineteenth Viceroy of Peru. Before this journey, he had surely received musical instruction while serving as a page in the house of Lemos and Andrade.[30] He may even have accompanied the grandees as their page when they attended the first production of *La púrpura de la rosa* in Madrid. Given the influence and standing of these patrons, Torrejón's teacher may well have been Hidalgo.[31]

The opera's performances in Lima are described in a printed newsletter offering the first operatic criticism published in the Americas:

The king's eighteen years, like the flowers of youth, are the first ones to be celebrated by the faithful recognition and truly Spanish loyalty of these dominions. On this day of public rejoicing, the City turned out in full-dress, and the nobility adorned the finery on its breasts with diamonds in gallant respect of its sovereign. His Excellency [the viceroy], in whom the generous flame of adoration for his King burns most brightly, attended all the demonstrations of his most dedicated observance; in the morning, with the Royal Audiencia, Courts, and Cabildo, he attended the solemn Mass that was sung in the Cathedral for the health and life of our King . . . . That night, in one of the patios of the palace, *La púrpura de la rosa* was performed, an elegant composition by D. Pedro Calderón, all in music, and performed with excellently skilled voices and rich display in the costumes, stage apparatus, perspective scenery, machines, and flights . . . . His Excellency paid the greatly swollen expenses of this *fiesta*, as well as those of the bullfights, with his usual inexhaustible generosity.[32]

This printed notice conveys the generic quality of an official report, praising the skilful singers, rich costumes, perspective scenery, movable sets, and stage machines – in other words, it conforms to what was typical of such notices about opera elsewhere in this period. The success of the enterprise is attributed largely to the viceroy's financial investment, but the name of the famous (and by 1701 long deceased) royal court dramatist, Calderón, is offered proudly as a guarantor of the opera's pedigree. Musicians were rarely acknowledged when their music was heard in Spanish court productions, and even the names of composers were rarely attached to opera libretti and printed notices in seventeenth-century Italy. But it is still somewhat surprising that Torrejón's name is left off, given his pre-eminence and the circulation of his sacred music (especially his vernacular *villancicos*) in Latin America. If he actually composed the opera, rather than merely compiling the manuscript, the opera would be his only extant secular composition.

In Torrejón's lifetime, a certain tension separated music that was defined as cultivated, correct, clean, and appropriate (contrapuntal polyphony setting religious texts) from a profane music associated with or suspected of low habits, dubious morality, and confusing looseness. This separation between correct music copied onto paper and preserved by the Church and music that was conspicuously not preserved in written form must be acknowledged as having shaped the context into which opera was introduced in Lima. Profane music of whatever species, but especially street music and dances (given their capacity to communicate by gestures, without texts or the mediation of an 'authorised' translation), was excluded early on from what might be termed the record of official culture, most likely because it could slip past and flourish outside ecclesiastical control. Festive public musical activity typically was generated within or around religious spaces in Lima, a city replete with churches and convents. But the central musical practices that infused performance with identity at all social levels were largely unwritten – rhythmic and timbric conventions, stylistic gestures, bass patterns, modes of embellishment, and vocal production all passed along via oral tradition. The tunes and rhythms of secular songs and dances also brought their associated meanings into pieces such as *La púrpura de la rosa* and the many vernacular sacred pieces whose manuscripts now lie collected in ecclesiastical archives.

Barely any comment about musical interpretation and technique has been transmitted to us from colonial Peru, with the exception of a few references in treatises and instruction books written by Spanish musicians and published in Spain.[33] Many performers in the Americas, especially the indispensable players of guitar and harp, did not read mensural or staff notation fluently, though Torrejón surely did. The notation of the Church's contrapuntal polyphony (*canto de órgano*) was the notation of learned musicians. Seventeenth-century theatrical musicians did not need it because they improvised, and, in most cases, harpists, guitarists, and even keyboard players worked from tablature or *cifra* when they used written music at all. Profane songs and *bailes* – the very stuff of Hispanic opera – resided in musicians' memories and bodies, and in the tunes, patterns, and gestures upon which they improvised. Thus, although the project of fully sung opera was without precedent in colonial Lima, it was possible thanks to the ability of Lima's improvising theatrical musicians and actress-singers. The music (whether by Torrejón, Hidalgo, or some admixture of the two) incorporates familiar, conventional gestures and patterns from a common Hispanic practice. The actress-singers learned their roles by rote; the opera's unfolding in reiterative sections of tuneful strophes made it easier to fashion affective shadings and ornamentation expressive of Calderón's elaborately Baroque poetry. Musicians in Lima shared well-known tunes, skills, and practices very similar to those Hidalgo's ensemble had deployed a half-century earlier in Madrid.

La púrpura de la rosa was a royal opera revived in the far distant locations of Madrid and Lima to celebrate dynastic alliances. Given his long service to the Habsburg cause, Monclova's choice of opera in Lima was extraordinary because he had already supported the requisite public acclamation of the Bourbon Philip V. By 1701 he had served in the colonies for twenty-two years, most of them in a Lima he termed 'la contera del mundo' (the furthest edge of the world). His official correspondence concentrates on military and administrative matters, the funds needed to restore the city, and the zealous pursuit of pirates, but private letters express nostalgic longing for the culture of the Madrid court of his youth. He surely remembered the many entertainments that Carpio had orga-nised, and he might have attended the first productions of both the Calderón–Hidalgo operas in 1660–1661. It is extremely likely that he had heard the 1679–1680 revival performances of *La púrpura de la rosa* in Madrid because the nobility were called to court for the celebrations following the marriage of Carlos II and in honour of the new queen. Monclova followed Carpio's example in producing this fully sung opera for a dynastic occasion. Moreover, just as the public entered the Coliseo theatre in the Buen Retiro palace and the theatre installed in the Palazzo Reale in Naples (see 'Italian Opera in Spanish Naples'), so Monclova opened the temporary theatre in his palace courtyard to the populace for *La púrpura de la rosa*.

Italian Opera in Spanish Naples

Naples was the administrative centre of the Spanish territories in Italy and, like Lima, was ruled by successive viceroys whose terms varied in duration. These representatives of a far-away sovereign changed so frequently that 'it was very difficult or even impossible to establish consistent patterns of patronage', as Fabris has noted,[34] and, with few exceptions, the interests and investments of individual viceroys have not yet been studied carefully. Some Spanish operas were performed in Naples before the eighteenth century, but the first thirty years of opera's history in this crowded musical metropolis unfold as the story of how interested patrons, producers, composers, and performers worked to create stable practical, financial, and political conditions for Italian opera. Italian opera is rightly under-stood as an *instrumentum regni* in Naples – though, with so many viceroys and shifting relationships within Neapolitan society, it is often unclear how individual operas or productions served or were exempt from the exigencies of the Spanish imperial program.

The viceroy who first brought opera to Naples, Iñigo Vélez de Guevara, eighth Count of Oñate (1597–1658), arrived from Rome in 1648 and encountered a Naples partly in ruins and with a starving populace after the ten-month Revolt of Masaniello against his tyrannical predecessor. Oñate was genuinely interested in theatre, but his highest priorities were the rebuilding of the city and renovation of the Palazzo Reale. Propagandistic festivities he ordered in summer 1649 culminated in a partly sung but elaborately staged series of tableaux, the *Trionfo di Partenope Liberata, Recitato in Musica nel Palazzo Reale*, ostensibly offered to celebrate the passage through Italy of Mariana de Austria, the young bride of Philip IV.[35] Of course, inviting the nobility to his palace allowed Oñate to shift their focus of interaction, diverting the nobles from their ingrained practice of staging theatricals independently and behind closed doors. Most of the operas in the first series he financed, beginning with *Didone, ovvero L'incendio di Troia* (between September and November 1650), were by Cavalli and performed by a company led by the Venetian theatrical engineer Giovan Battista Balbi (fl. 1636–1657). Oñate invited Balbi and his Febiarmonici to Naples in order to produce operas as elaborately as possible with innovations that might draw the nobility to his palace.[36]

Oñate imported opera to Naples as a complete package performed by a company from elsewhere ('comici forastieri italiani, chiamati Febi armonici, che rappresentano in musica') that stayed on after their first season with his direct financial support.[37] Their December 1652 production of Cavalli's *Veremonda* 'per ordine di Sua Eccellenza' in the Sala Grande of the Palazzo Reale had clear political intent.[38] First planned as a dynastic celebration for the Queen of Spain's birthday, it took on deeper shades of political meaning after the victory of the royal troops at Barcelona, though the victory could not have been foreseen when the opera was composed and rehearsed.

The calendar of opera productions in Naples was variable in the early years, but, after the death of Philip IV in 1665, opera increasingly responded to a closer association with dynastic celebration, the same association that motivated musical plays and operas elsewhere in the Spanish empire. Opera production was funded to honour the Spanish monarchy and encourage its fecundity. But the genre's fortunes were not guaranteed in Naples before the 1680s precisely because opera did not appeal to every Spanish viceroy. Many other kinds of public and private entertainment (the *cabalgata*, fireworks and maritime displays, equestrian games, carnival processions, processions on saints' days, Spanish *comedias*, and the Neapolitan *commedia*) were already institutionalised by protocol, religious observance, taste, or tradition. For example, the Count of Peñaranda (Gaspar de Bracamonte y Guzmán 1595–1676) preferred Spanish plays, so 'comedias 'all'uso di Spagna' were performed frequently during his time as viceroy by a Spanish company he paid to retain at the palace.[39] When the traditional 'gala' ceremony for the nobility was held on Prince Felipe Próspero's birthday at the palace in November 1659 (during Peñaranda's reign), no opera seems to have followed it. Likewise, when the nobility rode in a torch-lit procession with over one hundred riders to celebrate the Peace of the Pyrénées in the first week of December 1659, they were treated afterward to a traditional 'festino a ballo', not an opera. A Venetian opera, *L'Eritrea*, was staged a few weeks later on 26 December at the viceroy's palace for the invited nobility, but its Neapolitan libretto carries a dedication signed by 'Gli Armonici' to Antonio Fonseca, Count and Marquis del Vasto, Captain of the Guards, perhaps implying that it had already been performed at the public theatre with his sponsorship.[40]

Some degree of collaboration between the royal palace, site and symbol of the monarchy, and the public theatre was essential to opera's survival in Naples, but reliable mechanisms of production did not develop immediately. As was characteristic elsewhere in the Spanish dominions, theatrical impresarios were obliged to serve the palace, though they mostly did so with financial and material contributions from the viceroys who sponsored opera on two royal birthdays. The season began with the 6 November birthday of Carlos II (b. 1661, prince and later king); a second opera was designed for the 22 December birthday of Mariana de Austria (queen and later queen mother). The December opera most often continued into January at the public theatre, but in some years it did not even receive its première until early January, despite the 22 December dedication date printed in the libretto. Prior to 1696, the first performance or two of each opera was a protocoled event for the nobility and invited officials at the palace. Sometimes public performances continued at the palace, but most productions instead began at the palace and then were moved to the public Teatro di San Bartolomeo following their premières. During the short Neapolitan carnival, one or two operas were staged, but, before 1696, nearly all of them opened with a protocoled performance at the palace. Premières sponsored by the viceroy were the scaffold each season in an enduring political and financial relationship between Italian opera and representatives of the Spanish monarchy.

Opera in Naples was at once private and public, available to the invited nobility and then to anyone who could pay for a seat at subsequent performances. Prior to 1668, for example, performances were offered to the paying public in the Gioco della Pilotta attached to the palace (also known as the *teatro del Reale Parco* or the *Pallonetto*), a space that may have reminded Spaniards of their *corrales*.[41] Later on, operas produced inside the palace were sometimes public. During the 1680 carnival, for example, the Naples revival of Giovanni Legrenzi's (1626–1690) *Eteocle e Polinice* at the palace drew such crowds that second and third performances were added. The palace was opened to the public in this way because the opera was among the events celebrating a royal marriage, a 'festivity celebrating His Majesty, the King and should thus be enjoyed by all of his subjects'.[42] A similar sentiment had inspired the public revivals of *La púrpura de la rosa* in Madrid and Lima. A few years later, in a shrewd but typically generous move, Carpio allowed Alessandro Scarlatti's *L'Aldimiro* an expanded series of palace performances in November 1683 because the theatre at the palace première had been overflowing. People crowded in, hungry for novelty and with high expectations because *L'Aldimiro* was a new opera and the first of Carpio's first season; it would feature music by Scarlatti with special effects designed by Filippo Schor, and its cast included newly recruited singers.[43]

Beyond the palace, opera as a commercial venture was tested with varying degrees of financial and artistic success. The Santa Casa degli Incurabili (which ran the hospital for the mentally ill) held a monopoly on public commercial theatre, so its permission was required before tickets to any public performance could be offered for sale.[44] The Teatro di San Bartolomeo had been built in 1621 as a venue for spoken plays but reconditioned on Oñate's orders in 1652 with the investment of the Santa Casa. Following the Spanish model, a portion of the proceeds from the rental of theatre boxes supported this charity. Carnival was the most lucrative period in the Venetian operatic schedule, but the carnival in Naples was shorter, so carnival operas at the Teatro di San Bartolomeo had limited runs and thus could be more costly to produce. Drawing singers to Naples was another challenge, given the city's location at some distance from the operatic circuit in Northern Italy (Venice, Modena, Mantua, Bologna, Florence, etc.) where it was easier and less expensive for singers to travel.

The Venetian operas brought to Naples before the reign of the Marquis del Carpio were performed either by previously contracted itinerant companies or by a group of performers dubbed 'Febi Armonici' or just 'Armonici' but collected in Naples under the auspices of a performer or theatre manager. The series of libretto dedications signed by the stage architect and impresario Gennaro delle Chiave might indicate that the 'musici del teatro publico' worked as a stable company under his management. But notices about the performers are scarce, except for those about the infamous singer and prostitute Giulia De Caro, who had managed the company in 1673–1675, thanks to protection from the corrupt and gluttonous Viceroy Astorga and other lovers.[45] Most of the evidence suggests that operas by local composers were performed by local singers. But the frequent mention of 'musici forastieri' recruited by the viceroys or their agents points back to the plan devised by Oñate with Balbi. Little is known about contacts or agreements with agents or performers in Rome, Genoa, and Palermo, for example, probably because musicians, singers, and actors earned little and held such low social status. Naples was full of busy musicians and singers, thanks to its numerous noble palaces and churches, and the training offered in its conservatories, but the rule that singers in the Neapolitan royal chapel (a Spanish royal chapel) were prohibited from performing onstage proved an impediment to the organisation of opera productions for much of the viceregal period. Chapel singers, whether in Madrid or Naples, were not trained to sing onstage and were not encouraged to rub elbows with the likes of those who did, given the anti-theatrical prejudice. Nevertheless, three castrati from the chapel were forced to sing in *La Dori*, the first opera production sponsored by Viceroy Marquis de los Vélez in November 1675, in observance of the king's birthday. 'One or another of the castrati' ('Ogn'altro virtuoso eunuco') joined the cast, alongside singers from the 'teatro mercenario' because the chapel singers reportedly could not shrug off the viceroy's order.[46] Significantly, for carnival 1676, the viceroy instead paid travel expenses and a subsidy to import an opera troupe from Rome.[47] Musicians from the royal chapel performed in *Il Teodosio* for the royal birthday the following November in the Sala dei Viceré at the palace, and, if the diarist Fuidoro's report is accurate, their performance was open to both the nobility and other social strata.[48]

Operas designed originally for Venetian theatres and publics were subject to revision in Naples, but titles alone do not reveal the extent to which libretti and scores were reshaped and recomposed for the theatres, casts, and public in Naples, or how local musicians such as Filippo Coppola

(1628–1680), Francesco Provenzale (1624–1704), and Severo de Luca (fl. 1684–1734); the chapel master Pietro Andrea Ziani (1616–1684); or visiting composers such as Giovanni Buonaventura Viviani (1638–1692) intervened. Provenzale is named as the composer and praised in the preface to the libretto to *Il Theseo* (Naples, 1658, with a dedication to the viceroy García de Haro [y Sotomayor] de Avellaneda, count of Castrillo), which also names him as the composer of '*Ciro, Xerse,* and *Artemisia*', three previous operas that had 'enticed' the Neapolitan audience. It is likely that these titles represent three operas by Cavalli revised by Provenzale for Neapolitan production; much of *Il Ciro* was composed by Provenzale and ready for performance by Balbi's company before the end of Oñate's reign.[49] Even several years after the hurried departure of Balbi's company, Provenzale collaborated with a company constituted in Naples but called Febi Armonici (*L'Artemisia* and *Il Xerse* were staged at the palace in November and December 1657). A later maestro of the Royal Chapel, Ziani, may have revised his own *Le fatiche d'Ercole per Deianira* (Venice, 1662) when it was revived in 1679 to open the Neapolitan carnival. As seventeen years separated the Venetian and Neapolitan productions, and Ziani was already in failing health, it seems likely that Provenzale again contributed new music. The opera was extensively revised, according to Andrea Perrucci (1651–1704), dramaturge of the Teatro di San Bartolomeo, whose note to the reader explains that he had responded to local taste and modernised the Naples libretto, replacing aria texts from Venice with his new ones.[50]

Scarlatti's revisions to Legrenzi'ssss *Il Giustino*, carried out in collaboration with an unnamed poet (probably Perrucci or Giuseppe Domenico De Totis) for its 1684 Neapolitan production, point to a Spanish viceroy behind the scenes. First performed in Venice in 1683, *Il Giustino* was chosen for the king's birthday and start of the opera season in Naples in November 1684.[51] The opera began with a spectacular and lengthy new allegorical *loa* praising the Spanish monarchy, in which Atlas presides over the glorification of monarchy with arias and ensembles sung by four ancient rulers. The huge globe perched on Atlas's shoulders is suddenly shaken by an earthquake and breaks into four pieces representing the four regions of the Spanish empire – Europe, Asia, Africa, and America. While a giant statue of Carlos II is thrust outward, Monarchy (a soprano) sings to praise the king and the Habsburg cause. Every visual and musical element of this prologue had obvious significance in the positive representation of Spain's dominance. The allegory was absolutely typical of the Spanish stage, and Atlas was often associated with Carlos II. More striking is that

Figure 14.2 Atlas in the *loa* to the semi-opera *Fortunas de Andrómeda y Perseo*, ink drawing, Luigi Baccio del Bianco, from Pedro Calderón de la Barca, *Andrómeda y Perseo: fábula representada en el Coliseo del Real Palacio de Buen Retiro a obediencia de la Serenissima Señora Doña Maria Teresa de Austria Infanta de Castilla en festibo parabién que felices años goze la siempre Augusta Magestad de la Reyna Nuestra señora Doña Mariana de Austria*, ms. c. 1653, US-CAh, MS Typ 258, fol. 8.
Image from Houghton Library, Harvard University

all of these allegorical figures had appeared years before in *loas* that Viceroy del Carpio had produced in Madrid – Atlas in the *loa* to the semi-opera *Fortunas de Andrómeda y Perseo* (1653; see Figure 14.2), and the four festive choirs for the four parts of the empire in the *loa* to the zarzuela *El laurel de Apolo* that he produced in early 1658, for example. Beyond this *loa*, *Il Giustino* was given an enhanced staging with machines, effects, and sets designed by the viceroy's hand-picked production team (Schor, Nicolo Vaccaro, and Francesco della Torre). Conforming to both the Spanish and Neapolitan comic traditions, brand-new scenes for two hilarious comic characters were added as well. Overall, Scarlatti tightened up the opera's dramatic rhythm, strengthened the role of the female protagonist, and composed new arias and substitute arias for his cast, while retaining some of Legrenzi's music. *Il Giustino* shows how an opera designed for Venice was revised for Naples to assert a viceroy's personal and political agenda, raise the local standard of production, and delight local audiences. Not surprisingly, its long run of public performances at the Teatro di San Bartolomeo extended until mid-December.

In the final decades of the century, the investment of two viceroys – Carpio and his nephew Luis de la Cerda y Aragón, ninth Duke of Medinaceli (1660–1711) – transformed Naples 'from a way-post on the operatic itinerary into an operatic proving ground with high standards'.[52] Before moving to Naples, both Carpio and Medinaceli had come to appreciate Italian singing and skilled operatic voices in Rome, and both understood how opera might enhance personal elegance while supporting the Spanish cause. Carpio, the same zealous aristocrat who had produced zarzuelas, semi-opera, and the two Hidalgo operas in Madrid, was the first Spanish viceroy to arrive in Naples with prior experience as an opera producer, though the genre of Italian opera had been new to him before his arrival in Italy and visit to Venice during carnival 1677. He was immediately decisive in Naples, folding opera into his plan for the modernisation of public life and changing the mechanisms for opera production there. Intent on showcasing the best performers available for his first season (1683–1684), he borrowed the famous alto castrato Giovanni Francesco Grossi ('Siface', 1653–1697) from the Duke of Modena and financed the recruitment of other singers from Rome and Bologna, some of whom he had heard in Rome. He assigned several opera singers to salaried chapel positions and brought Scarlatti to Naples as the new maestro of the chapel and composer for the operas. Scarlatti, the most fluent aria composer of the age, was born in Palermo and thus already a Spanish subject, so it is unsurprising that Carpio had been among his early patrons in Rome. Three of the new operas by Scarlatti for Naples – *L'Aldimiro* (1683), *La Psiche* (1684), and *Il Fetonte* (1685) – reflected Carpio's personal history and were based on *comedias* by Calderón. Their allegorical *loas* revived favourite stage effects Carpio had featured in his Madrid productions years before. Both Carpio and later Medinaceli renovated or embellished theatres, installed their own productions teams and impresarios, recruited quality singers, and financed operas whose staging was innovative and exciting. It may not be coincidental that their productions occurred just as new urban guidebooks to the city's attractions were issued; perhaps opera became one more reason for opera-loving tourists to visit Naples.

* * *

Two operatic paradigms – one formed in Madrid, the other in Naples – retained their vitality among musicians, audiences, and patrons in the Spanish dominions beyond the close of the Habsburg era. Opera in Spanish and the conventions of the partly sung zarzuela, invented through the collaboration of Calderón and Hidalgo, proved durable in revival, even if sometimes with newly composed music. The second operatic model, Italian opera as energised in Naples by Scarlatti with support from the last Spanish viceroys, brought Naples to operatic prominence. Both of these very different models seem to have travelled to the Americas in the early eighteenth century. The older paradigm, Hispanic opera, not only reached Lima when *La púrpura de la rosa* distinguished the celebration of Philip V's birthday in 1701, but also was heard in New Spain when, apparently, *Celos aun del aire matan* was performed in Mexico to commemorate the same monarch's birthday in 1728. According to a notice in the December 1728 *Gaceta de México*, the news of Philip V's good health was carried over land and sea from Madrid via Havana and Veracruz before reaching Viceroy Juan de Acuña y Bejarano, Marquis de Casafuerte (1658–1734), in Mexico. The official birthday celebration began with the requisite pealing bells throughout the city, a mass of thanksgiving, and a *Te Deum*. Then royal, ecclesiastical, and municipal authorities gathered to attend three nights of protocoled performances of *Celos aun del aire matan* in the 'sumptuous theatre of [the viceroy's] royal palace'.[53]

Nothing is known about this production beyond what is stated in the *Gaceta*. It is possible that *Celos* was performed with Hidalgo's music on this occasion since his *tonos* and *villancicos* circulated in New Spain. Italian opera also reached Mexico, when Silvio Stampiglia's (1664–1725) *La Partenope, drama in musica* was performed there for Philip V's birthday, according to the title page of an undated bilingual *La Partenope* libretto printed in Mexico sometime early in the eighteenth century with the Italian text and a Spanish translation on facing pages.[54] A nineteenth-century bibliophile suggested 1711 as its date and listed an undocumented attribution to Manuel de Zumaya (also Sumaya; c. 1678–1755), a criollo composer and scholar who served as a singer, organist, and later chapel master at the cathedral in Mexico City.[55] If Zumaya composed or compiled the opera's music, no trace of his work has been recovered. Among the versions of Stampiglia's libretto in circulation in the early eighteenth century, the text of the Mexico City libretto is closest to that of *La Partenope* set by Neapolitan composer Luigi Mancia for Naples in 1699, though with small variations.[56] In New Spain during the early decades of the eighteenth century, theatrical singers were surely familiar with fashionable

Neapolitan music, just as were their counterparts in nearly every European musical centre.[57] Italian sonatas and Neapolitan arias were performed, absorbed, emulated, transmitted, and refashioned in the Atlantic world. The mellifluous siren queen Partenope was omnipresent as a symbol of Naples throughout the years of Spanish domination.[58] With uncanny buoyancy, the Neapolitan siren reached the Atlantic world and Mexico through a network of Spanish aristocrats enamoured of opera.

Notes

1 See Louise K. Stein, 'The Musicians of the Spanish Royal Chapel and Court Entertainments, 1590–1648', in Tess Knighton and Bernardo García García (eds.), *The Royal Chapel in the Time of the Habsburgs: Music and Court Ceremony in Early Modern Europe* (London: Boydell and Brewer, Ltd., 2005), 173–94.

2 This brief introduction summarises material first presented in Louise K. Stein, *Songs of Mortals, Dialogues of the Gods: Music and Theatre in Seventeenth-Century Spain* (Oxford: Clarendon Press, 1993).

3 Stein, *Songs of Mortals*, 191–205; Shirley B. Whitaker, 'Florentine Opera Comes to Spain: Lope de Vega's *La selva sin amor*', *Journal of Hispanic Philology*, 9/1 (1984), 43–66; Louise K. Stein, 'Opera and the Spanish Political Agenda', *Acta Musicologica* 63/2 (1991), 125–67; Lope de Vega, *La selva sin amor*, ed. Maria Grazia Profeti (Florence: Alinea Editrice, 1999).

4 Gregorio de Andrés, *El Marqués de Liche, bibliófilo y coleccionista de arte* (Madrid: Artes Gráficas Municipales, 1975) is based on limited Spanish sources and does not consider Carpio's years in Italy; his activity as patron and collector in Italy are summarised in Francis Haskell, *Patrons and Painters. A Study in the Relations between Italian Art and Society in the Age of the Baroque*, rev. edn. (New Haven and London: Yale University Press, 1980), 190–2; the extensive bibliography pertaining to Carpio's activity as a collector is given in a detailed documentary study by Leticia de Frutos Sastre, *El Templo de la Fama. Alegoría del marqués del Carpio* (Madrid: Fundación Caja Madrid, Fundación Arte Hispánico, 2009), to be supplemented by Alessandra Anselmi, 'Gaspar de Haro y Guzmán VII Marchese del Carpio: "Confieso que debo al arte la Magestad con que hoy triumpho"', *Roma moderna e contemporanea* 15/1–3 (2007), 187–253, and Jorge Fernández-Santos Ortiz-Iribas, 'The Politics of Art or the Art of Politics? The Marquis del Carpio in Rome and Naples (1677–1687)', in Piers Baker-Bates and Miles Pattenden (eds.), *The Spanish Presence in Sixteenth-Century Italy, Images of Iberia* (Farnham: Ashgate, 2015), 199–248.

5 On Carpio and music, see Thomas E. Griffin, 'Nuove fonti per la storia della musica a Napoli durante il regno del marchese del Carpio (1683–1687)', *RIM* 16/2 (1981), 207–28; Stein, '"De la *contera* del mundo": las navegaciones de la ópera

entre dos mundos y varias culturas', in Emilio Casares and Álvaro Torrente (eds.), *La ópera en España e Hispanoamérica*, 2 vols. (Madrid: ICCMU, 2001), vol. 1, 79–94; Stein, 'Three Paintings, a Double Lyre, Opera, and Eliche's Venus: Velázquez and Music at the Royal Court in Madrid', in Suzanne Stratton-Pruitt (ed.), *The Cambridge Companion to Diego Velázquez* (Cambridge and New York: Cambridge University Press, 2001), 170–93, 226–35; Stein, 'Opera and the Spanish Family: Private and Public Opera in Naples in the 1680s', in José Luis Colomer (ed.), *España y Nápoles. Coleccionismo y mecenazgo artístico de los virreyes en el siglo XVII* (Madrid: Centro de Estudios Europa Hispánica, 2009), 223–43; Stein, 'A Viceroy behind the Scenes: Opera, Production, Politics, and Financing in 1680s Naples', in Susan McClary (ed.), *Structures of Feeling in Seventeenth-Century Cultural Expression* (Toronto: University of Toronto Press, 2013), 209–49; Stein, '"*Para restaurar el nombre que han perdido estas Comedias*", The Marquis del Carpio, Alessandro Scarlatti, and Opera Revision in Naples,' in José-Luis Colomer, Giuseppe Galasso, and José Vicente Quirante (eds.), *Fiesta y ceremonia en la corte virreinal de Nápoles (siglos XVI y XVII)* (Madrid: Centro de Estudios Europa Hispánica, 2013), 415–46; and Stein '¿Escuchando a Calderón? Arias y Cantantes en *L'Aldimiro* y *La Psiche* de Alessandro Scarlatti', in Fausta Antonucci and Anna Tedesco (eds.), *La Comedia Nueva Spagnola e le scene italiane nel seicento: trame, drammaturgie, contesti a confronto* (Florence: Olschki, 2016), 199–219.

6 On this production and its music, see Stein, *Songs of Mortals*, 144–67.

7 Concerning theatrical songs and their sources, see Ibid., 354–60 and *passim*; Juan Vélez de Guevara, *Los celos hacen estrellas*, ed. J. E. Varey and Norman D. Shergold (London: Tamesis Books, Ltd., 1970); Louise K. Stein, 'El "manuscrito novena": sus textos, su contexto histórico-musical y el músico Joseph Peyró', *RM* 3/1–2 (1980), 197–234; Carmelo Caballero Fernández Rufete, 'Nuevas fuentes musicales del teatro calderoniano', *RM* 16/5 (1993), 2958–76; the facsimile edn. of Pedro Calderón de la Barca, *Andrómeda y Perseo*, ed. Rafael Maestre (Almagro: Instituto de Teatro, 1994); Carmelo Caballero Fernández Rufete, *Arded, corazón, arded. Tonos humanos del Barroco en la Península Ibérica* (Valladolid: Las Edades del Hombre, 1997); Alvaro Torrente and Pablo-L. Rodriguez, 'The "Guerra Manuscript" (c. 1680) and the rise of Solo Song in Spain', *JRMA* 123/2 (1998), 147–89; John Koegel, 'New Sources of Music from Spain and Colonial Mexico at the Sutro Library', *Notes*, Second Series, 55/3 (1999), 583–613; and Louise K. Stein, 'El manuscrito de música teatral de la Congregación de Nuestra Señora de la Novena. Su música, su carácter y su entorno cultural', in Antonio Álvarez Cañibano (ed.), *El manuscrito musical de la Congregación de Nuestra Señora de la Novena* (Madrid: Instituto Nacional de las Artes Escénicas y la Música, 2011), 53–101.

8 See Juan José Carreras, '"Conducir a Madrid a estos moldes": producción, dramaturgia y recepción de la fiesta teatral *Destinos vencen finezas* (1698/99)', *Revista de musicología* 18 (1995), 113–43; on modernity and the co-existence of

musical styles in Madrid's theatrical music, see Stein, 'El "manuscrito novena"', and Stein, 'Un manuscrito de música teatral reaparecido: *Veneno es de amor la envidia*', *RM* 5/2 (1982), 225–33; and Louise K. Stein and José Máximo Leza, 'Opera, Genre, and Context in Spain and Its American Colonies', in Anthony R. DelDonna and Pierpaolo Polzonetti (eds.), *The Cambridge Companion to Eighteenth-Century Opera* (Cambridge: Cambridge University Press, 2009), 244–69.

9 José María Domínguez Rodríguez, '"Comedias armónicas a la usanza de Italia": Alessandro Scarlatti's Music and the Spanish Nobility c. 1700', *EM* 37/2 (2009), 201–15.

10 Louise K. Stein, 'Henry Desmarest and the Spanish Context: Musical Harmony for a World at War', in Jean Duron and Yves Ferraton (eds.), *Henry Desmarest (1661–1741). Exils d'un musicien dans l'Europe du Grand Siècle* (Versailles: Éditions du Centre de Musique Baroque de Versailles; and Liège: Pierre Mardaga, 2005), 75–106; and Miguel Angel Marín-López, 'La recepción de Corelli en Madrid (c. 1680–c. 1810)', in Gregory Barnett, Antonella D'Ovidio, and Stefano La Via (eds.), *Arcangelo Corelli fra mito e realtà storica* (Florence: Olschki, 2007), 573–637.

11 Stein, *Songs of Mortals*, 205–57 ; Stein 'Opera and the Spanish Political Agenda'; Stein, 'Three Paintings, a Double Lyre, Opera, and Eliche's Venus'.

12 See the introductory essay to Tomás de Torrejón y Velasco, Juan Hidalgo and Pedro Calderón de la Barca, *La púrpura de la rosa*, ed. Louise K. Stein (Madrid: ICCMU and SGAE, 1999).

13 This opera has generated considerable bibliography since the 1930s, as noted in the introduction to Juan Hidalgo and Pedro Calderón de la Barca, *Celos aun del aire matan*, ed. Louise K. Stein (Middleton: A-R Editions, 2014), xxii.

14 On the relationship between the two operas and paintings in the Spanish royal collection, see Stein, *Songs of Mortals*, 212–16.

15 Stein, *Songs of Mortals*, 124–5, 133–8.

16 The first edition of the *Celos* libretto appeared in *Parte diez y nueve de comedias nuevas y escogidas de los mejores ingenios de Espana* (Madrid: Pablo de Val a costa de Domingo Palacio y Villegas, 1663); the cast list includes Bernarda Manuela, who played Pocris; María de Anaya, Mejera; and Bernarda Ramírez, Floreta. All three belonged to the theatrical company of Sebastián de Prado, sent by Philip IV to Paris for the entertainment of the infanta married to Louis XIV (the company left Madrid in April of 1660 and returned by April of 1661); see Stein (ed.), *Celos aun del aire matan*, x–xi.

17 Italian documents quoted in María Teresa Chaves Montoya, *El espectáculo teatral en la corte de Felipe IV* (Madrid: Ayuntamiento de Madrid, Área de Gobierno de la Artes, 2004), 287–9; see Stein (ed.), *Celos aun del aire matan*, x–xi, xxii.

18 John E. Varey and Norman D. Shergold, 'Introducción', to Juan Vélez de Guevara, *Los celos hacen estrellas*, cv–cviii; Alfred Francis Pribram and Moriz

Landwehr von Pragenau (eds.), *Privatbriefe Kaiser Leopold I an den Grafen F. E. Pötting: 1662–1673*, Fontes rerum austriacarum. Œsterreichische Geschichts-Quellen, herausgegeben von der historischen Kommission der Akademie der Wissenschaften in Wien. Zweite Abteilung, Diplomataria et acta, vol. 56, 276, 293, 295, 300, 312, 354. Although Leopold's ambassador noted in his diary on Sunday, 5 August 1660, that some of the royal musicians came to entertain him ('algunos músicos de la capilla real vinieron a divertirme con sus voçes y instrumentos'), he seems not to have noted anything about either of Hidalgo's operas; I have consulted Miguel Nieto Nuño (ed.), *Diario del Conde de Pötting, Embajador del Sacro Imperio en Madrid (1664–1674)*, 2 vols. (Madrid, 1990), vol. 1, 401. See also Andrea Sommer-Mathis, 'Calderón y el teatro imperial de Viena', in José Martínez Millán and Rubén González Cuerva (eds.), *La Dinastía de los Austria. Las relaciones entre la Monarquía Católica y el Imperio*, 3 vols. (Madrid: Ediciones Polifemo, 2011), vol. 3, 1965–1989. Andrea Sommer-Mathis, 'Feste am Wiener Hof unter der Regierung von Kaiser Leopold I und seiner ersten Frau Margarita Teresa (1666–1673)', in Fernando Checa Cremades (ed.), *Arte Barroco e ideal clásico: aspectos del arte cortesano en la segunda mitad del siglo XVII* (Madrid: Sociedad Estatal para la Acción Cultural Exterior; Rome: Real Academia de España, 2004), 231–56; and Henry W. Sullivan, *Calderón in the German Lands and the Low Countries: His Reception and Influence, 1654–1980* (Cambridge: Cambridge University Press, 2009), 95–6.

19 Concerning this production, its politics and reception, see Stein, 'Opera and the Spanish Family'.

20 On the first performances of *La púrpura de la rosa* in Madrid, see Stein, *Songs of Mortals*, 205–19.

21 John E. Varey and Norman D. Shergold, *Teatros y comedias en Madrid: 1666–1687. Estudio y documentos* (London: Tamesis Books, 1974), Fuentes para la Historia del Teatro en España 5, 177–9.

22 Stein, *Songs of Mortals*, 206.

23 On written history, catechism, and indoctrination, see especially, Bruce Mannheim, 'A Nation Surrounded', in Elizabeth Boone and Tom Cummins (eds.), *Native Traditions in the Post-conquest World* (Washington: Dumbarton Oaks, 1998), 381–418; Bruce Mannheim, 'Gramática colonial, contexto religioso', in Jean-Jacques Decoster (ed.), *Incas e indios cristianos: élites indígenas e identidades cristianas en los Andes coloniales* (Cusco: Centro de Estudios Regionales Andinos 'Bartolomé de las Casas', 2002), 209–20; Juan Carlos Estenssoro Fuchs, *Música y sociedad coloniales. Lima, 1680–1830* (Lima: Colmillo Blanco, 1989); John H. Elliott, *The Old World and the New 1492–1650* (Cambridge: Cambridge University Press, 1970); and Bruce Mannheim, *The Language of the Inka since the European Invasion* (Austin: University of Texas Press, 1991).

24 Concerning the travels of Hispanic opera and its patrons, see Louise K. Stein, "De la contera del mundo'.

25 See Louise K. Stein, '"*La música de dos orbes*": A Context for the First Opera of the Americas', *Opera Quarterly* 22/3–4 (2006), 433–58.

26 'Reconociendo su Exc, el general alboroso [*sic*] y público regocijo conque ha sido recebida, y celebrada en la Ciudad de Lima, noticia de tanta felicidad, rebozando en los semblantes de la lealtad Española la alegría común por el ingreso a la Monarchía de España del Rey N. S. D. Phelipe Quinto ... ha determinado anticipar el publico festivo obsequio, y fausta aclamación, sin esperar los caxones, donde vendrá el despacho, siguiendo el exemplar de la Coronada Villa de Madrid, que antes de ver a su Rey, y Señor en la Raya de sus Reynos, le juróm, y aclamó' (*Relación de algunas noticias de Europa* ...), quoted in José Antonio Rodríguez-Garrido, 'Teatro y Poder en el Palacio Virreinal de Lima (1672–1707)', (Ph.D. dissertation: Princeton University, 2003), 217; the bound volume containing these news sheets is explained and indexed in Mayellen Bresie, 'News-sheets Printed in Lima between 1700 and 1711 by José de Contreras y Alvarado, Royal Printer. A Descriptive Essay and Annotated List', *Bulletin of the New York Public Library* 78 (1974), 7–68.

27 Stein, '"*La música de dos orbes*"', 436–8.

28 Other sources also copied in the eighteenth century include the manuscript anthology of seventeen songs and anonymous *romances* (some of them versions of well-known songs from the Iberian peninsula) compiled by Gregorio de Zuola (d. 1709), a Spanish Franciscan who had worked in the missions and convents in Peru after 1666, in Cochabamba (Bolivia), Urquillos, and Cuzco; the examples of song and dance compiled by Amédée François Frézier in the reports of his travels, *Relation du voyage de la mer du sud aux côtes du Chily et du Perou, fait pendant les années 1712, 1713 & 1714* (Paris: Chez Jean-Geoffroy Nyon, 1716); and the section devoted to music in the second volume of the so-called Trujillo manuscript compiled by Baltasar Jaime Martínez de Compañón (c. 1785), which includes seventeen songs and three instrumental dances. See Robert Stevenson, *The Music of Perú, Aboriginal and Viceroyal Epochs* (Washington, DC: Pan American Union, 1959), 151–67; the Zuola manuscript as transcribed in Carlos Vega in 'Un códice peruano colonial del siglo XVII', *Revista Musical Chilena* XVI/81–2 (1962), 54–93, as well as in an earlier study by Vega, *La música de un códice colonial del siglo XVII* (Buenos Aires: Impr. de la Universidad, 1931).

29 I advanced this argument in 'Torrejón y Velasco, Hidalgo and Calderón de la Barca, *La púrpura de la rosa*', ed. Stein, and Stein, '"*La música de dos orbes*"'.

30 Lucas Ruiz de Ribayaz, a musician who travelled with Torrejón and the Count of Lemos to Peru, acknowledged that he had received his education while in service to the house of Lemos and Andrade; see his *Luz y norte musical para caminar por las cifras de la Guitarra Española y Arpa, tañer y cantar a compás por canto de órgano* (Madrid: Melchor Alvarez, 1677) [E-Mn, R-4025], fol. 2.

31 This suggestion was first offered by Robert Stevenson, 'Torrejón de Velasco, Tomás', *MGG1*, vol. 13 (1966), col. 570.

32 'Día de felicidad Pública, que comienza a contarse por los años felices de N. Rey, Señor D. Felipe V que prospere el cielo: que siendo 18. como flores de la edad, son los primeros que celebra el fiel reconocimiento, y lealtad Española en estos Reinos. Vistióse de gala la Ciudad, y la Nobleza esmaltó con Diamantes la fineza de los pechos en obsequio galante de su Señor. Su Excelencia, en quien arde más visible la llama generosa de la adoración a su Rey, passó a todas las demonstraciones de su maior culto; asistió la mañana con la Real Audiencia, Tribunales, y Cabildo a la solemne Misa, que se cantó en la Cathedral, por la salud, y vida de N. Rey y Señor, que Dios la continúe por dilatados años feliz. A la noche se celebró en uno de los patios de Palacio la Púrpura de la Rosa, composición elegante de D. Pedro Calderón, toda música, y executada con gran destreza de vozes y riqueza de galas, aparato de perspectivas, bastidores, tramoyas, y vuelos. La Loa fue también de música y representación, en que las Musas, y Deidades Coronaban a N. Invicto Filipo: costeando tan crecidos gastos en esta fiesta, como en la de los toros, la siempre inexhausta galantería de Su Excelencia.' *Diario de las noticias más sobresalientes en esta corte de Lima desde 20 de Octubre hasta 19 de Diciembre de este año de 1701* (Lima: Joseph de Contreras y Alvarado, 1701) [US- NYp, Humanities-Rare Books, KSD 76–235); Bresie, 'News-sheets Printed in Lima between 1700 and 1711', 30, summarises this news sheet as item number 14; see Rodríguez-Garrido, 'Teatro y Poder', 235–6; Stein, *'La música de dos orbes'*, 438, 454.

33 In his tutor for guitar and harp, Ruiz de Ribayaz described the centrality of memorisation and improvisation in the *tierras de ultramar*: 'que no en todas partes concurre lo que en Madrid; y que tiene experiencia el Autor (porque ha visto diferentes Reynos, Provincias remotas, y ultramarinas) que no saben ni practican dichas cifras, ni otras ningunas: porque aunque se tañe, y canta, no es más que de memoria, exceptuando a algunos que saben la Música de Canto de Organo'. Ruiz de Ribayaz, *Luz y norte musical,* fol. 7.

34 Dinko Fabris, *Music in Seventeenth-Century Naples: Francesco Provenzale (1624–1704)* (Aldershot, UK: Ashgate, 2007), 15.

35 Lorenzo Bianconi and Thomas Walker, 'Dalla *Finta pazza* alla *Veremonda*: Storie di Febiarmonici', *RIM* 10 (1975), 379–454: 388–90, describe the event and its sources in detail; see also Domenico Antonio D'Alessandro, 'L'opera in musica a Napoli dal 1650 al 1670', in Roberto Pane (ed.), *Seicento napoletano: Arte, costume, e ambiente* (Milan: Edizioni di comunità, 1984), 409–30.

36 Bianconi and Walker, 'Dalla *Finta pazza* alla *Veremonda*', 382–4; Ana Minguito Palomares, 'La política cultural del VIII conde de Oñate en Nápoles 1648–1653', in José Alcalá-Zamora and Ernest Belenguer (eds.), *Calderón de la Barca y la España del Barroco*, 2 vols. (Madrid: Centro de Estudios Políticos y Constitucionales, 2001), vol. 1, 957–74: 966–9; concerning Balbi and his

company, see Nicola Michelassi, 'Musici di Fortuna. I Mondi Teatrali di Giovan Battista Balbi e "La Finta pazza" tra Venezia e l'Europa 1637–1654' (Ph.D. dissertation, Università degli Studi di Firenze, 2003); and Nicola Michelassi, *La doppia 'Finta pazza': Il viaggio di un dramma veneziano nell'Europa del Seicento*, 2 vols. (Florence: Olschki, forthcoming).

37 Bianconi and Walker, 'Dalla *Finta pazza* alla *Veremonda*', 381–2; Ulissa Prota-Giurleo, *I Teatri di Napoli nel secolo XVII*, ed. Ermanno Bellucci and Giorgio Mancini, 3 vols. (Naples: Il Quartiere Edizioni, 2002), vol. 3, 15–16.

38 Bianconi and Walker, 'Dalla *Finta pazza* alla *Veremonda*'; Wendy Heller, 'Amazons, Astrology, and the House of Aragon: *Veremonda* tra Venezia e Napoli', in Dinko Fabris (ed.), *La circolazione dell'opera veneziana del Seicento* (Naples: Editoriale Scientifiche, 2005), 147–62.

39 Peñaranda supported the company of Adrián López with a monthly subsidy, and the Santa Casa degl'Incurabili allowed the company to keep all but a quarter of the proceeds from the sale of entry tickets for their productions; see Emilio Cotarelo y Mori, *Actores famosos del siglo XVII. Sebastián de Prado y su mujer Bernarda Ramírez* (Madrid: Tipografía de la Revista de archivos, bibliotecas, y museos, 1916), 33–4 and 37. When López was murdered on his way to the palace one evening by Spanish soldiers, Peñaranda was furious; he subsequently paid for the actor's funeral and masses for his soul.

40 The libretto by Giovanni Faustini was first set by Cavalli and performed in 1652 in Venice; Benedetto Croce, *I teatri di Napoli secolo XV–XVIII* (Naples: Luigi Pierro, 1891), 147–8; Lorenzo Bianconi, 'Funktionen des Operntheaters in Neapel bis 1700 und die Rolle Alessandro Scarlattis', in Wolfgang Osthoff and Jutta Ruile-Dronke (eds.), *Colloquium Alessandro Scarlatti Würzburg 1975* (Tutzing: Hans Schneider, 1979), 13–111: 52.

41 The palace interior had been partly ruined during the revolt and was under renovation, so a theatre was set up in this space attached to the palace; it may have seemed similar to a Spanish *corral* (Fabris, *Music in Seventeenth-Century Naples: Francesco Provenzale*, 155). Other rooms housed performances on occasion later on, including the 'Sala grande', the 'Sala del duca d'Alba', and the 'Salone dei Vicerè', but none of these housed a permanent theatre; see Pier Luigi Ciapparelli, 'I luoghi del teatro a Napoli nel seicento: le sale "private"' in Domenico Antonio D'Alessandro and Agostino Ziino (eds.), *La musica a Napoli durante il seicento* (Rome: Edizioni Torre d'Orfeo, 1987), 379–412: 384–92; Bianconi and Walker, 'Dalla *Finta pazza* alla *Veremonda*', 379.

42 '... essendo questo un festino della Maestà del Re N. S., a ragione dev'essere goduto da tutti'. Fuidoro, *Giornali*, I-Nn Ms X.B.19, fols. 96–7, quoted in Ulisse Prota-Giurleo, 'Breve storia del Teatro di Corte e della musica a Napoli nei secoli XVII–XVIII', in Felice De Filippis and Ulisse Prota-Giurleo, *Il teatro di corte del Palazzo Reale di Napoli* (Naples: L'Arte Tipografica, 1952), 17–146: 34, and Prota-Giurleo, *I Teatri di Napoli*, vol. 3, 114, 299.

43 See Stein '¿Escuchando a Calderón? Arias y Cantantes en *L'Aldimiro y La Psiche* de Alessandro Scarlatti'.

44 The *jus repraesentandi* was proclaimed by Philip II (1583) and reinforced by Philip IV; eighteenth-century documents reproducing the language from the original 1583 decree and subsequent decrees, consultations, or renewals are included in 'Appendice IV' of Francesco Cotticelli and Paologiovanni Maione, *Le Istituzioni Musicali a Napoli durante il Viceregno Austriaco (1707–1734)* (Naples: Luciano, 1993), 145–75.

45 Paologiovanni Maione, *Giulia de Caro 'Famosissima Armonica' e Il Bordello Sostenuto del Signor Don Antonio Muscettola* (Naples: Luciano, 1997), and Paologiovanni Maione, 'Giulia de Caro "seu Ciulla" da commediante a cantarina. Osservazioni sulla condizione degli "Armonici" nella seconda metà del Seicento"', *RIM* 32/1 (1997), 61–80.

46 See Paologiovanni Maione, 'Il mondo musicale seicentesco e le sue istituzioni: La Cappella Reale di Napoli 1650–1700', in Fabris (ed.), *La circolazione dell'opera veneziana*, 301–34: 320–3; Prota-Giurleo, *I Teatri di Napoli*, vol. 3, 272; on decorum and Spanish royal chapel musicians, see Stein, 'The Musicians of the Spanish Royal Chapel'.

47 Bianconi 'Funktionen des Operntheaters in Neapel bis 1700', 25; Bianconi and Walker, 'Dalla *Finta pazza* alla *Veremonda*', 387; Prota-Giurleo, *I Teatri di Napoli*, vol. 3, 272.

48 The diarist Innocenzo Fuidoro reported 'la notte in Palazzo li Musici della Cappella Regia rappresentorno *Il Teodosio* in musica, ove concorse Nobiltà infinita Napoletana e Spagnola e anche molta gente Civile del Popolo a goderla', quoted in Prota-Giurleo, *I Teatri di Napoli* vol. 3, 96, 277. The dedication in the libretto to *Il Teodosio* (I-Bu A.V.Tab.I.F.III.Vol.10.5) gives the location of the première in the sala dei viceré; see Bianconi 'Funktionen des Operntheaters in Neapel bis 1700', 25, 67.

49 Fabris, *Music in Seventeenth-Century Naples: Francesco Provenzale*, 154–9.

50 'Il Dottor Andrea Perruccio a chi legge' in *Le fatiche d'Ercolo per Deianira melodrama d'Aurelio Aureli. Riformato per il Teatro di S. Bartolomeo di Napoli dal Dottor Andrea Perruccio* (Naples: Carlo Porsile, 1679), fol. 3–3v, (I-Mb Racc. Dramm. Corniani Algarotti 314); Bianconi, 'Funktionen des Operntheaters in Neapel bis 1700', 69.

51 On the Legrenzi *Il Giustino* (libretto by Nicolò Beregan; February 1683, Teatro San Salvatore, Venice), see Rudolf Bossard, *Il Giustino; eine monographische Studie* (Baden-Baden: Koerner, 1988); Rudolf Bossard, 'I viaggi del Giustino', in Francesco Passadore and Franco Rossi (eds.), *Giovanni Legrenzi e la Cappella Ducale di San Marco* (Florence: Olschki, 1994), 495–544; Eleanor Selfridge-Field, *A New Chronology of Venetian Opera and Related Genres, 1660–1760* (Palo Alto: Stanford University Press, 2007), 159–60. On the revisions for Naples 1684 by Scarlatti and Carpio's production team, see Stein, *'Para restaurar el nombre que han perdido estas Comedias'*.

52 Stein, 'A Viceroy behind the Scenes', and Stein, 'How Opera Traveled', in Helen M. Greenwald (ed.), *The Oxford Handbook of Opera* (Oxford and New York: Oxford University Press, 2014), 843–61: 848. The consummate study of Medinaceli's patronage is José María Domínguez Rodríguez, *Roma, Nápoles, Madrid. Mecenazgo musical del Duque de Medinaceli, 1687–1710* (Kassel: Edition Reichenberger, 2013).

53 'La plausible [*sic* for 'apacible'] noticia de la salud del Rey Nro. Sr. y la de su Real familia, que conduxeron los pliegos que traxo a la Vera-Cruz una embarcación desde la Havana para S. Exc. y llegó a aquel Puerto el día 15, se celebró el 19 en esta corte (como assi mismo los años, que el mismo día cumplió S. M.) con general repique, Missa de gracias, y *Te Deum*, a que como es Costumbre, assistió la Real Audiencia, Tribunales, y Ayuntamiento, quienes también concurrieron por sus antiguedades, las tres noches immediatas, a la comedia *Zelos aun del ayre matan*, que a el misma [*sic*] aplauso hizo representar en el Sumptuoso Teatro de el Real Palacio el Excmo. Sr. Virrey.' *Gaceta de México desde primero, hasta fin de Diciembre de 1728* (México: Joseph Bernardo de Hogal, 1728), num. 13, 100–1, in *Gacetas de México*, ed. Francisco González de Cossio, 3vols. (Mexico: Secretaria de Educación Pública, 1949), vol. 1, 143–4.

54 *La Partenope Fiesta, que se hizo en el Real Palacio de México el día de San Phelipe, por los años del Rey nuestro Señor Don Phelipe V (que Dios guarde)* ... Mexico: Por los Herederos de la Viuda de Miguel de Ribera, (n.d.) (Mex-Mn / M8621 / PAR.f.). The title-page states in contradictory fashion that the opera was performed '*el día de San Felipe por los años del Rey nuestro Señor*' ('the day of Saint Philip for the birthday of the King our Lord'), but Saint Philip was celebrated at the beginning of May in this period (May 1), and Philip V's birthday was December 19. An exemplar is also held by the John Carter Brown Library at Brown University.

55 The date 1711 and attribution to Zumaya are by no means secure; they were assigned by a nineteenth-century bibliophile, José Mariano Beristáin de Souza, in his vast *Biblioteca Hispano-Americana septentrional* (1821), vol. 3 (Amecameca: Tipografía del Colegio Católico, 1883), 325, and reiterated by José Toribio Medina, *La imprenta en México 1539–1821* (Santiago, Chile, 1907–1912), vol. 3, 446, and all subsequent writers. In his entry for Zumaya, Beristáin de Souza also listed a now-lost *El Rodrigo*, 'Drama que se representó en el palacio real de México para celebrar el nacimiento del príncipe Luis Fernando', whose date he fixed as 1708. He identifies 'Ribera' as the printer of both items, though the extant *Partenope* was printed by 'Herederos de la Viuda de Miguel de Ribera'; this publisher operated 1714–1732, according to Ken Ward, Curator of Latin American Books, the John Carter Brown Library at Brown University, whose expertise I gratefully acknowledge.

56 On the European circulation of this libretto, see Robert Freeman, 'The Travels of *Partenope*', in Harold Powers (ed.), *Studies in Music History, Essays for*

Oliver Strunk (Princeton: Princeton University Press, 1968), 356–85; for the libretto's political context, see José María Domínguez Rodríguez, 'Cinco óperas para el príncipe. El ciclo de Stampiglia para el teatro de San Bartolomeo de Nápoles (1696–1702)', *Il Saggiatore Musicale* 19 (2012), 5–40.

57 Javier Marín López has noted, for example, that many of Zumaya's villancicos 'muestran su familiaridad con las innovaciones estilísticas italianas, de las que el compositor era plenamente consciente'; see 'Una deconocida colección de villancicos sacros novohispanos (1689–1812); El Fondo Estrada de la Catedral de México', in María Gembero Ustárroz and Emilio Ros-Fábregas (eds.), *La música y el Atlántico. Relaciones musicales entre España y Latinoamérica* (Granada: Universidad de Granada, 2007), 311–57 (325).

58 On this point, see Dinko Fabris, *Partenope da sirena a regina: il mito musicale di Napoli* (Naples: Cafagna Editore, 2016).

Further Reading

Adams, Martin. *Henry Purcell: The Origins and Development of His Musical Style.* Cambridge: Cambridge University Press, 1995.

Ahrendt, Rebekah. 'A Huguenot Impresario in the Dutch Republic'. In Michel Schuijer and Jed Wentz (eds.), *European Drama and Performance Studies: Dance and the Dutch Republic.* Paris: Classiques Garnier, 2015, 17–36.

Aikin, Judith P. 'Narcissus and Echo: A Mythological Subtext in Harsdörffer's Operatic Allegory *Seelewig* (1644)'. *ML* 72/3 (1991), 359–71.

Alm, Irene. 'Humanism and Theatrical Dance in Early Opera'. *Musica Disciplina* 49 (1995), 79–93.

  'Winged Feet and Mute Eloquence: Dance in Seventeenth-Century Venetian Opera', ed. Wendy Heller and Rebecca Harris-Warrick. *COJ* 15/3 (2003), 216–80.

Annibaldi, Claudio. 'Towards a Theory of Musical Patronage in the Renaissance and Baroque: The Perspective from Anthropology and Semiotics'. *Recercare* 10 (1998), 173–82.

Anthony, James R. 'Lully's Airs. French or Italian?'. *MT* 128/1729 (1987), 126–9.
French Baroque Music: From Beaujoyeulx to Rameau. Rev. edn. Portland: Amadeus Press, 1997.

Auld, Louis E. *The Lyric of Pierre Perrin, Founder of the French Opera.* 3 vols. Henryville: Institute of Medieval Music, 1986.

Austern, Linda. *Music in English Children's Drama of the Later Renaissance.* Philadelphia: Gordon and Breach, 1992.

Baker-Bates, Piers, and Miles Pattenden (eds.). *The Spanish Presence in Sixteenth-Century Italy, Images of Iberia.* Farnham: Ashgate, 2015.

Baldwin, Olive, and Thelma Wilson, 'The Subscription Musick of 1703–04'. *MT* 153/1921 (2012), 29–44.

Barthélémy, Maurice. 'L'opéra-comique des origines à la Querelle des Bouffons'. In Philippe Vendrix (ed.), *L'Opéra comique en France au XVIIIe siècle.* Liège: Mardaga, 1992, 9–78.

Bartoli Bacherini, Maria Adelaide. *'Per un regale evento': Spettacoli nuziali e opera in musica alla corte dei Medici.* Florence: Centro Di, 2000.

Bashford, Christina. 'Perrin and Cambert's *Ariane, ou Le Mariage de Bacchus* Re-Examined'. *ML* 72/1 (1991), 1–26.

Becker, Danièle. '"La selva sin amor": Favola pastorale, illustración de las teorías de Doni'. *RM* 10/2 (1987), 517–27.

Bergeron, Katherine. 'The Castrato as History'. *COJ* 8/2 (1996), 167–84.

Berton-Blivet, Nathalie. *Le Petit Opéra (1668–1723). Aux marges de la cantate et de l'opéra.* Ph.D, Université de Tours, 1996.

Besutti, Paola. *La corte musicale di Ferdinando Carlo Gonzaga, ultimo Duca di Mantova: Musici, cantanti e teatro d'opera tra il 1665 e il 1707*. Mantua: Gianluigi Arcari Editore, 1989.

'The "Sala degli Specchi" Uncovered: Monteverdi, the Gonzagas and the Palazzo Ducale, Mantua'. *EM* 27/3 (1999), 451–65.

Bianconi, Lorenzo. 'Funktionen des Operntheaters in Neapel bis 1700 und die Rolle Alessandro Scarlattis'. In Wolfgang Osthoff and Jutta Ruile-Dronke (eds.), *Colloquium Alessandro Scarlatti Würzburg 1975*. Tutzing: Hans Schneider, 1979, 13–111.

Bianconi, Lorenzo, and Giorgio Pestelli (eds.). *Opera Production and Its Resources*, trans. Lydia G. Cochrane. *The History of Italian Opera*. Vol. 4. Chicago and London: The University of Chicago Press, 1998.

Opera on Stage, trans. Kate Singleton. *The History of Italian Opera*. Vol. 5. Chicago and London: The University of Chicago Press, 2002.

Bianconi, Lorenzo, and Thomas Walker. 'Dalla *Finta pazza* alla *Veremonda*: Storie di Febiarmonici'. *RIM* 10 (1975), 379–454.

'Production, Consumption, and Political Function of Seventeenth-Century Opera'. *EMH* 4 (1984), 209–96.

Blumenthal, Arthur R. *Giulio Parigi's Stage Designs: Florence and the Early Baroque Spectacle*. New York and London: Garland Publishing, 1986.

Bjurström, Per. *Giacomo Torelli and Baroque Stage Design*. Stockholm: Almqvist, 1961.

Böhme, Erdmann Werner. *Die frühdeutsche Oper in Thüringen*. Stadtroda: Richter, 1931.

Bosi, Kathryn. 'Leone Tolosa and "Martel d'amore": A "balletto della duchessa" discovered'. *Recercare* 17 (2005), 5–70.

Bossard, Rudolf. *Il Giustino; eine monographische Studie*. Baden-Baden: Koerner, 1988.

'I viaggi del Giustino'. In Francesco Passadore and Franco Rossi (eds.), *Giovanni Legrenzi e la Cappella Ducale di San Marco*. Florence: Olschki, 1994, 495–544.

Boswell, Eleanore. *The Restoration Court Stage (1660–1702)*. Cambridge: Harvard University Press, 1932.

Bouquet-Boyer, Marie-Thérèse (ed.). *Les noces de Pélée et de Thétis, Venise, 1639 – Paris, 1654. Actes du colloque international de Chambéry et de Turin, 3–7 novembre 1999*. Bern, etc.: Peter Lang, 2001.

Braun, Werner. 'Johann Valentin Meders Opernexperiment in Reval 1680'. In Uwe Haensel (ed.), *Beiträge zur Musikgeschichte Nordeuropas. Kurt Gudewill zum 65. Geburtstag*. Wolfenbüttel and Zürich: Mösele, 1978, 69–78.

Vom Remter zum Gänsemarkt: aus der Frühgeschichte der alten Hamburger Oper (1677–1697). Saarbrücken: Saarbrücker Druckerei und Verlag, 1987.

'"Preußisches" im Pastorello musicale von 1663'. In Günther Walter (ed.), *Jahrbuch des Staatlichen Instituts für Musikforschung Preußischer Kulturbesitz. 2005*. Mainz: Schott Music, 2009, 115–23.

Brockpähler, Renate. *Handbuch zur Geschichte der Barockoper in Deutschland.* Emsdetten: Lechte [1964].

Brosius, Amy. '"Il suon, lo sguardo, il canto": Virtuose of the Roman Conversazioni in the Mid-Seventeenth Century'. Ph.D, University of New York, 2009.

Brown, Howard Mayer. 'How Opera Began: An Introduction to Jacopo Peri's *Euridice* (1600)'. In Eric Cochrane (ed.), *The Late Italian Renaissance, 1525–1630*. London: Macmillan, 1970, 401–43.

Buelow, George J. 'Hamburg Opera during Buxtehude's Lifetime: The Works of Johann Wolfgang Franck'. In Paul Walker (ed.), *Church, Stage, Studio: Music and Its Contexts in Seventeenth-Century Germany*. Ann Arbor: UMI Research Press, 1990, 127–41.

Bujić, Bojan. '"*Figura poetica molto vaga*": Structure and Meaning in Rinuccini's *Euridice*'. *EMH* 10 (1991), 29–62.

Burden, Michael. 'Casting Issues in the Original Production of Purcell's Opera "The Fairy-Queen"'. *ML* 84/4 (2003), 596–607.

(ed.). 'The Independent Masque 1700–1800: A Catalogue'. *Royal Musical Association Research Chronicle* 28/1 (1995), 59–159.

Performing the Music of Henry Purcell. Oxford: Clarendon Press, 1996.

Henry Purcell's Operas: The Complete Texts. Oxford: Oxford University Press, 2000.

Burgess, Geoffrey V. *Ritual in the Tragédie en musique from Lully's Cadmus et Hermione (1673) to Rameau's Zoroastre (1749)*. Ph.D, Cornell University, 1998.

Burney, Charles. *A General History of Music: From the Earliest Ages to the Present Period*, ed. Frank Mercer. 2 vols. London: G. T. Foulis, 1935.

Busch, Gudrun. 'Die Beer-Vockerodt-Kontroverse im Kontext der frühen mitteldeutschen Oper. Oder: Pietistische Opern-Kritik als Zeitzeichen'. In Rainer Lächele (ed.), *Das Echo Halles: kulturelle Wirkungen des Pietismus*. Tübingen: Bibliotheca-Academica Verlag, 2001, 131–70.

Buttrey, John. 'Dating Purcell's *Dido and Aeneas*'. *PRMA* 94 (1967–1968), 51–62.

'New Light on Robert Cambert, and His "Ballet et Musique"'. *EM* 23/2 (1995), 198–220.

Caballero Fernández Rufete, Carmelo. 'Nuevas fuentes musicales del teatro calderoniano'. *RM* 16/5 (1993), 2958–76.

Arded, corazón, arded. Tonos humanos del Barroco en la Península Ibérica. Valladolid: Las Edades del Hombre, 1997.

Caccini, Francesca. *La liberazione di Ruggiero dall'isola d'Alcina*. Florence: Pietro Cecconcelli, 1625; rpt. Florence: Studio per Edizioni Scelte, 1998.

Caccini, Giulio. *Le nuove musiche*. Florence: Giorgio Marescotti, 1601; rpt. Rome: Reale Accademia D'Italia, 1934.

Le nuove musiche, ed. and trans. H. Wiley Hitchcock. Madison: A-R Editions, 1970.

L'Euridice composta in musica in stile rappresentativo da Giulio Caccini detto Romano. Florence: Giorgio Marescotti, 1601; rpt. Bologna: Forni, 1968.

Cahusac, Louis de. *La Danse ancienne et moderne ou Traité historique de la danse*, ed. Nathalie Lecomte, Laura Naudeix, and Jean-Noël Laurenti. Paris: Desjonquères/Centre National Supérieur de la Danse, 2004, 219.

Calcagno, Mauro. *From Madrigal to Opera: Monteverdi's Staging of the Self*. Berkeley and Los Angeles: University of California Press, 2012.

Carter, Tim. '"In Love's harmonious consort"? Penelope and the Interpretation of *Il ritorno d'Ulisse in patria*'. *COJ* 5/1 (1993), 1–16.

'Re-Reading *Poppea*: Some Thoughts on Music and Meaning in Monteverdi's Last Opera'. *JRMA* 122/2 (1997), 173–204.

'Lamenting Ariadne?'. *EM* 27/3 (1999), 395–405.

'Singing Orfeo: On the Performers of Monteverdi's First Opera'. *Recercare* 11 (1999), 75–118.

Music, Patronage and Printing in Late Renaissance Florence. Aldershot and Burlington: Ashgate, 2000.

'*Per cagione di bene, et giustamente vivere*: Some Thoughts on the Musical Patronage of Giovanni de' Bardi'. In Piero Gargiulo, Alessandro Magini, and Stéphane Toussaint (eds.), *Neoplatonismo, musica, letteratura nel Rinascimento: I Bardi di Vernio e l'Accademia della Crusca; atti del Convegno Internazionale di Studi, Firenze-Vernio, 25–26 settembre 1998*. Paris: Société Marsile Ficin, 2000, 137–46.

Monteverdi's Musical Theatre. New Haven and London: Yale University Press, 2002.

'Rediscovering *Il rapimento di Cefalo*'. *JSCM* 9/1 (2003), https://sscm-jscm.org/v9/no1/carter.html.

Orpheus in the Marketplace: Jacopo Peri and the Economy of Late Renaissance Florence. Cambridge: Harvard University Press, 2013.

Understanding Italian Opera. New York: Oxford University Press, 2015.

Carter, Tim, and Zygmunt M. Szweykowski (eds.). *Composing Opera: From 'Dafne' to 'Ulisse errante'*. Cracow: Musica Iagellonica, 1994, 89–95.

Casares, Emilio, and Álvaro Torrente (eds.). *La ópera en España e Hispanoamérica*, 2 vols. Madrid: ICCMU, 2001.

Cavalieri, Emilio de'. *Rappresentatione di Anima, e di Corpo (1600): Emilio de' Cavalieri*, ed. Murray C. Bradshaw. Middleton: American Institute of Musicology, 2007.

Cessac, Catherine. *Elisabeth Jacquet de La Guerre: Une femme compositeur sous le règne de Louis XIV*. Arles: Actes Sud, 1995.

Marc-Antoine Charpentier. 2nd edn. Paris: Fayard, 2004.

'Les jeux à l'honneur de la victoire d'Elisabeth Jacquet de La Guerre: premier opéra-ballet?'. *Revue de Musicologie* 81/2 (1995), 235–47.

'Desmarets et Charpentier: deux musiciens des Jésuites à l'opéra'. In Jean Duron and Yves Ferraton (eds.), *Henry Desmarets (1661–1741). Exils d'un musicien dans l'Europe du Grand siècle*. Sprimont: CMBV-Mardaga, 1999, 279–300.

Chaves Montoya, María Teresa. *El espectáculo teatral en la corte de Felipe IV*. Madrid: Ayuntamiento de Madrid, Área de Gobierno de la Artes, 2004.

Chiarelli, Francesca. 'Before and after: Ottavio Rinuccini's *Mascherate* and Their Relationship to the Operatic Libretto'. *JSCM* 9/1 (2003), http://sscm- jscm.org/v9/no1/chiarelli.html.

Chrissochoidis, Ilias. 'La Musique du Diable (1711): An Obscure Specimen of Fantastic Literature Throws Light on the Elusive Opera Diva Marie-Louise Desmatins (fl. 1682–1708)'. *Society for Eighteenth-Century Music Newsletter* 11 (2007), 7–9.

Ciapparelli, Pier Luigi. 'I luoghi del teatro a Napoli nel seicento: le sale "private"'. In Domenico Antonio D'Alessandro and Agostino Ziino (eds.), *La musica a Napoli durante il seicento*. Rome: Edizioni Torre d'Orfeo, 1987, 379–412.

Clarke, Jan. *The Guénégaud Theatre in Paris (1673–1680)*. 3 vols. Lewiston, Queenston, and Lampeter: Edwin Mellen, 2007.

Clegg, Roger, and Lucie Skeaping. *Singing Simpkin and Other Bawdy Jigs: Musical Comedy on the Shakespearean Stage; Scripts, Music and Context*. Exeter: University of Exeter Press, 2014.

Coeyman, Barbara. 'Sites of Indoor Musical-Theatrical Production at Versailles'. *Eighteenth-Century Life* 17 (1993), 59–64.

Cohen, Sarah R. *Art, Dance, and the Body in French Culture of the Ancien Régime*. New York and Cambridge: Cambridge University Press, 2000.

Colzani, Alberto, Norbert Dubowy, Andrea Luppi, and Maurizio Padoan (eds.). *Il melodramma italiano in Italia e in Germania nell'età barocca. Atti del V. convegno internazionale sulla musica italiana nel secolo XVII, Loveno di Menaggio (Como), 28–30 giugno 1993*. Como: A.M.I.S., 1995.

Colzani, Alberto, Norbert Dubowy, Andrea Luppi, and Maurizio Padoan *Il teatro musicale italiano nel Sacro Romano Impero nei secoli XVII e XVIII*. Como: AMIS, 1999.

Cotticelli, Francesco, and Paologiovanni Maione, *Le Istituzioni Musicali a Napoli durante il Viceregno Austriaco (1707–1734)*. Naples: Luciano, 1993.

Couvreur, Manuel. *Jean-Baptiste Lully: musique et dramaturgie au service du prince*. Brussels: M. Vokar, 1992.

'Le récitatif lullyste et le modèle de la Comédie-Française'. *Entre théâtre et musique: récitatifs en Europe aux XVIIe et XVIIIe siècles. Cahiers d'histoire culturelle* 6 (1999), 33–45.

Covell, Roger. 'Seventeenth-Century Music for *The Tempest*'. *Studies in Music* 2 (1968), 43–65.

Cowart, Georgia. *The Origins of Modern Musical Criticism: French and Italian Music 1600–1750*. Ann Arbor: UMI Research Press, 1981.

The Triumph of Pleasure: Louis XIV and the Politics of Spectacle. Chicago and London: The University of Chicago Press, 2008.

Croce, Benedetto. *I teatri di Napoli: secolo XV–XVIII.* Naples: Luigi Pierro, 1891.

I teatri di Napoli: Dal Rinascimento alla fine del secolo decimottavo. Milan: Adelphi, 1992.

Cusick, Suzanne. '"There Was Not One Lady Who Failed to Shed a Tear": Arianna's Lament and the Construction of Modern Womanhood'. *EM* 22/1 (1994), 21–43.

Francesca Caccini at the Medici Court. Chicago and London: The University of Chicago Press, 2009.

D'Alessandro, Domenico Antonio. 'La musica a Napoli nel secolo XVII attraverso gli *avvisi* e i giornali'. In Lorenzo Bianconi and Renato Bossa (eds.), *Musica e cultura a Napoli dal XV al XIX secolo.* Florence: Olschki, 1983, 145–64.

'L'opera in musica a Napoli dal 1650 al 1670'. In Roberto Pane (ed.), *Seicento napoletano: Arte, costume, e ambiente.* Milan: Edizioni di comunità, 1984, 409–30.

Danchin, Pierre. 'The Foundation of the Royal Academy of Music in 1674 and Pierre Perrin's *Ariane*'. *Theatre Survey* 25/1 (1984), 55–67.

Daolmi, Davide. 'La drammaturgia al servizio della scenotecnica. Le "volubili scene" dell'opera barberiniana'. *Il Saggiatore Musicale* 13/1 (2006), 5–62, expanded version www.examenapium.it/barberini/barberini.pdf (accessed 19 April 2019).

Data, Isabella. 'Il "Rapimento di Proserpina" di Giulio Cesare Monteverdi e le feste a Casale nel 1611'. In Paola Besutti, Teresa M. Gialdroni, and Rodolfo Baroncini (eds.), *Claudio Monteverdi. Studi e prospettive: atti del convegno, Mantova, 21–24 ottobre 1993.* Florence: Olschki, 1998, 333–46.

De Caro, Gaspare. *Euridice: Momenti dell'Umanesimo civile fiorentino.* Bologna: Ut Orpheus Edizioni, 2006.

DelDonna, Anthony R., and Pierpaolo Polzonetti (eds.). *The Cambridge Companion to Eighteenth-Century Opera.* Cambridge: Cambridge University Press, 2009.

De Lucca, Valeria. 'The Power of the Prima Donna: Giulia Masotti's Repertory of Choice'. *JSCM* 17/1 (2011), http://sscm-jscm.org/jscm-issues/volume-17-no-1/the-power-of-the-prima-donna-giulia-masottis-repertory-of-choice/.

'Strategies of Women Patrons of Music and Theatre in Rome: Maria Mancini Colonna, Queen Christina of Sweden, and Women of Their Circles'. *Renaissance Studies* 25/3 (2011), 374–92.

De Paepe, Timothy. 'French Opera in Print and on Stage in Antwerp: Three Generations of Antwerp Book Publishers and Their Opera Librettos (1682–1714)'. *JSCM* 15/1 (2009), https://sscm-jscm.org/v15/no1/depaepe.html.

Die Musik in Geschichte und Gegenwart. Allgemeine Enzyklopädie der Musik. 17 vols. Friedrich Blume (ed.). Kassel: Bärenreiter, 1948–1968.

Die Musik in Geschichte und Gegenwart. Allgemeine Enzyklopädie der Musik. 29 vols. in two parts. 2nd rev. edn., ed. Ludwig Finscher. Kassel: Bärenreiter; Stuttgart: J. B. Metzler, 1994–2008.

Domínguez Rodríguez, José María. '"Comedias armónicas a la usanza de Italia": Alessandro Scarlatti's Music and the Spanish Nobility c. 1700'. *EM* 37/2 (2009), 201–15.

  'Cinco óperas para el príncipe. El ciclo de Stampiglia para el teatro de San Bartolomeo de Nápoles (1696–1702)'. *Il Saggiatore Musicale* 19/1 (2012), 5–40.

  Roma, Nápoles, Madrid: Mecenazgo musical del Duque de Medinaceli, 1687–1710. Kassel: Edition Reichenberger, 2013.

Dill, Charles. 'Eighteenth-Century Models of French Recitative'. *JRMA* 120/2 (1995), 232–50.

Doni, Giovanni Battista. *Lyra barberina αμΦιχορδος [amphichordos]*, ed. Anton Francesco Gori. 2 vols. Florence: Stamperia Imperiale, 1763; rpt. Bologna: Forni, 1974.

Dryden, John. *The Works of John Dryden*, ed. Earl Roy Miner and George R. Guffey. Vol. 15. *Plays: Albion and Albanius, Don Sebastian, Amphitryon*, ed. Earl R. Miner, George R. Guffey and Franklin B. Zimmerman. Berkeley, Los Angeles and London: University of California Press, 1976.

Dubowy, Norbert. 'Italienische Opern im mitteldeutschen Theater am Ende des 17. Jahrhunderts: Dresden und Leipzig'. In Friedhelm Brusniak (ed.), *Barockes Musiktheater im mitteldeutschen Raum im 17. und 18. Jahrhundert. Arolser Beiträge zur Musikforschung* 2. Cologne: Studio, 1994, 23–48.

Duckles, Vincent. 'English Song and the Challenge of Italian Monody'. In Vincent Duckles and Franklin B. Zimmerman (eds.), *Words to Music: Papers on English Seventeenth-Century Song*. Los Angeles: The William Andrew Clark Memorial Library, 1967, 3–42.

Ducrot, Ariane. 'Lully créateur de troupe'. *XVIIe Siècle* 98–9 (1973), 91–107.

Eccles, John. *Rinaldo and Armida*, ed. Steven Plank. Middleton: A-R Editions, 2011.

Emanuele, Marco. '*Arione* e il melodrama alla corte di Savoia'. *SM* 26/2 (1997), 313–29.

Emslie, McDonald. 'Nicholas Lanier's Innovations in English Song'. *ML* 41/1 (1960), 13–27.

Estenssoro Fuchs, Juan Carlos. *Música y sociedad coloniales. Lima, 1680–1830*. Lima: Colmillo Blanco, 1989.

Eubanks Winkler, Amanda. '"O Ravishing Delight": The Politics of Pleasure in *The Judgment of Paris*'. *COJ* 15/1 (2003), 15–31.

  (ed.). *Music for Macbeth*. Middleton: A-R Editions, 2004.

O Let Us Howle Some Heavy Note: Music for Witches, the Melancholic, and the Mad on the Seventeenth-Century English Stage. Bloomington: Indiana University Press, 2006.

'Enthusiasm and Its Discontents: Religion, Prophecy, and Madness in the Music for *Sophonisba* and *The Island Princess*'. *JM* 23/2 (2006), 317–30.

'Sexless Spirits?: Gender Ideology and Dryden's Musical Magic'. *MQ* 93/2 (2010), 297–328.

'A Thousand Voices: Performing Ariel'. In Dympna Callaghan (ed.), *A Feminist Companion to Shakespeare*. 2nd edn. Chichester: John Wiley & Sons, 2016, 520–38.

'The Intermedial Dramaturgy of Dramatick Opera: Understanding Genre through Performance'. *Restoration: Studies in English Literary Culture, 1660–1700* 42/2 (2018), 13–38.

Fabbri, Paolo. *Il secolo cantante: Per una storia del libretto d'opera nel Seicento*. 2nd edn. Rome: Bulzoni, 2003.

Fabbri, Paolo, and Angelo Pompilio (eds.). *Il corago, o vero alcune osservazioni per metter bene in scena le composizioni drammatiche*. Florence: Olschki, 1983.

Fabris, Dinko (ed.). *La circolazione dell'opera veneziana del Seicento*. Naples: Editoriale Scientifiche, 2005.

Music in Seventeenth-Century Naples: Francesco Provenzale (1624–1704). Aldershot: Ashgate, 2007.

'Relazioni musicali tra Venezia e Parigi da *Orfeo* a *Xerse*: il ruolo dei Bentivoglio', *I Musicisti veneziani e italiani a Parigi (1640–1670)*. Venice: Venetian Centre for Baroque Music, 2014, 6–15, www.vcbm.it/public/research_attachments/I_musicisti_veneziani_e_italiani_a_Parigi_-_Atti_della_giornata_di_studio.pdf (accessed 1 July 2019).

Partenope da sirena a regina: il mito musicale di Napoli. Naples: Cafagna Editore, 2016.

Fader, Don. 'The "Cabale du Dauphin," Campra, and Italian Comedy: The Courtly Politics of French Musical Patronage around 1700'. *ML* 86/3 (2005), 380–413.

Fajon, Robert. *L'Opéra à Paris du Roi Soleil à Louis le Bien-Aimé*. Geneva: Slatkine, 1984.

Farnsworth, Rodney. '"Hither, This Way": A Rhetorical-Musical Analysis of a Scene from Purcell's *King Arthur*'. *MQ* 74/1 (1990), 83–97.

Fischer, Christine (ed.). *'La liberazione di Ruggiero dall'isola d'Alcina'. Räume und Inszenierungen in Francesca Caccinis Ballettoper (Florenz, 1625)*. Zürich: Chronos Verlag, 2015.

Floros, Constantin, Hans Joachim Marx, and Peter Petersen (eds.), *Studien zur Barock Oper. Hamburger Jahrbuch für Musikwissenschaft*. Vol. 3. Hamburg: Verlag der Musikalienhandlung, 1978.

Fortune, Nigel (ed.). *Music and Theatre: Essays in Honour of Winton Dean*. Cambridge: Cambridge University Press, 2005.

Franck, Johann Wolfgang. *Hamburger Opernarien im szenischen Kontext: (Aeneas, 1680; Vespasian, 1681; Diocletian, 1682; Cara Mustapha, 1686)*, ed. Werner Braun. Saarbrücken: Saarbrücken Druckerei und Verlag, 1988.

Frandsen, Mary E. 'Eunuchi conjugium: The Marriage of a Castrato in Early Modern Germany'. *EMH* 24 (2005), 53–124.

Franko, Mark. *Dance as Text: Ideologies of the Baroque Body*. New York: Oxford University Press, 1993.

Freeman, Robert. 'The Travels of *Partenope*'. In Harold Powers (ed.), *Studies in Music History. Essays for Oliver Strunk*. Princeton: Princeton University Press, 1968, 356–85.

Freitas, Roger. 'The Eroticism of Emasculation: Confronting the Baroque Body of the Castrato'. *JM* 20/2 (2003), 196–249.

   Portrait of a Castrato: Politics, Patronage, and Music in the Life of Atto Melani. Cambridge: Cambridge University Press, 2009.

Gagliano, Marco da. *La Dafne di Marco da Gagliano*. Florence: Cristofano Marescotti, 1608; rpt. Bologna: Forni Editore, 1987.

   La Flora. Florence: Zanobi Pignoni, 1628; rpt. Bologna: Forni Editore, 1969.

   La Flora, ed. Suzanne Court. Middleton: A-R Editions, 2011.

Galilei, Vincenzo. *Dialogo della musica antica et della moderna*. Florence: Giorgio Marescotti, 1581; rpt. New York: Broude Brothers, 1967.

   Dialogue on Ancient and Modern Music, ed. and trans. Claude V. Palisca. New Haven: Yale University Press, 2003.

Gerbino, Giuseppe. 'The Quest for the Soprano Voice: Castrati in Renaissance Italy'. *SM* 33/2 (2004), 303–56.

Gherardi, Evaristo. *Le Théâtre Italien, ou le Recueil de toutes les scènes françoises*. Paris: Guillaume de Luyne, 1694.

   Le Théâtre italien de Gherardi, ou, Le Recueil général de toutes les comédies & scènes françaises jouées par les comédiens italiens du roi, pendant tout le temps qu'ils ont été au service. 6 vols. Paris: Jean-Bapt. Cusson et Pierre Witte, 1700.

Giustiniani, Vincenzo. *Discorso sopra la musica de' suoi tempi [1628]*, trans. Carol MacClintock. Rome: American Institute of Musicology, 1962.

Glixon, Beth L. 'Private Lives of Public Women: Prima Donnas in Mid-Seventeenth-Century Venice'. *ML* 76/4 (1995), 509–31.

   'Scenes from the Life of Silvia Gailarti Manni, a Seventeenth-Century *virtuosa*'. *EMH* 15 (1996), 97–146.

   'New Light on the Life and Career of Barbara Strozzi'. *MQ* 81/2 (1997), 311–55.

   (ed.). *Studies in Seventeenth-Century Opera*. Farnham: Ashgate, 2010.

   'Giulia Masotti, Venice, and the Rise of the Prima Donna'. *JSCM* 17/1 (2011), http://sscm-jscm.org/jscm-issues/volume-17-no-1/giulia-masotti-venice-and-the-rise-of-the-prima-donna/.

Glixon, Beth L., and Jonathan E. Glixon. 'Oil and Opera Don't Mix: The Biography of S. Aponal, a Seventeenth-Century Venetian Opera Theater'. In Susan Parisi (ed.), with collaboration of Ernest Harriss II and Calvin M. Bower, *Music in the Theater, Church, and Villa: Essays in Honor of Robert Lamar Weaver and Norma Wright Weaver*. Michigan: Harmonie Park Press, 2000, 131–44.

Inventing the Business of Opera: The Impresario and His World in Seventeenth-Century Venice. Oxford and New York: Oxford University Press, 2006.

Glixon, Jonathan E. '*Supereminet omnes*: New Light on the Life and Career of Vittoria Tarquini'. *Händel-Jahrbuch* 62 (2016), 385–98.

Mirrors of Heaven or Worldly Theaters? Venetian Nunneries and Their Music. Oxford and New York: Oxford University Press, 2017.

Gordon-Seifert, Catherine. 'Precious Eroticism and Hidden Morality: Salon Culture and the Mid-Seventeenth-Century French Air'. In Bonnie Blackburn and Laurie Stras (eds.), *Eroticism in Early Modern Music*. Farnham and Burlington: Ashgate, 2015, 227–60.

Grabu, Louis. *Albion and Albanius*, ed. Bryan White. The Purcell Society Edition Companion Series. Vol. 1. London: Stainer & Bell, 2007.

Griffin, Thomas E. 'Nuove fonti per la storia della musica a Napoli durante il regno del marchese del Carpio (1683–1687)'. *RIM* 16/2 (1981), 207–28.

Griffiths, Wanda R. 'Jacquet de la Guerre's Céphale et Procris: Style and Drama'. In Malcolm Cole and John Koegel (eds.), *Music in Performance and Society: Essays in Honor of Roland Jackson*. Warren: Harmonie Park Press, 1997, 251–68.

Grimarest, Jean-Léonor Le Gallois de. *Traité du recitatif dans la lecture, dans l'action publique, dans la declamation, et dans le chant. Avec un Traité des Accens, de la Quantité, & de la Ponctuation*. Paris: Jacques Le Fevre et Pierre Ribou, 1707.

Grove Music Online, ed. Laura Macy, www.grovemusic.com.

Hammond, Frederick. 'Bernini and the "Fiera di Farfa"'. In Irving Lavin (ed.), *Gianlorenzo Bernini: New Aspects of His Art and Thought*. University Park: The Pennsylvania State University Press, 1985, 115–78.

Music and Spectacle in Baroque Rome: Barberini Patronage under Urban VIII. New Haven: Yale University Press, 1994.

Hammond, Paul. 'Dryden's *Albion and Albanius*: The Apotheosis of Charles II'. In David Lindley (ed.), *The Court Masque*. Manchester: Manchester University Press, 1984, 169–83.

Harness, Kelley. 'Le tre *Euridici*: Characterization and Allegory in the *Euridici* of Peri and Caccini'. *JSCM* 9/1 (2003), https://sscm-jscm.org/v9/no1/harness.html.

Echoes of Women's Voices: Music, Art, and Female Patronage in Early Modern Florence. Chicago: The University of Chicago Press, 2006.

Harris, Ellen T. *Henry Purcell's Dido and Aeneas*. Oxford: Clarendon Press, 1987.

Harris-Warrick, Rebecca. 'Staging Venice'. *COJ* 15/3 (2003), 297–316.

    Dance and Drama in French Baroque Opera: A History. Cambridge: Cambridge University Press, 2016.

Harris-Warrick, Rebecca, and Carol G. Marsh. *Musical Theatre at the Court of Louis XIV: Le Mariage de la Grosse Cathos*. Cambridge: Cambridge University Press, 1994.

Haun, Eugene. *But Hark! More Harmony: The Libretti of Restoration Opera in English*. Ypsilanti: Eastern Michigan University Press, 1971.

Heikamp, Detlef. 'Il Teatro Mediceo degli Uffizi'. *Bollettino del Centro Internazionale di architettura Andrea Palladio* 16 (1974), 323–32.

Heller, Wendy. 'Tacitus Incognito: Opera as History in *L'incoronazione di Poppea*'. *JAMS* 52/1 (1999), 39–96.

    'Dancing Desire on the Venetian Stage'. *COJ* 15/3 (2003), 281–95.

    Emblems of Eloquence: Opera and Women's Voices in Seventeenth-Century Venice. Berkeley, Los Angeles, and London: University of California Press, 2003.

    'Truth and Verisimilitude in Venetian Opera'. In Victoria Johnson, Jane F. Fulcher, and Thomas Ertman (eds.), *Opera and Society in Italy and France from Monteverdi to Bourdieu*. Cambridge: Cambridge University Press, 2007, 34–52.

Herr, Corinna, Herbert Seifert, Andreas Sommer-Mathis, and Reinhard Strohm (eds.). *Italian Opera in Central Europe 1614–1780*. 3 vols. Berlin: Berliner Wissenschafts-Verlag, 2006–2008.

Herissone, Rebecca. 'Playford, Purcell, and the Functions of Music Publishing in Restoration England'. *JAMS* 63/2 (2010), 243–90.

Hewitt, Barnard (ed.). *The Renaissance Stage: Documents of Serlio, Sabbattini and Furttenbach*. Coral Gables: University of Miami Press, 1968.

Hidalgo, Juan, and Pedro Calderón de la Barca. *Celos aun del aire matan*, ed. Louise K. Stein. Middleton: A-R Editions, 2014.

Hill, John Walter. *Roman Monody, Cantata, and Opera from the Circles around Cardinal Montalto*. New York and Oxford : Oxford University Press, 1997.

    'Beyond Isomorphism toward a Better Theory of Recitative'. *JSCM* 9/1 (2003), https://sscm-jscm.org/v9/no1/hill.html.

Holford-Strevens, Leofranc. '"Her Eyes Became Two Spouts": Classical Antecedents of Renaissance Laments'. *EM* 27/3 (1999), 379–93.

Holman, Peter. *Four and Twenty Fiddlers: The Violin at the English Court 1540–1690*. Rev. edn. Oxford: Clarendon Press, 1995.

Hook, Lucyle. 'Motteux and the Classical Masque'. In Shirley Strum Kenny (ed.), *British Theatre and the Other Arts, 1660–1800*. Washington, DC: Folger Shakespeare Library, 1984, 105–15.

Howard, Patricia. 'Quinault, Lully, and the Precieuses: Images of Women in Seventeenth-Century France'. In Susan Cook and Judy S. Tsou (eds.), *Cecilia*

Reclaimed: Feminist Perspectives on Gender and Music (Urbana: University of Illinois Press, 1994), 70–89.

Hume, Robert D. 'The Nature of the Dorset Garden Theatre'. *Theatre Notebook* 36/3 (1982), 99–109.

'The Politics of Opera in Late Seventeenth-Century London'. *COJ* 10/1 (1998), 15–43.

Ingegneri, Angelo. *Della Poesia Rappresentativa e del Modo di Rappresentare le Favole Sceniche*, ed. Maria Lisa Doglio. Ferrara: Edizioni Panini, 1989.

Isherwood, Robert M. *Music in the Service of the King: France in the Seventeenth Century*. Ithaca: Cornell University Press, 1973.

Italian Opera Librettos: 1640–1770, ed. Howard Mayer Brown. 16 vols. New York: Garland, 1978–1984.

Ivanovich, Cristoforo. *Memorie teatrali di Venezia*, ed. Norbert Dubowy. Venice: Nicola Pezzana, 1688; rpt. Lucca: LIM, 1993.

Jeanneret, Christine. 'Gender Ambivalence and the Expression of Passions in the Performances of Early Roman Cantatas by Castrati and Female Singers'. In Tom Cochrane, Bernardino Fantini, and Klaus R. Scherer (eds.), *The Emotional Power of Music. Multidisciplinary Perspectives on Musical Arousal, Expression, and Social Control*. Oxford: Oxford University Press, 2013, 85–101, appendix 359–69.

Katz, Ruth. *Divining the Powers of Music: Aesthetic Theory and the Origins of Opera*. New York: Pendragon Press, 1986.

Kaufold, Claudia, Nicole K. Strohmann, and Colin Timms (eds.). *Agostino Steffani: europäischer Komponist, hannoverscher Diplomat und Bischof der Leibniz-Zeit / Hanoverian Diplomat and Bishop in the Age of Leibniz*. Göttingen: V&R Unipress, 2017.

Kendall, Yvonne. 'Theatre, Dance and Music in Late Cinquecento Milan'. *EM* 32/1 (2004), 74–95.

Kendrick, Robert. 'What's So Sacred about "Sacred" Opera? Reflections on the Fate of a (Sub)Genre'. *JSCM* 9/1 (2003), https://sscm-jscm.org/v9/no1/kendrick.html.

Kerman, Joseph. *Opera as Drama*. New York: Knopf, 1956; rev. edn. Berkeley: University of California Press, 1988.

Kimbell, David. *Italian Opera*. Cambridge: Cambridge University Press, 1991.

King, Helen. *The One-Sex Body on Trial: The Classical and Early Modern Evidence*. Farnham and Burlington: Ashgate, 2013.

Kintzler, Catherine. *Poétique de l'opéra français de Corneille à Rousseau*. 2nd edn. Paris: Minerve, 2005.

Kirkendale, Warren. 'Zur Biographie des ersten Orfeo, Francesco Rasi'. In Ludwig Finscher (ed.), *Claudio Monteverdi. Festschrift Reinhold Hammerstein zum 70. Geburtstag*. Laaber: Laaber-Verlag, 1986, 297–335.

The Court Musicians in Florence during the Principate of the Medici. Florence: Olschki, 1993.

Emilio de' Cavalieri, 'Gentiluomo Romano': His Life and Letters, His Role as Superintendent of All the Arts at the Medici Court, and His Musical Compositions. Florence: Olschki, 2001.

Klaper, Michael. 'Der Beginn der Operngeschichte in Paris? Anmerkungen zu *La finta pazza* (1645)'. In Laurine Quetin and Albert Gier (eds.), *Le livret en question. Le livret en question. [Actes d'un colloque tenu à Bamberg du 18 au 20 janvier 2007 sur le thème 'Perspectives de la librettologie'].* Musicorum 5 (2006–2007). Tours: Presses universitaires François-Rabelais, 2007, 77–104.

'New light on the history of *L'Orfeo* (Buti-Rossi)'. In Alessandro Di Profio and Damien Colas (eds.), *D'une scène à l'autre: l'opéra italien en Europe.* 2 vols. Liège: Mardaga, 2008, vol. 1, 27–40.

Kusser, Johann Sigismund. *Adonis*, ed. Samantha Owens. Middleton: A-R Editions, 2009.

Lacroix, Paul. *Ballets et mascarades de cour de Henri III à Louis XIV (1581–1652).* 6 vols. Geneva: J. Gay et fils, 1868–1870.

La Gorce, Jérôme. 'Une Académie de musique en province au temps du Roi-Soleil: l'Opéra de Rouen'. In Marc Honegger and Christian Meyer (eds.), *La musique et le rite sacré et profane. Vol. 2: Communications libres. Actes du 13. Congrès de la Société Internationale de Musicologie Strasbourg, 29 août–3 septembre 1982.* Strasbourg: Association de Publication près les Universités de Strasbourg, 1986, 465–96.

L'Opéra à Paris au temps de Louis XIV. Paris: Desjonquères, 1992.

Jean-Baptiste Lully. Paris: Fayard, 2002.

'Recherches sur les débuts de l'opéra de Metz: privilèges, répertoires et troupes (1699–1732)'. In Yves Ferraton (ed.), *Itinéraires musicaux en Lorraine, sources, événements, compositeurs.* Langres: D. Guéniot, 2002, 41–58.

Landi, Stefano. *Il S. Alessio, dramma musicale.* Rome: Paolo Masotti, 1634; rpt Bologna: Forni Editore, 1970, new edn. 2003.

Lattarico, Jean-François. *Busenello, un théâtre de la rhétorique.* Paris: Garnier, 2013.

Law, Hedy. 'Orphée at the Forains. Silencing and Silences in Old Régime France'. In Kirsten Gibson and Ian Biddle (eds.), *Cultural Histories of Noise, Sound and Listening in Europe, 1300–1918.* Abingdon and New York: Routledge, 2017, 111–26.

Lawrence, W. J. 'Foreign Singers and Musicians at the Court of Charles II'. *MQ* 9/2 (1923), 217–22.

Le Blanc, Judith. *Avatars d'opéras: parodies et circulation des airs chantés sur les scènes parisiennes.* Paris: Classiques Garnier, 2014.

Le Blanc, Judith, and Herbert Schneider (eds.). *Pratiques du timbre et de la parodie d'opéra en Europe: XVIe–XIXe siècles.* Hildesheim, Zürich, and New York: G. Olms, 2014.

Le Cerf de La Viéville, Jean-Laurent. See Raguenet.

Lecomte, Nathalie. *Entre cours et jardins d'illusion. Le ballet en Europe 1515–1715.* Pantin: Centre national de la danse, 2014.

Leech, Peter. 'Musicians in the Catholic Chapel of Catherine of Braganza, 1662–92'. *EM* 29/4 (2001), 570–87.

Lefkowitz, Murray. 'Shadwell and Locke's *Psyche*: The French Connection'. *PRMA* 106 (1979–1980), 42–55.

Leopold, Silke. *Geschichte der Oper. Vol. 1: Die Oper im 17. Jahrhundert.* Laaber: Laaber-Verlag, 2006.

Lindley, David. *Shakespeare and Music.* London: Thompson Learning, 2006.

Locke, Matthew. *The English opera, or, The vocal musick in Psyche with the instrumental therein intermix'd : to which is adjoyned the instrumental musick in The tempest.* London: Printed by T. Ratcliff and N. Thompson for the author, 1675.

   Dramatic Music, ed. Michael Tilmouth, Musica Britannica. Vol. 51. London: Stainer and Bell, 1986.

Louvat-Molozay, Bénédicte. *Théâtre et musique. Dramaturgie de l'insertion musicale dans le théâtre français (1550–1680).* Paris: H. Champion, 2002, 365–400.

Lowerre, Kathryn. *Music and Musicians on the London Stage, 1695–1705.* Farnham: Ashgate, 2009.

   'Dramatick Opera and Theatrical Reform: Dennis's *Rinaldo and Armida* and Motteux's *The Island Princess*'. *Theatre Notebook* 59/1 (2005), 23–40.

Lowerre, Kathryn. (ed.). *The Lively Arts of the London Stage, 1675–1725.* Farnham: Ashgate, 2014.

Luckett, Richard. 'Exotick but Rational Entertainments: The English Dramatick Operas'. In Marie Axton and Raymond Williams (eds.), *English Drama: Forms and Development: Essays in Honour of Muriel Clara Bradbrook.* Cambridge: Cambridge University Press, 1977, 123–41.

   'A New Source for "Venus and Adonis"'. *MT* 130/1752 (1989), 76–9.

Lully, Jean-Baptiste. *Œuvres complètes. Série II. Comédies-ballets et autres divertissements*, vol. 6, ed. John S. Powell, Herbert Schneider, and Laura Naudeix. Hildesheim, Zürich, New York: G. Olms, 2007.

Mabbett, Margaret. 'Italian Musicians in Restoration England (1660–90)'. *ML* 67/3 (1986), 237–47.

MacNeil, Anne. 'The Divine Madness of Isabella Andreini'. *JRMA* 120/2 (1995), 195–215.

   'Weeping at the Water's Edge'. *EM* 27/3 (1999), 406–17.

   Music and Women of the Commedia dell'Arte in the Late Sixteenth Century. Oxford and New York: Oxford University Press, 2003.

Maione, Paologiovanni. *Giulia de Caro 'Famosissima Armonica' e Il Bordello Sostenuto del Signor Don Antonio Muscettola.* Naples: Luciano, 1997.

'Giulia de Caro "seu Ciulla" da commediante a cantarina. Osservazioni sulla condizione degli "Armonici" nella seconda metà del Seicento'. *RIM* 32/1 (1997), 61–80.

Mamone, Sara. *Dèi, semidei, uomini. Lo spettacolo a Firenze tra neoplatonismo e realtà borghese (XV–XVII secolo)*. Rome: Bulzoni, 2003.

Mancini, Franco, Maria Teresa Muraro, and Elena Povoledo. *I teatri di Venezia*. 2 vols. Venice: Corbo e Fiore, 1995–1996.

Marx, Hans Joachim, and Dorothea Schröder (eds.). *Die Hamburger Gänsemarkt-Oper. Katalog der Textbücher (1678–1748)*. Laaber: Laaber-Verlag, 1995.

Maul, Michael. 'Die Gebrüder Uffenbach zu Besuch in der Gänsemarktoper – Bemerkungen zu einem altbekannten Reisebericht'. In Hans Joachim Marx and Wolfgang Sandberger (eds.), *Göttinger Händel-Beiträge*. Vol. 12. Göttingen: Vandenhoeck & Ruprecht, 2008, 183–95.

  Barockoper in Leipzig (1693–1720). 2 vols. Freiburg im Breisgau: Rombach, 2009.

Mazzocchi, Domenico. *La catena d'Adone*. Rome: Fr. Corbelletti, 1626; rpt. Bologna: Forni Editore, 1969.

Mazzocchi, Domenico, and Virgilio Marazzoli. *L'Egisto, ovvero, Chi soffre speri*, ed. Howard Mayer Brown and Eric Weimer. New York: Garland Publishing, 1982.

McClary, Susan (ed.). *Structures of Feeling in Seventeenth-Century Cultural Expression*. Toronto: University of Toronto Press, 2013.

McGowan, Margaret M. *L'Art du ballet de cour en France: 1581–1643*. Paris: Editions du CNRS, 1978.

  'Échanges entre le ballet de cour et le théâtre au milieu du XVIIe siècle'. In Irène Mamczarz (ed.), *Les Premiers opéras en Europe et les formes dramatiques apparentées*. Paris: Klincksieck, 1992, 153–69.

Megale, Teresa. 'Altre novità su Anna Francesca Costa e sull'allestimento dell'*Ergirodo*'. *Medioevo e Rinascimento* 7/n.s. 4 (1993), 137–42.

Mei, Girolamo. *Girolamo Mei (1519–1594): Letters on Ancient and Modern Music to Vincenzo Galilei and Giovanni Bardi: A Study with Annotated Text*, ed. and trans. Claude V. Palisca. 2nd edn. Rome: American Institute of Musicology, 1977 [1960].

Ménestrier, Claude-François. *Des Représentations en musique anciennes et modernes*. Paris: René Guignard, 1681.

Mersenne, Marin. *Harmonie universelle*. Part 1. Paris: Jean Cramoisy, 1636.

  Harmonie universelle. Part 2. Paris: Pierre Ballard, 1637.

Mesnard, Jean. 'La Musicalité du texte dans la tragédie classique'. In Irène Mamczarcz (ed.), *Les premiers opéras en Europe et les formes dramatiques apparentées*. Paris: Klincksieck, 1992, 117–32.

Michelassi, Nicola. '*La Finta pazza* a Firenze: Commedie "spagnole" e "veneziane" nel teatro di Baldracca (1641–1665)'. *Studi secenteschi* 41 (2000), 313–53.

Musici di Fortuna. I Mondi Teatrali di Giovan Battista Balbi e 'La Finta pazza' tra Venezia e l'Europa 1637–1654. Ph.D, Università degli Studi di Firenze, 2003.

'La finta pazza: un dramma incognito in giro per l'Europa'. In Davide Conrieri (ed.), *Gli Incogniti e l'Europa*. Bologna: I libri di Emil, 2011, 145–208: 188.

La doppia 'Finta pazza': Il viaggio di un dramma veneziano nell'Europa del Seicento. 2 vols. Florence: Olschki, forthcoming.

Milesi, Francesco (ed.). *Giacomo Torelli: L'invenzione scenica nell'Europa barocca*. Fano: Fondazione Cassa di Risparmio, 2000.

Milhous, Judith. *Thomas Betterton and the Management of Lincoln's Inn Fields, 1695–1708*. Carbondale and Edwardsville: Southern Illinois University Press, 1979.

'The Multimedia Spectacular on the Restoration Stage'. In Shirley Strum Kenny (ed.), *British Theatre and the Other Arts 1660–1800*. Washington, DC: Folger Shakespeare Library, 1984, 41–66.

Minguito Palomares, Ana. 'La política cultural del VIII conde de Oñate en Nápoles 1648–1653'. In José Alcalá-Zamora and Ernest Belenguer (eds.), *Calderón de la Barca y la España del Barroco*. 2 vols. Madrid: Centro de Estudios Políticos y Constitucionales, 2001, vol. 1, 957–74.

Moureau, François. 'Parties et parodies musicales à la Comédie-Française sous Louis XIV'. *Revue d'Histoire du Théâtre* 57 (2005), 227–42.

Muir, Edward. 'Why Venice? Venetian Society and the Success of Early Opera'. *Journal of Interdisciplinary History* 3/36 (2006), 331–53.

Muraro, Maria Teresa (ed.). *Studi sul teatro veneto fra Rinascimento ed età barocca*. Florence: Olschki, 1971.

Venezia e il melodramma nel seicento. Florence: Olschki, 1976.

L'opera italiana a Vienna prima di Metastasio. Florence: Leo S. Olschki, 1989.

Murata, Margaret. *Operas for the Papal Court, 1631–1668*. Ann Arbor: UMI Research Press, 1981.

'Why the First Opera Given in Paris Wasn't Roman'. *COJ* 7/2 (1995), 87–105.

'*Dal ridicolo al diletto signorile*. Rospigliosi and the Intermedio in Rome'. In Caroline Panel-Giron and Anne-Madeleine Goulet (eds.), *La Musique à Rome au XVIIe siècle*. Rome: École française de Rome, 2012, 269–89.

'Encountering Opera'. In Michael Klaper and Nastasia Tietze (eds.), *The Beginnings of Opera in Europe*. Turnhout: Brepols, forthcoming.

Nagler, Alois M. *A Source Book in Theatrical History*. New York: Dover, 1959.

Theatre Festivals of the Medici. New Haven: Yale University Press, 1964.

Nancy, Sarah. *La voix féminine et le plaisir de l'écoute en France aux XVIIe et XVIIIe siècles*. Paris: Classiques Garnier, 2012.

Naudeix, Laura. *Dramaturgie de la tragédie en musique (1673–1764)*. Paris: H. Champion, 2004.

'Le jeu du chanteur dans l'esthétique spectaculaire de l'opéra lulliste'. In Jacqueline Waeber (ed.), *Musique et Geste en France de Lully à la Révolution*. Bern: Peter Lang, 2009, 43–54.

'La "mélodie harmonieuse des cieux": musiciens visibles ou cachés dans le ballet français du XVIIe siècle.' In Bénédicte Louvat-Molozay and Xavier Bisaro (eds.), *Les Sons du théâtre, Angleterre et France (XVIe–XVIIIe siècle). Éléments d'une histoire de l'écoute*. Rennes: Presses Universitaires de Rennes, 2013, 73–84.

'Qui est l'auteur d'un ballet de cour? du *Paradis d'amour* (1572) aux *Fâcheux* (1662)'. In Sabine Chaouche, Estelle Doudet, and Olivier Spina (eds.), *Écrire pour la scène (XVe–XVIIIe siècle)*. Paris: Garnier, 2017, 97–113.

(ed.), *Molière à la cour. Les Amants magnifiques en 1670*. Rennes: Presses Universitaires de Rennes, 2020.

Nestola, Barbara. *Les Italiens à la Cour de France: de Marie de Médicis au Régent Philippe d'Orléans*. Versailles: CMBV, 2004.

'L'*Egisto* fantasma di Cavalli: nuova luce sulla rappresentazione parigina di *Egisto ovvero Chi soffre speri* di Mazzocchi e Marazzoli (1646)'. *Recercare* 19/ 1–2 (2007), 125–46.

Neubacher, Jürgen. 'Drei wieder zugängliche Ariensammelbände als Quellen für das Repertoire der Hamburger Gänsemarkt-Oper'. In Hans Joachim Marx (ed.), *Beiträge zur Musikgeschichte Hamburgs vom Mittelalter bis in die Neuzeit. Hamburger Jahrbuch für Musikwissenschaft*. Vol. 18. Frankfurt am Main: Peter Lang, 2001, 195–206.

Nevile, Jennifer. 'Cavalieri's theatrical ballo "O che nuovo miracolo": A Reconstruction'. *Dance Chronicle* 21/3 (1998), 353–88.

Norman, Buford. *Touched by the Graces: The Libretti of Philippe Quinault in the Context of French Classicism*. Birmingham, AL: Summa Publications, 2001.

'Le rôle de Quinault dans la création de l'opéra français'. In Jean Duron (ed.), '*Cadmus & Hermione' (1673) de Jean-Baptiste Lully et Philippe Quinault: livret, études et commentaires*. Wavre: Mardaga, 2008, 71–95.

Orgel, Stephen, and Roy Strong. *Inigo Jones: The Theatre of the Stuart Court Masque*. 2 vols. London: Sotheby Parke Bernet, 1973.

Ossi, Massimo. '*Dalle Macchine . . . la Maraviglia*: Bernardo Buontalenti's *Il Rapimento di Cefalo* at the Medici Theater in 1600'. In Mark A. Radice (ed.), *Opera in Context*. Portland: Amadeus, 1998, 15–35.

Page, Janet. 'Sirens on the Danube: Giulia Masotti and Women Singers at the Imperial Court'. *JSCM* 17/1 (2011), http://sscm-jscm.org/jscm-issues/ volume-17-no-1/sirens-on-the-danube-giulia-masotti-and-women-singers- at-the-imperial-court/.

Palisca, Claude V. 'The *Camerata fiorentina*: A Reappraisal'. *SM* 1 (1972), 203–36.

'The Musical Humanism of Giovanni Bardi'. In Hagop Meyvalian (ed.), *Poesia e musica nell'estetica del XVI e XVII secolo*. Florence: Artiminio, 1979, 45–72.

Humanism in Italian Renaissance Musical Thought. New Haven and London: Yale University Press, 1985.

The Florentine Camerata: Documentary Studies and Translations. New Haven: Yale University Press, 1989.

Studies in the History of Italian Music and Music Theory. Oxford: Clarendon Press; New York: Oxford University Press, 1994.

Pampaloni, Cristina. 'Giovanni castrati nell'Assisi del Settecento'. *Musica/Realtà* 8 (1987), 133–54.

Parisot, François-Georges. 'Le Mariage d'Henri de Lorraine et de Marguerite de Gonzague-Mantoue 1606. Les fêtes et le témoignage de Jacques Bellange'. In Jean Jacquot (ed.), *Les fêtes de la Renaissance. Journées internationales d'études Abbaye de Royaumont, 8–13 juillet 1955*. Paris: Éditions du CNRS, 1956, 153–89.

Peri, Jacopo. *Le musiche di Jacopo Peri sopra L'Euridice*. Florence: Giorgio Marescotti, 1600; rpt. Rome: Reale Accademia D'Italia, 1934 and Bologna: Forni, 1969.

Euridice, ed. Howard Mayer Brown. Madison: A-R Editions, 1981.

Perrucci, Andrea. *Dell'Arte Rappresentativa*, ed. Anton Giulio Bragaglia. Florence: Sansoni, 1961.

Pinnock, Andrew. 'Play into Opera: Purcell's *The Indian Queen*'. *EM* 18/1 (1990), 3–21.

'The Rival Maids: Anne Killigrew, Anne Kingsmill and the Making of the Court Masque *Venus and Adonis* (Music by John Blow)'. *EM* 46/4 (2018), 631–52.

Pirrotta, Nino, and Elena Povoledo. *Music and Theatre from Poliziano to Monteverdi*, trans. Karen Eales. Cambridge: Cambridge University Press, 1982.

Plank, Steven E. '"And Now about the Cauldron Sing": Music and the Supernatural on the Restoration Stage'. *EM* 18/3 (1990), 392–407.

Porter, William V. 'Peri and Corsi's *Dafne*: Some New Discoveries and Observations'. *JAMS* 18/2 (1965), 170–96.

Powell, John. S. *Music and theatre in France, 1600–1680*. Oxford: Oxford University Press, 2000.

'The Opera Parodies of Florent Carton Dancourt'. *COJ*, 13/2 (2001), 87–114.

Prest, Julia. *Theatre under Louis XIV: Cross-Casting and the Performance of Gender in Drama, Ballet and Opera*. New York: Palgrave MacMillan, 2006.

'The Politics of Ballet at the Court of Louis XIV'. In Jennifer Nevile (ed.), *Dance, Spectacle, and the Body Politick, 1250–1750*. Bloomington: Indiana University Press, 2008, 229–40.

Price, Curtis. *Music in the Restoration Theatre: With a Catalogue of Instrumental Music in the Plays, 1665–1713*. Ann Arbor: UMI Research Press, 1979.

Henry Purcell and the London Stage. Cambridge: Cambridge University Press, 1984.

'*Dido and Aeneas*: Questions of Style and Evidence'. *EM* 22/1 (1994), 115–25.

Profeti, Maria Grazia (ed.). *Commedia e musica tra Spagna e Italia*. Florence: Alinea, 2009.

Prota-Giurleo, Ulisse. 'Breve storia del Teatro di Corte e della musica a Napoli nei secoli XVII–XVIII'. In Felice De Filippis and Ulisse Prota-Giurleo, *Il teatro di corte del Palazzo Reale di Napoli*. Naples: L'Arte Tipografica, 1952, 17–146.

Prota-Giurleo, Ulisse, Ermanno Belluci, and Giorgio Mancini. *I Teatri di Napoli nel secolo XVII*. 3 vols. Naples: Il Quartiere Edizioni, 2002.

Prunières, Henry. *L'opéra italien en France avant Lulli*. Paris: Librairie ancienne Honoré Champion, 1913.

   Le Ballet de cour en France avant Benserade et Lully, suivi du ballet de 'La Délivrance de Renaud' de Pierre Guédron. Paris: H. Laurens, 1914.

Purcell, Henry. *The Works of Henry Purcell*. Vol. 3, *Dido and Aeneas*, ed. Margaret Laurie. Borough Green: Novello, 1979.

   The Works of Henry Purcell. Vol. 19, *The Indian Queen*, ed. Margaret Laurie and Andrew Pinnock. London: Novello, 1994.

   Venus and Adonis, ed. Bruce Wood. The Purcell Society Edition Companion Series. Vol. 2. London: Stainer & Bell, 2008.

Quinault, Philippe. *Alceste, suivi de la Querelle d'Alceste: Anciens et modernes avant 1680*, ed. Buford Norman, William Brooks, and Jeanne Morgan Zarucchi. Geneva: Droz, 1994.

   Philippe Quinault: Livrets d'opéra, ed. Buford Norman. 2 vols. Toulouse: Société de Littérature Classique, 1999.

Radice, Mark A. 'Sites for Music in Purcell's Dorset Garden Theatre'. *MQ* 81/3 (1997), 430–48.

   (ed.). *Opera in Context*. Portland: Amadeus, 1998.

Raguenet, François, and Jean-Laurent Le Cerf de La Viéville. *La Première Querelle de la musique italienne (1702–1706)*, ed. Laura Naudeix. Paris: Garnier, 2018.

Reardon, Colleen. *Holy Concord within Sacred Walls: Nuns and Music in Siena, 1575–1700*. Oxford and New York: Oxford University Press, 2002.

   'Launching the Career of a *secondo uomo* in Late Seventeenth-Century Italy'. *JSCM* 16/1 (2010), par. 5.5, at http://www.sscm-jscm.org/v16/no1/reardon.html.

   'Camilla in Siena and Senesino's Début'. *SM* n.s. 2/2 (2011), 281–325.

   'Letters from the Road: Giulia Masotti and Cardinal Sigismondo Chigi'. *JSCM* 17/1 (2011), http://sscm-jscm.org/jscm-issues/volume-17-no-1/letters-from-the-road-giulia-masotti-and-cardinal-sigismondo-chigi/.

   'Siena Cathedral and Its Castrati'. In Kristine K. Forney and Jeremy L. Smith (eds.), *Sleuthing the Muse: Essays in Honor of William F. Prizer*. Hillsdale: Pendragon, 2012, 201–17.

'Getting Past No or Getting to Yes: Nuns, Divas, and Negotiation Tactics in Early Modern Italy'. In Karen Nelson (ed.), *Attending to Early Modern Women: Conflict and Concord*. Newark: University of Delaware Press, 2013, 23–43.

A Sociable Moment: Opera and Festive Culture in Baroque Siena. New York: Oxford University Press, 2016.

Ricci, Corrado. *I teatri di Bologna nei secoli XVII e XVIII: storia aneddotica*. Bologna: Successori Monti: 1888.

Rock, Judith. *Terpsichore at Louis-le-Grand: Baroque Dance on a Jesuit Stage in Paris*. Saint Louis: Institute of Jesuit Sources, 1996.

Rodríguez-Garrido, José Antonio. *Teatro y Poder en el Palacio Virreinal de Lima (1672–1707)*. Ph.D, Princeton University, 2003.

Rosand, David, and Ellen Rosand. 'Barbara di Santa Sofia and Il Prete Genovese: On the Identity of a Portrait by Bernardo Strozzi'. *Art Bulletin* 63/2 (1981), 249–58.

Rosand, Ellen. 'Barbara Strozzi, *virtuosissima cantatrice*: The Composer's Voice'. *JAMS* 31/2 (1978), 241–81.

'L'Orfeo: the Metamorphosis of a Musical Myth'. *Israel Studies in Musicology* 2 (1980), 101–30.

'Seneca and the Interpretation of *L'incoronazione di Poppea*'. *JAMS* 38/1 (1985), 34–71.

Opera in Seventeenth-Century Venice: The Creation of a Genre. Berkeley, Los Angeles, and London: University of California Press, 1991.

Monteverdi's Last Operas. A Venetian Trilogy. Berkeley, Los Angeles, and London: University of California Press, 2007.

Rosand, Ellen. (ed.). *Readying Cavalli's Operas for the Stage: Edition, Production*. Aldershot: Ashgate, 2013.

Rosow, Lois. 'French Baroque Recitative as an Expression of Tragic Declamation'. *EM* 11/4, 468–79.

'Lully's Musical Architecture: Act IV of *Persée*'. *JSCM* 10/1 (2004), https://sscm-jscm.org/v10/no1/rosow.html.

Rospigliosi, Giulio. *Melodrammi profani*, ed. Danilo Romei. Florence: Studio Editoriale Fiorentino, 1998.

Melodrammi sacri, ed. Danilo Romei. Florence: Studio Editoriale Fiorentino, 1999.

Rosselli, John. *The Opera Industry in Italy from Cimarosa to Verdi: The Role of the Impresario*. Cambridge: Cambridge University Press, 1984.

'The Castrati as a Professional Group and a Social Phenomenon'. *Acta Musicologica* 60/2 (1988), 143–79.

Singers of Italian Opera: The History of a Profession. Cambridge: Cambridge University Press, 1992.

Rossi, Luigi. *Il palazzo incantato, overo, La guerriera amanta*, ed. Howard Mayer Brown. New York: Garland, 1977.

Il palagio d'Atlante overo la Guerriera amante (ms. Sec. 17). Bologna: Forni Editore, 1983.

Rossi, Michelangelo. *Erminia sul Giordano*. Rome: P. Masotti, 1637; rpt. Bologna: Forni Editore, [1969].

Rothmund, Elisabeth. '"Dafne" und kein Ende: Heinrich Schütz, Martin Opitz und die verfehlte erste deutsche Oper'. *Schütz-Jahrbuch* 20 (1998), 12–47.

Russano Hanning, Barbara. 'Glorious Apollo: Poetic and Political Themes in the First Opera'. *Renaissance Quarterly* 32/4 (1979), 485–513.

   Of Poetry and Music's Power: Humanism and the Creation of Opera. Ann Arbor: UMI Research Press, 1980.

Sartori, Claudio. 'La prima diva della lirica italiana: Anna Renzi'. *Rivista musicale italiana* 2/3 (1968), 430–52.

Sartorio, Antonio. *Giulio Cesare in Egitto*, ed. Craig Monson. Collegium Musicum (Yale University). 2nd ser., vol. 12. Madison: A-R Editions, 1991.

Saslow, James M. *The Medici Wedding of 1589: Florentine Festival as 'Theatrum Mundi.'* New Haven and London: Yale University Press, 1996.

Savage, Roger. 'The Shakespeare-Purcell *Fairy Queen*: A Defence and Recommendation'. *EM* 1/1 (1973), 200–22.

   'Sea Spectacles on Dry Land: The 1580s to the 1690s'. In Margaret Shewring and Linda Briggs (eds.), *Waterborne Pageants and Festivities in the Renaissance. Essays in Honour of J.R. Mulryne*. Farnham and Burlington: Ashgate, 2013, 359–71.

Savage, Roger, and Matteo Sansone (eds.). '*Il Corago* and the Staging of Early Opera: Four Chapters from an Anonymous Treatise *circa* 1630'. *EM* 17/4 (1989), 494–511.

Scheitler, Irmgard. 'Harsdörffer und die Musik'. In Stefan Keppler-Tasaki and Ursula Kocher (eds.), *Georg Philipp Harsdörffers Universalität*. Berlin: De Gruyter, 2011, 213–36.

   'Martin Opitz und Heinrich Schütz: Dafne – ein Schauspiel'. *Archiv für Musikwissenschaft* 68/3 (2011), 205–26.

   'Würzburg, der Jesuitenorden und die Anfänge der Oper'. *Schütz-Jahrbuch* 37 (2015), 39–62.

Schildt, Maria. 'Hedwig Eleonora and Music at the Swedish Court, 1654–1726'. In Kristoffer Neville and Lisa Skogh (eds.), *Queen Hedwig Eleonora and the Arts: Court Culture in Seventeenth-Century Northern Europe*. London: Routledge, 2017, 179–89.

Schmidt, Gustav Friedrich. *Neue Beiträge zur Geschichte der Musik und des Theaters am Herzoglichen Hofe zu Braunschweig-Wolfenbüttel. Ergänzungen und Berichtigungen zu Chrysanders Abhandlung . . . Erste Folge. Chronologisches Verzeichnis der in Wolfenbüttel, Braunschweig, Salzthal, Bevern und Blankenburg aufgeführten Opern, Ballette und Schauspiele (Komödien) mit Musik bis zur Mitte des 18. Jahrhunderts*. Munich: Wilhelm Berntheisel, 1929.

Die frühdeutsche Oper und die musikdramatische Kunst Georg Caspar Schürmanns. 2 vols. Regensburg: Verlag Gustav Bosse, 1933–1934.

Schnapper, Antoine (ed.). *La scenografia barocca.* Bologna: CLUEB, 1982.

Schneider, Herbert, and Jérôme de La Gorce (eds.). *Jean-Baptiste Lully: Actes du colloque/ Kongressbericht: Saint-Germain-en-Laye – Heidelberg 1987.* Laaber: Laaber-Verlag, 1990.

Schrammek, Bernhard. *Zwischen Kirche und Karneval. Biographie, soziales Umfeld und Werk des römischen Kapellmeisters Virgilio Mazzocchi (1597–1646).* Kassel: Bärenreiter, 2001.

Schröder, Dorothea. *Zeitgeschichte auf der Opernbühne: barockes Musiktheater in Hamburg im Dienst von Politik und Diplomatie (1690–1745).* Göttingen: Vandenhoeck & Ruprecht, 1998.

Schroedter, Stephanie. 'The French Art of Dancing as Described in the German Dance Instruction Manuals of the Early 18th Century'. In Stephanie Schroedter, Marie-Thérèse Mourey, and Giles Bennett (eds.), *Barocktanz im Zeichen französisch-deutschen Kulturtransfers.* Hildesheim: Olms, 2008, 412–72.

Schulze, Walter. *Die Quellen der Hamburger Oper (1678–1738). Eine bibliographisch-statistische Studie zur Geschichte der ersten stehenden deutschen Oper.* Hamburg-Oldenburg: G. Stalling, 1938.

Scott, Virginia. *The Commedia dell'Arte in Paris. 1644–1697.* Charlottesville and London: University Press of Virginia, 1990.

Sebastiani, Johann. *Pastorello musicale oder Verliebtes Schäferspiel,* ed. Michael Maul. Beeskow: Ortus Musikverlag, 2005.

Seifert, Herbert. *Die Opera am Wiener Kaiserhof im 17. Jahrhundert.* Tutzing: Schneider, 1985.

Selfridge-Field, Eleanor. *A New Chronology of Venetian Opera and Related Genres, 1660–1760.* Palo Alto: Stanford University Press, 2007.

Shergold, Norman D. 'The First Performance of Calderón's *El mayor encanto amor*'. *Bulletin of Hispanic Studies* 35/1 (1958), 24–7.

Solerti, Angelo (ed.). *Le origini del melodrama.* Turin: Fratelli Bocca, 1903; rpt. Bologna: Forni, 1969.

Sommi, Leone de'. *Quattro dialoghi in materia di rappresentazioni sceniche,* ed. Ferruccio Marotti. Milan: Il Polifilo, 1968.

Spencer, Christopher (ed.). *Five Restoration Adaptations of Shakespeare.* Urbana: University of Illinois Press, 1965.

Spink, Ian. *English Song: Dowland to Purcell.* 2nd edn. New York: Taplinger Publishing Company, 1984.

Stangalino, Sara Elisa. *I drammi musicali di Nicolò Minato per Francesco Cavalli.* Ph.D., University of Bologna, 2011.

Stein, Louise K. 'El "manuscrito novena": sus textos, su contexto histórico-musical y el músico Joseph Peyró'. *RM* 3/1–2 (1980), 197–234.

'Un manuscrito de música teatral reaparecido: *Veneno es de amor la envidia*'.
  RM 5/2 (1982), 225–33.

'Opera and the Spanish Political Agenda'. *Acta Musicologica* 63/2 (1991),
  125–67.

*Songs of Mortals, Dialogues of the Gods: Music and Theatre in Seventeenth-
  Century Spain*. Oxford: Clarendon Press, 1993.

'"De la *contera* del mundo": las navegaciones de la ópera entre dos mundos y
  varias culturas'. In Emilio Casares and Álvaro Torrente (eds.), *La ópera en
  España e Hispanoamérica*. 2 vols. Madrid: ICCMU, 2001, vol. 1, 79–94.

'Three Paintings, a Double Lyre, Opera, and Eliche's Venus: Velázquez and
  Music at the Royal Court in Madrid'. In Suzanne Stratton-Pruitt (ed.), *The
  Cambridge Companion to Diego Velázquez*. Cambridge and New York:
  Cambridge University Press, 2001, 170–93.

'Henry Desmarets and the Spanish Context: Musical Harmony for a World at
  War'. In Jean Duron and Yves Ferraton (eds.), *Henry Desmarets
  (1661–1741). Exils d'un musicien dans l'Europe du Grand Siècle*. Versailles:
  Éditions du Centre de Musique Baroque de Versailles; Liège: Pierre
  Mardaga, 2005, 75–106.

'The Musicians of the Spanish Royal Chapel and Court Entertainments,
  1590–1648'. In Tess Knighton and Bernardo García García (eds.), *The Royal
  Chapel in the Time of the Habsburgs: Music and Court Ceremony in Early
  Modern Europe*. London: Boydell and Brewer, Ltd., 2005, 173–94.

'"*La música de dos orbes*": A Context for the First Opera of the Americas'. *OQ*
  22/3–4 (2006), 433–58.

'Opera and the Spanish Family: Private and Public Opera in Naples in the
  1680s'. In José Luis Colomer (ed.), *España y Nápoles. Coleccionismo y
  mecenazgo artístico de los virreyes en el siglo XVII*. Madrid: Centro de
  Estudios Europa Hispánica, 2009, 223–43.

'El manuscrito de música teatral de la Congregación de Nuestra Señora de la
  Novena. Su música, su carácter y su entorno cultural'. In Antonio Álvarez
  Cañibano (ed.), *El manuscrito musical de la Congregación de Nuestra Señora
  de la Novena*. Madrid: Instituto Nacional de las Artes Escénicas y la Música,
  2011, 53–101.

'"*Para restaurar el nombre que han perdido estas Comedias,*" The Marquis del
  Carpio, Alessandro Scarlatti, and Opera Revision in Naples'. In José-Luis
  Colomer, Giuseppe Galasso, and José Vicente Quirante (eds.), *Fiesta y
  ceremonia en la corte virreinal de Nápoles (siglos XVI y XVII)*. Madrid:
  Centro de Estudios Europa Hispánica, 2013, 415–46.

'A Viceroy behind the Scenes: Opera, Production, Politics, and Financing in
  1680s Naples'. In Susan McClary (ed.), *Structures of Feeling in Seventeenth-
  Century Cultural Expression*. Toronto: University of Toronto Press, 2013,
  209–49.

'How Opera Traveled'. In Helen M. Greenwald (ed.), *The Oxford Handbook of Opera*. Oxford and New York: Oxford University Press, 2014, 843–61.

'¿Escuchando a Calderón? Arias y Cantantes en *L'Aldimiro* y *La Psiche* de Alessandro Scarlatti'. In Fausta Antonucci and Anna Tedesco (eds.), *La Comedia Nueva Spagnola e le scene italiane nel seicento: trame, drammaturgie, contesti a confronto*. Florence: Olschki, 2016, 199–219.

Stein, Louise K., and José Máximo Leza, 'Opera, Genre, and Context in Spain and its American Colonies'. In Anthony R. DelDonna and Pierpaolo Polzonetti (eds.), *The Cambridge Companion to Eighteenth-Century Opera*. Cambridge: Cambridge University Press, 2009, 244–69.

Steude, Wolfram. 'Heinrich Schütz und die erste deutsche Oper'. In Frank Heidelberger, Wolfgang Osthoff, and Reinhard Wiesend (eds.), *Von Isaac bis Bach. Studien zur älteren deutschen Musikgeschichte. Festschrift Martin Just zum 60. Geburtstag*. Kassel: Bärenreiter, 1991, 169–79.

Sternfeld, Frederick W. 'The First Printed Opera Libretto'. *ML* 59/2 (1978), 121–38.

Strainchamps, Edmond. 'New Light on the Accademia degli Elevati of Florence'. *MQ* 62/4 (1976), 507–35.

'The Life and Death of Caterina Martinelli: New Light on Monteverdi's "Arianna"'. *EMH* 5 (1985), 155–86.

Strohm, Reinhard. 'Italian Operisti North of the Alps'. In Reinhard Strohm (ed.), *The Eighteenth-Century Diaspora of Italian Musicians*. Turnhout: Brepols, 2001, 1–59.

Strozzi, Giulio, and Francesco Sacrati. *La finta pazza*, ed. Nicola Usula. Ricordi: Milano, 2018.

Strunk, Oliver (ed.). *Source Readings in Music History*. Rev. edn., ed. Leo Treitler. New York: Norton, 1998.

Talbot, Michael. 'A Venetian Operatic Contract of 1714'. In Michael Talbot (ed.), *The Business of Music*. Liverpool: Liverpool University Press, 2002, 10–61.

Tamburini, Elena. *The Island Princess: British Library Add. MS 15318, a Semi-Opera*, ed. Curtis Price and Robert Hume. Music for London Entertainment 1660–1800. Series C, English Opera and Masque. Vol. 2. Tunbridge Wells: R. Macnutt, 1985.

'A partire dall'"Arianna" monteverdiana pensando ai comici. Luoghi teatrali alla corte di Mantova'. In Paola Besutti, Teresa M. Gialdroni, and Rodolfo Baroncini (eds.), *Claudio Monteverdi. Studi e prospettive*. Florence: Olschki, 1998, 415–29.

Thomas, Downing A. *Aesthetics of Opera in the Ancien Régime, 1647–1785*. Cambridge: Cambridge University Press, 2002.

Thorp, Jennifer. 'Dance in Late 17th-Century London: Priestly Muddles'. *EM* 26/2 (1998), 198–212.

'Dance in the London Theaters c. 1700–1750'. In Jennifer Nevile (ed.), *Dance, Spectacle, and the Body Politick 1250–1750*. Bloomington: Indiana University Press, 2008, 136–52.

Timms, Colin. *Polymath of the Baroque: Agostino Steffani and His Music*. New York and Oxford: Oxford University Press, 2003.

Tomlinson, Gary. *Monteverdi and the End of the Renaissance*. Berkeley: University of California Press, 1987.

Music in Renaissance Magic: Toward a Historiography of Others. Chicago: The University of Chicago Press, 1993.

'Pastoral and Musical Magic in the Birth of Opera'. In Thomas Bauman and Marita McClymonds (eds.), *Opera and the Enlightenment*. Cambridge: Cambridge University Press, 1995, 7–20.

'Renaissance Humanism and Music'. In James Haar (ed.), *European Music, 1520–1640*. Woodbridge and Rochester: Boydell Press, 2006, 1–19.

Torrejón y Velasco, Tomás de, Juan Hidalgo, and Pedro Calderón de la Barca. *La púrpura de la rosa*, ed. Louise K. Stein. Madrid: ICCMU and SGAE, 1999.

Torrente, Álvaro. *La música en el siglo XVII*. Madrid: Fondo de Cultura Económica, 2016.

Torrente, Alvaro, and Pablo-L. Rodriguez. 'The "Guerra Manuscript" (c. 1680) and the Rise of Solo Song in Spain'. *JRMA* 123/2 (1998), 147–89.

Tosi, Pier Francesco. *Opinioni de' cantori antichi e moderni*. Bologna: Lelio dalla Volpe, 1723; rpt. New York: Broude Brothers, 1968.

Observations on the Florid Song: Or Sentiments on the Ancient and Modern Singers, trans. J. E. Galliard. 2nd edn. London: J. Wilcox, 1743.

Treadwell, Nina. *Music and Wonder at the Medici Court: The 1589 Interludes for La pellegrina*. Bloomington: Indiana University Press, 2008.

Trinchieri Camiz, Franca. '"La bella cantatrice": I ritratti di Leonora Barone e Barbara Strozzi a confronto'. In Francesco Passadore and Franco Rossi (eds.), *Musica, Scienza e idee nella Serenissima durante il Seicento*. Venezia: Edizioni Fondazione Levi, 1996, 285–94.

Trott, David. 'Réflexions sur les conditions de la parodie d'opéra en France entre 1669 et 1752'. In Letizia Cagiano Norci and Delia Gambelli (eds.), *Le Théâtre en musique et son double (1600–1762)*. Paris: H. Champion, 2005, 105–19.

Varey, John E., and Norman D. Shergold. *Teatros y comedias en Madrid: 1666–1687. Estudio y documentos*. London: Tamesis Books, 1974.

Varwig, Bettina. 'Schütz's *Dafne* and the German Operatic Imagination'. In Nikolaus Bacht (ed.), *Music, Theatre and Politics in Germany, 1850–1950*. Aldershot: Ashgate, 2006, 117–38.

'Echos in und um *Dafne*.' *Schütz-Jahrbuch* 33 (2011), 105–10.

Vega, Lope de. *La selva sin amor*, ed. Maria Grazia Profeti. Florence: Alinea Editrice, 1999.

Vélez de Guevara, Juan. *Los celos hacen estrellas*, ed. John E. Varey and Norman D. Shergold. London: Tamesis Books, Ltd., 1970.

Vittori, Loreto. *La Galatea*, ed. Thomas Dunn. Middleton: A-R Editions, 2002.

Waczkat, Andreas. 'Simon Dachs Liederspiele und die Anfänge der deutschen Oper'. In Axel E. Walter (ed.), *Simon Dach (1605–1659). Werk und Nachwirken*. Tübingen: Max Niemeyer Verlag, 2008, 321–36.

Walker, Daniel P. 'Ficino's *Spiritus* and Music'. *Annales musicologiques* 1 (1953), 131–50.

(ed.). *Musique des Intermèdes de 'La Pellegrina'*. Paris: Éditions du Centre National de la Recherche Scientifique, 1963.

Walkling, Andrew R. 'Masque and Politics at the Restoration Court: John Crowne's *Calisto*'. *EM* 24/1 (1996), 27–62.

Masque and Opera in England, 1656–1688. New York: Routledge, 2017.

'The Ups and Downs of Louis Grabu'. *Royal Musical Association Research Chronicle* 48/1 (2017), 1–64.

English Dramatick Opera, 1661–1706. London and New York: Routledge, 2019.

Walls, Peter. *Music in the English Courtly Masque, 1604–1640*. Oxford: Clarendon Press, 1996.

Watanabe-O'Kelly, Helen. *Court Culture in Dresden: From Renaissance to Baroque*. Houndmills, Basingstoke, and New York: Palgrave, 2002.

Weaver, Robert Lamar, and Norma Wright Weaver. *A Chronology of Music in the Florentine Theater, 1590–1750: Operas, Prologues, Finales, Intermezzos and Plays with Incidental Music*. Detroit: Information Coordinators, 1978.

Wendt, Joachim R. M. *Materialien zur Geschichte der frühen Hamburger Oper*. Vol. 1: *Eigentümer und Pächter*. Aurich: Wendt, 2002.

Westrup, Jack A. 'Foreign Musicians in Stuart England'. *MQ* 27/1 (1941), 79–89.

Purcell, rev. edn. London: Dent & Sons, 1980.

Whenham, John. *Claudio Monteverdi: Orfeo*. Cambridge: Cambridge University Press, 1986.

Whenham, John, and Richard Wistreich (eds.). *The Cambridge Companion to Monteverdi*. Cambridge: Cambridge University Press, 2007.

Whitaker, Shirley B. 'Florentine Opera Comes to Spain: Lope de Vega's *La selva sin amor*'. *Journal of Hispanic Philology* 9/1 (1984), 43–66.

White, Bryan. 'Grabu's *Albion and Albanius* and the Operas of Lully: "... acquainted with all the performance of the French Opera's"'. *EM* 30/3 (2002), 410–27.

'Letter from Aleppo: Dating the Chelsea School Performance of *Dido and Aeneas*'. *EM* 37/3 (2009), 417–28.

Wilbourne, Emily. *Seventeenth-Century Opera and the Sound of the Commedia dell'Arte*. Chicago: The University of Chicago Press, 2016.

Winn, James A. 'Heroic Song: A Proposal for a Revised History of English Theater and Opera, 1656–1711'. *ECS* 30/2 (1996/1997), 113–37.

'"A Versifying Maid of Honour": Anne Finch and the Libretto for *Venus and Adonis*'. *The Review of English Studies* 59/238 (2008), 67–85.

Queen Anne: Patroness of Arts. New York: Oxford University Press, 2014.

Wisch, Barbara, and Susan Scott Munshower (eds.). *'All the world's a stage': Art and Pageantry in the Renaissance and Baroque*. Vol. 2: *Theatrical Spectacle and Spectacular Theater*. University Park: Papers in Art History from The Pennsylvania State University, vol. 6, 1990.

Wistreich, Richard. '"La voce è grata assai, ma. . .": Monteverdi on Singing'. *EM* 22/1 (1994), 7–20.

Wood, Bruce. 'A Mangled Chime: The Accidental Death of the Opera Libretto in Civil War England'. *EM* 36/2 (2008), 265–84.

Wood, Bruce, and Andrew Pinnock. '"Unscarr'd by Turning Times"? The Dating of Purcell's *Dido and Aeneas*'. *EM* 20/3 (1992), 372–90: 387.

'*The Fairy Queen*: A Fresh Look at the Issues'. *EM* 21/1 (1993), 44–52, 54–62.

Wood, Caroline. 'Orchestra and Spectacle in the Tragédie en Musique, 1673–1715: Oracle, Sommeil and Tempête'. *Proceedings of the Royal Musical Association* 108 (1981–1982), 25–46.

Music and Drama in the Tragédies en Musique, 1673–1715. New York and London: Garland, 1996.

Wood, Caroline, and Graham Sadler. *French Baroque Opera: A Reader*. Aldershot: Ashgate, 2000.

Zaslaw, Neal. 'The First Opera in Paris: A Study in the Politics of Art'. In John Hajdu Heyer (ed.), *Jean-Baptiste Lully and the Music of the French Baroque, Essays in Honor of James R. Anthony*. Cambridge: Cambridge University Press, 1989, 7–23.

Index

For EU product safety concerns, contact us at Calle de José Abascal, 56–1°,
28003 Madrid, Spain or eugpsr@cambridge.org.

www.ingramcontent.com/pod-product-compliance
Ingram Content Group UK Ltd.
Pitfield, Milton Keynes, MK11 3LW, UK
UKHW051259040726
472853UK00011B/634